CHILDREN OF POVERTY

Studies on the Effects of Single Parenthood, the Feminization of Poverty, and Homelessness

edited by

STUART BRUCHEY
Allan Nevins Professor Emeritus
Columbia University

CHILD MALTREATMENT AND PSYCHOLOGICAL DISTRESS AMONG URBAN HOMELESS YOUTH

LISA A. RUSSELL

Routledge
Taylor & Francis Group
LONDON AND NEW YORK

First published 1998 by Garland Publishing, Inc.

Published 2018 by Routledge
2 Park Square, Milton Park, Abingdon, Oxon OX14 4RN
52 Vanderbilt Avenue, New York, NY 10017

First issued in paperback 2018

Routledge is an imprint of the Taylor & Francis Group, an informa business

Library of Congress Cataloging-in-Publication Data

Russell, Lisa A., 1959–
Child maltreatment and psychological distress among urban homeless youth / Lisa Russell.
p. cm. — (Children of poverty)
Revision of thesis (Ph. D.)—University of California at Los Angeles, 1995.
Includes bibliographical references and index.
ISBN 0-8153-3016-2 (alk. paper)
1. Homeless youth—Abuse of—California—Los Angeles. 2. Homeless youth—California—Los Angeles—Psychology. 3. Homeless youth—California—Los Angeles—Social conditions. 4. Child abuse—California—Los Angeles. I. Title. II. Series.
HV4506.C2R87 1998
362.76'086'942—dc21

97-35335

ISBN 13: 978-1-138-99120-0 (pbk)
ISBN 13: 978-0-8153-3016-5 (hbk)

Dedicated to the memory of Brandon
and to other adolescents who have lost their way.

Contents

Tables and Figures

Tables:

Figures:

Foreword

Thousands of young people experience homelessness in the United States every year. Yet our understanding of this group remains fragmented and incomplete.

Although sparse, evidence suggests that homelessness is not the grand adventure that some readers might imagine. Not only do many of these young people have difficulty meeting their basic needs for food and safe shelter, but they are also at great risk for violent and traumatic injury, infectious diseases, pregnancy, and other health problems. Many have emotional problems such as depression, suicide attempts, psychotic symptoms, and disturbing symptoms of post-traumatic stress. Many also have serious problems related to their own alcohol and other drug use. At times, many are very lonely and afraid.

Services for homeless young men and women are usually scarce, inadequate, or inappropriate. Despite best efforts by many service providers, agency staff may not have the training or resources to deal with overlapping serious emotional and substance use problems. In addition, their legal status as minors limits access to needed housing, educational systems, medical and mental health services, and social welfare programs.

Lisa Russell's *Child Maltreatment and Psychological Distress Among Urban Homeless Youth* is a very timely book and a unique resource for anyone who wants detailed information about homeless youth. As is well documented here, there is no typical homeless youth and there is no single cause for youth homelessness. Rather, there are many factors which result in young people leaving their family or institutional homes including abuse, neglect, family conflict and disruption, and parent drug and alcohol abuse. More importantly, however, this book gives us a rare understanding about the youths' mental health and histories and relates those histories to earlier exposure to violence, abuse, and neglect.

Marjorie J. Robertson, Ph.D.
Alcohol Research Group, Berkeley, and
School of Medicine, San Francisco
University of California

September, 1997

Preface

The conceptual inquiry for this book began during my health education internship with the High Risk Youth Project in Los Angeles, a collaborative program of the Los Angeles Free Clinic and the Division of Adolescent Medicine of Children's Hospital. During my work with the Project's young clients and exceptional staff, I became aware of the complexity of past and present experiences, environmental and social stressors and supports, and internal processes which influence health behaviors and health itself for many young people. Of particular interest to me was the relationship between child abuse and neglect and mental health. The experience with the High Risk Youth Project led me to pursue doctoral work in the behavioral science area of public health and an interdisciplinary fellowship in child abuse and neglect at the University of California, Los Angeles. This book is a slightly revised form of my dissertation. Specifically, I have added selected updates to the literature review and an index. It is my great hope that the content will be useful in improving the efforts to provide safe and healthy environments where young people can grow and self-determine a positive future.

Lisa A. Russell, Ph.D., MPH
Department of Applied Health Science
Indiana University

September, 1997

Preface

The conceptual origins for this book began during my [illegible] internship with the [illegible] Youth [illegible] in Los Angeles, a collaborative program of the Los Angeles Free Clinic and the Division of Adolescent Medicine at Children's Hospital. During my work with the project's youth [illegible] staff, I [illegible] the complexity of [illegible] environments and social stressors [illegible] [illegible] [illegible] between child [illegible] and mental health. [illegible] [illegible] University of California, Los Angeles. This book is [illegible] revised form of my dissertation, specifically [illegible] selected updates to the literature review and [illegible] [illegible] [illegible]

Lisa A. [illegible], PhD, MPH
[illegible] of [illegible] Health Science
[illegible] University

September [illegible]

Acknowledgments

The principal investigators of the Hollywood Homeless Youth Study were Milton Greenblatt, M.D.; Julia M. Robertson, M.D.; and Marjorie J. Robertson, Ph.D. Funding of the original study was provided by the California State Department of Mental Health (Grant No. 85-76258, Milton Greenblatt, M.D. and Julia M. Robertson, M.D., Principal Investigators), N.I.A.A.A. Professional Services (Contract No. 87MO23952101D, Marjorie J. Robertson, Ph.D., Principal Investigator), and the Los Angeles County-Olive View Medical Center, Department of Psychiatry. The thoughts presented in this book do not necessarily represent those of the principal investigators of the Hollywood Homeless Youth Study or those of the Study's funding agencies.

Special thanks to Dr. M. Audrey Burnam for directing me to Dr. Marjorie J. Robertson and her study; to Dr. Marjorie J. Robertson for allowing me access to the Hollywood Homeless Youth Study data and for her faith in me; to my doctoral study guidance committee members: Drs. Snehendu B. Kar, Bertrand Raven, and Emil Berkanovic for giving me a solid foundation; to my dissertation committee members: Drs. Judith M. Siegel, Susan Sorenson, Carol Aneshensel, Gail Wyatt, and Norma Feshbach for their skill and encouragement and for challenging me to grow; to Dr. Linda B. Bourque for her generous mentoring; to Dr. Roland Summit for his wisdom and experience; to Dr. Julia Pennbridge for assisting my initial efforts to collect my own sample and for lending a kind and thoughtful ear over the years; to Susan Pearlman, Laurie Goodman, Nina Mancina, and Susan Rabinowitz for introducing me to the world of high-risk youth and for being wonderful friends; to the staffs of for his technical assistance and encouragement; and to Gloria Krauss and Jessica Novak for their superb clerical assistance;

Personal and heartfelt thanks to Arlyne Garbe for extraordinary caregiving and to my family and friends for their support, patience and love.

Child Maltreatment and Psychological Distress among Urban Homeless Youth

I
Introduction

This book describes a secondary analysis of survey data collected from a modified snowball sample of 96 homeless and runaway youth. The sample contains youth from selected street and social service sites located within a geographically defined region of Los Angeles. The analysis examines the area of inquiry defined by the intersection of three somewhat disparate fields of research. These fields include the literatures on homeless and runaway youth; child maltreatment; and stress, coping and resiliency.

Specifically, this is a descriptive study which investigates potential relationships between the experience of specific types of child maltreatment and the experience of symptoms of psychological distress within a homeless youth sample. Measures of child maltreatment include assessment of intrafamilial and extrafamilial violence, physical and sexual abuse, and neglect. Indices of psychological distress encompass evaluations of depression, post-traumatic stress disorder (PTSD), suicide ideation and attempts, conduct disorders, trait anxiety, and substance abuse. Of particular interest is the examination of the data for factors which are associated with relative resiliency to the experience of child maltreatment and the factors which are associated with gender differences in the experience of child maltreatment, symptoms of psychological distress, and resiliency.

The runaway and homeless youth literature contributes contextual information which may be useful when interpreting the results of this investigation. However, the homeless youth literature has been plagued by both methodological and conceptual weaknesses. Most of the research has been limited by sampling difficulties and instrumentation weaknesses, and the much of the peer-reviewed empirical literature has arisen from a handful of research groups observing a few local shelter populations. These studies often are anecdotal in nature and only occasionally address descriptive analyses. This research contributes to the growing sophistication of the methodologies used to study homeless and runaway youth by sampling both street and social service agency sites and by using standardized measures of psychological distress. Due to the limited interest in the runaway and homeless youth literature and the inherent methodological difficulties in studying this population, the development or application of theories relevant to adaptation has been rather slow. The analysis presented here attempts to enhance the runaway and homeless youth literature with its application of stress and coping theories to the understanding of the effects of child maltreatment.

The child abuse and neglect literature, although more mature than the homeless youth literature, also has been faced with methodological and conceptual problems. For instance, the definition of what constitutes abuse has varied widely across studies. Theoretical models have been elaborated which attempt to explain the observed sequelae of child maltreatment. Nevertheless, like the empirical studies, these models have tended to focus exclusively on the effects of child sexual abuse. Less theory development has been accomplished to describe the intrapsychic and interpersonal processes which may follow exposure to neglect, physical abuse, or domestic violence. Many of the studies of the consequences of child maltreatment have used clinical samples of adults and children; few studies have used samples of adolescents. Only a handful of these studies have been of homeless youth, nearly all of which were conducted with shelter samples. In addition, investigating child maltreatment involves serious legal and ethical dilemmas regarding the protection of human subjects from harm. The desire and mandate to protect these subjects often result in the compromise of research designs and population choice. This phenomenon contributes to the slow progress of knowledge and creation of appropriate services for maltreatment survivors. Needless to say, the opportunity to examine the correlates of child maltreatment in a well-designed study of homeless and runaway youth is rare.

Finally, the stress, coping, and resiliency literature offers the most expansive literature coverage, both theoretically and empirically, to the subject of this investigation. This literature contributes general theoretical frameworks for analyzing and comparing the effects of specific stressors such as child maltreatment. It is not, of course, without its methodological and conceptual limitations as well. For instance, the definitions of stress and coping are complicated by a lack of consensus within the field as to what constitutes the antecedents, the events, and the consequences of a stressful experience for the purpose of study and how these reflect the actual process of stress. The identification of factors which moderate or mediate the psychological effects of various stressors other than child maltreatment broadens the empirical base from which research questions and hypotheses may be drawn. Although the stress and coping literature has begun to address various populations, including youth, it is quite unusual to find it examining homeless youth or abused and neglected youth. One of the primary goals of this study is to contribute to the understanding of the relationship of exposure to child maltreatment and psychological distress as an example of the stress and coping processes which may exist among homeless youth.

Both the homeless youth and child abuse literatures have been virtually ignored by those in the public health field. In an age of growing conservatism, it may become more and more difficult to persuade public policymakers to allocate scarce resources to helping a sub-population of the homeless described merely by its high prevalence of substance abuse, mental illness, and criminal activity rather than as survivors of multiple abuses. As concern about urban crime escalates, the call for resources has emanated from law enforcement, and the solution to the homeless problem has often been left to the legal system.

Secondary and tertiary prevention programs designed to ameliorate the negative effects and continuation of homelessness are scarce and costly, considering the poor prognoses for many of those served. In addition, most homeless youth do not qualify for the social services offered in these programs due to age and legal status restrictions. They are likewise ineligible for services targeting homeless adults or children, and, because of the lack of legitimate economic roles for adolescents, may be forced to participate in illegal activities for survival. Finally, those with multiple psychological and behavioral symptoms of distress often do not meet the criteria for placement in either short or long-term shelters.

Due to the high prevalence of abusive life experiences, risk-taking behaviors, and health care needs in this population, it seems evident that homeless youth would be of concern to those in the public health sector.

Public health interventions targeting homeless and runaway youth must attend to the diversity of this population's needs. This study attempts to provide useful information to assist in the development of effective interventions and the allocation of resources.

II
Literature Review

Homeless Youth

This section on homeless youth reviews the literature on the population of young people who are characterized as being without stable living situations, including runaways, throwaways, push-outs, system kids, street kids, and unaccompanied youth. There is no consensus on a definition of homelessness for youth. The studies reviewed cover samples which include youth who are newly homeless, sporadically homeless, and chronically homeless through a variety of paths.

The investigation presented in this book was not designed to examine the many factors which may cause homelessness among youth. The focus of this study is on the exposure of homeless youth to child maltreatment and symptoms of psychological distress. First, however, there is a brief overview to describe the scope and spectrum of homelessness among youth as defined in the academic literature.

Incidence and Prevalence

The actual number of homeless youth present at any given time in any given region in the United States is unknown. This is due to some of the same methodological problems which plague the adult homeless literature, i.e., the lack of consensus regarding the definition of the population under study, varied and limited methods for producing population estimates, and a lack of a mechanism for centralized reporting (Brennan, Huizinga, and Elliot, 1978; Rothman and David, 1985). For example, until the 1990 Census, there was no specific government agency which was responsible for enumerating or characterizing homeless adults. In the 1990 Census, homeless adults were sampled from emergency shelters. This practice was widely criticized in the popular media for its inability to represent those homeless adults who do not use shelters and its underestimation of the total homeless adult population. Rossi (1989) has described the strengths and weaknesses of various sampling methodologies used for homeless adults and has concluded that the true size of the homeless population is not calculable. Rossi adds that variations in the definition of "homeless" contribute to the wide fluctuation in population estimates and reflect social values of what is considered unacceptable shelter. For instance, some operationalizations of homelessness have included the marginally housed, i.e., those who are at high risk of losing that housing, and some have not.

Regardless of the definition of homelessness used, Rossi (1989) contends that homelessness is a statistical rarity in the overall population, affecting less than 2% of the adult population and that studying statistically rare events can be costly because of the numbers of persons who must be screened before encountering the desired characteristic. These costs may be reduced by screening in locations where the homeless are known to congregate, but this technique may underestimate those homeless who are the least socially enmeshed and who may exist hidden from others. Nevertheless, Rossi suggests that sampling of the homeless should focus on areas of known geographic concentration. Rossi also recommends that identification strategies for homeless adults rely on the self-reports of qualifying characteristics of housing instability, rather than the observations of any physically apparent characteristic of the persons. Other factors affecting the estimation of the homeless population include the often transient nature of homelessness and the geographic mobility and uneven geographic distribution of homeless individuals.

Elements which have influenced the definition of homeless youth in the academic literature often have focused on the cause of homelessness. For instance, some studies differentiate between those youth who have left their family homes and those youth whose families have left them and whether the separation is consensual. Youth who have become homeless with their families are typically classified within the genre of homeless families, whereas youth who have become homeless on their own are categorized as homeless youth. Youth living apart from their families have been described based on the type and duration of use of shelters and other housing (e.g., emergency shelters, abandoned buildings, foster care, friend's house etc.). "Youth living apart from their families" includes youth who are believed to be at risk for homelessness such as those removed from the family home by child protective services and those who are abducted from the home or family neighborhood.

Notwithstanding these definitional limitations, there is evidence that suggests that the size of the homeless and runaway youth population is significant. In 1976, the Opinion Research Corporation conducted a nationwide telephone survey of a probability sample of 62,895 households which revealed an annual incidence of overnight runaway behavior of 1.7 percent of youth aged ten to seventeen (or between 519,000 and 635,000 individual runaways) (Opinion Research Corporation, 1976). A 1983 U.S. Department of Health and Human Services report on runaway and homeless youth estimated the incidence of the nation's runaway and homeless youth to be between 733,000 and 1,300,000 per year (U.S.D.H.H.S., 1983). Since this estimate was based on reports from service providers, the U.S.D.H.H.S. report emphasized the conservative nature of the estimate. For example, this incidence rate is not believed to include those youth who have been reported missing or those who have not sought services. The report estimates that only one in twelve runaway youth have contact with shelters which receive federal funds. In addition, the majority of these youth are believed to return home within a few days, whereas an unknown number do not (National Network of Homeless and Runaway Youth, 1985).

Estimates of the incidence of homeless youth in California have ranged from 12,700 to 128,000 (Olson-Raymer, 1986) and in Los Angeles County from 10,000 to 20,000, depending on the season (Pursley, 1981). However, a recent study based the estimate of homeless youth on the enumeration of runaway/homeless youths receiving services in Los Angeles County for a twelve-month period coupled with the U.S.D.H.H.S. estimate that 11 out of 12 do not seek services. These investigators submitted that there may be at least 34,800 homeless youth in Los Angeles County each year (Pennbridge, Yates, David and MacKenzie, 1990). In spite of the large estimates of the size of the homeless youth population, it is considered to be the most understudied subgroup among the homeless population (Institute of Medicine, 1988).

Only recently has the small literature on runaway youth incorporated definitions of homelessness into their studies. This may be because of the political implications of the label "homeless". In a legal sense, no minor can be homeless; the minor is either in the custody of their parent(s) or guardian(s) or the State via the child welfare system. In spite of this, the Runaway Youth Act, which provides for some funding of services to youth, was renamed to include homeless youth in 1980. In doing so, one may argue that the federal government has acknowledged the existence of minors who have not benefitted from the protective services of the child welfare system.

Currently, the label "homeless" may elicit a more sympathetic response than the term "runaway" which may bring to mind images of juvenile delinquency and criminal activity. Perhaps "homeless" youth are more likely to be seen as victims of circumstance and deserving of government assistance than "runaway" youth. These two classifications may not be useful distinctions since the youth themselves are not so easily categorized and often fit both definitions.

Many service providers distinguish between "runaways" and "homeless" youth as reflected in the definitions developed by the National Network of Runaway and Youth Services (Robertson, 1991) and the National Center for Missing and Exploited Children (Burgess, Hartman and McCormack 1986):

> *Runaways* are children and youth who have left home at least overnight without parental or caretaker permission.
>
> *Throwaways* are children and youth who have been forced to leave their homes or have been ignored by their caretakers.
>
> *Homeless Youth* are youth who are not residing in their parental, foster or institutional homes due to unilateral or bilateral estrangement or abandonment. Runaways, throwaways or abducted youth may become homeless.

Implicit in these distinctions are the differences in choice or intent in leaving home and access to a stable living situation. These distinctions often are blurred in reality, especially for the youth, and, as such, are problematic to measure accurately. The terms "runaway" and "homeless youth" sometimes are used by service providers to infer differences in the amount of time spent away from home, with "runaway" denoting the shorter stay away from home.

Also, definitions often differ with respect to the age range studied or discussed (Brennan, et al., 1978; Pennbridge et al., 1990; Robertson, 1989). For instance, the findings of those investigators describing shelter samples reflect the intake policies of the shelters studied. Some homeless youth shelters restrict their intake to youth under 18 years old, others include youth under 25 years old.

For purposes of this study, eligibility criteria were conceptualized based on adaptations of definitions used in studies of homeless adults. Youth who met the inclusion criteria of the Hollywood Homeless Youth study were minors who spent the night prior to the interview either in a formal emergency shelter, in improvised shelter (including abandoned buildings, vehicles, public places, or other somewhat protective sites not normally considered conventional dwelling places), or on the streets (i.e., outdoor areas such as parks or beaches) (Robertson, 1989). This definition excludes those youth who are homeless with their families. The choice of age range to study (i.e., those under 18 years old) is based on the frequency with which it is used to delimit the choice of samples in homeless adult studies and the access of minors without legal status to services, employment, and many other resources (Robertson, 1989).

The limited empirical information that is available on runaway/homeless youth is almost exclusively derived from client samples of runaway and homeless agencies (e.g., Feitel, Margetson, Chamas and Lipman, 1992; Kipke, Montgomery, and MacKenzie, 1993; Maxwell, 1992; Schweitzer and Hier, 1993; Shaffer and Caton, 1984; Yates, MacKenzie, Pennbridge, and Cohen, 1988). These client samples are likely to misrepresent those who do not use these services. The data often have been collected by chart review or are furnished by questioning the service providers rather than the youth, resulting in somewhat impressionistic data. In addition, many of the studies have employed unstandardized measures of psychological distress and problem behaviors which lack acceptable estimates of validity and reliability (Jones 1988).

Demographic Profile

Despite definitional variations across studies of homeless youth, some demographic patterns have emerged in the studies reviewed (Caton, 1986; Pennbridge et al., 1990; Robertson, 1991; Sommer, 1984). For example, there is a slight tendency for females to be predominant in shelter samples and males to be predominant in street samples. The ages of the respondents usually range from 13 to 17 years but may drop as low as 9 years. Ethnicity tends to reflect the distribution of the area sampled or overrepresent minority populations, if the sample is taken from a shelter. In contrast, the ethnicity of those being served by drop-in centers is predominately white. Education tends to reflect participation in remedial and special education classes with most youth having completed the ninth grade. Family socioeconomic status can be from any stratum, with some tendency toward lower strata. Family composition shows some bias toward single, female parents or large, reconstituted (i.e., stepparent) families. Cities of origin vary with the sample source. Shelter youth are mostly from the immediate geographical surroundings of the area sampled and outreach/drop-in center youth originate from outside the county. Runaway behavior has been reported to be most frequent in the Northwest and West-Midwest of the nation. Episodic homelessness (i.e., multiple episodes, sometimes constituting lengthy periods) characterizes over three-quarters of some samples.

Recent anecdotal (and previously published) observations by service providers across the country have suggested that homeless youth who seek social services are, in general, younger, more ethnically varied, more emotionally disturbed, and have been homeless longer than those clients previously encountered (Rothman and David, 1985; Yates et al., 1988). This phenomenon could be due to changes in the observers themselves or to changes in referral patterns rather than to a true change in the population.

Although it is not the purpose of this book to evaluate the etiology of homelessness, it may be instructive to review the literature concerned with the antecedents of homelessness in order to understand the different family and social contexts which may exist among homeless and runaway youth. The identification of various precursors to youth homelessness has shaped the way that the medical and social service professions view and treat homeless youth and their families. In particular, the discovery of histories of abuse and neglect among homeless youth appear to have influenced the focus of etiological models of youth homelessness and intervention strategies.

Etiological Models of Runaway Behavior

Three etiological perspectives have been described in the runaway literature: (1) the individual psychopathology of the runaway, (2) the pathological environment and the social structure, and (3) the sociopsychological interplay between the individual personality and the social environment (Janus, McCormack, Burgess and Hartman, 1987). The first etiological perspective is illustrated in the second edition of the American Psychiatric Association's Diagnostic and Statistical Manual for Mental Disorders (i.e., DSM-II) which includes "runaway" as its own diagnostic category (American Psychiatric Association, 1968). In the current version (i.e., DSM-IV), runaway behavior is incorporated as a component in the diagnosis of a personal conduct disorder as an example of rule violation if the runaway behavior occurred more than once or was lengthy and was not in response to physical or sexual abuse at home (American Psychiatric Association, 1994). The relative abundance of psychological symptomatology detected in runaway youth compared with school-based samples of youth has been used to promote an emphasis on intraindividual causality of psychopathology and treatment for the youth.

The second view holds that runaway behavior is a rational reaction to a hostile and abusive environment resulting from basic social inequities and is a perspective often supported by service providers. The third school suggests that the behavior results from a complex relationship between specific socioenvironmental conditions and the individual personality, where the individual is capable of responding in either an adaptive or maladaptive manner, depending on the environmental conditions. Policymakers adhering to the latter view would suggest that prevention and treatment must address both the individual and the environment.

Jones (1988) and others have taken these etiological perspectives a step further in describing a set of typologies which classify patterns of runaway behaviors and suggest treatment strategies. The Family Dynamics Typology includes (1) runaways who are "running from" a destructive situation, family conflict or crisis, an unsharable problem, abuse, and/or neglect and (2) youth who are abandoned, thrown out, or pushed out. This typology fits with the pathological environment and social structure etiology described above. The Personal Characteristics Typology, or intraindividual etiology, includes youth who are in search of adventure, alternative life-styles, opportunities for aggressive conduct, or who are negatively peer influenced or psychiatrically disabled. The Temporal Model Typology categorizes youth who run for various lengths of time at varying frequencies, including crisis runaways, multiple runaways, and long-term homeless youth. The temporal model typology is applicable across etiologies.

These etiological distinctions may be of limited value since many homeless youth fit into more than a single descriptive category. The evaluation of the scope and cause of youth homelessness and the assignment of treatment modalities require the consideration of all of these precipitating factors. The elucidation of typologies has, however, emphasized both the diversity of antecedent problems inherent in this population and the need for a constellation of intervention strategies which can be assembled in different ways according to needs of the youth and, if feasible, the family.

The description of typologies of runaway and homeless youth highlights the inadequacy of the social policies which emphasize reunification of runaway and homeless youth with their families. While in many instances, this solution is both feasible and the most desirable outcome for all parties, often times reunification is neither beneficial nor desired by either party. The alternatives to reunification are suspect as well. When reunification efforts fail, service agencies may refer these young people for placement in foster care or a group home by the local child protective service agency. It is these child protective services, however, which are reputed to lack sufficient monitoring and resources to ensure quality care. Since repeat runaway episodes have been found to be associated with foster care placement (Caton, 1986), foster care may not prevent further runaway episodes and homelessness.

Shane (1989) concluded from a study of over 500 clients of homeless and runaway youth services in New Jersey that the majority (64%) never return home because of the high prevalence of family dysfunction. In an analysis of recipients of homeless and runaway youth services in Los Angeles County, Pennbridge and colleagues found that 31.7% of the sheltered youth and 15.5% of those served by outreach or drop-in agencies were reunified with some family member (Pennbridge et al., 1990). The short-term runaways have had the highest probability of familial reunification (approximately 57%). Slightly over one-third of the shelter youth could be considered "short-term runaways", i.e., youth who have run away once or twice. Over one-third of the youth served in the shelters sampled by Pennbridge were considered "homeless youth" (i.e., youth, with or without histories of abuse, who have been away from home for two months or more; have been abandoned, pushed out, or thrown out; or have been emancipated). Additionally, 67% of the outreach/drop-in center youth in the study had no home or placement to which they could return (Pennbridge et al., 1990).

In order to address the needs of more homeless and runaway youth, Shane (1989) suggested the provision of varying levels of intervention. These interventions would include programs targeting prevention efforts for at-risk families and their children; improved access to family (and youth) support mechanisms such as long-term shelters; and supported emancipation for youth in appropriate cases. Emancipated youth would be eligible for various social benefits currently available exclusively to adults such as health care, low-cost housing, and educational and vocational training programs. For those youth who require only temporary shelter (usually limited to a maximum of 14 days) before reunification or some other resolution is possible, more crisis shelters are needed in underserved areas. Pennbridge et al. (1990) found that the providers of the 72 emergency shelter beds available to youth in Los Angeles County were able to serve scarcely more than one-third of the more than 4,500 requests they received in one year.

Child Maltreatment

Studies indicate a high prevalence of child abuse among runaway/homeless youth. At least half of the youth seeking services from runaway and homeless youth agencies have experienced some form of abuse, and from 19% to 50% of these youth have been identified as neglected (Hartman, Burgess and McCormack, 1987; Kennedy, 1991; Kurtz et al., 1991; Pennbridge et al., 1990; Powers, Eckenrode and Jaklitsch, 1990; Robertson, 1991; Shane, 1989; Sibthorpe, Drinkwater, Gardner, and Bammer,1995; Stiffman, 1989; Yates et al. 1988). The above-mentioned researchers cite the rates of family violence to be approximately 19%, neglect from 19% to 50%, physical abuse from 16% to 73%, and sexual abuse from 5% to 36% among the samples of runaway and homeless youth studied. The fluctuations in abuse rates among samples from runaway and homeless youth service agencies may reflect differences in the sampling, recruitment, and data collection procedures. For example, these studies vary with regard to the instruments used, the source of data (e.g., agency staff vs. youth), the method of data collection (questionnaire vs. interview), the degree of structure and standardization of questions, the timing of assessment (e.g., at client intake vs. at exit), the threat of the initiation of an abuse report to child protective authorities, the fear of loss of service eligibility, and the degree of response anonymity available. In contrast to the high prevalence of maltreatment among runaway and homeless youth, junior high school students have anonymously reported maltreatment rates of 10.3% for physical abuse, 4.1% for sexual abuse, and 3.9% for physical and sexual abuse combined (Hibbard, Brack, Rauch and Orr, 1988).

Substance Use

Studies of substance use among street-involved youth in the U.S. have revealed that these youth are almost five times as likely to be heavy drinkers and three times as likely to be daily users of marihuana, as compared to a national sample of same aged school youth (McKirnan and Johnson, 1986). Prevalence estimates of excessive alcohol use and daily use of marijuana are 41% and 23% respectively. A study by Smart and colleagues showed that 46% of Toronto street youth reported clinically significant patterns of alcohol use (Smart, Adlaf, Porterfield and Canale, 1990). These street youth revealed rates of illicit drug use ten times higher compared with Toronto school students. Fifty-four percent of a homeless youth street sample obtained by the Stanford Center for the Study of Families, Children and Youth reported "regular use" of both alcohol and drugs (1991). In contrast, 21% and 12% of Stanford's shelter sample of homeless youth disclosed regular use of alcohol and drugs, respectively. A study of clinic youth yielded a diagnosis of drug abuse in 57% of the clinic's runaway clientele compared to 14% of the nonrunaways (Yates et al., 1988). With the exception of the study by Yates and colleagues, these studies utilized standardized semi-structured or structured interviews to assess substance use. The Stanford Study collected their data using structured interviews, but information regarding the measures used has not been reported. A study of client case histories from 17 shelters across the nation revealed an association between parental alcohol abuse and homeless youth alcohol abuse (van Houten and Golembiewski, 1978). Sixty percent of this sample had a parent with a history of substance abuse or criminality.

Psychological Distress

Smart and colleagues (1990) reported that approximately one-third of a sample of street youth revealed experiencing frequent feelings of depression and 42% had attempted suicide; yet 68% related that they felt good about themselves. An analysis of intake data in a high-risk youth clinic revealed that, among runaways, 84% were assessed as depressed and 18% reported that they had attempted suicide (Yates et al., 1988); these levels of depression and suicide attempts were approximately four times greater than those in the nonrunaway clinic comparison group. Kennedy's study of client records from a runaway and homeless youth agency revealed that 45% of the population had previously attempted suicide (Kennedy, 1991). The Stanford Study of Homeless Families,

Children and Youth (1991) reported that 39% of their shelter sample of homeless youth disclosed prior suicide attempts during interviews. In contrast, 62% of the Stanford Study's street youth sample reported previous suicide attempts. Among these studies, Smart and colleagues were the only researchers who described the use of standardized instruments to assess mental health.

Physical Illness

Medical chart data from an outpatient adolescent health clinic revealed that homeless and runaway youth were significantly more likely to receive a diagnosis of infection with a sexually transmitted disease, pelvic inflammatory disease, hepatitis, asthma, pneumonia, scabies, trauma, and rape as their nonrunaway cohorts visiting the clinic (Yates et al., 1988). At 13%, the prevalence of pregnancy was similar for both groups. Because of the pressure to participate in illegal and often dangerous activities (e.g., drug dealing, theft, prostitution), these youth are also at high risk for assault, sexual exploitation, homicide, and HIV infection. As with homeless adults, homeless youth are susceptible to malnutrition and gastrointestinal disorders associated with inadequate food sources.

The above overview attempts to describe the complexity of the problem of homeless and runaway youth in North American culture and is meant to be a context in which to place the research questions of this book. These research questions focus on the experience of abusive and neglectful events and psychological distress among homeless youth. The next review highlights the literature on child abuse and neglect and its effects on the mental health of its survivors. In particular, this section probes for the identification of factors which may mitigate the effects of the traumatic event or promote resiliency to these effects.

Child Abuse and Neglect

This section provides an overview of the child abuse and neglect literature with particular emphasis on the prevalence and incidence of child maltreatment in the general population and among adolescents, the psychological and behavioral correlates, and the factors which may mediate or moderate psychological sequelae. Since the causality of child abuse and neglect is not requisite to understanding this book, models of etiology are not reviewed.

Incidence and Prevalence

As with the case of homeless youth, there is little standardization in the definition of child abuse and neglect employed across empirical studies, and the reliable assessment of accurate prevalence and incidence rates has been highly problematic. Rates also may vary according to whether maltreatment "caseness" required (1) disclosure by a survivor during data collection, (2) reporting to child protective authorities, or (3) substantiation by authorities (i.e., met state legal criteria for child maltreatment). According to the findings from the Study of the National Incidence and Prevalence of Child Abuse and Neglect (United States Department of Health and Human Services (USDHHS), 1988), approximately 25.2 children per 1,000 (or a total of more than one and one-half million children) were the subjects of substantiated case reports to child protective services nationwide. About two-thirds (63%) of these cases pertained to neglect, and less than half (43%) were due to emotional abuse (categories are not mutually exclusive). Physical abuse was the most frequently documented abuse type, followed by emotional abuse and sexual abuse. Physical neglect was the most frequently documented type of neglect, followed by educational and emotional neglect. Sixty percent of the countable cases involved moderate injuries, ten percent involved serious injuries, and less than 1% involved fatalities. A recent study of the National Incidence and Prevalence of Child Abuse and Neglect (U.S.D.H.H.S., 1994), the national annual incidence of neglect, physical abuse, and sexual abuse among reported and substantiated cases of maltreatment among minor children were 52%, 23%, and 14%, respectively, in 1992.

Although the 1988 U.S.D.H.H.S. study reports a 66% increase in all maltreatment cases (i.e., for all cases of fatal and nonfatal abuse and neglect) over the 1980 incidence rate and a 74% increase in the incidence of abuse cases, one cannot determine if this reflects an increase of abuse or an increase in reporting. Since the U.S.D.H.H.S. studies reflect data only from substantiated reports and because many cases do not get reported (Finkelhor, 1984), they probably significantly underestimate the actual incidences of child abuse and neglect. Other epidemiological estimates have originated mostly from community-based adult populations and have most often assessed the lifetime prevalence of sexual abuse and exploitation.

Among college student samples, the prevalence of child sexual abuse (variously defined) has ranged from 8-35% for women and from 5-30%

for men; among community samples of adults, the prevalence of child sexual abuse has ranged from 6-62% for women and from 3-16% for men (Peters, Wyatt and Finkelhor, 1986). For non-Hispanic White women responding to community surveys, the prevalence of childhood sexual assault (of the contact type) has been found to range from 5.3% to 67% and, for non-Hispanic White men, from 2 to 3.8% (Russell, 1986; Siegel, Sorenson, Golding, Burnam and Stein, 1987; Wyatt, 1985). In addition, these general population surveys revealed that over half of the sexual abuse perpetrators were acquaintances of the victim. Both Siegel et al. (1987) and Wyatt (1985) reported that approximately half of their respondents who revealed histories of childhood sexual assault had experienced more than one assault. The rather wide range of sexual abuse rates has been attributed to variations in the definitions of sexual assault, the age of the respondent, the degree of probing during interviews (Siegel et al., 1987); the age of the perpetrator relative to the age of the respondent, and the sample composition (Wyatt and Peters, 1986). Similar inconsistencies in data collection procedures have been noted across national samples (Wynkoop, Capps and Priest, 1995). Nevertheless, a review of the prevalence rates of child sexual abuse reported in surveys of nonclinical populations of adults from 19 countries suggests that abuse rates are comparable to those reported in North American research (Finkelhor, 1994).

Ethnicity/Race

Two studies reviewed found no significant differences in the prevalence rates of child sexual abuse between racial/ethnic groups (Hall and Flannery, 1984; Jones and McCurdy, 1992; Wyatt, 1985); one study reviewed found no relationship between race/ethnicity and exposure to child physical abuse (Jones and McCurdy, 1992). However, Siegel et al. (1987) reported higher rates of child sexual assault among non-Hispanic White respondents (8.7%) than among Hispanic respondents (3.0%). Studies of reported cases of child abuse have also found that non-Hispanic Whites are the modal ethnic group among reported cases of sexual abuse and emotional maltreatment (American Association for Protecting Children, 1988; Powers and Eckenrode, 1988); however, at least one of these studies has indicated that Hispanic and African-American abuse victims tend to be over-represented in those cases which are reported (Powers and Eckenrode, 1988). These ethnic differences may partially reflect differences in reporting practices rather than actual differences in exposure.

Gender

When all ethnic groups are considered in the general population, Finkelhor (1984) estimated that for every male who is sexually abused as a child, there are 2-3 females who are sexually abused. Studies of community surveys and of maltreatment cases reported to child protective authorities indicate that females tend to be sexually abused more often than males (Finkelhor, Hotaling, Lewis and Smith, 1990; Jones and McCurdy, 1992; Siegel et al., 1987). The existence of a relationship between the gender of the abuse survivor and the reporting of physical or emotional abuse to child protective authorities has been equivocal (Jones and McCurdy, 1992; Powers and Eckenrode, 1988).

Socioeconomic Status

Studies suggest that the occurrence of neglect and physical abuse is associated with a child's lower socioeconomic status (Giovannoni and Billingsley, 1970; Wolock and Horowitz, 1979). However, a child's socioeconomic status does not appear to be related to exposure to sexual abuse (Finkelhor and Baron, 1986; Hall and Flannery, 1984; Jones and McCurdy, 1992).

Age

The 1988 Study of the National Incidence and Prevalence of Child Abuse and Neglect demonstrated that the incidence of all types of child maltreatment and resultant injuries of moderate severity increase as the child's age increase (U.S.D.H.H.S., 1988). The rates of reported cases of educational neglect, emotional neglect, physical abuse, sexual abuse, and emotional abuse steadily rise from infancy to age 17 and peak between the ages of 12 and 17. According to findings from the National Incidence and Severity of Child Abuse and Neglect (U.S.D.H.H.S., 1981), adolescent maltreatment accounts for 42% of the substantiated reports of child abuse, 41% of all serious injuries and 24% of all fatalities in reported and substantiated child abuse cases. Despite the significant level of injuries and lethal abuse inflicted on adolescents, they are the least likely age group to be reported to child protection authorities (Powers & Eckenrode, 1988; Schellenbach & Guerney, 1987).

Compared with other age groups, scant research has been conducted on child abuse and neglect in adolescent populations. In addition, child protective service representatives have communicated that reports involving adolescents are given a lower priority than reports involving younger children. One study found that, for adolescents, suspected child abuse cases are more likely to be reported if the alleged victim is female, from an ethnic minority or from a low socioeconomic background (Powers and Eckenrode, 1988). The lack of recognition of adolescent maltreatment may be due to several factors: (1) adolescents themselves may be reluctant to report abuse or neglect since they may not view themselves as victims of maltreatment if familial maltreatment has become normalized; (2) adolescents may be ashamed or embarrassed to disclose maltreatment for fear of the social stigma and rejection which may occur (especially among peers); (3) adolescents may fear disclosing due to family/perpetrator reprisal and rejection and/or family economic and psychological disruption; and (4) adolescents may be perceived to be more developmentally capable of self-protection and self-determination and, consequently, less vulnerable than smaller children.

Gender and Abuse Characteristics

Finkelhor (1984) found gender differences in the experience of sexual abuse among the American Humane Association's reported and substantiated cases of childhood sexual abuse. Compared with female victims of sexual abuse, Finkelhor discovered that male victims were more often victimized by a nonfamily member, more likely to be physically abused, more likely to come from a poor home headed by a single parent, and more likely to have their abuse reported to the police rather than the child protective services. Like female survivors of sexual abuse, male survivors were most often victimized by adult males.

Pierce and Pierce (1985) also discovered gender differences in their review of substantiated child sexual abuse cases reported to a child abuse hotline. Female victims were more likely to live with and be sexually abused by their natural fathers, less likely to have physical contact with the perpetrator, more likely to be placed in protective custody and receive more counseling than male victims. Perpetrators of sexual abuse of female children were more likely to be imprisoned than the victimizers of male children. As with Finkelhor's study, male sexual abuse victims were more likely to be physically threatened and abused and less likely to live with a father figure. Both studies revealed tendencies for male sexual abuse survivors to be younger at the time of the abuse report and to reside with other sexually abused children compared with female survivors.

In an examination of medical records from a tertiary care hospital, Farber and colleagues found no relationships between gender of the sexually abused child and the relationship to the perpetrator, source of referral of the child, the number of abusers, the number of victims, the persistence of the abuse or the existence of physical abuse (Farber, Showers, Johnson, Joseph and Oshins, 1984). The discrepancy between Farber's results and those of Pierce and Pierce and Finkelhor may be due to the differences in sample source and study design. For instance, many factors may influence which sexual abuse victims receive referrals to a tertiary care facility, and these factors may mask gender differences in the experience of sexual abuse which are detectable earlier in the discovery process. In addition, the case control design used by Farber and colleagues does not allow the analysis of gender differences in the frequencies of referrals from different sources. Gender differences discovered in reported and substantiated cases of sexual abuse may be reflections of differential reporting and substantiation rather than actual gender differences in the experience of sexual abuse.

Psychological Sequelae

Researchers disagree on the potential for significant psychological sequelae from child abuse, and many abuse survivors fail to meet criteria for a diagnosis of a psychiatric disorder according to the Diagnostic and Statistical Manual of Mental Disorders (DSM-III) (American Psychiatric Association, 1980). Nevertheless, the bulk of the research conducted in the past decade indicates that there can be serious developmental and adaptational consequences of child abuse (Tong, Oates & McDowell, 1987). For example, studies have reported the prevalence of at least one psychiatric disorder in sexual abuse populations to range from 20 to 80 percent (Silverman, Reinherz, & Giaconia, 1996; Sirles, Smith and Kusama, 1989; Tufts' New England Medical Center: Division of Child Psychiatry, 1984).

Clinical Issues

Due to the rather large spectrum of psychological and behavioral symptoms which survivors of abuse and neglect may display, these survivors often come to the attention of professionals not specifically trained in evaluating a client/patient for a history of child abuse and neglect. Many clinicians believe that effective treatment of the psychological and behavioral consequences of exposure to traumatic events relies, in part, on the accurate identification of the underlying trauma (Horowitz, 1986). Considering the correlations between many psychological distress symptoms and the experience of child abuse and neglect, it would seem to be prudent to evaluate patients for the exposure. Schaefer, Sobieraj, and Hollyfield (1988), for example, reported that approximately one-third of the adult male alcoholics in their sample of veterans had experienced childhood physical abuse, and Cohen and Densen-Gerber (1982) reported that 84% of their sample of adult drug abusers in treatment acknowledged a history of childhood sexual abuse, physical abuse and/or neglect. Cavaiola and Schiff (1988) reported that 30% of their adolescent chemical dependency in-patients were identified as victims of physical and/or sexual abuse.

Indicators of Psychological Distress

Psychological and behavioral correlates of child maltreatment which have been noted in the clinical and empirical literature include: depression, anxiety, low self-esteem, self-hatred, guilt, self-blame, sense of helplessness, high external locus of control, anger, rage, depersonalization, dissociation, personality disorders (e.g., borderline and multiple personality disorder), post-traumatic stress disorder (PTSD), conduct disorders, avoidant behavior, alienation, decreased ability to concentrate, low empathy, sleep or eating disorders, heightened number of somatic symptoms, developmental disorders affecting cognition and speech, poor school performance, sexual identity confusion, poor peer relationships, poor self and body image, problems with intimacy and sexual relationships, runaway behavior, promiscuity, prostitution, criminal activity, substance abuse, self-mutilation, suicide attempts, social withdrawal, repeated victimization, and aggressive/possibly abusive or exploitative behavior (Ageton, 1983; Briere and Elliott, 1994; Briere and Runtz, 1988; Burgess, Hartman and McCormack, 1987; Edwards and Donaldson, 1989; Fergusson, Horwood and Lynskey, 1996; Lindberg and Distad, 1985; Cohen and Mannarino, 1988; Coons, 1986; Shapiro, 1987; Goodwin, 1981; McCormack, Janus and Burgess, 1986; Mullen, Martin, Anderson, Romans and Herbison, 1994; Peters, 1988; Rimsza, Berg and Locke, 1988; Roesler and McKenzie, 1994; Stein, Golding, Siegel, Burnam and Sorenson, 1988; Straker and Jacobson, 1981; Tong, Oates and McDowell, 1987; Toth, Manly and Cicchetti, 1992; Urquiza and Goodlin, 1994).

Symptom Onset

The literature on the psychological effects of child maltreatment has focused on the sequelae of child sexual abuse. The psychiatric symptomatology discovered among child/adolescent survivors of child abuse is often referred to as the "short-term" or "proximal" effect of the abuse. Browne and Finkelhor (1986) prefer to label the psychiatric symptoms manifested within two years of the abuse termination as "initial" effects; they argue that the label "short-term" may incorrectly imply that the effects are of short duration. Conversely, symptoms revealed by adult survivors frequently are labeled "long-term" sequelae to abuse. Neither the mechanisms by which proximal symptoms disappear, remain or evolve into other long-term symptoms nor the processes by which the presentation of some symptoms is delayed have been well identified and elaborated.

Proximal Effects

Meta-analyses of the proximal effects of child sexual abuse revealed that the symptoms which tend to differentiate child abuse survivors from non-abused psychiatric patients and non-abused community children include anxiety disorder, low self-esteem, depression, post-traumatic stress disorder (PTSD), suicide ideation and behavior, and sexualized behavior (Beitchman, Zucker, Hood, daCosta and Akman, 1991; Green, 1993; Wolfe and Brit, 1995). Of these symptoms, sexualized behavior is the sole symptom which appears to be unique to child sexual abuse survivors when compared with other clinical samples of children (Beitchman et al., 1991; Browne and Finkelhor, 1986). In children, sexualized behavior may be manifested by sexual play, masturbation, seductive behavior or sexually aggressive behavior; in adolescents, sexualized behavior may also include frequent sexual contacts with numerous partners.

Distal Effects

Long-term sequelae of child sexual abuse in adults and adolescents have included sexual dysfunction and dissatisfaction, sexual orientation confusion, depression, lowered self-esteem, borderline personality disorder, multiple personality disorder, substance abuse, and increased risk of offending and victimization; long-term effects of child sexual abuse accompanied by significant force or threats consist of anxiety, fear, and suicide ideation and attempts (Beitchman et al., 1991; Beitchman et al., 1992; Fergusson et al., 1996; Green, 1993; Jumper, 1995; Siegel et al., 1987; Wyatt, 1985). The bulk of the research detailing the psychological effects of child sexual abuse among children and adolescents has been based on samples of psychiatric patients and child protective service clients; whereas the parallel studies among adults have utilized samples of undergraduates and community residents as well as psychiatric patients. It has been suggested that studies based on psychiatric samples may over-estimate the amount of psychopathology associated with child abuse if only the most disturbed survivors seek professional psychological treatment.

Homeless and Runaway Youth

The few studies which have examined the psychological and behavioral correlates of child abuse among youth who utilize the services of runaway and homeless youth agencies have described similar abuse associated symptoms to those described above (Janus et al., 1987; McCormack et al., 1986; Powers and Jaklitsch, 1989; Powers et al., 1990; Stiffman, 1989). The psychological and behavioral symptoms associated with sexual abuse among runaway and homeless youth include fear of adult men, sexual dysfunction and confusion, and sexual acting-out. Increased somatization, suicide ideation and behavior, avoidant coping, depression, anxiety, feelings of futurelessness, guilt, aggressive and nonaggressive problem behaviors, and parental drug abuse were associated with undifferentiated maltreatment. Substance use was not associated with maltreatment in these studies.

Witnessing Family Violence

The rare studies of the psychological and behavioral correlates of witnessing family violence have produced data which suggest that, among children residing in a shelter for battered women, those who have witnessed but have not been victims of family violence experience increased anxiety, depression and decreased self-esteem compared to non-abused children (Brown et al., 1983). Children who were both witnesses and victims of family violence displayed the highest levels of depression and behavioral problems, even after socioeconomic status was controlled among the three comparison groups (Emery, 1989; Hughes, 1988). Jaffe and colleagues (1990) found that child observers of wife abuse reported beliefs of personal responsibility for the violence and for their mother's protection; these young witnesses also displayed stronger tendencies to view violence as an appropriate means of conflict resolution compared with children from nonviolent families. Kalmuss (1984) reported that, for both men and women, witnessing marital violence was more predictive of perpetration of and victimization by severe marital aggression in adulthood than was being hit by parents during adolescence.

Specificity of Psychological Indicators

There are no indicators (or combinations thereof) of psychological distress which are pathognomonic for exposure to any type of child abuse, neither can their absence be construed as evidence of a lack of exposure to child abuse, neglect, or family violence (Green, 1993). In fact, the only symptoms which tend to differentiate between sexual abuse and physical abuse exposure are symptoms associated with sexual dysfunction and aggressive behavior, respectively (Briere and Runtz, 1990). The association of aggressive behavior with physical abuse may be a reflection of gender differences in abuse exposure in study samples (Beitchman et al., 1991). The degree of specificity of any of these symptoms is relatively unknown because of the failure of most studies to assess and control for exposure to more than one type of child abuse. As reflected by the commonality of distress symptoms exhibited by survivors of physical and sexual abuse, the underlying psychological abuse common to both types of abuse may be responsible for the bulk of the psychic damage inflicted (Claussen and Crittenden, 1991; Garbarino, 1980).

Although numerous studies of children and adults suggest an association between exposure to child abuse and psychological distress, some studies have either found no relationship between child abuse and distress or a relationship limited to specific measures of distress (Hibbard and Hartman, 1992). For instance, standardized measures of depression, anxiety and self-esteem failed to discriminate between sexually abused female children recruited from a rape crisis center and non-abused age-matched children (Cohen and Mannarino, 1988). In a study of female college undergraduates, standardized measures of depression, self-esteem, locus of control and parental support did not differ significantly between sexually abused and non-abused women (Fromuth and Burkhart, 1989). These two studies differ from the vast majority of other studies of the sequelae of child sexual abuse in their methodologies, and this may contribute to the disparities in the findings. The abused sample in Cohen and Mannarino's study consisted primarily of children abused by non-parent relatives, whereas the participants of comparable studies have often been abused by a parent or caretaker. Fromuth and Burkhart's study differs from other studies in that it includes non-contact sexual abuse in its sexual abuse definition. It has also been suggested that general measures of psychological distress may not be sensitive enough to detect the symptoms associated with sexual abuse (Beitchman et al., 1991).

Moderators and Mediators of Psychological Effects

Moderators and mediators of the effects of child maltreatment have been examined infrequently. Factors which have been found to influence the psychological effects of the abuse experience may be divided into three categories: the victim's sociodemographic and preexisting psychological characteristics, the victim's family characteristics, and the abuse characteristics (Beitchman et al., 1991 and 1992; Briere and Runtz, 1988; Browne and Finkelhor, 1986; Burgess et al., 1987; Cohen and Mannarino, 1988; Conte and Schuerman, 1987; Edwards and Donaldson, 1989; Fromuth, 1986; Kinard, 1982; McCormack et al., 1986; Rimsza, Berg and Locke, 1988; Sirles et al., 1989; Tong et al., 1987). The bulk of the published research has focused on moderators and mediators of the relationship between child sexual abuse and psychological distress.

Gender

The studies which examine the potential role of moderating factors in the experience of child sexual abuse and the subsequent development of psychological distress most frequently have examined the moderating effects of the gender of the survivor. Gender was not found to affect the relationship between previous sexual assault and current psychiatric symptoms in Burnam and colleagues' (1988) community survey nor in Briere and Runtz's (1988) study of crisis center adult clients, both of which used standardized structured interviews. In addition, subject gender did not moderate effect size variance in Jumper's (1995) meta-analysis of the relationship of child sexual abuse to adult psychological adjustment.

On the other hand, reviews of the child and adult sexual abuse literatures (Beitchman et al., 1991 and 1992) and a community-based study of adults (Stein et al., 1988) suggest that sexually abused males tend to display symptoms of externalizing symptoms of distress (e.g., conduct disorder, substance abuse) more frequently than sexually abused females. Female survivors of sexual abuse, on the other hand, tended to report internalizing symptoms of distress (e.g., depression, anxiety) more frequently than male survivors. It is not clear whether these findings indicate a global propensity of troubled males to exhibit externalizing behaviors compared with troubled females or perhaps a greater likelihood that sexually abused males experience concomitant physical abuse than sexually abused females.

Several researchers have examined gender as a moderator of the experience and effects of sexual abuse among several shelter samples of runaway and homeless youth (Hartman, C.R. et al., 1987; Janus et al., 1987; McCormack et al., 1986; Powers et al., 1990). Data were collected using structured interviews of youth or semi-structured questionnaires of shelter staff; some measures were standardized, but most were not.

A female homeless youth's response to sexual abuse tends to be characterized by running away, blaming others, viewing the abuse as uncontrollable and unpredictable, participating in prostitution and petty theft, acting aggressively towards others, and using drugs or alcohol (Hartman, C.R. et al., 1987; McCormack et al., 1986). In contrast, male victims have tended to react by experiencing self-blame for the abuse, replicating their sexual exploitation on others, having increased somatization and suicide ideation, having decreased perceived control over events, withdrawing from interpersonal relationships, and concealing their sexual abuse history and their emotions. Hartman and her colleagues suggest that these gender variations in response reflect differences in the psychological manipulation employed by the perpetrators of their abuse experiences. For example, male victims of extrafamilial sexual abuse may be led to believe that they are willing participants rather than victims and are, therefore, responsible for their own involvement in the activities. This dynamic is even more apt to exist if the male victim is coerced into recruiting other victims. McCormack and her colleague interpreted their results as evidence that, among homeless youth, female victims of sexual abuse may act in an aggressive manner as a ". . . violation of female sex role expectations . . . and a challenge to the authority of the family and other social institutions . . .."

Age at Onset

The evidence supporting a relationship between the age at abuse onset and the development of subsequent psychopathology is equivocal, at best (Adams-Tucker, 1982; Beitchman et al., 1991, 1992; Browne and Finkelhor, 1986; Burnam et al., 1988; Kendall-Tackett, Williams and

Finkelhor, 1993; Hartman, Leon, and Finn, 1987; Rimsza et al., 1988; Ruch and Chandler, 1982; Wolfe and Birt, 1995; Wozencraft et al., 1991). In a review of the studies of adult survivors of sexual abuse, Beitchman et al. (1992) reported a trend which indicated that postpubertal abuse is more traumatic than prepubertal abuse. However, in a review of the studies of child and adolescent sexual abuse survivors, Beitchman et al. (1991) presented evidence that children who were molested before adolescence were the most disturbed. The apparent discrepancy between these two reviews may be due to several factors: age at abuse onset is often confounded with duration of abuse, amount of force used, and severity of the abuse. Abuse onset may significantly precede the age at which the abuse is reported, a proxy measure often used instead of age at abuse onset. In addition, the nature and timing of the indicators of psychological distress resulting from sexual abuse may differ between children and adults, making comparisons between the two age groups difficult. Age at abuse onset may be a useful measure to estimate the developmental stage which may have been first affected by the abuse, but it cannot replace knowledge of the duration of family dysfunction which may have preceded the abuse and may significantly effect psychological outcomes. In addition, there is some evidence to suggest that the amount of force accompanying sexual abuse and the degree of intrusiveness of the abuse increase with the victim's age (Gomes-Schwartz, Horowitz and Sauzier, 1985; Peters, 1976).

Compliance

The abuse survivor's level of compliance with the abuser's demands has also been found to influence the degree of psychological distress experienced subsequent to the abuse. For instance, this compliance may range from fighting back and getting help to participation, enjoyment and the recruitment of others. Higher levels of compliance have generally been associated with greater levels of psychological distress, particularly guilt, self-blame and aggressive behaviors (Burgess et al., 1987; MacFarlane, 1978).

Sociodemographic Characteristics

With regard to the effects of sexual abuse survivor race/ethnicity and socioeconomic status on psychological outcome, the evidence is ambiguous. Wyatt (1986) did not find ethnicity and educational level to significantly effect the relationship between sexual abuse and psychological distress. Russell and her colleagues found that, among survivors of sexual abuse, African-American women reported more distress than White women; however, these African-American women were also more likely to experience more intrusive and more forced abuse compared with the White women in the sample (Russell, Schurman and Trocki, 1988). Russell's findings were not explained by differences in social class.

Family Characteristics

Family composition, parental psychopathology, parental substance use, available social support (especially from a significant adult) and the existence of a parental/caretaker role model for coping are examples of family characteristics which may influence the risk of being abused and the effects of abuse on adaptation. Survivors of child sexual abuse are more likely than non-abused children to have divorced or separated biological parents, parents with psychological problems, and parents who abuse alcohol and/or drugs (Adams-Tucker, 1981; Beitchman et al., 1991 and 1992; Burgess et al., 1987; Gruber and Jones, 1983). Family cohesion and the availability of a significant and understanding adult with adaptive coping skills have been found to significantly mitigate the negative effects of sexual abuse (Conte and Schuerman, 1987; Freidrich, Beilke and Urquiza, 1988; Fromuth, 1986; Spaccarelli and Kim, 1995).

Abuser Characteristics

The abuser characteristics (age, gender, substance abuse) and the survivor's relationship with the abuser (e.g., degree of dependency, closeness and trust before abuse) have also been found to affect the level of subsequent psychological distress, especially the ability to trust adults. In general, survivors of sexual abuse perpetrated by biological fathers or stepfathers are more likely to report symptoms of psychological distress than survivors who were victimized by other offenders (Adams-Tucker, 1982; Briere and Runtz, 1988; Gorcey, Santiago, McCall-Perez, 1986; Sirles et al., 1989; Wozencraft et al., 1991). The relationship of the perpetrator with the victim is often associated with the gender and age of the victim; boys and older children are more likely to be sexually assaulted by non-relatives (Mian, Wehrspann, Klajner-Diamond, LeBaron and Winder, 1986; Pierce and Pierce, 1985; Tong et al., 1987). Intrafamilial sexual abuse may also be associated with abuse of greater duration and frequency, greater family psychopathology and less available support for the abused child (Russell, 1986).

The few studies that have examined the psychological effects of perpetrator gender have found that male offenders are associated with the greatest amount of psychopathology and recalled trauma in sexual abuse survivors (Finkelhor, 1984; Seidner and Calhoun, 1984). However, perpetrator gender has not been necessarily associated with the severity of abuse (Rudin, Zalewski, Bodmer-Turner, 1995). Two studies which analyzed the impact of perpetrator age on the effects of sexual abuse among college students revealed that students reported feeling more traumatized when the offenders were adults (vs. adolescents) (Finkelhor, 1979; Fromuth, 1983). These results held after controlling for perpetrator gender, use of force, type of sex act, and age of the victim (Finkelhor, 1979). One may speculate that increased psychological distress may be associated with the number of sexual abuse offenders involved; however, none of the studies reviewed examined this. Sirles and her colleagues (1989) found that offender alcohol abuse was related to the diagnosis of psychiatric disorders among sexually abused children visiting an outpatient psychiatry clinic.

Abuse Characteristics

Other abuse-related mediators of distress include the degree and type of coercion involved, the degree of intrusiveness, the number of abuse occurrences, and the duration of the abusive relationship(s). It has been suggested that the more types of abuse exposure (i.e., physical, emotional and sexual abuse, family violence, and neglect), the more terror associated with the abuse experience (often associated with the amount of force used), the more intrusive the physical contact (e.g., oral, vaginal or anal intercourse) and the greater the exposure to abuse (frequency and duration), the greater the resultant psychological distress experienced (Adams-Tucker, 1982; Bagley and Ramsay, 1985; Briere and Runtz, 1988; Boney-McCoy and Finkelhor, 1995; Burgess et al. 1984; Collings, 1995; Fergusson et al., 1996; Finkelhor, 1979; Fromuth, 1986; Goodman, Dutton and Harris, 1997; Gorcey et al., 1986; Groth, 1978; Hartman, M. et al., 1987; Herman, Russell and Trocki, 1986; Peters, 1988; Rimsza et al., 1988; Sirles et al., 1989; Tong et al., 1987; Wolfe and Birt, 1995). In addition, exposure to multiple types of abuse or trauma is likely to affect psychological adjustment independently of the type of abuse being examined. For instance, Higgins and McCabe (1994) found that level of family violence predicted adult adjustment independent of child sexual abuse.

Perpetrator identity, abuse duration, type of sexual acts, and the use of force may be interrelated. For instance, survivors of sexual abuse perpetrated by stepfathers have tended to experience more force or threats of force and more intrusive sexual acts; survivors of sexual abuse by either fathers or stepfathers have often experienced abuse of longer duration and frequency than survivors of other offenders (Russell, 1986). Beitchman and his colleagues (1991 and 1992) have concluded that the mediating roles of many of the abuse-specific and victim-specific characteristics in the development of psychological symptomatology are ambiguous and that future studies need to assess these characteristics and control for their covariates. In particular, researchers suggest that the etiological roles of the survivor's gender, age at abuse onset, duration and frequency of abuse in the survivor's psychopathology require further definition.

Miscellaneous Factors

Mediating factors which occur as a result of the abuse may consist of the survivor's disclosure and the familial and institutional response to that disclosure, the meaning and attributions of the abuse to the survivor, and the survivor's residential and caretaker stability. Sexual abuse survivors whose disclosure of the abuse resulted in negative parental reactions or removal from their homes have been found to suffer the greatest amount of psychological distress (Adams-Tucker, 1982; Fromuth, 1986; MacFarlane, 1978; Peters, 1988; Tufts' New England Medical Center, 1984). However, Lamb and Edgar-Smith (1994) reported that the timing of the first disclosure, the recalled response to the first disclosure, and the number of lifetime disclosures were not associated with adult socioemotional functioning. The recipient of and the perceived response to the first disclosure differed by whether the first disclosure occurred during childhood or adulthood.

In another study, negative parental response to disclosure was related to the survivor's removal from home (Tufts' New England Medical Center, 1984). In contrast, Wozencraft and her colleagues (1991) found that suicide ideation was more frequent among those sexual abuse survivors who had not been removed from home. Examination of the context and meaning of a child's removal from home may help to explain these contradictory findings. Although little systematic research has examined the effect that the meaning that abuse events has on survivor adjustment; attributions of self-blame have been associated with more severe psychological distress in some sexual abuse survivors (Gold, 1986) and may be more frequent when the sexual abuse involves penetration (Spaccarelli, 1994). More recently, negative cognitive appraisals of threat, harm or loss (including negative self-evaluations) associated with child sexual abuse have been significantly associated with internalizing symptoms among adolescent women (Spaccarelli, 1995).

Exposure to Physical Abuse Without Sexual Abuse

Few studies have examined the moderators of the psychological effects of physical abuse in the absence of sexual abuse. There is limited evidence that abuse and victim characteristics influence psychological outcomes of physical abuse. Children who are younger at the onset of the abuse, exposed to a longer term of abuse, more severely injured, and maintained in a unstable home environment have been found to suffer the greatest problems with emotional adjustment (Kinard, 1982).

Methodological Issues

Sampling

The child abuse literature which focuses on prevalence estimates and on the psychological impact of the abuse has been fraught with methodological problems. Empirical studies in child abuse have tended to rely on small non-probability samples from single sources which are of limited external validity and have largely been comprised of clinical case studies and anecdotal data from providers. This reliance on clinical samples has probably been for two reasons: (1) clinical samples were readily available, tended to contain many child abuse cases and required fewer resources in order to obtain data and (2) researchers did not realize how prevalent child abuse was within the general population. It is suspected that clinical samples overestimate the degree of psychopathology associated with abuse since well-adapted survivors probably do not seek therapeutic services.

Study design

Many of the child abuse research designs have failed to include any comparison groups or standardized norms for their measures of psychological distress, and those that have included comparison groups may have been hampered by their inability to thoroughly exclude cases of abuse from them. The lack of comparative data with non-abused subjects makes it difficult to interpret the uniqueness and significance of the descriptive data collected from abused subjects. The selection of non-abused clinic patients as comparisons for abused patients has had the advantage of being able to control for the potential effect of having agency contact or being labeled as having a psychosocial problem. The disadvantage of this practice may be that factors which covary with abuse may also covary with other traumatic experiences which are prevalent in a clinical population but not in the general population. For example, measures of anxiety may distinguish children with a history of abuse from those without such a history in the general population but not in a psychiatric population because of covariance with the experience of being a psychiatric in-patient (Lamphear, 1986).

Definitions of Abuse

Studies of the prevalence and effects of child abuse are difficult to compare because of a failure to adequately describe the methodology used. In particular, these methodologies exhibit a lack of consensus and/or a lack of specificity in defining what constitutes abuse for purposes of the research. Validation of the abuse is often difficult to achieve as well, especially considering that many cases never come to the attention of child protection authorities.

Broad definitions of abuse used in the inclusionary criteria for participation in a study allow the researcher to assess the impact of different levels and types of abusive acts and facilitate multiple analyses which are comparable to the definitions used in other studies. These more general definitions of child abuse permit the discovery of the impact of the seemingly less abusive acts and support the validation of the victim role for the survivors of these abuses (Wyatt and Peters, 1986).

Dimensions of abuse which vary the most across child abuse studies include age of the victims, age of the perpetrators relative to the age of the victim, degree of consent (vs. coercion) from adolescent victims, type(s) of abuse and degree of physical contact, and types of perpetrators included (i.e., relative, acquaintance, or stranger). Most researchers include maltreatment perpetrated by parents in their inclusion criteria for child abuse, and some include abuse committed by other caretakers. Non-caretaker and non-relative perpetrators are less likely to be included in the operationalization of child abuse, but they may comprise anywhere from

30% to 50% of all child abuse (Finkelhor and Baron, 1986). Abuse by older children or by peers is rarely assessed by child abuse researchers.

Response Rates

Response rates in abuse studies are likely to be affected by the degree of anonymity or confidentiality available to the respondent, the wording and ordering of the questions, the degree of rapport established with the researcher during data collection, and the perceived social and legal ramifications of disclosure. For instance, an informed consent which specifies that child protective authorities must be contacted if an adolescent respondent discloses abuse may be expected to stifle disclosures among those who feel most threatened by the potential consequences.

In general, two hypotheses about response rates in child abuse studies prevail (Peters, Wyatt, and Finkelhor, 1986): (1) survivors of child abuse tend to avoid answering questions about child abuse because of the potentially negative social and psychological consequences of disclosure or (2) survivors of child abuse tend to seek out opportunities to discuss their abuse experiences in supportive and non-judgmental environments. The first hypothesis suggests that prevalence rates of abuse would be underestimated providing that only abuse survivors remove themselves from participation. The second hypothesis implies that an overestimation of the prevalence rate of abuse could occur if non-abused individuals selected out of the study because of a lack of topic relevance. The likelihood of either of these hypotheses being true depends on the amount of abuse-specific information used to describe the study during participant recruitment and on the psychological needs of the abuse survivor at the time of the study. Peters and colleagues' (1986) review of the child sexual abuse literature suggests that survivors of child sexual abuse do not respond consistently in either direction to the topic of child sexual abuse in empirical studies.

Response Bias

The retrospective study designs are subject to recall error of the abuse itself and of any antecedent circumstances such as pre-abuse baseline measures of psychological functioning. Recall error may be a function of mood, psychological functioning, information storage and retrieval ability, and the meaning of the abuse for the developmental stage of the respondent. For instance, Femina and her colleagues (1990) conducted a

9-year longitudinal study of incarcerated youth from adolescence into young adulthood in order to assess their abuse reporting patterns over time. The results revealed a tendency among the incarcerated to underreport histories of abuse in adulthood compared with substantiated reports collected during adolescence. Contrary to some expectations, the incarcerated adolescents were not found to overreport their abuse experiences in bids for sympathy. The subjects who denied or minimized previous abuse experiences acknowledged that the reasons for their altered disclosure included the desire to forget the abuse, the wish to avoid humiliation, and the concern for protecting their parents. These researchers suggest that abuse questions be as neutral as possible with regard to the inference of blame and responsibility for the abuse. Finkelhor (1986) suggests that retrospective collection of pre-abuse data may be optimized by using memory anchors and multiple data sources. Recall ability also has been associated with abuse characteristics. In a prospective study of women's memories of child sexual abuse, women were more likely to recall past child sexual abuse if they were older at the time of the abuse, the perpetrator was a "stranger", and force was used during the abuse (Williams, 1995).

Temporal Sequence

Longitudinal designs allow researchers to follow the natural course of abuse consequences. However, the natural course of symptom development after abuse experiences is not known, so the timing of data collection subsequent to abuse exposure may also affect what symptoms of distress, if any, are detected. Although symptoms of psychological maladjustment have been detectable in many survivors long after the abuse experience (Tong et al., 1987), it is not clear what differentiates these individuals from those who display only short-term symptomatology. It has been suggested in the literature that preexisting psychological distress may be exacerbated by the exposure to child abuse, and this phenomenon is responsible for the apparent persistence of abuse associated symptoms. Prospective designs, although costly, may reveal the existence of a relationship between pre-abuse psychological distress, the experience of abuse, and subsequent psychological functioning. Steele (1986) argues that the effect of researcher attention on the long-term development of subjects in a child abuse study may mitigate the negative effects of the abuse. One may take this argument one step further and wonder if such attention would mask the actual differences in psychological adaptation and distress trajectories between the victims of child abuse and non-abused children because of the victims' greater need for this attention.

Data Collection

The method of data collection may also affect the quantity and quality of the data collected. For instance the quality of an interview to assess a history of child abuse most likely depends on the effect of rapport with the interviewer, the amount of probing and clarifying of questions and answers permitted, the number of specific screening questions used, and the degree of confidentiality involved in the data collection, storage and reporting. The use of questionnaires has typically been recommended for the collection of sensitive information because of the ability to maintain the anonymity of the respondent. However, there may not be as much incentive to complete a questionnaire in solitude as there is to complete an interview with another person; and questionnaires cannot respond sympathetically to traumatic disclosures nor clarify question wording.

In a review of child sexual abuse prevalence studies, Wyatt and Peters (1986) reported that the use of face-to-face interviews and multiple questions for abuse screening tended to produce the highest prevalence rates compared with methods using questionnaires and single question screeners. Face-to-face interviews were postulated to be most effective at eliciting abuse information when the interviewer is well-trained, ethnically homologous with the respondent, non-judgmental, and sensitive to the difficulties in disclosing an abuse history. Multiple screening questions for abuse are believed to identify more abuse histories by allowing the respondent more time to consider disclosing, more opportunities for the respondent to recognize a descriptive match between his/her abuse experience and the question, and more cues to assist in recalling the abuse event(s) (Peters et al., 1986).

Measures

With regard to standardized measures, the normative distribution of some outcome measures specific to child abuse may be unknown, such as sexualized play among pre-adolescent children, since standardized measures of child abuse are still being developed (Finkelhor, 1986). Researchers have varied in their requirements that child sexual abuse cases be substantiated before inclusion in studies of the consequences of child maltreatment. Although, Leiter and colleagues (1994) found no significant differences on a variety of school and delinquency outcome measures between substantiated and unsubstantiated child abuse cases among school aged children.

Psychological measures used, if standardized at all, often lack either face validity or convergent validity for the population being surveyed or interviewed. Often times, the source of the data is the subjective and incomplete information found in a medical, social service, law enforcement, or court record. The ordering of the questions as well as the pattern of exclusions have been suspected to affect disclosure of abuse and psychological distress by virtue of their psychological impact and/or presumptive logic, respectively (Haugaard and Emery, 1989; Lamphear, 1986; Wyatt and Peters, 1986). However, Haugaard and Emery (1989) found no evidence that the order of abuse questions relative to the dependent psychological measures affected the relationships uncovered in their survey of college undergraduates.

Potential mediators and moderators of the abuse experience on adaptation are often ignored in measurement. For example, organic disease/damage, IQ, developmental level, race/ethnicity, age, gender, source of subjects, socioeconomic status, and home circumstances are infrequently examined or controlled. Competing independent factors such as exposure to other traumatic events or major life events or high levels of chronic role strain have rarely been assessed. Finally, much of this research literature has focused on the effects of sexual abuse on females, ignoring the impact of this and other types of abuse and neglect on both females and males.

Theoretical Models of the Psychological Effects of Abuse:

Before completing this review of the relevant child abuse literature, a few studies which advance theoretical explanations for the psychological and behavioral correlates of child abuse and neglect are discussed. The discussion includes a review of developmental theory, attribution theory, learned helplessness, and the four traumagenic dynamics model of the effects of child sexual abuse.

Developmental Disruption Theory

Wolfe (1987) postulates that the psychological and behavioral disorders found in abused children may be better understood if the abuse is examined for how it disrupts a particular developmental process. The disruption of any developmental process is hypothesized to affect subsequent developmental progression. Wolfe states that it is primarily the effects that abuse has on the psychological development of the child that causes lasting psychological disorder, rather than its effects on physical development. Variations in adaptation are explained by the presence of mediators of the abuse such as efficacious coping skills and social support. The existence of these mediators depends on the mastery of related developmental tasks. Since abuse often occurs in a family experiencing a history of multiple stressors, it may be difficult to distinguish the unique effects that abuse may have on the developing child. Wolfe organizes his description of the interactive relationship between psychological development, abuse and psychological outcomes around three primary dimensions of child development: behavioral, socioemotional and social-cognitive.

For example, the facets of self-control and aggression in behavioral development are posited to be most affected by abuse. If punishment is overly punitive and inconsistent, the child may not learn socially acceptable impulse control and may learn that aggression is an appropriate response to feelings of frustration. A parent's inconsistent response to a child's behavior may result in an inability of the child to feel secure and trusting of others. This lack of trust of others coupled with poor self-control may hinder the development of social competence. There is evidence that early exposure to punitive and inconsistent disciplinary measures, family violence and physical abuse may lead to aggressive behavior in early childhood (Egeland and Sroufe, 1981; Maccoby and Martin, 1983; Parke and Slaby, 1983) and antisocial and violent behavior in adolescence (Lewis, Pincus, and Glaser, 1979; Loeber, Weisman and Reid, 1983; Tarter, Hegedus, Winsten, and Alterman, 1984).

Wolfe submits that child abuse impairs the development of the attachment, empathy and affective dimensions of socioemotional maturation and the intellectual and moral aspects of sociocognitive development. Child abuse experienced during infancy or early childhood has been associated with poor attachment between the child and the caregiver (Egeland and Sroufe, 1981). The impairment of parent-child attachment is believed to limit the child's stress reduction resources (Lipsitt, 1983) and may predispose the child to psychological adaptation problems (Achenback and Edelbrock, 1981) and future abuse (Starr, 1982). Abused children have been found to be less empathic towards others compared with non-abused children (Main and George, 1985). In the presence of obviously distressed children, abused toddlers were likely to behave aggressively or fearfully towards these distressed children, whereas non-abused toddlers displayed concern (Barahal, Waterman and Martin, 1981). The evidence for the notion that affect development is impaired as a result of child abuse comes from studies which demonstrate higher levels of depression and hopelessness among abused children compared with non-abused children (Kazdin, Moser, Colbus and Bell, 1985). Children who had histories of abuse and who had also experienced recent abuse were found to display the highest levels of depressive symptomatology.

With regard to the evidence that abuse affects the intellectual and moral aspects of sociocognitive development, studies of children's attributions have revealed that abused children tend to view the intentions of their peers' actions toward them as hostile, regardless of the true intent (Dodge, Murphy and Buchsbaum, 1984). Abused children have been found to perceive acts which precipitated psychological distress to be unfair when it happened to others but not when it happened to them. In contrast, neglected children judged the inequitable distribution of toys to be unfair for themselves but not for others (Dodge and Frame, 1982). Deficits have also been noted in the cognitive, verbal and social skills of abused children compared with non-abused children (Hoffman-Plotkin and Twentyman, 1984; Parke and Slaby, 1983). These deficits have been attributed to the suppression of cognitive and social stimulation in the abusive home environment.

Wolfe's developmental perspective of the effects of child abuse has contributed a much needed framework for understanding how child abuse may disrupt the normal developmental process. Nevertheless, the interactive relationship between development, abuse, and adaptation makes it difficult to disentangle the individual effects and understand the underlying process. Wolfe's circular explanation of the relationship between abuse, psychological development and psychological disorder does not specifically account for the existence of inherent individual differences which may affect variations in resilience to the effects of abuse. Most of the supporting evidence presented by Wolfe is derived from child survivors. It is not clear from the model what the long-term effects of these developmental disruptions might be. Ideally, future studies on the sequelae of child abuse will examine the effects of the disruption of developmental progress before, during and after the abuse onset. In addition, it appears that the model assumes that the abuse experienced was intrafamilial physical abuse, and it does not attempt to explain the effects of extrafamilial abuse, sexual abuse, or family violence per se.

Based on case studies of child sexual abuse survivors, Green (1996) postulated that the impact of intrafamilial sexual abuse across the lifespan might be understood in terms of exposure to two traumatic elements: (1) the repeated sexual assaults combined with (2) the chronic pathological family interaction. Green suggested that exposure to the sexual assaults results in the observed anxiety-related symptoms and exposure to the family dysfunction produces a defensive organization which becomes incorporated into the survivor's personality.

Attribution Theory

Of the cognitive theoretical models, attribution theory has had some empirical support in explaining the psychological correlates of child abuse and neglect. Attribution theory posits that individuals make attributions about behaviors and their consequences in three dimensions: locus of causality (internal vs. external to the person), controllability (within the person's control or not), and stability (particular to the environment or to the individual) (Weiner, 1979). Gold (1986) found that women who were sexually abused in childhood and who reported psychological distress tended to make internal, stable, and global self-attributions about the abuse and about other subsequent bad events (some may refer to this as an attributional style or personality trait). For instance, these sexually abused women may blame themselves for the abuse experience and subsequently develop an attributional style whereby they consistently attribute the cause of all negative events to themselves. Gold suggests that their reported levels of distress and low self-esteem may be due to the self-attributions which they make for bad events. Meyer and Taylor's (1986) findings with rape victims support the hypothesis that it is not the causal attributions which result in behavioral self-blame but those which result in characterological self-blame which are associated with poor adjustment. In other words, long term psychological distress does not result from self-blame for an act committed but from self-blame for possessing some inherently undesirable trait.

Learned Helplessness

Of the learning theoretical models, the reformulated theory of learned helplessness (which incorporates concepts from attribution theory) has also had some empirical support in explaining the psychological and behavioral correlates of child abuse and neglect. This theory proposes that individuals exposed to outcomes that are unrelated to their efforts learn that these outcomes are uncontrollable. This, in turn, leads to the expectation that outcomes will persist to be independent of their actions in the future. This expectation produces motivational, cognitive, and emotional deficits which are manifested as reduced initiative, inability to see past and present relationships between responses and outcomes, and uncontrollable anxiety. When outcomes are perceived as uncontrollable, an attribution is made for helplessness (Abramson, Seligman and Teasdale, 1978).

For instance, Kelley (1986) suggested that because of the unequal power positions with their adult sexual abusers, children learn that the abuse is independent of their actions and because of this learned non-contingency about present and past events, experience feelings of helplessness and a lack of control. Subsequently, the child attributes this non-contingency to internal (self), stable (across time), and global (across situations) processes. These attributions depend on the degree of self-blame experienced (often-times characterological rather than behavioral), the chronicity of the abuse, and the number of abusers and abusive situations, respectively. It is the child's expectation of future non-contingency that is believed to account for prevalence of child abuse victims who marry abusive spouses and/or participate in intergenerational abuse. Kelley cites that the support for the application of the reformulated theory of learned helplessness to the understanding of the effects of child abuse is based on clinical anecdotes from child abuse survivors and the existing empirical evidence supporting the application of attribution theory. Kelley submits that the psychological correlates reported in the literature are consistent with the symptoms of learned helplessness: fear, low self-esteem, guilt, anxiety, and depression. The experience of powerlessness to protect oneself is postulated to create the psychological maladaptation. Implicit in the theory of learned helplessness is that the learning about the noncontingency of the abuse may take place over a period of time with many exposures to acute abuse events. The reaction of helplessness and anxiety is elicited across events and across time.

Although many of the symptoms associated with child maltreatment are consistent with the symptoms of learned helplessness, the ability of attribution theory or the theory of learned helplessness to predict some of the other psychological and behavioral effects is unclear. For example, once attributions are made for the abuse, how are these attributions translated into emotions, cognitions and behaviors which account for the presence of sexualized or aggressive behaviors or substance abuse? Researchers applying attribution theory to understanding the effects of child abuse posit that maladaptation from abuse occurs because of attributions of self-blame. However, this does not account for the maladaptive symptoms detected in the absence of self-blame among female runaway abuse victims (Hartman, C.R. et al., 1987). In addition, neither theory specifically accounts for some of the potential moderators and mediators of the effects of abuse. These moderators and mediators include the developmental stage of the child maltreatment survivor, the survivor's gender, the degree of family and institutional support available and abuse-related characteristics. It may be argued, however, that adaptation depends upon the attributions made for the abuse and that these attributions are based on the characteristics of the abuse and the survivor. The majority of the research on the effects of child abuse that is based on attribution theory or the theory of learned helplessness has been limited to studying the effects of sexual abuse among adult women. Little is known about whether these theories are applicable to the understanding of the effects of other traumatic stressors or other types of child maltreatment among children and adults of both genders. Lastly, the theory of learned helplessness focuses on the etiology of one end of a spectrum of responses, helplessness, rather than also including explicit interpretations of the etiology of competence and adaptation.

Four Traumagenic Dynamics Model

Finkelhor and Browne's Four Traumagenic Dynamics (1988) is a model which incorporates the components of PTSD in an attempt to explain the spectrum of psychological symptoms associated with child sexual abuse. The model was developed in response to the inability of the PTSD model to specifically account for many of the symptoms associated with child sexual abuse noted by clinicians and researchers and the inability of many substantiated child abuse victims to qualify for psychological treatment using the PTSD criteria for diagnosis. Some of the sequelae of child sexual abuse which the PTSD standard does not recognize include self-blame, sexualized behavior/sexual problems, suicidality, substance abuse, revictimization, aggressive conduct, and cognitive disorders. The PTSD criteria as defined by the DSM-III (American Psychiatric Association, 1980) require the existence of a recognizable and universally traumatic stressor, the reexperiencing of the trauma associated with the stressor, the numbing of affect, and at least two of the following symptoms:

hyperalertness
sleep problems
survival guilt
difficulties with memory or concentration
avoidance of activities reminiscent of the traumatic event or the exacerbation of symptoms when exposed to cues of the traumatic event.

Finkelhor and Browne's model adds the following four trauma-inducing components to the PTSD formulation to describe the trauma of child sexual abuse: (1) traumatic sexualization in which the child's sexuality is influenced in inappropriate and interpersonally dysfunctional manners; (2) betrayal in which the child discovers that someone upon whom they depend has intentionally hurt him/her; (3) stigmatization in which the child receives negative messages about him/herself and (4) powerlessness in which the child's will, desires, and sense of efficacy are dominated and controlled and the child experiences the threat of injury or annihilation. These factors are broadly conceptualized, overlapping themes around which symptoms of psychological distress may be organized. These four dynamics are believed to occur in varying degrees, depending on the abuse characteristics, and their combined effect colors the abuse survivor's cognitive and emotional perspective of his/her relationship with the world. As the main sources of trauma in child sexual abuse, the absence of any of the dynamics may account for better adaptation.

The Four Traumagenic Dynamics Framework predicts that sexual abuse involving force, seduction to participate, older perpetrators, or perpetrators in a position of trust with the child will be the most psychologically damaging. It may be recalled from the discussion of moderators and mediators of abuse effects that there is evidence to support these predictions. Evidence which supports the existence of traumatic sexualization resulting from child abuse has included the discovery of non-normative sexual knowledge and behaviors among small children (Adams-Tucker, 1981) and the problems surrounding sexual functioning and intimacy among adult survivors (Briere, 1984). The internalization of the social stigmatization associated with sexual abuse has been suggested by the tendency for abuse survivors to associate with other stigmatized groups, such as criminals, prostitutes and drug abusers (Briere, 1984; Silbert and Pines, 1983). The experience of powerlessness in the ability to control the abuse is believed to be responsible for the development of symptoms associated with PTSD (Briere, 1984; Justice and Justice, 1979; Summit, 1983). The lack of control over the abuse exposure may damage the feelings of self-efficacy associated with existing coping skills and with one's ability to protect oneself. The damage to self-efficacy may be result in impaired performance at work or school. Decreased self-efficacy associated with declining school and work performance has been observed in child abuse survivors (Adams-Tucker, 1981). Lastly, the experience of powerless may result in either further victimization (Fromuth, 1986), if it is manifested as helplessness, or aggressive and victimizing behavior towards others as an attempt to gain control over the abuse situation (Groth, 1978).

Finkelhor and Browne's model is unique in that it specifically accounts for the traumatic sexualization which may antecede sexual dysfunction among sexual abuse survivors. It fails, however, to establish linkages with the traumatic processes which may be involved with other types of child abuse and neglect, family violence, or other types of overwhelming life events. It also neglects to account for the observed differences in impact relative to the age/developmental stage at the time of exposure, for the processes by which some survivors may actively and passively affect the degree of negative impact, and for the various ways that the impact may be manifested. The four Traumagenic Dynamics Framework lacks an underlying theory which interconnects the four dynamics; rather, it is more of a collection of explanations for observed phenomena. As such, it allows for the application of other theories within and between these dynamics. Like the other cognitive-based theoretical frameworks, the Traumagenic Dynamic Framework may underestimate the role that affect plays in the development of psychological distress resulting from abuse. For instance, none of the theoretical models reviewed thus far have specifically discussed the etiology of dissociation, an important phenomenon from a psychoanalytic perspective. The potential contribution of psychoanalytic theories to the study of child maltreatment is explicated in the forthcoming section on traumatic stress.

Although psychological theories are beginning to guide some of the work which examines the adaptational consequences of child abuse and neglect, it is unusual to see the application of stress and coping theories in the child abuse literature. In contrast, traumatic stress researchers demonstrate a good deal of interest in the child abuse literature. Additionally, the theoretical base which is evolving specific to child abuse tends to center on the deviant and pathological responses of survivors, rather than on the resilient and adaptive responses. In order to broaden the theoretical foundation for this book, this review includes a synopsis of the stress and coping theoretical and empirical literature. This literature provides a context for the analysis of both moderating and mediating mechanisms which either exacerbate or mollify the traumatic impact of child abuse, neglect and family violence.

Stress, Coping, and Resiliency

The stress and coping literature, in its broadness, seems to provide the best conceptual and methodological linkages applicable to the data available for this study. It contributes a framework which can accommodate multiple theoretical paradigms as well as the examination of various stressors and stress reactions. Use of this literature allows comparisons to be made between the stress reactions documented in the child abuse and homeless youth literatures and the stress experiences of other populations. The following review of the literature highlights the major stress and coping theoretical perspectives, issues, and findings. This review incorporates discussion concerning the theoretical models which describe the effects of traumatic stressors and the mechanisms which may be involved in resilience to particular stressors. Included in this section is coverage of research concerned with identifying moderators and mediators of the stress experience. The effect of gender on the stress experience is of particular relevance to this book. In contrast with previous sections, the review begins with a discussion of the major theoretical perspectives in the stress and coping literature and concludes with the empirical findings relevant to distress and the effects of gender and age on the stress process.

Theoretical Models of Stress and Coping

One of the first observations which may be made regarding the stress literature is the conceptual and methodological difficulties of defining the components of the process. These components include the stressor, the person's appraisal of the stressor, the person's response (if any), and any resultant psychological or physiological distress. Attempts to operationalize these elements have resulted in theoretical and practical overlap between them. Although this makes investigation challenging, it draws attention to the inherent complexity of the stress process.

General Adaptation Syndrome

Selye (1973) described the stress process as one which challenges an organism to adapt or readjust (the general adaptation syndrome). In this model, exposure to a noxious stimulus, or stressor, elicits an alarm reaction which, depending on the presence of conditioning factors, leads to adaptation to the stressor. Reexposure or prolonged exposure to the stressor may lead to resistance, but extensive reexposure may lead to exhaustion, illness and death. A key concept in the general adaptation syndrome is that the body's adaptive resources are finite and can be exhausted.

Selye and his colleagues believed that failures at adaptation resulted in either or both physical and psychological distress. Due to the moderating effects of specific conditioning factors; such as genetic predisposition, gender, age and diet; the stress process was perceived to vary across stressor types and across individuals. Selye used the term "stress" to describe the complex reactions an organism has to an environmental challenge. Although much of the early stress research focused on physiological responses to stressors, the application of Selye's General Adaptation Syndrome to psychological stressors was inevitable. Indeed, there is evidence that both physical and psychological stressors can affect similar physiological and psychological distress symptoms (Baum, Singer and Baum, 1981). For purposes of reviewing the stress literature as it applies to this book, the focus remains on psychological and behavioral outcomes rather than biological indicators.

As researchers from sociology and psychology entered this arena of study, the stress process became defined by social, psychological as well as physiological constructs. Operationalizations of the components of the stress process varied across and within these academic disciplines. Although consensus on these definitions is still lacking today, a few of the more popular perspectives are presented. The review centers around empirically supported examples of two general paradigms: (1) the transactional models and (2) the structural models.

Transactional Model

The most significant of the transactional models has been described by Lazarus and Folkman (1984). In this model, stress is conceptualized to arise from the reciprocal interaction of the person with the environment over time. Potential stressors are assessed for situational meaning and implications for personal well-being, i.e., primary appraisal. Primary appraisal is influenced by the perceived threat from, attitudes toward, control over and prior experience with the stressor (Baum, Singer and Baum, 1981). Secondary appraisal involves the evaluation of available coping resources which may be implemented to alter the person-environment relationship or to manage any emotional distress. The transactional models distinguish themselves from structural models in that they do not emphasize either a stimulus or a response orientation. Rather, the focus of inquiry is on the process by which events are related to psychological distress via appraisal and coping. According to this perspective, an abused child facing another encounter with an abusive parent might appraise the event as threatening and out of her/his control. An inability to obtain support from the other parent might result in the child's decision to escape the situation by running away (e.g., altering the child's exposure to the stressor) or taking drugs (e.g., managing emotional distress). Holman and Stokols (1994) extended the application of a person-environment transactional model to the understanding of self-destructive behaviors and revictimization among survivors of child sexual abuse by proposing that mental and/or physical escape from the abuse may impair the development of a positive self-identity and attachment to the socio-physical environment if the abuse results in global shifts away from active efforts to control the environmental.

Structural Model

A primary example of the structural paradigm is the stress model proposed by Pearlin and coworkers (1981). These researchers describe the stress process as one which results in distress by affecting changes in a person's sociostructural roles. A major stressor is postulated to exacerbate preexisting role strains which diminishes self-esteem and a sense of mastery or control. It is through this mechanism that individuals are rendered vulnerable to the symptoms of distress. Coping and social support are seen to affect changes in distress only by their influence on this antecedent process of diminished self-esteem and sense of mastery. Major stressors may create new strains or exacerbate existing strains and can deplete social support networks, economic resources and other coping mechanisms. For example, escalating family violence may add strain to a child who is struggling to maintain a normal school life. The strain of maintaining the school role may result in psychological distress by decreasing the child's sense of mastery and self-esteem.

Pearlin and others (Bourque and Back, 1977; Pearlin et al., 1981) noted that it seemed to be the off-schedule (or unpredictable) life events, such as mid-life spouse bereavement, which resulted in the most role disruption and subsequent distress. Pearlin and colleagues also noted that vulnerability to the negative effects of life strain depended to some degree on the availability of valued roles other than those being threatened or disrupted. Although work by Thoits (1995) suggests that the psychological response to life events may depend more on the meaning and sequencing of life events than the salience of the role-identity involved. Consistent with Pearlin and colleague's sociostructural perspective, there is evidence that one's exposure to particular stressful events and strains and one's possession of high levels of self-esteem and mastery are differentially distributed across socioeconomic strata (Pearlin and Lieberman, 1979; Ulbrich, Warheit, and Zimmerman, 1989).

Stressors

Stress researchers have devised various ways of defining the noxious agents that Selye described. Lazarus and Cohen (1977) characterized a typology of three stressor types: cataclysmic phenomena, powerful events and daily hassles. Stressors which had sudden onsets, tended to occur as single or clustered events and affected large numbers of people, such as natural disasters, were considered to be cataclysmic phenomena. Events which were equally challenging but tended to affect separate individuals, such as bereavement, were typed as powerful events. Daily hassles incorporated the chronic and repetitive irritants or challenges associated with daily life which do not require large amounts of change. An example of a daily hassle would be exposure to an automobile traffic jam. Similarly, Pearlin (1985) categorized life strains into three groupings: chronic problems of daily life; predictable life cycle events and less expected and often undesirable life crises.

Other investigators distinguish stressors based on their desirability, frequency of occurrence, severity, controllability, and temporal characteristics. Though there are mixed results with regard to which aspects of life events are the most stress-inducing, the features of uncontrollability (Brown and Siegel, 1988; Paykel, 1974), threat (Brown and Harris, 1978), role exits (Paykel, 1974), loss and undesirability (Brown and Harris, 1978; Burt and Bjorck, 1987; Cohen, 1987; Rutter,

1981) have been associated with psychological distress, especially depression, in some studies. Pearlin (1985) submits that it is not these life event characteristics or even their impact on role transitions, per se, which induce psychological distress. Rather, it is their effect on the more constant aspects or conditions of life.

Developmental Issues

Investigators have also begun to consider the effect of developmental tasks on the stress process and the effect of stress and coping on developmental progression (Aneshensel and Gore, 1991; Rutter, 1981; Wolfe, 1987). Rutter (1981) suggests that previous experience with a stressor may influence a person's response via the following developmental processes: the stressor may (1) precipitate distress which may persist for reasons independent of the stressor; (2) initiate physiological changes which cause later dysfunction; (3) contribute to persistent behavioral change which becomes maladaptive over time; (4) be detrimental to family conditions or stability which may lead to disorder; and (5) modify sensitivity to stress or alter the ability to cope effectively with future stressors. Wolfe (1987) adds that experience with a stressor may alter a person's self concept which affects the response to new stressors and influences a person's choice of stressor exposure. It is for these reasons that Aneshensel and Gore (1991) have suggested that the qualitative nature of the stress process in adolescents may differ from that in adults.

Another example of a structural model of stress and coping is Aneshensel and Gore's model (1991) which was developed to describe the stress process in adolescents. This model reflects the potential effect that the normative developmental tasks may have on the stress process for adolescents. These developmental tasks include developing autonomy from the family, establishing an identity and exploring intimacy in peer relationships (Patterson and McCubbin, 1987). Aneshensel and Gore propose the following model of stress and coping in adolescence: (1) normal developmental processes can precipitate role and relationship changes; (2) these role and relationship changes mediate the effect of developmental transitions on health outcomes (3) certain factors act to moderate the relationship between developmental change, role transitions and health outcomes and (4) these moderators can be affected by normal development or by role transitions. These moderating factors include: non-normative life stress and strains, social support, coping resources, individual characteristics and demographics, social attributes, cohort history and the context of the stress.

Coping

Regardless of the theoretical paradigm, coping may be described as the cognitive and behavioral attempts to diminish, endure or master challenges which drain an individual's resources (Kessler, Price and Wortman, 1985). Three common factors underlie most coping typologies: actions taken to alter one's relationship with the stressor, changes made in perceiving this relationship and efforts taken to manage associated emotional distress (Kessler, Price and Wortman, 1985). These dimensions are not mutually exclusive and may occur together or sequentially. Actions to alter one's relationship with the stressor include information seeking, behavioral avoidance and problem solving involving alteration of the stressor. Redefining the situation and searching for meaning can be examples of alterations in perceptions of the relationship. Cognitive avoidance and tension reduction strategies can be considered types of emotional management coping techniques. Successful coping, i.e., adaptation to the challenges of the stressor, has been associated with familiarity with the stressor, the temporal and physical discreteness of a stressor, knowledge of the efficacy of various coping strategies, accurate expectations of outcomes and the cultural and role context of the situation (Lazarus, 1975).

Theoretical Models of Traumatic Stress

The stress and coping models discussed thus far have been applied to studies investigating both "normative" and "non-normative" life events and strains. That is to say, they have focused on life stresses that a majority of a community population would be likely to experience at some point in their lives as well as those life events which are off-schedule or unscheduled and out of the ordinary experiences. However, the bulk of these applications have been to normative life stresses. The review next examines the models which represent the conceptual trends with regard to traumatic stressors, a type of non-normative life event, and their psychological and behavioral sequelae. Traumatic life events or crises have been defined as being discrete, negative, unexpected, undesirable, uncontrollable life events which are outside of what is considered the normative life experience, such as child abuse, rape, disasters, war, and concentration camp imprisonment. Other definitions have emphasized the components of the trauma process rather than the discreteness of the traumatic event.

Psychodynamic Models

Freud (1893) conceptualized that the intensity of an undesirable life event determines whether a stimulus barrier is violated and whether the ego is overwhelmed in its efforts to master the event. He suggested that attempts are made to repress the unacceptable idea of the life event into the unconscious. Failure at repression was believed to result in anxiety and the experience of unbearable affect. The constriction of this unbearable affect is then likely to occur. Pierre Janet (1889), Freud's contemporary, suggested that the strong emotions elicited by an undesirable life event interfere with the appraisal and response which are adaptive for the situation (van der Kolk, Brown, and van der Hart, 1989). Janet also postulated that failure to completely face the experience leads to the dissociation of the traumatic recollections with subsequent fragmentary reliving of the original event. Horowitz (1986) also believed that the response to traumatic events involves the phases of reliving and denial manifested as intrusive reexperiencing of the event and numbing of affect. Horowitz suggested that effective resolution of this response sequence depended on the intentional recollection of the trauma and the reintegration of its memory and associated affect into cognitive schemas adaptive to daily functioning.

A Cognitive Model

McCann and colleagues (1988 and 1990) elaborated upon Horowitz's idea of cognitive schemata and their relation to psychological adaptation after traumatic events. Their constructivist self-development theory (i.e., CSD theory) of psychological adaptation is based on the composite theoretical and empirical findings collected from studies of rape, child abuse, domestic violence, criminal victimization, disasters, and the Vietnam war. The premise for this model is schema theory. Schema theory states that individuals actively organize the information received about the self, others and the environment into core beliefs and expectations in order to understand the information and create meaning. These stable cognitive entities are called schemata, and they are shaped by one's early life experiences. Subsequent exposure to similar life experiences can activate latent schemata and their associated cognitions. These cognitions may influence mood and behavior and the way new information is organized and stored. New information may be processed and incorporated with old schemata to maintain cognitive consistency or cause the modification of these older schemata in order to avoid cognitive dissonance. Discrepancies of fit between schema and information result in conflict and arousal. The emotional arousal may be reduced by avoiding the information which is discrepant with schemata, reinterpreting the meaning of the information to maximize harmony with schemata or modifying schemata to better fit with the new information. The organization of cognitions and information into schemata is believed to influence the organization of behaviors as well (Wortman, 1983).

McCann and her associates describe that schemata develop in response to all life experiences within the following primary areas of psychological and social functioning: safety, trust, power, esteem and intimacy. Life experiences include all information regarding interactions with other people and the environment. The development of these schemata are also molded by a person's gender and sociocultural history. Schemata are predicted to form within the psychological and interpersonal functioning areas in the order given above which correspond with a person's developmental stages.

Schemata are associated with emotions, and these may be positive or negative. Survivors of traumatic stress may possess negative schemata within one or several of the five areas of functioning. Psychological response patterns vary according to the positive and negative schemata about self and others within these areas. The role that these schemata play in psychological adaptation to the traumatic event depends on the phenomenological context of the person's situation.

Life experiences, therefore, are postulated to shape, support or change prior schemata. These schemata exert influence on psychological adaptation. The model suggests five major classifications of traumatic stress response reflective of psychological adaptation: emotional, cognitive, biological, behavioral and interpersonal. Persons are believed to be motivated to behave in ways which are congruent with or confirming of existing schemata.

Psychological adaptation is suggested to affect a person's exposure to future life experiences. For example, within the area of safety, negative schemata may be developed in response to sexual assault which reflect beliefs and expectancies about the inability to protect oneself. These negative schemata may precipitate anxiety symptoms and fragmentary intrusive replaying of the sexual assault in a subconscious attempt to reconcile this negative event with previous positive safety schemata. Exposure to cues reminiscent of the sexual assault may elicit unwarranted fear responses and the inability to distinguish threatening situations from nonthreatening situations and to mobilize adequate coping resources. This may result in the exposure to other negative life events. These negative safety schema may also result in the inability to trust others and a behavioral response of social withdrawal.

CSD theory, together with the previously reviewed psychoanalytic and cognitive stress models, provide a framework for understanding how schemata may affect the appraisal of traumatic events and psychological adaptation and how psychological adaptation may affect interpersonal relations and subsequent exposure to life experiences. It is broad enough to be applicable to all types of family violence and to other traumatic stressors, and it accounts for variations in response due to the survivor's developmental stage. This schema model may be used to understand the process of resilience as well as psychological distress, and it can accommodate the existence of suspected mediating and moderating factors. CSD theory is particularly valuable to the study of child maltreatment because it gives more definition to the emotional, behavioral, and interpersonal dimensions of response, unlike the other cognition-based theoretical models. Nevertheless, it may be argued that by focusing on cognitive structures such as schemata, CSD theory still underestimates the importance of affective processes in the development of psychological distress. Cognitive models, in general, may undervalue the roles of those affective processes which operate at the subconscious level in the formation of distress.

Methodological and Conceptual Issues

The early studies which examined the associations between exposure to life events and psychiatric illness found only modest relationships, and daily hassles were often better predictors of distress than major life events (Kanner, Coyne, Schaefer, and Lazarus, 1981). It has been speculated that these modest relationships have been due to methodological and conceptual flaws in the studies. Namely, these flaws have included imprecise definitions of life events and psychological distress, incorrect analytic techniques and the failure to specify moderators and mediators (Tennant, Bebbington, and Hurry, 1981).

For example, tests of reliability of reporting of life events have revealed variable agreement between the subject and a close informant about the occurrence of an event and its severity (Brown and Harris, 1978; Cohen, 1987; Hudgens, Robins, and Delong, 1970). Test-retest methods of assessing the reliability of life event measures have generally shown moderate to low reliability within individuals as well (Horowitz, Schaffer, Hiroto, Wilner, and Levin, 1977). These low reliability scores may be attributed, at least partially, to the lack of specificity of some life event scales and to the use of clinical samples with psychiatrically unstable patients. A review of studies which compared life event data obtained from both checklist and interview indicated that life events are reported more frequently on checklists (Gorman, 1993). Empirical validity of life event scales appears to be compromised most often by the degree of ambiguity and reliability of event measures (Tennant et al., 1981).

It has been speculated that self-reports of life events have been hampered by recall bias and retrospective contamination in which the reporting of the event and its context are affected by respondent memory, mood or current mental status (Brown, 1974). A respondent's efforts to assign meaning to past events or current problems may result in spurious associations between measures of distress and recalled events. Johnson and Bradlyn (1988) reported that, although a respondent's ability to accurately recall past life events decreased over time, recall was improved when data were collected by interview rather than by questionnaire. The use of time anchors may also improve the recall and time placement of life events.

The temporal assessment of life events in relation to psychological distress has also been an issue. Due to the cross-sectional design of the early stress and coping studies, the direction of causality could not be ascertained. Prospectively designed studies demonstrated evidence that the relationship between life events and psychological distress is bidirectional: exposure to negative life events may precipitate or aggravate psychological distress and distress may predispose an individual to experience negative life events (Billings and Moos, 1982; Hammen, Mayol, deMayo, and Marks, 1986; Kessler, 1997).

Life stressors have often been treated as discrete events, which may obscure the detection of those events which occur so frequently as to provide almost chronic exposure to a threat to adaptation. Distress onset has also been measured as if it were discrete in spite of evidence that the bulk of depressive symptoms found in the community is chronic in occurrence (Aneshensel, 1985; Ormel and Sanderman, 1989). High levels of chronic distress within a sample may mask the detection of those reacting to acute life stress (Ormel and Sanderman, 1989).

Other temporal questions include: what is the best length for an evaluation period after an event? In other words, is distress evident immediately after exposure to a life event? Or is there an incubation period before distress develops? Or will different symptoms be detected at different times of assessment? How long will distress be detectable before resolution has occurred? Is the coping strategy or distress detected due to a past event, the anticipation of an event or the failure for a desirable event to occur?

The measurement of distress or maladaptation has ranged from the evaluation of nonspecific symptoms of distress to symptoms of specific psychiatric disorders and diagnostic case status. The assessment of psychological reactions to life events has tended to not include definitions and measurements of symptoms of adaptation. These evaluations have included nonstandardized clinical interviews as well as standardized semi-structured and structured interviews and questionnaires. Specific psychiatric disorders which have been assessed include depression and dysphoria, suicide ideation and attempts, anxiety, substance abuse, conduct disorders and schizophrenia. Of these, depression has been evaluated most frequently. Using depression as an example of outcome measures, the measurement advantages and disadvantages are described for two different standardized methodologies.

Standardized psychiatric interviews and self-report symptom scales have both been used in the estimation of depression following major life events. Proponents of the interview methodology praise its relative reliability and ability to give a diagnostic case status which may reflect a clinically significant diagnosis. The Diagnostic Interview Schedule, or DIS, is an example of the standardized interview methodology. Diagnoses are based on the number of symptoms, their severity, duration and configuration. Symptom scales, on the other hand, are less directly associated with a diagnosable depressive disorder. An example of a symptom scale is the Center for Epidemiological Studies Depression Scale, or CES-D. Although these symptom scales more closely reflect the respondent's threshold for the symptoms of depression, they do not yield data which can be easily translated into psychiatrically defined case status. Standardized interviews and symptom scales can both provide a continuum of depressive symptoms which may indicate a predisposition to depressive disorders, a subclinical affective disorder, or stages before or after psychiatric disorders (Aneshensel, 1985).

The measurement of coping has also been an issue in stress and coping research. Coping has conceptual and methodological overlap with life events and psychological distress. For example, in some studies of adolescent stress and depression, drug abuse, truancy and theft have been viewed as controllable negative life events (Cohen, Burt, and Bjorck, 1987). They could also be perceived as coping strategies or symptoms of psychological disorders. Coping efforts may precipitate, be a symptom of, or exacerbate psychological distress (Kessler, Price and Wortman 1985). The criterion of successful coping has often been the avoidance of disorder, but this becomes a circular argument if one explains the avoidance of disorder as occurring because of successful coping (Rutter, 1981). Controversy has also arisen regarding whether coping reflects a trait of the individual or the state of that individual in a particular situation. The ability to assess coping is affected by these issues as well as the extent to which a person is aware of his/her own coping efforts and able to accurately report them (Kessler, Price and Wortman, 1985).

The inclusion of various mediating and moderating variables in these analyses has, in some instances, increased the amount of variance in psychological distress that is accounted for by life events. These constructs have included perceived control, self-esteem, and social support. Control, although variously defined, has generated considerable empirical support and has appeared in numerous theoretical models: locus of control theory (Rotter, 1975), self-efficacy theory (Bandura, 1977), stress and coping theory (Lazarus and Folkman, 1984), mastery within stress and coping theory (Pearlin et al., 1981), hardiness (Kobasa, Maddi, and Kahn, 1982), learned helplessness theory (Abramson, Seligman, and Teasdale, 1978; Seligman, 1975), a conceptual framework for the long-term psychological effects of traumatic child abuse (Carlson, Furby, Armstrong, and Shlaes, 1997), and attribution theory (Weiner, 1979). Although far from unequivocal, the sum of the empirical evidence suggests that those who appraise life events and their consequences as being beyond their control are more likely to use emotion-focused coping and are more susceptible to the effects of stressors (Thoits, 1995).

The constructs of loss and danger have been described in the literature as being event characteristics which are associated with negative psychological impact. It has also been suggested that it is the appraisal of the loss and danger aspects of events which are associated with decreases in perceived control and attendant depression. Self-esteem is viewed alternately as a symptom of a depressive disorder and a mediator of depression, and there is empirical evidence which supports both perspectives. Several investigators of psychological distress have found evidence supporting the predictive power of social support and self-esteem when combined with measures of life stress and personality (Aneshensel and Stone, 1982; Brown, Andrews, Harris, Alder, and Bridge, 1986). Vilhjalmsson (1993) argues that conceptualizing social support as a strain which directly increases the risk of depression, rather than as a moderator of the effects of other stressors, is most consistent with the available data from community studies.

In general, little is known about how appraisal affects the choice of coping endeavors, how disposition affects appraisal and coping and vice versa, how people avoid or create life stresses, what determines coping choices (especially adaptive ones), how coping choices are acquired and changed (Kessler, Price and Wortman, 1985), and what the determinants and dimensions of the meanings of stressors might be (Park and Folkman, 1997; Thoits, 1995). In addition, the role of fear as a mediator in the stress and coping process has been relatively unexplored. The degree of fear elicited by a stressor may represent the level of threat or challenge associated with the stressor as perceived by the person. This fear may influence the subsequent choice of coping strategies (Lang, 1977) and how information about the stressors is processed, stored, and retrieved (Foa, Steketee, and Rothbaum, 1989). As with most appraisals of life event characteristics, there is conceptual overlap between the emotion elicited by the life event, such as fear, and psychological distress. Fear may be a precursor to, a symptom of, or the result of distress. Intuitively, transactional stress and coping models are satisfying in that they attempt to account for the conceptual congruity between steps of the stress process. Although this may be a more accurate reflection of reality, it presents fairly difficult methodological problems. This review now takes a closer look at the empirical findings relevant to general stress and coping theories and their applications in adult samples. The research reviewed here emphasizes studies which have used objective or standardized measures and comparison groups.

Adults

It is important to bear in mind that in spite of evidence suggesting that stressful life events play a role in the onset of psychological and physiological distress, most people exposed to such events do not develop detectable psychological distress (Kessler, Price and Wortman, 1985; Paykel, 1978). Of those who do suffer from distress following major life stress, between 20% and 40% fail to recuperate entirely in spite of the passage of time (Silver and Wortman, 1980). Furthermore, psychological distress is likely to be determined by many factors besides the life event in question.

Research findings indicate that chronic difficulties (or daily hassles) and major life events are independently associated with somatic and mental health (Brown and Harris, 1978; DeLongis, Coyne, Dakof, Folkman and Lazarus, 1982) but that daily hassles account for more variation in psychological distress than do major life events (Kanner et al., 1981). There is also evidence that negative daily events mediate the relationship between negative life events and psychological distress (Wagner, Compas and Howell, 1988), yet negative life events have been found to be associated with increases in symptoms of psychological distress, even when initial levels of distress are controlled (Billings and Moos, 1982). The relationship between particular coping strategies and distress outcomes has been variable (Stone, Helder and Schneider, 1988). Pearlin and Schooler (1978) suggest that adaptive coping may have more to do with the variety of coping strategies in one's collection than with using any one particular strategy.

There is also evidence of an inoculation effect that experience with stress may have on the adaptation to future stressors. Burgess and Holstrom (1979) found that recovery from rape occurred more rapidly among women who had experienced the loss of a parent, spouse or child through death, divorce or separation compared with those who had no history of such losses. However, adaptation took longer for women who had been criminally assaulted prior to the rape compared with women who had not experienced a previous assault.

Several groups of factors have been found to moderate the effects of stressors on a person. These factors include social support, coping, appraisal and various individual characteristics (Thoits, 1995). These individual characteristics include age, sex, genetic factors, temperament and intelligence (particularly as related to problem solving skills) (Rutter, 1981). There is evidence, for example, that there may be a genetic predisposition to criminality (Crowe, 1974; Hutchings and Mednick, 1974) and that temperament affects a child's ability to elicit supportive responses from a parent (Dunn, 1980; Rutter, 1977). Since the stress moderating effects of gender among adolescents is salient to this book, the review now focuses on the studies which describe stress and coping within adolescents and children and which describe the effects of gender on the stress process.

Adolescents and Children

Research in stress and coping among adolescents has more or less followed the path of the stress research among adults and has focused on variations in exposure to stressors and in vulnerability to stressors (Aneshensel and Gore, 1991). As with the research on adults, the majority of the evidence supports the relationship between the experience of life stress and psychological distress among adolescents (Compas, Wagner, Slavin, and Vannatta, 1986; Brown and Siegel, 1988; Swearington and Cohen, 1985; Thoits, 1983). In other studies with youthful samples, the relationship between life events and distress has been demonstrated to be mediated by the occurrence of negative daily events (Wagner, Compas and Howell, 1988); and previous distress has been predictive of exposure to negative life events and maladaptation (Swearington and Cohen, 1985). These studies also replicate the findings with adult samples.

With regard to differences in the stress experience across childhood and adolescence, it has been noted that the number of daily life strains experienced increases through adolescence while the number of major life events remains fairly stable among high school students (Compas, Davis and Forsythe, 1985). There has been no evidence of increased vulnerability to distress relative to developmental stage among children of parental divorce (Wallerstein and Kelly, 1980). However, studies indicate that significant life stress produces various symptoms of distress in children, depending on the child's age. For example, Cohen and colleagues (1987) reported that young adolescents were more likely to act-out when maladapted after significant life stress, and older adolescents were more likely to display internalized symptoms of maladaptation similar to adults. Brown and Harris (1978) reported that younger children tended to display more delayed reactions to bereavement compared with older children. Kagan (1988) found that life stressors, in general, tended to induce fear in younger children and anger in older children.

Among youth, negative life events have been associated with decreased self-esteem (Greenberg, Siegel and Leitch, 1983), depression, anxiety, drug use, self-destructive tendencies, suicide (Cohen-Sandler, Berman and King, 1982; Freidrich, Reams and Jacobs, 1982; Isherwood,

Adam and Hornblow, 1982; Mullins, Siegel and Hodges, 1985; Wills, McNamara and Vaccaro, 1995), poor academic performance, somatization, delinquency, substance use, conflict with parents and fighting (Barrera, 1981; Bruns and Geist, 1984; Fontana and Dovidio, 1984; Gad and Johnson, 1980). Spirito and colleagues found that high school students and adolescent psychiatric inpatients agreed on the most frequent sources of life stress: school, parents, friends and boyfriend/girlfriend (Spirito, Overholser, and Stark, 1989). For suicidal and distressed adolescents, the most salient problem area was with their parents and the most frequently used coping strategies included social withdrawal, problem solving and emotional regulation. Distressed adolescents tended to use wishful thinking and resignation more frequently than the suicidal adolescents. In a comparison between adolescents who had attempted suicide and those who had not, adolescents who had attempted suicide were more likely to report recent exposure to intense life stress, to inaccurately appraise the controllability of stressful events and to describe maladaptive behaviors as ways of coping (Wilson, Stelzer, Bergman, Kral, Inayatullah and Elliot, 1995). The suicidal adolescents were as likely as the non-suicidal comparison group to identify adaptive coping strategies but were less likely to use them.

Rutter (1981) reported that an increased incidence of psychiatric disorders in children has been associated with various environmental factors; these factors may potentiate the effects of other life stresses. For instance, marital discord, low socioeconomic status, large family size with overcrowding, paternal criminality, maternal psychiatric disorder and admission of the child into the care of local authorities have all been associated with an elevated risk of psychopathology. Factors which have not been well defined in the child stress and coping literature are those which protect the child from experiencing distress or maladaptation. A review of the child resiliency literature reveals three dimensions around which the protective factors described in these studies cluster. These dimensions include: (1) dispositional attributes of the child; (2) family cohesion and warmth; and (3) the availability of a supportive adult. For instance, although there is conceptual overlap between the protective factor and stressor, empirical findings suggest that children with at least one supportive parental relationship have significantly less conduct disorders following family conflict than those who did not (Rutter, 1979).

Gender

Women have been reported to be twice as likely to reveal intense levels of psychiatric distress, especially depression, than men (Kessler and McRae, 1981). For adults, these gender differences have been attributed to variations in vulnerability, coping strategies, exposure due to role demands, and reporting of symptoms of distress between men and women. Studies which have examined potential mediators of stress and coping across gender differences have provided evidence which largely refutes the notion that women are intrinsically or biologically more vulnerable to stressful events. The studies reviewed reflect the influence of two major perspectives used to explain gender differences in stress and coping, socialization theory and role constraint theory (Rosario, Shinn, Morch, and Huckabee, 1988). Socialization theory posits that gender differences in distress and coping are products of cultural socialization in which women are taught to use less effective coping strategies. Role constraint theory suggests that observed gender differences in stress and coping are due to actual differences in role demands.

Gender differences in response to stress among adults, when detected, tend to be determined by the context of the life events in question. For example, no gender differences were discovered with relation to distress following job loss, divorce or widowhood in Kessler's meta-analysis of several community surveys (Kessler et al., 1984). Women did report more distress than men following a loss of someone close to them such as the death of a loved one other than a spouse. One explanation for this observation is that women tend to give and derive more support from their social networks than men (Kessler and McLeod, 1984; Kessler, Price and Wortman, 1985). These social networks may provide women with more coping resources but may also provide women with more sources of stress.

Thoits (1986) found in a community survey of adult heads of household that when number and types of roles held were controlled, men and women reported experiencing similar amounts of distress overall. Gender differences in distress were found only in the context of work rather than family life. Radloff and Rae (1979) found that women respondents from their community survey reported exposure to more stressors associated with depression than male respondents did. These stressors were related to depression for both men and women. When exposure to these stressors was controlled, women were still more likely to report depressive symptoms than men. This may be due to structural differences in coping resources between men and women, an aspect which was not assessed in this study.

Women and men have been found to use equal amounts of emotion-focused coping. Men, on the other hand, have been found to use more problem-focused coping in their work roles (Folkman and Lazarus, 1980). Women tend to engage in tension reduction coping (e.g., substance use, relaxation, eating, exercise). Dressler (1985) found that among black adults in the rural South, active coping mitigated the effects of stress for women but exacerbated the effects of stress for men. Dressler suggested that the efficacy of coping strategies is influenced by the sociocultural norms in the community. In medical settings, women have been found to seek information more readily than men (Billings and Moos, 1985). Among clinically depressed adults, Fondacaro and Moos (1987) found that women tended to report more coping using affective regulation, information/support seeking and problem solving and less coping using emotional discharge than men. Other researchers of adult populations have either found no relationship between gender and coping or contradictory findings (Billings and Moos, 1985; Heppner, Reeder, and Larson, 1983; Stone, Helder and Schneider, 1988).

Brems and Johnson (1989) found that, for college undergraduates, male sex-role orientation was associated with the use of denial as a defensive coping mechanism and femaleness was related to turning against the self. Men were found to view their problem solving abilities more favorably than females, also. In contrast, Hamilton and Fagot (1988) found no gender differences in coping behaviors for chronic stressors among their undergraduate sample. One explanation for these discrepant results may be that Brems and Johnson did not assess coping in the context of actual life events but in the context of hypothetical non-specific problems.

Studies of stress and coping in prepubertal children suggest that, in general, males are more vulnerable to disorder following life stress than females (Garmezy, 1988; Rutter, 1981). It has been suggested that this may be the result of the communication of adult expectations for coping which reflect gender differences. Werner (1984) reports that the observed male vulnerability in childhood is reversed in adolescence, when girls tend to be the more vulnerable of the sexes. Consistent with studies of adult females (Billings and Moos, 1982), a study of adolescent coping among high school students has reported that females use more emotional regulation in coping with peer problems and more social support than males (Stark, Spirito, Williams and Guevremont, 1989). Male adolescents were also found to appraise events as less extreme in desirability, rely more on wishful thinking for coping and to view resignation as more efficacious than female adolescents. No age differences in stress and coping were detected within this adolescent sample. In a study of high school volunteers conducted by Compas and colleagues, female adolescents reported more negative life events than males. This relationship held only for middle adolescent females (ages 12-17) and males (ages 12-14).

Rather than focusing exclusively on the mechanisms by which individuals become psychologically damaged as a result of traumatic life events such as child abuse and neglect and family violence, the review now shifts towards examining theoretical models which seek to explain the existence of those children who exhibit more adaptive responses. It is from these children that one may learn, perhaps, the keys to their recovery and effective functioning for purposes of application to interventions.

Resilience

The underlying concept of resiliency is the belief that some children emerge from highly stressful conditions as competent, well-adapted individuals. Masten and colleagues (1988) describe a definition of resiliency to be "an inherent human capacity to recover from adversity, to restore equilibrium of functioning". Others have added that this capacity is a phenomenon that may develop at various times in the context of the person-environment transaction over the lifespan (Egeland, Carlson, and Sroufe, 1993). Still others have described resilience more simply as *normal* development under trying conditions (Fonagy, Steele, Steele, Higgitt, and Target, 1994). Since conceptualizations of resilience vary in scope and focus, there is little consensus on a single definition of resiliency. Is resiliency demonstrated by the lack of psychopathology or the presence of competence? or both? What does it mean to be highly functioning in some dimensions of competence but not in others? If resiliency and vulnerability are opposite ends of a spectrum, what characterizes each step in the spectrum as well as the extremes? Due to a historical focus on maladaptation resulting from stress, there is probably better agreement on the criteria used to determine psychopathology, as a dimension of incompetence, than there is on the criteria for competence and adaptation.

In addition, there is concern that vulnerability factors and protective factors are not being treated as conceptually or methodologically distinct from stressors or measures of psychological adaptation (Seifer and Sameroff, 1987; Tennant and Bebbington, 1978). In other words, vulnerability factors which can produce distress in isolation of provoking agents are, in fact, stressors themselves, and the measurement of protective factors is often confounded with the measurement of psychological adaptation. In some studies, for example, socioeconomic status may be conceptualized as a protective factor when it is high, and in other studies socioeconomic status may be conceptualized as a stressor when it is low. Self-esteem may be viewed to be a moderator of the stress process or an indicator of psychological distress. It seems plausible, then, that uncontrollable discrete stressors are less likely to be confounded with measures of maladjustment.

The outcome measures of resiliency against high-risk conditions have ranged from the absence of psychopathology or of maladaptive behavior to specifically-designed measures of social competence, academic success, and emotional adjustment (Luthar & Zigler, 1991; Rutter, 1987). While an emphasis on competence, a more positive approach than absence of maladjustment, is commendable, it is also a relatively new concept which seems problematic to operationalize in a culturally and developmentally valid way. In addition, demonstration of social competence probably does not preclude the existence of less observable psychopathology (e.g., internalizing symptoms). Thus, social competence, alone, may be an incomplete measure of resiliency or adjustment. Besides the conceptual difficulties in defining adaptation or competence, there are also methodological problems in assessing the nature, timing, and degree of exposure to risk and multiple stressors (Luthar, 1993). For instance, resiliency to traumatic stressors such as rape and sexual abuse has been challenging to measure because of the tendency to under-report stigmatized victimization and to conceal distress (Lyons, 1991).

There is evidence from the child abuse and disaster literatures that a life event's characteristics may influence the degree of psychological distress experienced by the survivors. Sowder (1985) identified the following disaster event characteristics which were related to maladjustment: the level of fright induced, the length of exposure, unexpectedness and uncontrollability, the duration of threat before and after actual exposure, the depletion of available coping resources, the degree of alteration of the environment, the causative agent of the event and the symbolic meaning of the event. Although these event qualities were described in relation to disasters, they represent characteristics relevant to other traumatic events also. DeLongis and colleagues (1982) have found that the relationship between event characteristics and adjustment is often mediated by personal attributes. There is also evidence that, in general, the intensity of the trauma exposure is the best predictor of adaptation and resiliency factors operate best under conditions of low trauma intensity or exposure (Pynoos, Frederick, Nader, Arroyo, and Steinberg, 1987). In addition, factors which may precipitate maladjustment following trauma may not be responsible for the sequence of symptoms or the course of recovery (Lyons, 1991).

Models of Resiliency

Garmezy, Masten and Tellegen (1984) have described three mathematical models of stress resistance, two of which detail the potential processes by which personal attributes and stress may have an impact on adjustment. The compensatory model predicts that high exposure to stressors is likely to decrease levels of competence and that various personal attributes work to raise levels of competence in a simple additive fashion. In other words, persons who possess a protective factor are higher in competence than those without the factor with the same levels of stress exposure. An example relevant to the stressor of child abuse would be the prospective study of two children with identical exposure to abuse but different levels of psychological adaptation, as measured throughout the varying levels of exposure to abuse. In this model, the child with the consistently higher level of adaptation would be the child possessing a given protective attribute or factor, such as an ongoing relationship with a trusted, supportive adult.

The immunity vs. vulnerability (or "protective factor") model describes that the relationship between stress and personal attributes in predicting adjustment is an interactive one where the presence of a given factor mediates a protective effect of increasing stress on adaptation. Gender may be a factor which can confer either protection or vulnerability to a stressor. For instance, a child with escalating exposure to abuse may not experience any significant decreases in competence unless the child is female. The challenge model submits that a curvilinear relationship exists between stress and adjustment, whereby moderate levels of stress could increase competence. In this model, a child exposed to a moderate amount of abuse would be predicted to be more competent than those who had experienced small or large amounts of maltreatment.

Masten and colleagues (1988) added four more mathematical models of stress and competence to the above array; two of these models also describe the effect of personal attributes on the stress and competence relationship. The first model predicts that it is the presence of the attribute alone, and not the level of stress, which determines the level of competence in a linear fashion. An example might be the comparison of two children with different problem-solving capabilities who were exposed to equivalent but increasing amounts of abuse. Each child would possess levels of competence reflecting their different cognitive abilities, but these levels of adaptation would not vary with the increasing levels of abuse.

The second model states that it is the level of stress exposure, not the absence of a protective attribute, that inversely influences competence. An illustration of this model would be that children would demonstrate decreasing competence with increasing abuse exposure regardless of differences in personal or environmental attributes. The third model, or cumulative effects model, posits that small amounts of stress exposure will have minimal effects on competence but that a clustering of stress events will result in a curvilinear decrease in competence. This model may be depicted by the child who adapts to the occasional outburst of family violence with fairly high levels of adaptation but, upon exposure to the repeated and frequent sexual and physical maltreatment beginning on her twelfth birthday, rapidly and exponentially loses the level of competence she once had.

The last model, or vulnerability model, describes that the relationship between stress and personal attributes in predicting adjustment is an interactive one where the presence of a given factor facilitates high competence under low levels of stress but mediates a deleterious effect on adaptation when stress increases. In this model, a highly empathic child may demonstrate high levels of social competence at low levels of abuse because of his/her ability to empathize with others. This child may be more likely to lose that high level of competence when the abuse escalates to involve her little sister compared with a child who is less empathic. None of these models is considered to be mutually exclusive of the others. It has been suggested, however, that because the interaction effects observed thus far have contributed little in explaining the variance in adjustment, then the more parsimonious main effects models should be followed (Luthar and Zigler, 1991). However, it seems premature to close the doors on the application of interactive models to the study of child maltreatment.

Masten and her colleagues (1988) found that the results of their study of grade school children showed consistent patterns which supported the application of their mathematical models. The patterns of adaptation discovered depended on the standard for competence used and the particular moderators examined. When the criterion for competence was classroom disruptiveness and the attributes of IQ, socioeconomic status and parenting quality were examined in relation to life stress, the results supported the protective vs. vulnerability model. When engagement in school activities was the criterion of competence and the same moderators were examined, the results could be explained by the vulnerability model. Attributes such as IQ predicted competence as measured by scholastic achievement, regardless of life stress level. This result supported one of the main effects models described.

Masten's findings also suggested that attributes may be protective for one sex and detrimental or less protective for the other in affecting competence. For example, girls appeared to benefit more from adept maternal parenting than boys did; and girls who did not have skilled maternal parenting were more likely to display aggressive behavior than boys under similar circumstances. In general, children with more personal and environmental protective factors exhibited better adaptation in the school setting. Adaptation, here, was measured as the degree of social involvement, the level of scholastic achievement and the frequency of disruptive or aggressive behavior. Overall, females tended to show higher levels of competence, especially social competence, than boys. This result is consistent with the findings of other studies of stress and adaptation in this age group (Rutter, 1979; Werner and Smith, 1982). Both response style (e.g., aggressive vs. disengaging) and social competence are likely to affect the amount of social support received from significant others as well as the possibility of exposure to more stress. The authors found that higher levels of intelligence, socioeconomic status and parental competency acted as protective factors against disruptive and aggressive behavior. Masten and her colleagues speculate that this finding may be the result of differences in learned response behavior across classes and cultures.

The identification of protective factors in other studies of resiliency in children has included intellectual ability, gender, aspects of temperament, humor, ego-control, social skills, interpersonal awareness and empathy, social expressiveness, internal locus of control, task-related self-efficacy, self-worth and self-esteem, autonomy, good problem-solving skills, education and skills training, religious faith, absence of organic deficits, good familial relationships, parental availability and competence, sensitive and responsive caregivers, family harmony and cohesion, future planning, presence of a significant and/or supportive other, identification with a resilient role model, positive school experiences, availability of opportunities at major life transitions, social and resource-related supports for children and parents, higher parental education, and good parental coping skills (Cicchetti, Rogosch, Lynch, and Holt, 1993; Egeland, et al., 1993; Fonagy et al., 1994; Masten, Garmezy, Tellegren, Pelligrini, Larkin, & Larsen, 1988; Murphy & Moriarity, 1976; Rutter, 1987; Werner, 1986; Werner, 1992; Wertlieb, Weigel & Feldstein, 1987). In addition, Werner (1984) found that resilient children were notably more able to find acceptable meaning in their lives after traumatic events than were non-resilient children. Virtually all of these protective mechanisms have been discussed in the child abuse literature as well. In their study of maltreated children, Herrenkohl and her colleagues (1994) concluded that resilience depended on an interaction between maturational, individual, and environmental processes and that the manifestation of resilience tended to be limited to particular domains of adaptation.

Rutter (1987) perceives the concepts of vulnerability and resiliency as not just opposite ends of a spectrum, but as outcomes which reflect a process of risk (stressor) negotiation and modification of response. It is this process which needs elucidation. Rutter continues by describing resilience not as a fixed personal characteristic but, rather, as an attribute which varies within a person across situations, ages, developmental stages etc.. Likewise, factors which function as protective mechanisms in one situation may function as vulnerability mechanisms in another. As one may notice, however, some of the protective factors identified above are neither attributes of a person nor are they under a person's control. Protective factors could be viewed as operating on or between particular planes: e.g., macro-societal, familial, micro-societal, intraindividual, situational etc. and as being variously attributable to the stressed person.

Conceptually, some of these protective factors function as moderating mechanisms, i.e., they are antecedent factors which interact with other conditions in affecting adaptation. Others act as mediating mechanisms which are produced during the stress exposure and influence the relationship or transaction between antecedent factors, stress exposure, and adjustment. Rutter (1987) describes four possible mechanisms by which protective factors may mediate the effect of risk on adaptation. The first is the reduction of the impact of the risk factor by altering the meaning (e.g., attributions) or danger of that stressor for that child. For example, there has been ongoing discussion in the child abuse literature which posits that the psychic damage is rendered through the meaning of the abuse rather than through the physical injuries, per se (Garbarino, Guttman, and Seeley, 1988). One of the concepts of this first mechanism is the alteration of the risk. This is demonstrated in the child sexual abuse prevention programs which have attempted to inoculate children with controlled exposure to low risk situations under conditions favorable to successful coping. This mechanism may also involve the alteration of exposure to the stressor. Alteration of exposure may involve psychological distancing rather than physical distancing and may account for phenomena such as social withdrawal and dissociation among abuse survivors.

The second mediating mechanism serves to reduce the negative sequelae which follow risk exposure and continue or heighten the risk impact. For example, the child abuse literature discusses the potentially negative chain of events which may follow disclosure (Summit, 1988). These negative consequences of disclosure may be the disbelief and stigmatization by others. The third mechanism affects self-esteem and self-efficacy via the support derived from secure and harmonious love relationships (for children, this could be a non-abusive parental or adult relationship), the successful accomplishment of valued tasks (e.g., recreational, educational, or social), and adaptive coping with life turning points which may affect a risk trajectory (e.g., entrance into a new school). The final mechanism involves the availability of opportunities which may result from successful coping and adaptation (e.g., avoiding teen pregnancy or taking advantage of educational opportunities which result in better job preparedness).

Masten's (1988) and Garmezy's (1984) mathematical models reflect attempts to anticipate the possible mathematical relationships between traumatic events, adaptation and vulnerability factors and do not venture to describe the dynamics of resiliency. The psychodynamic/cognitive processing model of traumatic victimization (McCann et al., 1988) described in the stress and coping section provides a framework for understanding how traumatic events may affect adaptation through their effects on schemata. This schema model, in conjunction with Masten's mathematical models, is used to guide the analytic approach for this book. It is hoped that this strategy facilitates the description of specific mechanisms which may affect the impact of child maltreatment in homeless youth.

The next chapter details the research questions and hypotheses for this study and the theoretical, empirical, and methodological basis for their development. Specifically, rationales for the following are elaborated: (1) the prediction of psychological and behavioral correlates of child abuse/assault, neglect, and family violence; (2) the prediction of protective and vulnerability factors and the discussion of the mechanisms by which they may mediate or moderate the relationship between child abuse/assault, neglect, and family violence and measures of distress, and (3) the prediction of gender differences in circumstances surrounding the abusive processes as well as in measures of distress and the discussion of the potential mechanisms by which these differences occur.

Summary of the Literature Review

Homeless Youth

A review of the literature on homeless and runaway youth reveals that these youth are relatively understudied and underserved compared with other youth or other homeless populations. Among the existing studies, consensus on the definitions of homeless and runaway youth has been lacking, and sampling frames have been limited to social service agencies. Therefore, epidemiological estimates of the homeless youth phenomenon vary widely. The estimated number of homeless youth in Los Angeles County each year has ranged from 10,000 to 34,800. Demographically, homeless youth are quite heterogeneous and often reflect the characteristics of the surrounding community. A review of the literature coupled with conversations with local service providers and researchers revealed the following trends in the composition of the homeless youth population: over representation of minority youth; increasing numbers of pre-teen or early teenage youth; history of remedial or special education; longer periods of homelessness; lower family socioeconomic status; and running from families headed by single female parents or from large reconstituted families.

In general, the literature suggests that homeless youth experience a wide variety of problems which may precede, co-occur with, or result from their homelessness. Such problems include exposure to domestic violence, physical and sexual abuse, neglect, substance abuse, depression and suicide attempts. Once youth become enmeshed in street life they are subject to becoming victims of further sexual and emotional exploitation, illness, injury and death. The potential interrelationships between different subtypes of maltreatment and symptoms of psychological distress are the focus of the book.

Although studies of homeless adults suggest that some adults experience their first homelessness during adolescence, the likelihood of a homeless youth becoming a homeless adult is unknown (Robertson, 1991). Effective interventions directed at homeless youth may require that the entire spectrum of interrelated problems which hinder the adaptation of these youth be addressed. This idea is in opposition to the current trend of intervention programs and program funding which focus on single problem areas.

The research presented in this book contributes to the homeless youth literature by virtue of its methodological improvements on other studies and by its examination of the correlates of child maltreatment using a stress and coping paradigm. A modified snowball sample consisting of homeless youth encountered at social service agencies and in street settings are used in the analyses. The inclusion of youth sampled from street settings distinguishes this study from those which sampled clients of social service agencies alone. The data have been derived from face-to-face interviews with the homeless youth rather than a review of agency case records or provider interviews. In contrast to many other studies of homeless youth, the measures used for this study's secondary analyses generally consist of structured and semi-structured items which have known distributions in clinical and community samples. Child maltreatment has been broadly defined to include dimensions which are rarely assessed in studies of homeless youth, such as domestic violence and neglect.

Child Abuse and Neglect

The prevalence of child maltreatment among homeless and runaway youth appears to be as high or higher than that in the general population. Studies of mandated child abuse reporters and child protective service staff members indicate that child abuse cases involving adolescents tend to be reported less often and, if reported, given the lowest priority compared with cases involving younger children. This phenomenon is believed to be due to the perception that adolescents are capable of protecting themselves from harm. In addition, maltreatment cases affecting homeless or runaway youth may be given the lowest priority because they are difficult to engage and are already living away from their homes and intrafamilial abusers.

A review of the literature on the psychological sequelae of child maltreatment reveals that most studies are of pre-teen children or adults and have focused on the psychological sequelae of female child intrafamilial or caretaker sexual abuse alone. Taken together, the majority of the clinical reports and empirical studies suggest that there may be serious developmental and adaptational consequences of child maltreatment for children and adults. No single symptom or constellation of symptoms is pathognomonic for child maltreatment or its subtypes. The only psychological or behavioral effects which somewhat differentiate between subtypes of abuse have been aggressive behavior and sexualized behavior or dysfunction; these symptoms have tended to be associated with physical abuse and sexual abuse, respectively. There are relatively few published reports on the psychological consequences of neglect or exposure to family violence.

The identification of factors which may moderate or mediate the effects of child maltreatment has been an important direction in child abuse research. Knowledge of these factors may assist clinicians and other service providers in their attempts to triage survivors into appropriate care. However, research which examines mediators and moderators is still in its infancy and has almost exclusively focused on the effects of child sexual abuse. The sum total of the research to date suggests that the effects of child sexual abuse are amplified if the perpetrator is the child's father or stepfather, force is used, penetration occurs, and parental response to disclosure is unsupportive. The independent effects of these factors have been difficult to assess because of their interrelatedness with one another. There remain many unanswered questions with regard to the relative impact of other mediators and moderators of child sexual abuse such as the survivor's gender and developmental stage and age at abuse onset.

Much of the research on the psychological sequelae of child maltreatment has suffered from significant methodological weaknesses. These flaws have included the failure to clearly operationalize abuse, include a comparison group, exclude abused individuals from the comparison group, control for pre-existing psychopathology, use standardized measures for assessing psychopathology, assess the time elapsed between the cessation of abuse and data collection, and use more than one source of data. Studies have been difficult to compare because of wide variations in choice of sample sources, measurement period, outcome measures, data collection, and abuse assessment. It is conceivable that recall error may be reduced among adolescents due to the relative recency of maltreatment and other childhood events. On the other hand, one might argue that adolescents may be more subject to the effects of proximal psychological symptoms on recall compared with adults. Nevertheless, the opportunity to study child maltreatment and psychological distress among a sample of homeless youth is rare.

For the most part, studies of the psychological consequences of child maltreatment have been atheoretical. More recently, researchers have begun to describe the theoretical basis for their studies or have suggested theoretical models which can account for certain psychiatric symptoms associated with child sexual abuse. The models reviewed exemplified the different theoretical perspectives found in the child maltreatment literature. These different theoretical positions arose from cognitive, developmental, learning and psychodynamic traditions and include a developmental disruption model (Wolfe, 1987), attribution theory (Gold, 1986; Weiner, 1979), the reformulated theory of learned helplessness (Abramson, Seligman and Teasdale, 1978), and the Four Traumagenic Dynamics Model (Finkelhor and Brown, 1988).

Stress and Coping

A review of theoretical models which represent the structural (Pearlin et al., 1981) and transactional perspectives (Lazarus and Folkman et al., 1984; Aneshensel and Gore, 1991) introduces this section. Since these models have largely been used to explain the effects of "normative" life stress, the review also includes a description of a schema model of traumatic stress (McCann et al., 1988). The application of stress and coping theoretical models to the study of the effects of child maltreatment provides a broad theoretical and empirical base in which to place the findings from the stress and coping literature and child maltreatment literature. The traumatic stress model, in particular, affords the comparison between different types of maltreatment experiences and contribute a contextual framework for understanding the possible cognitive, behavioral, and affective processes which underlie any observed relationships described in this book.

Like the child maltreatment literature, the stress and coping literature has suffered from definitional problems. The operationalization of the components of the stress process has been difficult because of the increasing evidence that the stress process has transactional properties. In other words, all dimensions are interrelated; and that which affects one dimension, affects all dimensions in some fashion. For any given stress situation, this has led to blurred distinctions between the descriptions of stressors, coping strategies, appraisal, response, and any resultant psychological distress. Across stress situations and time periods, a behavior may be viewed as an effective coping strategy in response to stress in one context and an indicator of maladaptation in another context.

Early studies found only modest relationships between exposure to life events and psychiatric illness. Stronger relationships have been found when measures of life events were modified to enhance their reliability and validity, data collection was done by interview, time anchors were embedded in the measures to boost recall accuracy, measures of psychological distress were standardized, and potential moderating and mediating variables were assessed. In particular, social support, coping, appraisal and various individual characteristics have been found to moderate the relationship between life event exposure and symptoms of psychopathology.

Both major life events and daily hassles have been found to be independently associated with somatic and mental health. There is also evidence which suggests that daily hassles mediate the relationship between major life events and psychological distress. It appears that pre-existing distress may be related to exposure to negative life events and to subsequent distress, but negative life events themselves may contribute to the development of distress irrespective of previous distress levels. In addition, no single coping strategy has been found to be adaptive across situations; rather, the possession of a constellation of coping skills may be most adaptive.

A review of the empirical studies of stress and coping did not support the notion of increased vulnerability to distress relative to developmental stage. However, distress may be manifested differently across developmental periods and its expression may be modified by the gender of the individual. Three dimensions of protective factors have been identified which appear to mitigate the effects of life stresses in children:

(1) pro-social dispositional attributes of the child; (2) strong family cohesion; and (3) the availability of a supportive adult.

Women have been reported to be more likely to reveal intense levels of specific symptoms of psychiatric distress, especially depression, than men. For adults, these gender differences have been attributed to variations in vulnerability, coping resources and strategies, exposure due to role demands, expression of distress, and willingness to disclose symptoms between men and women; yet little evidence exists that women are biologically more vulnerable to the effects of stress compared with men. Gender differences in response to stress among adults, when detected, tend to be determined by the context of the life events in question.

Rather than focus exclusively on the mechanisms by which individuals become psychologically damaged as a result of traumatic life events such as child maltreatment and family violence, the review also includes an examination of the stress resilience literature which attempts to document the adaptive responses among survivors. Due to the historical research emphasis on stress-induced psychopathology, there is better agreement among investigators on the criteria for psychopathology than there is for competence and adaptation. Some researchers have used the absence of detectable psychopathology as the criteria for resilience; others have attempted to devise measures of adaptation or social competence as indicators of resilience. However, the absence of one these indicators of maladaptation does not necessarily imply the absence of the other; the use of both criteria may be a better measure of overall resilience to a given stressor. In addition, there is a lack of consensus among researchers as to whether resilience is a function of a fixed characteristic of an individual or a malleable attribute which is influenced by environmental and social factors.

Seven mathematical models of resiliency based on empirical results are presented in the review. These models were developed by Garmezy et al. (1984) and Masten et al. (1988) to predict variations in the relationships between a stressor, adaptation, and protective or vulnerability factors over time. The ability of a model to predict the observed results is often dependent on which measures are used to represent the different components of the stress process. Factors which operate as vulnerability mechanisms in one situation may act as resiliency mechanisms in another.

Data from the child abuse and disaster literatures suggest that a life event's characteristics may influence the degree of psychological distress experienced by the survivors. These event characteristics include: the level of fright induced, the length of exposure, unexpectedness and uncontrollability, the duration of the threat before and after actual exposure, the depletion of available coping resources, the degree of alteration of the environment, the causative agent of the event and the symbolic meaning of the event. The relationship between the dimensions of an event and adjustment has been found to be mediated by attributes of the survivor. The best predictor of adaptation appears to be the intensity of the trauma exposure, and resiliency factors are most effective under conditions of low trauma intensity or exposure. Researchers in resiliency posit that factors which may precipitate initial maladjustment may not be those which perpetuate symptoms.

Empirical studies of resiliency have revealed that stress-mitigating factors may operate on or between particular environment planes (e.g., macro-societal, familial, micro-societal, intraindividual or situational). Protective factors may mediate the effects of stress by altering the meaning or danger of that stressor for the individual, reducing the negative sequelae of stressors, or enhancing the availability of opportunities which may result from successful coping and adaptation. One of the major methodological concerns in resiliency research is that the operationalization of vulnerability and protective factors often has been confounded with the definition of stressors or measures of psychological adaptation.

The original study presented in this book contributes to the resiliency literature by describing the factors which may moderate or mediate the effects of child maltreatment among homeless youth. The analyses differentiate risk and protective factors and examine the impact that survivor gender has on child maltreatment and psychological sequelae.

III
Research Questions

The research questions are organized around three main themes: (1) description of the sociodemographic, maltreatment, and psychological characteristics of the sample; (2) analysis of the relationships between maltreatment, symptoms of psychological distress, and any mediators or moderators; and (3) examination of the relationships between gender, the experience of maltreatment, and the psychological and behavioral correlates of maltreatment.

Definition of Terms

Homeless youth: any legal minor (i.e., less than 18 years of age) who spent the previous night in a formal emergency shelter, an improvised shelter, or on the streets.

Child maltreatment: exposure to physical abuse, contact sexual abuse, neglect, and/or domestic violence. This definition excludes exposure to psychological abuse and includes maltreatment perpetrated by any cohabitants and any non-cohabitants.

Psychological distress: symptoms of trait anxiety, current and lifetime depression, lifetime suicide ideation and attempts, lifetime substance abuse and/or dependency, lifetime conduct disorder (excluding runaway behavior), and lifetime post-traumatic stress disorder (PTSD).

Research Questions

1a. What are the characteristics of this homeless youth sample in terms of sociodemographic characteristics, exposure to maltreatment events, and symptoms of problem behaviors and psychological distress?

1b. Do the characteristics described in 1a differ by subsample, i.e. those youth encountered in street settings vs. youth interviewed at social service agency sites?

The research literature suggests that there are demographic differences between youth encountered in street settings and those seeking social services (Caton, 1986; Pennbridge et al., 1990; Robertson, 1991). For instance, there is a slight tendency for females to be predominant in shelter samples and males to be predominant in street samples. Race/ethnicity tends to reflect the distribution of the area sampled or to emphasize minority populations, if the sample is taken from a shelter; in contrast, the race of those being served by drop-in centers is primarily white. Shelter youth tend to be from the immediate geographical surroundings of the area sampled and outreach/drop-in center youth originate from outside the local area (e.g., county).

1c. What sociodemographic and family characteristics, in particular, characterize those youth who were ever exposed to maltreatment events and/or experienced symptoms of psychological distress?

Abuse

Although some researchers have found no racial/ethnic differences between those who have experienced childhood sexual abuse (Jones and McCurdy, 1992; Wyatt, 1985) or childhood physical abuse (Jones and McCurdy, 1992) and those who have not, the only research on sexual assaults among Latinos/Hispanics found higher rates of childhood sexual abuse among non-Hispanic Whites compared with Hispanics (Siegel et al., 1987). Prevalence studies indicate that female children are exposed to more sexual abuse than male children (Finkelhor et al., 1990). While low socioeconomic status may be associated with child neglect and physical abuse (Giovannoni and Billingsley, 1970; Wolock and Horowitz, 1979), socioeconomic status does not appear to be associated with child sexual abuse (Finkelhor and Baron, 1986; Jones and McCurdy, 1992).

Depression
Female adults and adolescents (not children) tend to report symptoms of depression more often than male adults and adolescents (Kandel and Davies, 1982; Kessler and McRae, 1981). Socioeconomic status appears to be inversely related to depressive symptoms among teenagers, and adolescents tend to have a higher rate of depression than adults and younger children (Angold, 1988; Kandel and Davies, 1982). The search for a relationship between depression and ethnicity among children and adolescents has resulted in inconclusive findings. Female adolescents attempt suicide more often than males but do not complete suicide as often as males of the same age; older white adolescent males are the most likely to commit suicide and younger black adolescent females are the least likely to do so (Stillion, McDowell and May, 1989). Completed suicides tend to increase with age, and attempted suicides decrease with age (Curran, 1987).

Suicide
A large multicity study of youth in shelters and on the street found that family member's substance use was associated with a youth's prior suicide attempts independent of the youth's own substance use (Greene and Ringwalt, 1996).

PTSD
Studies of demographic correlates of PTSD have focused on age, developmental stage and gender; however, the scant findings have been contradictory (Breslau, Davis, Andreski and Peterson, 1991; Lyons, 1987). For instance, Lyons presents evidence which suggests that boys are more susceptible to PTSD than girls; yet Breslau and colleagues found that being female was a risk factor for developing symptoms of PTSD among adults. Perhaps vulnerability to PTSD depends on both gender and developmental stage.

Substance Use
Substance use steadily increases with age throughout adolescence until the age of 25, after which there is a distinct decline in use (Kandel, 1982). Female adolescents tend to report less drug and alcohol use than male adolescents; however, both genders tend to report marijuana use at approximately the same rates (Kandel, 1982). Studies of relationships between substance use and race/ethnicity among adolescents have yielded equivocal results (Joshi and Scott, 1988). Some studies suggest that

African-American adolescents and adults and Latino adolescents have higher rates of drug abuse/dependence than other ethnic groups (Joshi and Scott, 1988; Robins et al., 1984).

Conduct Disorder
Male children tend to be diagnosed with conduct disorder more often than female children, and youth living in poverty tend to be diagnosed with conduct disorder more frequently than other children (Offord, 1985).

2a. Is the experience of maltreatment events associated with problem behaviors or symptoms of psychological distress in this homeless youth sample?

H1: The exposure to maltreatment events is associated with the experience of symptoms of depression, suicide ideation and attempts, substance abuse and/or dependency, PTSD, and conduct disorder.

One of the psychological sequelae which has been specifically associated with child physical abuse is aggressive conduct (Briere and Runtz, 1990). Children who have witnessed family violence have been found to have increased levels of depression compared with non-witnesses (Brown, Pelcovitz, and Kaplan, 1983). Children who were witnesses as well as victims had the highest levels of depression (Emery, 1989; Hughes, 1988). Survivors of child sexual abuse have been reported to display symptoms of PTSD (Briere and Runtz, 1988), depression, suicide ideation and behavior, and substance abuse more often than non-victims (Beitchman et al., 1991).

H1b: The exposure to child sexual abuse is associated with greater numbers of sexual partners for the past year.
One of the distinguishing sequelae of child sexual abuse is sexualized behavior; sexualized behavior may manifest itself as sexual contact with numerous different partners (Beitchman et al., 1991; Browne and Finkelhor, 1986).

H1c: The symptoms of psychological distress are found to co-occur with one another.

Although it is not apparent which precedes the other, there is substantial evidence that alcohol and drug use co-occur with depression among adolescents (Joshi and Scott, 1988). Substance abuse has also been associated with symptoms of PTSD, suicide ideation and attempts, and conduct disorder (Greene and Ringwalt, 1996; Stiffman, Earls, Powell and Robins, 1987). Among maltreated youth, PTSD has been found to co-occur with other anxiety disorders, psychotic disorder, attention-deficit hyperactivity disorder, and suicide ideation (Famularo, Fenton, Kinscherff, and Augustyn, 1996). Among older youth, suicide attempts have been associated with mood disorders, psychotic disorders, disruptive disorders, and substance abuse disorders (Brent, 1995).

H2: The onset of symptoms of psychological distress is recalled to have occurred after the first child maltreatment exposure according to the retrospective reports.

Symptoms of psychological distress have been found to both precede and succeed the experience of sexual assault. Symptoms of major depression, alcohol abuse or dependence, drug abuse or dependence, and phobia have been found to differentiate the abused from the non-abused both before and after the sexual assault. Symptoms of antisocial personality tended to distinguish between the abused and the non-abused before the assault (Burnam et al., 1988).

H3a. Exposure to sexual assault covaries with involvement in sex work (i.e., pornography or prostitution).

Some studies indicate that childhood sexual abuse survivors may be at risk for subsequent sexual assault or exploitation (Siegel et al., 1987; Silbert and Pines, 1983; Urquiza and Goodlin, 1994; Widom and Kuhns, 1996; Wyatt, 1985).

H3b. Sexual assault survivors who have been sexually revictimized do not differ in demographic characteristics and symptoms of psychological distress from other sexual assault survivors.

Sorenson and colleagues found no differences in demographic characteristics and rates of mental disorders between adults who had single lifetime exposures to sexual assault and those who had had multiple exposures (Sorenson, Siegel, Golding and Stein, 1991). Although, prior victimization (sexual or nonsexual) was associated with symptoms of PTSD among a nationally representative sample of children who were child sexual abuse survivors (Boney-McCoy and Finkelhor, 1995).

H3b. Sexual revictimization is positively related to pregnancy and multiple sexual partners and inversely related to use of condoms.

Sexual revictimization has been associated with unintended pregnancies and multiple sexual partners (Wyatt, Guthrie and Notgrass, 1992).

2b. What factors appear to affect the degree of vulnerability or resiliency of these homeless youth to child maltreatment?

H1: The following protective factors moderate or mediate the association between the maltreatment experience and the mental health outcomes:

(1) history of mental health treatment
(2) use of health care and social services
(3) perceived family psychopathology or substance abuse
(4) institutional placement (i.e., juvenile detention, group home, foster care)
(5) educational level of parents
(6) length of homelessness
(7) income in last month
(8) availability of food, shelter, clothing

Family composition, parental psychopathology, parental substance use, available social support (especially from a significant adult) and the existence of a parental/caretaker role model for coping are examples of family characteristics which may influence the effects of abuse on adaptation. Survivors of child sexual abuse are more likely than non-abused children to have divorced or separated biological parents, parents with psychological problems, and parents who abuse alcohol and/or drugs (Adams-Tucker, 1981; Beitchman et al., 1991 and 1992; Burgess et al., 1987; Gruber and Jones, 1983). Family cohesion and the availability of a significant and understanding adult with adaptive coping skills have been found to significantly mitigate the negative effects of sexual abuse (Conte and Schuerman, 1987; Friedrich, Beilke and Urquiza, 1988; Fromuth, 1986).

Low socioeconomic status and admission of a child into the care of local authorities have been associated with an elevated risk of psychopathology (Rutter, Yule, Quinton, Rowlands, Yule, and Berger, 1975). Sexual abuse survivors whose disclosure of the abuse resulted in negative parental reactions or removal from their homes have been found to suffer the greatest amount of psychological distress (Adams-Tucker, 1982; Fromuth, 1986; MacFarlane, 1978; Peters, 1988; Tufts' New England Medical Center, 1984). In one study, negative parental response to disclosure was related to the survivor's removal from home (Tufts' New England Medical Center, 1984). In contrast, Wozencraft and colleagues (1991) found that suicide ideation was more frequent among sexual abuse survivors who had not been removed from home. With regard to physical abuse, children who are younger at the onset of abuse and are maintained in a unstable home environment have been found to suffer the greatest problems with emotional adjustment (Kinard, 1982).

Wagner and colleagues (1988) found that the relationship between life events and distress is mediated by negative daily events among youth.

For homeless youth, the unavailability of shelter, food, clothing, and water may be conceptualized as negative daily events.

H2: The following maltreatment characteristics mediate the association between exposure to sexual assault and the mental health outcomes:

(1) relationship of perpetrator
(2) degree of violence
(3) degree of intrusiveness
(4) frequency of exposure
(5) age at first event exposure
(6) age of perpetrator relative to respondent
(7) number of perpetrators

In general, survivors of sexual abuse perpetrated by biological fathers or stepfathers are more likely to report symptoms of psychological distress than survivors who were victimized by other offenders (Adams-Tucker, 1982; Briere and Runtz, 1988; Gorcey, Santiago, McCall-Perez, 1986; Sirles et al., 1989; Wozencraft, Wagner and Pellegrin, 1991). The relationship of the perpetrator with the victim is often associated with the gender and age of the victim; boys and older children are more likely to be sexually assaulted by non-relatives (Mian, Wehrspann, Klajner-Diamond, LeBaron and Winder, 1986; Pierce and Pierce, 1985; Tong et al., 1987). Intrafamilial sexual abuse may also be associated with abuse of greater duration and frequency, greater family psychopathology and less available support for the abused child (Russell, 1986). Although there is evidence that survivor age at first exposure may moderate the effects of child sexual abuse, it is unclear whether age represents a mechanism of developmental process, of duration of exposure, of response to disclosure, or of something else.

Male offenders have been associated with the greatest amount of psychopathology and recalled trauma in both male and female sexual abuse survivors (Finkelhor, 1984; Seidner and Calhoun, 1984). Two studies which analyzed the impact of perpetrator age on the effects of sexual abuse among college students revealed that students reported feeling more traumatized when the offenders were adults (vs. adolescents) (Finkelhor, 1979; Fromuth, 1983). These results held after controlling for perpetrator gender, use of force, type of sex act, and age of the victim (Finkelhor, 1979).

Other abuse-related mediators of distress include the degree and type of coercion involved, the degree of intrusiveness, the number of abuse occurrences, and the duration of the abusive relationship(s). It has been suggested that the more types of abuse exposure (i.e., physical, emotional and sexual abuse, family violence, and neglect), the more terror associated with the abuse experience (often associated with the amount of force used), the more intrusive the physical contact (e.g., oral, vaginal or anal penetration) and the greater the exposure to abuse (frequency and duration), the greater the resultant psychological distress experienced (Adams-Tucker, 1982; Bagley and Ramsay, 1985; Briere and Runtz, 1988; Burgess, et al., 1984; Collings, 1995; Finkelhor, 1979; Fromuth, 1986; Goodman, Dutton and Harris, 1997; Gorcey, Santiago, McCall-Perez, 1986; Groth, 1978; Hartman, M., et al., 1987; Herman, Russell, Trocki, 1986; Peters, 1988; Rimsza, Berg and Locke, 1988; Sirles et al., 1989; Tong, Oates and McDowell, 1987; Wolfe and Birt, 1995).

Perpetrator identity, abuse duration, type of sexual acts, and the use of force may be interrelated. For instance, survivors of sexual abuse perpetrated by stepfathers have tended to experience more force or threats of force and more intrusive sexual acts; survivors of sexual abuse by either fathers or stepfathers have often experienced abuse of longer duration and frequency than survivors of other offenders (Russell, 1986). Children who are exposed to a longer term of physical abuse and are more severely injured have been found to suffer the greatest problems with emotional adjustment (Kinard, 1982).

H3: The following coping characteristics mediate the association between exposure to the child maltreatment and the mental health outcomes:

(1) fighting back during a physical assault

(2) choosing to leave home vs. being told to leave home

Perceived compliance with an assault has been associated with greater levels of psychological distress, particularly guilt, self-blame and aggressive behaviors (Burgess et al., 1987; MacFarlane, 1978).

3a. Does gender predict different circumstances surrounding the maltreatment experienced by this homeless youth sample?

H1: Males are more likely to be identified as survivors of neglect, whereas females are more likely to be identified as survivors of sexual abuse.

In a study of runaway and homeless youth, service providers tended to identify males as survivors of neglect and females as survivors of sexual abuse (Powers et al., 1990). Among community surveys and reported child abuse cases, female respondents have been more likely to be identified as survivors of sexual abuse than male respondents (Finkelhor et al., 1990; U.S.D.H.H.S., 1981).

H2: Male survivors of child maltreatment are more likely to be identified as "throwaways/push-outs" or homeless, whereas female survivors are more likely to be identified as "runaways".

Male survivors of child maltreatment have been found to be at greater risk for being forced out of their family homes compared with female survivors who tend to run away (Hartman, C.R., et al., 1987; Powers et al., 1990). However, this finding may be mediated by the type of maltreatment and other aspects of the environment from which the youth is running. McCormack and her colleagues (1986) reported that male victims of child sexual abuse run away more frequently than female victims.

H3: Female survivors of child maltreatment are more likely to have been reported to child protective authorities and more likely to have been removed from home.

Female survivors of child sexual abuse are more likely to be viewed as truthful during disclosure (Wood, Orsack, Murphy, and Cross, 1996) and to be reported to child protective services than male survivors (Finkelhor, 1984). Pierce and Pierce (1985) found that female survivors of child sexual abuse are more frequently removed from home than male survivors.

H4: Compared with female survivors, male survivors of sexual assaults have:

(1) experienced more physical assaults
(2) been victimized more often by non-family members
(3) been younger at the onset of abuse
(4) been more likely to be sexually penetrated

There is evidence that male survivors of sexual abuse experience more physical abuse and are victimized more often by non-family members compared with female survivors (Finkelhor, 1984; Mian et al., 1986; Pierce and Pierce, 1985; Tong et al., 1987). Male survivors of sexual abuse have also been found to experience more physical contact/penetration and to be younger at the onset of abuse compared with female survivors (Finkelhor, 1984; Pierce and Pierce, 1985).

H5: Female respondents have been exposed to physical assaults at the same rate as male respondents.

Powers and her colleagues (1990) found no gender differences among runaway and homeless youth in their exposure to physical abuse and family violence or in the gender of their perpetrators of physical abuse and family violence.

3b. Does gender predict different psychological responses to maltreatment among this homeless youth sample?

H1: Female survivors of sexual abuse are more likely to report the following specific behaviors: prostitution, acts of physical aggression, and petty theft; whereas male survivors are more likely to report self-blame for non-specific negative events, internalizing symptoms of distress, somatic symptoms (e.g., sleep and eating problems), and self-hatred.

Among runaway and homeless youth, female sexual abuse survivors have been found to be more likely to have symptoms of anxiety, participate in criminal activities such as prostitution and petty theft, commit acts of verbal and physical aggression, use drugs or alcohol, blame others for their abuse, and become involved in the juvenile justice system compared with non-abused females. In contrast, male victims of child sexual abuse have been characterized by somatic symptoms, anxiety, self-blame for their abuse, social withdrawal, suicidality and the fear of adult men compared with non-abused males (Hartman, C.R., et al., 1987; Janus et al., 1987; McCormack et al., 1986). Janus et al. (1987) found that, among homeless youth, male survivors of child sexual abuse displayed increased somatization, suicide ideation, self-blame, and social withdrawal compared with female survivors and non-victims.

IV
Methodology[1]

Study History

This study analyzes data which were collected in 1987 under the direction of Drs. Milton Greenblatt, Julia M. Robertson, and Marjorie J. Robertson. The original study was funded by the California State Department of Mental Health (Grant No. 85-76258, Milton Greenblatt, M.D. and Julia M. Robertson, M.D., Principal Investigators), N.I.A.A.A. Professional Services (Contract No. 87MO23952101D, Marjorie J. Robertson, Ph.D.), and the Los Angeles County-Olive View Medical Center, Department of Psychiatry.

Research Design and Sample Type

The research team used a survey design for purposes of describing the mental health and social characteristics of the homeless youth population in Hollywood, California. Traditional research methodologies which depend on the ability to identify the target population do not lend themselves to easy application in research on the homeless. Many of these methods rely on population lists generated by residential phone numbers, census tracts of home addresses, known and stable distributions of target individuals in the community, moderate to high statistical frequency of target individuals, and/or on physically consistent and observable characteristics. None of these methods would accurately identify the homeless youth population. The homeless youth population was considered to be "unlistable" because of the impossibility of identifying what constituted the homeless youth universe.

Homelessness is a statistical rarity in the overall population (Rossi, 1989), and studying statistically rare events can be costly because of the numbers of persons which must be screened before encountering the desired characteristic. These costs may be reduced by screening in locations where the homeless are known to congregate. Consequently, a non-probability sample of the snow-ball type or what Rossi (1989) would describe as a "partial count" of the homeless youth population was devised. It is important to note that, for purposes of establishing the relative independence of the units of analysis, this sample was a snowball sample of sites, not individuals. One may still argue, however, that the assumption of independence inherent to many analytic techniques may not be guaranteed here.

In order to improve upon the external validity of the empirical studies which report samples collected at single sites, usually service establishments, the decision to sample from multiple heterogeneous sites was made. Sampling exclusively from service sites would have presented two problems: (1) only 32 emergency beds for homeless youth existed in Hollywood at the time of the study and (2) some shelters maintained policies which excluded housing youth who were suspected of either alcohol or substance use. These conditions could have led to difficulties in obtaining a moderate sample size with adequate representation of substance users, a primary objective of the original study. Due to the investigators' inability to collect a true probability sample, however, any inferences to the homeless youth population must be done with caution.

Sample Selection Criteria

The target population was defined as homeless adolescents who were minors (i.e., those less than eighteen years old) who had spent the previous night either in a formal shelter, in improvised shelter (including abandoned buildings, vehicles, public places, or other unconventional living places), or on the streets (including places such as parks or beaches) and were encountered within a given geographic area in Hollywood, CA. This definition of homeless adolescents included those who were alone, with family members (either their parent(s) or their children), or with friends. However, none of the homeless youth encountered were homeless with blood relatives.

The area surveyed included: (1) all of the newly incorporated city of West Hollywood and (2) parts of the city of Los Angeles bounded by Franklin Avenue on the north, Melrose Avenue on the south, La Brea

Avenue on the west, and Western Avenue on the east. This area was chosen based on service providers' beliefs about where the homeless youth perceived the boundaries of the "Hollywood area" to be. The Hollywood area was selected because it is presumed to have the highest concentration of homeless youth in Los Angeles County (Robertson et al., 1984).

Sampling Frame

A multistage sampling scheme was devised in which sites where homeless adolescents could be found were identified, listed, and sampled. All eligible adolescents within each site were subsequently identified and interviewed.

Stage One: A list of service providers to the homeless youth population in Los Angeles was assembled from a roster of members of the Coordinating Council for Homeless Youth Services[2] and the list of Resources for Runaway and Homeless Youth of the *Child Abuse and Neglect Treatment Resource Directory*, Department of Children's Services (see Robertson, 1989). A project staff member contacted the director or administrator of each agency on the list of service providers either by phone or in person.

These administrators were asked whether their agencies provided services to homeless adolescents in the Hollywood or West Hollywood area and whether they would be willing to participate in the study. They were asked to describe the outer boundaries as well as the "heart" of Hollywood as they thought their clients viewed them and to identify specific locations in this area where they believed homeless youth spent time for any reason (e.g., for purposes of hanging out, eating or sleeping). In addition, providers were requested to name additional service providers in the area. Any previously unidentified agencies were added to the provider list and contacted.

A final list of twenty-one service providers was compiled. The potential sampling sites were characterized by the service providers according to the type of place (e.g., fast food establishment), type of homeless youth likely to be found there (i.e., based on socioeconomic, family, and mental health characteristics), types of activities they tended to do there, and what time of day they were likely to be there. This first stage produced a list of possible sampling sites including seven service sites (three shelters, two meal programs, and two daytime congregating areas), fourteen "street" sites (two fast-food establishments, two parks, eight abandoned buildings, and sections of Hollywood and Santa Monica Boulevards).

Stage Two: Homeless youth respondents were used as informants of possible sampling sites to provide an "insider's" view of the population's locations. Toward the end of each interview, each respondent was requested to identify all of the places in Hollywood where they or other homeless youth spent time. Site characteristics were identified as described above. Non-duplicate sites named during this stage were added to the site list and sampled. The homeless informants identified ten additional sampling sites which were not duplicated in the provider site list. These included seven fast-food restaurants, two street corners, and one park.

The final sampling frame consisted of thirty-one survey sites. Sampling sites included both "street" and "shelter" sites: seven service sites (three shelters, two meal programs, and two drop-in centers) and twenty-four street sites (three fast-food establishments, three parks, eight abandoned buildings, two popular corners and long sections of Hollywood and Santa Monica Boulevards). Of the final list of potential survey sites, only one shelter refused access to the researchers. The homeless informants rarely identified specific "squats" (abandoned buildings used as a primary nighttime shelter) as potential survey sites. When questioned further, these youths explained that their reluctance to divulge this information was due to their fear of being invaded by other homeless persons or raided by the police, should the information be leaked or sold. It should be noted that these sites were probably "under-represented" in this snowball sample.

Sample Size and Response Rate

A minimum of two and a maximum of five visits were conducted at each sample site, with the goal being to interview at least one eligible respondent at each site. Abandoned buildings were only sampled twice because of the limited availability of the police escort. A census of homeless adolescents was taken at each site, and all of those present were screened for eligibility. Unfortunately, no information is available regarding the number or characteristics of youth who were screened out of the study. A total of one-hundred homeless adolescents were selected into the sample; of these, one refused to be interviewed. Ninety-nine homeless adolescents were interviewed. Three cases failed to meet either the age or homelessness criteria and were eliminated from the sample. Of the remaining ninety-six cases, three had broken off the interview. The resulting completion rate was 96%. It is believed that the $10.00 incentive given to the participants coupled with the superior skill of the interviewers contributed greatly to the high response rate.

Interview Team and Training

The interview team consisted of five interviewers, three women and two men, and a female field supervisor. All of the interviewers were Caucasian. Interviewers were experienced in interviewing homeless persons or other hard-to-engage populations, or they had backgrounds involving adolescents in clinical settings. The interview team included a postdoctoral fellow who was a social psychologist, a graduate student with clinical experience with adolescents, a psychiatric technician with experience on adolescent inpatient wards, a professional interviewer experienced with homeless adults, and an undergraduate with a specialized interest in homeless adolescents. The team supervisor was a research psychologist with experience in survey research with homeless adults.

Thirty-two hours of intensive classroom training was given to all of the interviewers. This training involved lectures, exercises, role playing, and mock interviews. The content of the instruction included an overview of survey research and the current project, standardized interviewing procedures (i.e., interpersonal aspects of interviewing in a non-biasing manner), procedures specific to particular instruments (e.g., sections of the Diagnostic Interview Schedule), probing strategies, and instructions for conduct in the field.

Instrumentation

The Homeless Adolescent Interview Schedule (HAIS) is a comprehensive instrument designed specifically for this study. The HAIS included sections on alcohol and drug use, mental health, physical health, homelessness history, subsistence adaptation, family and social history, residential instability, criminal history, and victimization.

Standardized Instruments:

NIMH Diagnostic Interview Schedule (DIS) sections concerning: depression, alcohol use, drug use, suicide ideation and attempts, and post-traumatic stress

Diagnostic Instrument for Children and Adolescents (DICA): conduct disorders section

Childhood Depression Inventory (CDI): assesses depressive symptoms experienced within the past two weeks

Revised Children's Manifest Anxiety Scale (RCMAS): assesses trait anxiety disorder

Non-standardized items:

Homelessness history, adaptation, victimization, protective strategies, health status, service utilization, and migration and mobility were adapted from the instrument used in the Los Angeles Skid Row Homeless Study (Farr, et al., 1986).

Questions regarding education, treatment of alcohol, drug, and mental (ADM) disorders, family ADM problems and treatment history, and health status and treatment history were adapted from a mental health survey of adolescents using inner-city health clinics (Stiffman, et al., 1987).

Certain questions on homelessness history, health status, suicide behavior, income and employment, and migration were adapted from the instrument used with homeless adults in Los Angeles County (Robertson, et al., 1985).

Some questions on current and prior substance use were adapted from the National Longitudinal Survey of Youth (Mensch and Kandel, 1988). Questions on sexual assault were modified from the Los Angeles Epidemiologic Catchment Area Project supplement on sexual assault (Siegel, et al., 1986).

Expert consultants guided the development of items assessing special topic areas such as physical and sexual abuse, sexual exploitation (via prostitution and pornography), consequences of family ADM problems, suicide, AIDS, and residential history.

All interviews were conducted in English. The field supervisor, who was bilingual, screened all potential respondents. Although, preparations had been made to interview in Spanish, it was not necessary since all eligible respondents spoke English. When permission was granted, a small subsample of the interviews (approximately 20%) were audio recorded on cassette tapes to allow closer monitoring of the interviews and to provide a source of qualitative information which details the context of the structured responses.

Data Collection

Between May 25 and July 1, 1987, 2-hour in-person interviews were conducted by trained, experienced interviewers from the University of California School of Public Health and the Department of Psychiatry, Los Angeles. All interviews were conducted between 6:00 a.m. and 12:00 midnight. Service providers perceived the existence of seasonal increases in the size of the population during the summer months, so sampling during these dates may be considered advantageous. It is also possible that the characteristics of the population may vary with the seasons, as well.

The data collection procedure involved establishing a somewhat unique sampling strategy for each locale. Street sites, for example, were sectored off by block or other geographic markers. Each sector was then "swept" to identify potential respondents. In the case of abandoned buildings, a special unit of police escorts entered the buildings first to establish the safety of the environment for the interviewers. If anyone was present, the interview team would enter and conduct screening for the survey. During the first round of visits to each site, the entire interview team was brought to each site. It became evident that, for most street sites, future sampling rounds did not require such a large and potentially intrusive interview team to cover the respondents efficiently and effectively.

At each site, individuals were screened for eligibility and, if eligible, offered a $10.00 incentive to participate in the study. Informed consent included a discussion of the length of the interview (approximately two hours), the purpose and nature of the questions (which include the very sensitive areas of sexual behavior, sexual abuse, substance use, mental health etc.), the confidentiality of the data, and the legal requirements which mandated the reporting of any disclosed child abuse to child protective authorities. While this information may have served as a powerful disincentive to participate or to be truthful in the interview, it should be noted that it was communicated to the respondents that the disclosure of their identities was at their discretion. Interviewers and respondents were matched on gender, when feasible.

Keeping in mind that the sampling sites were not independent and that this population is highly mobile between sites, it was considered possible that duplication of respondent interviews could occur. Consequently, the interview supervisor was present at each site for each round of sampling and screened all potential respondents for duplication by physical recognition. This was possible because of the small sample size and the brief period of data collection (five weeks). The presence of the supervisor also insured the consistent application of the screening criteria, uniform monitoring of all interviews, immediate resolution of matters of judgement, and that no interviewers were ever in the field alone.

The greatest dilemma encountered in the field was the accurate application of the age criteria (i.e., finding respondents who were under 18 years old) during screening. Self-reported age and identification documents were both found to be highly unreliable. Service providers and respondents described that reported age is manipulated according to what advantage may be obtained. Some homeless youth misrepresent their age as being older in order to buy alcohol, obtain services for adults, or to avoid detention. It was discovered that several homeless youths misrepresented their age during screening because of fear of detention. This, of course, resulted in their exclusion from the study. They later confessed the misrepresentation to the project director. One youth misrepresented his age as being younger in order to be included in the study and obtain the ten dollar incentive. He was discovered during the several follow-up questions which were used to confirm age. He also subsequently admitted his falsehood and motive. The reported response rate may be overestimated given that some eligible adolescents may have been eliminated because of age misrepresentation. In addition, two non-homeless adolescents were also deleted from the original sample after careful review of their interviews revealed that they could not have been homeless. These two had also misrepresented themselves during screening.

Two open-ended questions were placed at the end of the interview to provide an opportunity for informal debriefing at the end of the interview. These questions were: "Do you have any advice for other adolescents?" and "What words of advice would you give people who are trying to help homeless adolescents such as yourself?" Respondents were allowed as much time as they desired for open discussion at the end of the interview, and many youth continued to talk with the interviewers for quite some time. Respondents who appeared to be psychologically disturbed by the interviews were evaluated by either the clinical social worker or psychiatric technician who were members of the interview team. Staff clinicians at the Department of Psychiatry of the Los Angeles County - Olive View Medical Center were on call should severe problems with a respondent exist. Respondents were all given the telephone numbers of the researchers and clinicians and encouraged to call if they experienced overwhelming psychological distress subsequent to the interview. None of the respondents contacted the research/clinical team.

Data Recording and Quality Control

Ten percent of the cases were randomly selected and compared with the original interviews, as a measure of quality control. In addition, twenty percent of the entries for each case were contrasted with the original coding sheets (less than .5% error was found). Data cleaning was then accomplished using programs which identified out-of-range values for certain variables, skip-pattern mistakes, and logical errors.

Demographic Description of the Sample

The modal characteristics of the sample are as follows: 61% are male, 60% are White, and 58% have a birthplace outside of California. The mean age of the sample is 16.1 years (range 13-17 years).

Comparison of the Study Sample with Similar Samples

Local homeless youth service providers have speculated that there are sociodemographic differences between those homeless youth who use formal over-night shelter services, those who use outreach/drop-in services, and those who use neither. A study of homeless youth in Los Angeles suggests that shelter populations contain more females, ethnic minorities, and youth originating from outside of California than local outreach populations (Pennbridge et al., 1990). Outreach/drop-in centers tend to have older youths than youth shelters because youth shelters usually restrict their clientele eligibility to those under eighteen years of age. Service providers have suggested that they believe that the outreach/drop-in centers have a more chronically homeless youth population than the youth shelters. Little is known about the sub-population of homeless youth believed to exist who rarely, if ever, appear in the service samples. It is postulated that these youth may more closely resemble those who are older and more chronically homeless.

Compared with the demographic characteristics of Hollywood shelter and outreach samples (Pennbridge et al., 1990), the Hollywood Homeless Youth Sample (HHYS) most closely resembles the outreach sample in terms of gender, race/ethnicity, and birthplace/origin (Table 4.1). The age distribution of the HHYS is more similar to that of the shelter sample because of the age exclusion criteria used in collecting the snowball sample (i.e., respondents must be <18 years old).

Operationalization of Constructs

Due to the nature of secondary analysis, some of the operationalizations are less than optimal for the objectives of this study. However, given the sampling difficulties inherent in homeless populations, the information available may be considered well worth examining. Measures relevant to the study's constructs are described below.

Definition of Measures

Sociodemographic and other personal characteristics: age, gender, education (i.e., last completed year of school, ever held back in school, ever in special education program/class), employment, income of last thirty days, race/ethnicity, place of birth, institutional placements, reasons for detention, plans to attend school/currently attending school, perceived health at the time of the interview and since left home; ever perceived problem with mental health or substance use

Homelessness characteristics: reason left home, unilateral vs. bilateral decision to leave home, reason for homelessness, age at first and last homelessness episode onset, number of episodes, cumulative lifetime exposure, length of current episode, patterns of homelessness, mobility and migration, homelessness after release from institutional placement, subsistence problems (e.g., food, clothing, medical care, hygiene), actions taken for self-protection (e.g., sleeping during the day, avoiding certain people and places, carrying a weapon), alone or with others, street gang affiliation

Service utilization: use of formal shelters or mental or physical health services in the year prior to the interview; location of interview (i.e., service agencies vs. street site); ever spent a night in a mental hospital; have a regular medical provider

Family characteristics: age of mother at respondent's birth, marital status of respondent's biological parents, mortality of respondent's biological parents, educational level of respondent's biological parents, number of siblings, respondent's belief that a relative had a problem with mental disorders or substance use

Child maltreatment: lifetime exposure to physical assaults, sexual assaults, neglect, and/or witnessing domestic violence; sexual revictimization; sexual and physical assault: age at exposure onset, frequency, relationship of perpetrator(s), number of perpetrators, relative age of perpetrator(s), degree of violence, degree of intrusiveness, number of types of assaults; fighting back during physical assault

Symptoms of psychological distress (symptom counts were either dichotomized at the median or constructed as present vs. not present): lifetime major depression, suicide ideation and attempts, substance abuse and/or dependency, conduct disorder, PTSD; current depression, trait anxiety; age at symptom onset; number of current and lifetime diagnoses; current: self-esteem, loneliness, hopelessness, body image, disturbances with sleeping or eating, conviction of being loved (subscales created from the CDI); lifetime: self-worth, self-blame, self-hate, hopelessness, sleep disturbances (subscales created from the DIS)

Adaptation: school performance

Risk-taking: involvement in sex work and age at onset, engagement in unprotected sexual encounters, number of sexual partners, history of pregnancy, history of sexually transmitted disease

Analysis of the Data

Due to (1) the uncertainty of independence between responses, (2) the inability to calculate the probability of sampling a homeless youth, and (3) the small sample size, the analyses emphasize describing the HHYS sample rather than making statistical inferences to the entire population of homeless youth. Analyses include cross-tabulations, Pearson Chi-square or Fisher's Exact Test statistics, and odds ratios when the levels of significance are less than .10. Cross-tabulation cell differences which exceed 10% may be referred to as suggestive in the absence of a statistically significant Chi-square or Fisher's Exact Test. It is recognized that conducting multiple analyses increases the probability of observing spurious associations. All results are viewed with an emphasis on hypothesis-generation for future studies rather than on hypothesis-testing.

Methodological Strengths of the Study

This study is unusual in that it contributes information about homeless youth who use social services and those who do not, and it employs standardized measures of child maltreatment and psychological distress. Data were collected by highly trained interviewers during face-to-face interviews using well-defined multiple indicators of maltreatment and psychological distress; all of these factors are associated with enhanced measurement reliability and validity. In addition, multiple types of child maltreatment have been assessed, including neglect, domestic violence, extrafamilial, and intrafamilial. Potential moderators and mediators of the psychological consequences of maltreatment are analyzed.

Generalizability

The Hollywood Homeless Youth sample is a vast improvement over the single source samples which are prevalent in the homeless youth literature. The HHYS sample includes youth encountered in street sites as well as in homeless youth service sites. Most studies of homeless youth focus exclusively on the clients of youth service sites. Although the HHYS sample is not a probability sample, it is likely to provide better representation of the homeless youth population than the ubiquitous shelter samples. It is recognized, however, that the HHYS sample, by virtue of its snowball composition, probably under-represents those homeless youth who are the least socially involved with other homeless youth and service providers and those homeless youth who are precariously housed (e.g., youth who may have spent the night previous to the interview with a pimp, "john", or other individual.) Anecdotal evidence from service providers suggests that the numbers of homeless youth in Hollywood increase during the summer months. It seems plausible that these summertime homeless youths may differ in some characteristics from those who are homeless in Hollywood during the rest of the year, although there are no published data which address this issue. Since this sample was collected mostly during the month of June, it is possible that it somehow more closely reflects those homeless youth who appear in Hollywood during the summer months than those who remain during the rest of the year.

As noted earlier, there was some evidence of misrepresentation of age and homelessness status which affected some respondents' eligibilities to participate in the study. It is estimated that this phenomenon resulted in the inadvertent exclusion of some adolescents who would have been eligible and the inclusion of some who were not eligible. The net bias was believed to have been that more eligible adolescents were excluded than ineligible adolescents included. Due to the limited availability of police escort services for sampling of abandoned buildings and squats, only two such sites were sampled. In addition, the appearance of a police escort, while necessary for interviewer safety, may have influenced the respondents' answers to eligibility screening questions as well as other items on sensitive topics or illegal behaviors.

Limitations of the Study Design

Because of the cross-sectional design of the study, assertions about causal relationships cannot be made. However, the temporal direction of some relationships may be explored with caution based on respondent recall of the sequence of events.

Reliability and Validity of Measures

This section addresses the following topics related to the reliability and validity of the measures used in this study: single data source, standardized interaction between interviewers and respondents, confidentiality/anonymity, literacy, illegal or sensitive topics, social desirability, recall bias, interviewer observations, and known psychometric properties of the measures.

The only source of data is from the respondents themselves, and much of the data rely on the respondent's recollection of events. Consequently, no other source of data exists with which to confirm the validity of these data. In addition, some measures request information about which the respondent may have limited knowledge. For example, data collected regarding substance abuse by family members and the mental health of family members are possibly inaccurate estimates.

In order to enhance the validity and reliability of the data, efforts were made to maintain high levels of confidentiality and standardized interaction during interviews. The introductions, informed consent statement, questions, probes and transitions were scripted to ensure consistent delivery. In order to enhance the probability of honest reporting of sensitive and illegal experiences, guarantees of confidentiality were made to all respondents and identifying information was deliberately not collected. At the end of the interview, if the respondent had indicated a history of abuse, the interviewer was required to inform the respondent of the researcher's legal mandate to report the incident(s). Because no identifying information had been collected during the interview, the respondent's voluntary participation was requested in order to obtain the names of the respondent and perpetrators. It is difficult to know whether the informed consent procedure influenced a respondent's subsequent disclosure of maltreatment in spite of the assurances of anonymity of the data.

The interview was designed to gradually introduce the more sensitive topics after rapport had been established and anonymity affirmed. The more sensitive and specific question areas (e.g., information about physical and sexual abuse) were placed towards the end of the interview and were preceded by more general questions.

Although the interviews were conducted in private to reduce the social influence of others on the respondents' answers, the concern of response bias due to efforts to be socially desirable to the interviewer remained. A measure of social desirability was embedded in the drug portion of the schedule in order to assess this type of response bias. Service providers had warned the researchers that respondents may exaggerate their experiences when reporting. Consequently, respondents were asked whether they had experience taking a bogus drug called "adrenachromes"; none of the respondents reported using this drug. On the whole, there was little evidence of over-reporting of behaviors or experiences. Ten percent of the sample, however, refused to answer questions dealing with sexual abuse, resulting in a probable underestimation of the phenomenon. Other sensitive or illegal experiences may have been underreported due to fear of shocking or offending the interviewer. The nine-item lie scale of the Revised Manifest Anxiety Scale (RCMAS) was evaluated as another measure of honest reporting. Seventy-six percent reported that two or fewer items were true, and only 5.5% reported that five or more unlikely statements were true.

In order to reduce recall bias, questions were time-bound requiring an estimate of the time since the behavior or experience occurred. Multiple questions were asked around specific behaviors to stimulate recall and help to clarify any difference in subcultural definitions between the interviewer and the respondent. These effects could not, however, compensate for a respondent who was developmentally or psychologically unable to recall actual events or experiences or to make the associations requested in a question. For example, a respondent may have had psychogenic amnesia or dissociation regarding the abuse experienced in childhood and have been unable to recall it or to associate current problems/feelings with the event(s).

The interviewers observed each respondent's dress, physical appearance (weight), predominant affect, motor behavior, speech (amount and flow), attention, literacy, other general impressions and response to the interview. None of the respondents appeared to be completely unable to comprehend and respond to the interview.

The instrument consisted primarily of closed-ended structured interview questions. The Children's Depression Inventory (CDI), a standardized instrument, was designed to be self-administered, however, the interviewer had the prerogative to read these items aloud to the respondent if it was deemed necessary. Literacy was assessed during the beginning the interview when the respondent was requested to recite the race/ethnic groups and types of drugs listed on cards given by the interviewer. Determination of sufficient literacy for purposes of the interview was accomplished without any set criteria and was based on the interviewer's subjective assessment.

Most of the standardized measures have known properties of validity and reliability for normative samples of non-homeless adolescents (e.g., Children's Depression Inventory or CDI, Revised Children's Manifest Anxiety Scale or RCMAS, and the Diagnostic Interview for Children and Adolescents or DICA); and some have known properties for adults only (e.g., Diagnostic Interview Schedule or DIS). In response to the recommendations of other researchers in this area, symptoms or symptom clusters derived from these measures are treated as descriptive categories rather than as bases for formal diagnoses (based on DSM-III criteria) to avoid premature labeling of persons during an atypical or crisis situation (Dennis, 1987). Therefore, rather than be assigned to a diagnostic category, respondents are referred to as "meeting the criteria" for a particular diagnosis based on this instrument. The instrument was pretested on homeless adolescents in another geographic region of Los Angeles County in order to evaluate the instrument and the newly trained interviewers, but the validity and reliability of the measures were not systematically assessed at the time. Selected indicators of validity and reliability of some of the measures used in the HHYS are reported and discussed in the discussion chapter.

The standardized measures have some known psychometric properties when used with other populations. For instance, the DICA has had excellent inter-interview reliability in the diagnosis of conduct disorder among psychiatric in-patients between the ages of 7 and 17 (kappa=1.00) (Welner, Reich, Herjanic, Jung and Amado, 1987). This same study reported an agreement of 81.5% between the diagnosis predicted by the DICA and the hospital discharge diagnosis. Herjanic and Reich (1982) found that the results obtained from parents given the DICA tended to disagree with those results from the child's DICA. In general, children reported their aggressive behaviors less frequently and their covert conduct transgressions (e.g., stealing) more frequently than their parents did.

The CDI, a measure of depression in children, is one of the most extensively used and researched measures around. It has high internal consistency (Cronbach's alpha >.80) and moderate test-retest reliability from 1 week to 6 months, depending on the age and gender of the respondent (Kazdin, 1988). The CDI is able to distinguish psychiatric groups of children from non-patients, and it correlates well with related constructs such as self-esteem, negative cognitive attributions, hopelessness, anxiety, and social withdrawal. Among non-patient samples, approximately 10% of the sample is expected to score 19 or above on the scale (Kazdin, 1988; Smucker, Craighead, Craighead and Green, 1986; Ollendick and Yule, 1990). These high-scoring individuals tend to exhibit difficulties in areas associated with depression, such as anxiety and low self-esteem (Doerfler, Felner, Raley and Evans, 1988). The CDI is designed to evaluate the severity of depression based on the number of symptoms reported rather than provide a diagnosis of depression. The CDI does not uniformly distinguish depression from other diagnoses or from maladjustment (Kazdin, 1988).

The DIS was designed to discriminate psychiatric diagnoses from temporary discomforts and from physical illness among the general adult population (Robins et al., 1984). Diagnoses arising from the DIS have had moderate to good agreement with those produced by psychiatrists using the DSM-III assessment criteria with a general community sample (major depression Y=0.54, alcohol abuse and/or dependence Y=0.71, drug abuse and/or dependence Y=0.72) (Helzer and Robins, 1988).

The RCMAS was designed to assess trait anxiety. RCMAS anxiety scores have not been found to differ across school grade (i.e. from grades 2 through 11) or race, and the lie subscale has not varied with respondent gender (Reynolds and Richmond, 1978). Reynolds and Richmond also found that the RCMAS had excellent reliability estimates (KR_{20}=.85). In addition, the RCMAS has been shown to correlate strongly and significantly with the trait anxiety subscale of the STAIC (Spielberger, 1973) and has not been shown to correlate significantly with the state anxiety subscale of the STAI (Reynolds, 1980).

Notes

[1]The methodology used for the Hollywood Homeless Youth Study as described by Robertson (1989) is presented here with augmentation by the book's author.

[2]A coalition of private and public agencies that serve the homeless and runaway youth population in Los Angeles.

Table 4.1 Local Service Samples[a] vs. the Hollywood Homeless Youth Sample[b]

	Shelters %	Outreach & Drop-in %	HHYS %
Gender			
Males:	45.8	70.7	61.5
Females:	54.2	29.3	38.5
Race/Ethnicity			
White	48.7	58.4	59.4
African American	27.6	15.4	14.6
Hispanic/Latino	16.0	20.6	12.5
Native American	1.8	2.6	7.3
Asian/Pacific Islander	3.8	1.7	5.2
Other/Unknown	2.0	1.3	1.0
Birthplace/Origin			
L.A. Cty	60.6	21.8	26.0
Other CA Cty	12.1	15.0	13.5
Out of CA	26.2	60.9	59.4
Other/Unk	1.0	2.3	1.1
Age			
0-9 yr	0.1	0.0	0.0
10-11 yr	0.4	0.3	0.0
12-13 yr	8.7	2.5	2.1
14-15 yr	39.2	9.6	26.0
16-17 yr	51.0	41.6	71.9
18+ yr	0.6	46.0	0.0
Total *n*	2902	7613	96

[a] (Pennbridge et al., 1990)

[b] HHYS snowball sample from shelter, drop-in, and street sites

V
Results

Results are presented in sub-sections which cover the basic research questions: (1) describing the sample[1] with emphasis on the context of homelessness, history of child maltreatment, and psychological distress; (2) examining associations between child maltreatment and psychological distress; and (3) examining potential mediators and moderators of the association between child maltreatment and psychological distress. Due to the density of the descriptive results, a results summary follows a detailed account of the analyses. The results summary reviews both significant associations and non-significant trends.

When reading the results chapter, tests of significance should be regarded with caution for three reasons: (1) the sample is a non-probability sample and may not accurately represent the homeless youth population in Hollywood, CA, (2) responses from different individuals may not be independent of one another, and (3) the small sample size does not allow for much statistical power to determine significant sub-group differences. Consequently, cross-tabulation cell differences which exceed 10% may be referred to as suggestive in the absence of a statistically significant Chi-square or Fisher's exact test, and all results are viewed with an emphasis on hypothesis-generation for future studies rather than on hypothesis-testing. Chi-square values which are not cited in the text may be found in the tables. Chi-square values and odds ratios are reported only for relationships which reach levels of significance less than .10.

Sample Characteristics

Demographics and Educational Background

The modal characteristics of the sample are as follows: 61% are male, 59% are White, and 60% have a birthplace outside of California (Table 5.1). The mean age of the sample is 16.1 years (range 13-17 years). Gender and race/ethnicity covaried with age whereby men tended to be older than women and African-Americans tended to be younger than youth of other racial or ethnic heritage. Eighteen percent of the sample either identified themselves as gay, lesbian, or bisexual or reported involvement in same sex sexual activities in the year preceding the interview.

The mean grade level completed is 9.2, 28% have been held back at some point in school, and 27% have been in a special education program (Table 5.2). Modal (42%) school performance was average. School performance tended to be higher among younger respondents and among respondents who had histories of placement in foster or group care. Seventy-eight percent of the sample had been suspended, and 37% had been expelled from school. Seventy-one percent of the sample reported having plans to return to school some day; 12% were in school at the time of the interview.

Ten percent of the respondents identified themselves as emancipated minors, i.e., possessing the legal status of adults. Four percent of the sample had been previously married; none were currently married and living with their spouses. Thirty-one percent of the female respondents had given birth to one or more children; none were living with their children at the time of the interview.

Family History

With regard to the respondent's biological parents, 17% of the sample never knew one or both of their parents (Table 5.3). Twenty-seven percent of the sample had parents who were still married to each other. Fourteen percent of the respondents had lost a mother to death, and 11% had lost a father. Sixty-seven percent of the respondents' mothers and 77% of the fathers had at least a 12th grade education. Over half of the respondents were born to mothers who were 20 years of age or younger at the time of their births, and two out of three had living siblings. Mother's age at the birth of the respondent was positively related to the educational level of the respondent's father and the respondent's lifetime homelessness exposure, and it was inversely related to the respondent's placement in foster care.

History of Institutional Placements

Over three-quarters of the sample had spent some time in an institutional placement, such as foster care, group care, and/or juvenile detention (Table 5.4). Among those who had been in placement, the median number of times in any institutional placement was four. One-third of the sample had been in multiple types of placements. The most common placement was juvenile detention (22% of the total sample). History of placement in a juvenile detention facility covaried with chronic homelessness. Number of institutional placements was positively related to the number of episodes of homelessness, the lifetime total number of days of homelessness, and history of hospitalization for mental health problems, and was inversely related to age at first homeless episode.

Detention by Law Enforcement and Participation in Violence

Over half of the respondents had been detained by the police overnight at least once (Table 5.5). The most common reason for recent detention was the alleged commitment of a "minor" offense (e.g. running away, trespassing, to protect the respondent etc.) (Tables 5.6 and 5.7). Contrary to many media portrayals of youth and homeless persons, the majority of offenses (83%) for which respondents were detained overnight by law enforcement authorities were for *non*-violent offenses, and two-thirds of the sample had *never* been detained for violent offenses.

This is not to suggest that violence on the streets and in communities is not a serious problem. Eighty-eight percent of the Hollywood Homeless Youth Study sample (HHYS) acknowledged having engaged in physical violence, and 76% of the sample disclosed having hurt someone in a physical altercation. Two-thirds of the sample reported having threatened someone with physical injury, and approximately half of the respondents had robbed someone under threat of physical injury. Fifty-four percent of the respondents disclosed that they had 'been in a gang' sometime in their lives. Participation in violent activities when living on the streets is probably necessary for self-defense and for acquiring the means for survival.

History of Homelessness

Although cumulative lifetime homelessness was less than one year for 62% of the sample (median of six and one-half months) (Table 5.8), 48% had been homeless at least five times (with 23% homeless more than ten times). Eighty-three percent of the sample had been either episodically or chronically homeless. The range of lifetime homelessness was from five days to seven years. Almost all (92%) of the respondents considered themselves to be "homeless". Less than 10% of the sample was missing data on homelessness characteristics; therefore, no special analyses were conducted on those respondents with missing data.

First Homeless Episode

Respondents reported that their age at their first homeless episode ranged from 5 to 17 years with a mean of 13 years (Table 5.9); 86% recalled leaving their homes by choice. Half of the sample reported that the event or condition which precipitated their first homeless episode was family conflict; 22% recalled that physical or sexual abuse was the reason for their homelessness. Over two-thirds of the sample was homeless for 30 days or less the first time.

Current Homeless Episode

The range of respondent ages at the onset of the current homeless episode was from 10-17 years with a mean of 15 years. Sixty-five percent of the sample reported leaving home by choice (Table 5.10). Being asked to leave home was positively related to a history of hospitalization for mental health problems and was inversely related to age at first homelessness. Women were as likely as men to be asked to leave home. As with the first homelessness episode, the modal reason for being homeless at the time of the interview was reported to be family conflict (36%). Almost half of the sample had been homeless between one and twelve months during the current episode, and over half reported being homeless with friends. Abandoned buildings ("squats") were most often cited (32%) as the place usually used for sleeping when the respondent could not afford a room or an apartment. The majority of the respondents (60%) had not slept in a shelter or mission in the thirty days preceding the interview; few (16%) reported regular use of shelters. Respondents who were younger or had lower incomes in the month preceding the interview were more likely to report recent use of shelters. Most respondents reported that their typical sleeping place was in improvised shelters as opposed to more protective settings such as shelters, missions, someone's home, hotel/motels, or juvenile hall.

Mobility and Migration

Half of the sample had moved to Los Angeles county within the past year; 41% had lived in Los Angeles county for one year or less in their lifetimes (Table 5.11). Over half of the respondents (57%) had experienced between 3-30 intercity moves in their lifetimes. Almost three-quarters of the sample (73%) had spent at least one night in the past year in their family home; 59% had spent at least one night on the street/outdoors/or in a public place. Forty-six percent of the respondents had spent at least one night in the past year in a "squat". Few had spent one night in the past year in a foster home (11%), a group home (7%), or other institutional (12%) care. Sixty-percent of the sample had not spent any nights in an emergency shelter in the past year. Four out of five respondents spent some time outside of Hollywood during an average 24-hour day. However, 92% of the sample usually slept in the Hollywood area.

Main Sources of Food

Over half (57%) reported that they had experienced one or more days with nothing to eat (Table 5.12). The sample's modal sources of food were shelters or other free meal programs (53%).

Subsistence Characteristics

Half of the sample reported having legal sources of income (e.g. legal job, family, and friends) in the 30 days prior to the interview (Table 5.13). Income for the previous thirty days ranged from 0 to $1500 with a median of $100. Having problems obtaining adequate clothing, food, and facilities for personal hygiene were positively related to length and chronicity of lifetime homelessness exposure and inversely related to age at first homelessness exposure.

Health Care Resources and Use

About one-third of the respondents recalled having medical insurance (including Medi-Cal); one-half reported having a specific place and/or person which provides medical care (Table 5.14). Over half of the sample had received medical care in the past year; one-quarter had received help for a mental health problem. Few had received help for alcohol use (16%) or drug use (9%) in the past year. One-quarter of the sample had ever spent a night in a mental hospital; less than 10% had ever spent the night in a drug treatment or alcohol treatment facility.

Risk-Taking Profiles

Forty-three percent of the respondents reported having had their first sexual encounters before the age of 12. The number of sexual partners in the year preceding the interview ranged from 0 to over 95 with a mean and median of 4 partners (Table 5.15). Sex was exchanged for money by 29% of the sample, for food or shelter by 22% of the sample, and for drugs by 11% of the sample. Eight percent reported having posed for sexual photographs or movies. Almost half (44%) of the women had been pregnant at least once; 33% of the women had given birth at least once. One out of five respondents recalled having had a sexually transmitted disease. One out of three respondents had been tested for HIV-antibodies; 3.6% of those tested were positive for HIV-antibodies. Over one-third of the sample reported never using birth control; only one-third used a condom regularly during the last year. One out of five respondents had driven a car while under the influence of alcohol, and one out of three had injected drugs.

Perceived Health of Self and Relatives

Three-quarters of the sample rated their health as fair or poor; although, most respondents (73%) felt that their health was the same as before they became homeless (Table 5.16). One out of three respondents reported having had a mental problem; only one out of six felt that they needed help with their mental problems. Three out of four respondents had used alcohol and/or drugs before they became homeless. Most participants did not perceive that they had used greater quantities of substances since becoming homeless.

A relative(s) was perceived to have an alcohol, drug, or mental problem by 50%, 29%, and 32% of the sample, respectively (Table 5.17). Fifty-nine percent of the sample thought that a drug, alcohol, and/or mental health problem existed within their family (excluding themselves); 39% of the respondents believed that two problems existed within their families. For many of the respondents, the relative with the substance use problem was a parent and this problem contributed to verbal arguments and physical violence between the parent, the respondent, and others.

Daily Stressors

Almost all respondents reported taking at least one action to avoid being harmed while living on the streets. In order of prevalence, these actions were (1) always being with someone who is trusted (77%), (2) avoiding certain places (67%), (3) avoiding certain people (50%), (4) carrying a weapon (50%), and (5) staying awake at night/sleeping during the day (24%) (Table 5.18). Over half of the respondents do three or more of these things to avoid being harmed.

About half of the respondents reported that getting food and clothes was usually or sometimes a problem; most respondents (63%) claimed that finding a place to clean up was rarely or never a problem. The majority (68%) said that getting medical care was rarely or never a problem. However, 46% of the sample claimed to have trouble getting at least three out of these four basic needs.

Child Maltreatment

Only eight percent of the sample reported that no child maltreatment (i.e., neglect, physical and sexual abuse, or witness to domestic violence as defined by the questionnaire items) occurred (Tables 5.19 and 5.20). One out of five respondents disclosed being neglected (unspecified); nearly one out of two respondents reported being physically neglected by their parents (Table 5.21).

Over three-quarters of the sample recalled being physically assaulted by relatives, caretakers (or their friends or relatives), friends, strangers, or cohabitants (Table 5.22). Half of those who recalled physical assaults had experienced a level of violence which was life-threatening, i.e., threatened with a weapon, stabbed, or shot. Nearly one-third of those who were physically assaulted sought professional medical attention for their injuries; this proportion was the same regardless of whether the assault perpetrator was a cohabiting relative or friend or a non-resident. Twenty-two percent of those who disclosed histories of physical abuse had been locked in a small room, and one out of six had been tied up. Almost all (94%) of those assaulted had been victimized more than once. Two-thirds of those assaulted recalled being between two and ten years of age at the first assault and having more than one perpetrator. For half of those assaulted, both adults and peers were the perpetrators; for 75% of those responding, the perpetrators included at least one parent.

Thirty-four percent of the sample disclosed histories of sexual assault involving physical contact perpetrated by relatives, caretakers (or their friends or relatives), friends, strangers, or cohabitants (Table 5.23). Three out of four of those recalling sexual assaults had had genital contact with the perpetrator; one out of two had been sexually penetrated. One out of five survivors' assaults exclusively involved being touched by the perpetrator. Two out of three assault survivors had been assaulted more than once. Forty-one percent of those who disclosed sexual assault had been assaulted by more than one perpetrator; 39% had been assaulted by more than one perpetrator and on more than one occasion. Slightly more than half (57%) of the sexual assault survivors recalled their first sexual assault as occurring during puberty or early adolescence (at 11-16 years of age). For two-thirds of the sexual assault survivors, their perpetrators were exclusively adults. One-third of those disclosing histories of sexual assault identified the perpetrator(s) as being a parent figure, usually the respondent's father.

Nearly one out of two respondents reported witnessing violence in their homes (Table 5.24). Half of those who witnessed domestic violence disclosed that the violence was exclusively between adults. Three out of four witnesses recalled that the violence was limited to two specific individuals in the home, one of whom tended to be a father figure and/or the mother's boyfriend. For 42% of the witnesses, the targets of the violence were women and female children: the respondent's mother and sisters. Only ten percent of the witnesses recalled male adults and children as being the sole targets of violence; when male adults and children were the sole targets of the violence, the targets were identified as brothers of the respondent. Almost all of the witnesses had observed domestic violent exchanges involving hitting with a hand (95%); half of the witnesses (48%) had seen someone beaten. One out of four witnesses had observed someone threaten another with a weapon in the home. One out of eight witnesses had seen persons burned, stabbed, shot, or raped in the home.

Twelve percent of the sample refused to answer questions on child maltreatment. Those who refused to answer were slightly more likely to be older, more educated, African-American, young men who had been told to leave home and had not used youth shelter services in the month preceding the interview. Respondents interviewed at drop-in centers and whose current homeless episode was longer in duration were moderately more likely to refuse to answer the items on child maltreatment.

Characteristics of Histories of Physical Assaults Without Sexual Assaults

For youth whose first exposure to physical assaults was before adolescence, assaults were most often perpetrated by multiple persons, including one or both parents/caretakers. Youth whose first physical assault occurred during adolescence tended to describe their attacks as being committed by a single non-parent perpetrator. Regardless of age at onset of physical assaults, life-threatening levels of violence were most often reported when the perpetrators were multiple and included both adults and peers. Very few respondents who disclosed histories of physical assault had been assaulted only once. Young women's histories of physical assault tended to mirror those of youth who had been exposed after adolescence, and young men's histories of physical assault tended to replicate those of youth who had been exposed before adolescence. Levels of violence associated with physical assaults did not covary with respondent gender, and women and men were equally likely to fight back during physical assaults. Respondents who reported histories of both physical and sexual assaults were more likely to disclose exposure to neglect and family violence than respondents who did not report a history of sexual assault.

Characteristics of Histories of Sexual Assaults Which Included Physical Assaults

For youth who were initially exposed to sexual assaults between the ages of three and nine, the assaults tended to involve sexual penetration perpetrated by their fathers. Exposure to sexual assaults during adolescence, i.e., between the ages of 11 and 17, was most often perpetrated by multiple adult and peer perpetrators in a single assault which did not include sexual penetration. For youth whose first exposure to sexual assaults occurred during adolescence, assaults perpetrated by single adults were most likely to entail life-threatening levels of physical violence. Although, it is unclear from the data whether the physical assaults described by the respondents occurred in the context of sexual assaults or as separate attacks. There was no observed relationship between age at onset for sexual assault and age at onset for physical assault.

Young women's histories of sexual assault most frequently mirrored those of youth who had been exposed before adolescence, but young women exposed before adolescence were more likely to experience a single assault than were young men. Life-threatening levels of violence were more often described by female survivors of sexual assault than by male survivors. Young men's histories of sexual assault most frequently mirrored those of youth who had been exposed during adolescence, but young men exposed after adolescence were more likely to experience multiple assaults than were young women. The greater likelihood of sexual revictimization among male sexual assault survivors compared with female survivors may be due, in part, to their more frequent involvement in sex work (i.e., pornography and prostitution).

Responses to Child Maltreatment

Three-quarters of those who disclosed physical assault reported that they fought the perpetrator of the physical attack (Table 5.25). Nearly one of two who disclosed histories of child maltreatment left home because of the maltreatment. Suspected child maltreatment was reported to the authorities for half of those who revealed histories of maltreatment (Table 5.26). Seventeen percent of the disclosed neglect cases, 36% of the disclosed physical assault cases, 29% of the disclosed sexual assault cases, and 40% of the disclosed domestic violence cases were reported to the authorities. The prevalence of reporting did not vary significantly according to whether the perpetrators were residents of the respondent's home. Almost half of those respondents whose maltreatment was reported were removed from the home by authorities. When the parent was the suspected perpetrator, 50% of the reported neglect cases, 50% of the reported physical assault cases, 25% of the reported sexual assault cases, and 40% of the reported domestic violence cases resulted in the removal of the respondent from the home (Table 5.27). It could not be determined which perpetrators were also custodial parents. Only a handful of maltreatment reports resulted in the arrest of the perpetrator.

Psychological Distress

Approximately 23% of the sample had symptoms of current depression. DSM-IIIR criteria were met for a lifetime diagnosis of an episode of major depression, alcohol abuse or dependence, drug abuse or dependence, and conduct disorder by 26%, 48%, 39%, and 84% of the sample, respectively (Table 5.28). In order to make the diagnosis of conduct disorder meaningful for this sample, the diagnostic criteria were adjusted to exclude behaviors which were necessary for survival on the streets and which may have been necessary to escape maltreatment at home, i.e., symptoms had to be present for over one year when the respondent was not homeless, and running away was not included as a symptom leading to diagnosis. Taking these exclusions into account, the prevalence of conduct disorder then decreases from 84% to 68%. Thirty-eight percent of the sample had at least one symptom of post-traumatic stress disorder (PTSD) in the previous 12 months as measured by an adaptation of the DIS; 18% of the sample met DSM-IIIR criteria for a lifetime diagnosis of PTSD (with two of three required symptoms of avoidance or numbing of stimuli). Two out of three respondents reported having had suicide thoughts; about half (47%) of the respondents reported attempting suicide at least once.

Only seven percent of the respondents met DSM-III diagnostic criteria for trait anxiety. Seventy-five percent of the respondents did not meet the diagnostic criteria for either current depression or trait anxiety; 17% of the sample had no lifetime diagnoses of substance abuse or dependence, major depression, conduct disorder, or PTSD (Table 5.29). Two out of three respondents met caseness criteria for multiple lifetime diagnoses.

Two out of three respondents had had symptoms of dysphoria; one in three reported symptoms of dysthymia (Table 5.30). The most commonly experienced symptoms of major depression included guilt, sleep disturbance, and thoughts of death. One in four respondents who met criteria for a diagnosis of PTSD disclosed having symptoms after more than one traumatic event (Table 5.31). Seeing a person killed, being physically or sexually assaulted, and experiencing the death of a friend or family member were the traumatic events most commonly cited as causing the PTSD symptoms.

Forty-one percent of the sample had no symptoms of any drug dependence or abuse (Table 5.32); an additional 21% of the sample had symptoms of drug use which did not meet criteria for a diagnosis of drug abuse and/or dependence. Among youth who met DSM-III criteria for drug abuse and/or dependence caseness, the diagnosis was most often made for use of cannabis (83%), amphetamines (33%), cocaine (22%), and opioids (22%); 42% met caseness criteria for more than one drug. Over 80% of those who disclosed any drug use reported use of cannabis, psychedelics, cocaine, or amphetamines during the year preceding the interview (Table 5.33) and reported use of more than one drug in the six months preceding the interview. Twenty-eight percent of all respondents had no symptoms of alcohol dependence and/or abuse; another 20% of the sample had symptoms of alcohol use which did not meet criteria for a diagnosis of alcohol abuse and/or dependence (Table 5.32). Less than ten percent of the sample was missing data on indicators of psychological distress; therefore, no special analyses were conducted on those respondents with missing data.

Location of Interview by Sample Characteristics[2]

The sample was stratified into three groups which reflected the locations of the interviews: (1) 50% were from drop-in centers for homeless/runaway youth, (2) 23% were from emergency shelters for homeless/runaway youth, and (3) 27% were from street locations. Drop-in centers included social service agencies which may provide safe shelter for a few hours, food and/or case management. Emergency shelters provided short-term (usually less than two weeks) overnight shelter, food and case management. Street locations included street corners, fast food establishments, parks, and abandoned buildings (i.e., "squats"). In order to assess the differences and similarities between service samples and street samples, respondents interviewed in shelters and drop-in centers were compared with those recruited from street sites. The street subsample was characterized as being predominantly comprised of older male youth who were born in a state other then California, who voluntarily left home, and who have been episodically homeless. Respondents in the street subsample were also likely to report symptoms of substance abuse and conduct disorder.

Interview Location by Demographic Characteristics

The odds of interviewing a non-white youth in a shelter were 2.5 times greater than those of encountering a white, non-Latino respondent; yet the odds of recruiting a white, non-Latino respondent at a drop-in center were 2.6 times that of interviewing non-white youth (Table 5.34). Respondents who had been born outside the United States were 8.4 more times more likely to be interviewed in shelters than were youth born in the United States. California natives were 3.1 times more likely to be encountered in shelters than were other United States citizens. Although not statistically significant, female respondents were slightly more likely to be interviewed in shelters than male youth, and younger respondents (i.e., 13-15 years old) tended to be recruited from drop-in centers and shelters more readily than older respondents (i.e., 16-17 years old). Survivors of sexual assaults were more likely to be encountered in shelters and drop-in centers than at street sites. Youth who identified themselves as gay, lesbian, or bisexual were more likely to be interviewed at street and drop-in sites than at youth shelter sites. Of the respondents who had not used youth shelter services in the year preceding the interview, two-thirds were interviewed at youth drop-in centers.

Interview Location by Characteristics of Homelessness

Respondents who had been told to leave home were 4.1 times more likely to be encountered at drop-in centers and 3.2 times more likely to be interviewed in a shelter than were youth who left home on their own (Table 5.35). Respondents who reported being 'homeless alone' were 2.7 times more likely to be encountered in a shelter than those who were 'homeless with others'. The odds of encountering a respondent who had been homeless (lifetime) for one year or more in a drop-in center or shelter were 4.0 times and 2.0 times, respectively, higher than those of finding a youth who had been homeless for less than one year. The odds of recruiting a temporarily homeless youth from a drop-in center or shelter were 5.4 and 4.5 times higher, respectively, than those of recruiting an episodically homeless youth. Chronically homeless respondents were 5.8 times and 2.5 times more likely to be encountered at drop-in centers and shelters, respectively, than episodically homeless youth but 1.8 times less likely to be interviewed in a shelter than temporarily homeless youth. There appeared to be no difference in the odds of recruiting a chronically homeless youth from those of a temporarily homeless youth in a drop-in center.

Interview Location by Psychological Distress

The odds of interviewing youth who reported higher symptoms of current depression, lifetime major depression, and trait anxiety in a shelter were

3.6, 4.0, and 5.1 times higher than those of interviewing youth who reported lower symptoms (Table 5.36). The likelihood of encountering youth who reported more symptoms of lifetime major depression in a drop-in center was 1.8 times greater than the likelihood of recruiting youth who reported fewer symptoms.

There were some trends suggested by the data which did not reach statistical significance: youth sampled in shelters appeared to be more likely to report greater numbers of symptoms of current and lifetime depression and lifetime PTSD as well as meet diagnostic criteria for lifetime PTSD. Youth encountered in shelters were less likely to report elevated symptoms of conduct disorder and meet diagnostic criteria for lifetime alcohol or drug abuse and/or dependence. Youth interviewed at street sites were less likely to report elevated symptoms of lifetime PTSD or depression or meet diagnostic criteria for lifetime PTSD. Youth sampled in drop-in centers were less likely to report elevated symptoms of current depression and more likely to meet diagnostic criteria for lifetime drug abuse and/or dependence.

Homelessness Characteristics by Selected Demographic Characteristics

Although not statistically significant, the chronically homeless (> 1 episode, > or = 1 year lifetime homelessness) respondents were slightly more likely to be white, non-Latino women than those who were temporarily homeless (Table 5.37). Episodically homeless youth tended to be white, non-Latino and younger (i.e., 13-15 years old) compared with those who were temporarily homeless. Respondents who reported cumulative homelessness of one year or longer tended to be older (i.e., 16-17 years old), white, non-Latino, women.

Child Maltreatment by Selected Respondent Characteristics

When all types of child maltreatment are considered simultaneously in one hierarchical variable, male respondents were 2.4 times more likely to disclose histories of physical assault (without sexual assault) than were female respondents (Table 5.38). The odds of a female respondent disclosing a history of sexual assault (with or without physical assault) were 1.7 times that of a male respondent. Respondents who revealed histories of sexual assault were almost five times more likely to have fathers who had less than 12th grade educations compared with respondents who reported histories of physical assault (without sexual assault) and compared with those who reported negative histories of physical and sexual assault. The relationship between history of sexual assault and mother's educational level showed a similar trend to that with father's educational level but was not statistically significant.

Slight tendencies were noted for those disclosing histories of physical assault to have spent time in a group home and in juvenile detention and for those disclosing histories of sexual assault to be younger (13-15 years of age) and to have parents who were divorced. Respondents who disclosed histories of sexual assault were moderately more likely to have had below average grades in school and slightly more likely to have had longer lifetime histories of homelessness (although age at first homeless episode did not differ from others). Youth whose mothers were young (i.e., 20 years old or younger) at the time of their births were more likely to disclose histories of neglect than other youth.

Psychological Distress by Selected Respondent Characteristics[2]

The odds of female respondents having higher numbers of trait anxiety symptoms or of meeting diagnostic criteria for current depression were 2.2 and 2.8 times higher, respectively, than for male respondents (Table 5.39). The odds of female respondents disclosing histories of suicide thoughts and attempts were 2.6 and 2.8 times higher, respectively, than for male respondents. Male youth were three times and two times more likely to meet lifetime diagnostic criteria for drug abuse and/or dependence and conduct disorder (χ=2.730, p<.10, O.R.=0.477, n=95) caseness, respectively, than were female youth. Younger participants (aged 13-15 years) were 2.5 times more likely to report higher numbers of symptoms of lifetime major depression than older participants (aged

16-17 years). In contrast, older respondents were three and two times more likely to disclose histories of suicide attempts and higher numbers of symptoms of alcohol abuse and/or dependence, respectively, than younger respondents.

The odds of participants meeting diagnostic criteria for lifetime depression caseness and having a tenth grade education or greater are four times higher than for those with less than a tenth grade education; yet the odds of respondents having less than a tenth grade education and meeting diagnostic criteria for current depression caseness are four times higher than for respondents with at least a tenth grade education. The odds of respondents with lower incomes (<$100 in the past month) having higher numbers of trait anxiety symptoms was 4.4 times higher than for respondents with higher incomes (>=$100 in the past month). Participants with lower incomes were 2.2, 2.3, and 2.2 times more likely to have higher numbers of symptoms of lifetime depression and to disclose histories of suicide thoughts and attempts, respectively, than participants with higher incomes. The odds of participants who had spent days without food disclosing histories of suicide attempts were 3.9 times higher than for those who had not spent days without food.

Youth who believed that a relative(s) had a problem with alcohol use were 3.2 times more likely to meet diagnostic criteria for drug abuse and/or dependence and 2.1 times more likely to report elevated symptoms than other youth (Table 5.40). The odds of participants who reported that relative(s) had drug problems meeting diagnostic criteria for lifetime drug abuse and/or dependence and conduct disorder were 4.0 and 2.9, respectively, higher than for those who did not report the belief that relative(s) had drug problems. Belief that a relative(s) had a problem with mental health significantly and positively covaried with virtually every indicator of psychological distress except alcohol. Youth who disclosed gang affiliation were more likely to meet diagnostic criteria for alcohol abuse (χ=10.015, p<.01, O.R.=3.974, n=92) and conduct disorder (χ=7.436, p<.01, O.R.=3.478, n=83). Receipt of mental health treatment in the year preceding the interview covaried positively with indicators of trait anxiety (χ=11.366, p<.001, O.R.=6.702, n=88), lifetime major depression (χ=7.390, p<.01, O.R.=3.929, n=91), and current depression (χ=16.270, p<.0001, O.R.=8.957, n=85). The associations between other indicators of psychological distress and sociodemographic and economic characteristics of the respondents were not statistically significant.

Several trends which did not achieve statistical significance were observed. For instance, respondents who were born in countries other than the United States appeared to be less likely to meet diagnostic criteria for drug abuse and/or dependence than those born in the United States and younger respondents tended to have higher numbers of symptoms of trait anxiety than older participants. Young women were more likely to report symptoms of lifetime major depression and PTSD than young men. Youth who identified themselves as gay, lesbian, or bisexual or who described engaging in same-sex sexual activities in the year preceding the interview were more likely to describe histories of suicide thoughts and symptoms of drug abuse and/or dependence and conduct disorder and were less likely to report histories of suicide attempts or elevated symptoms of trait anxiety or current depression.

Respondents who had spent days without food were more likely to report histories of suicide thoughts. Higher income tended to covary with elevated symptoms of drug abuse. Youth who disclosed gang affiliation were more likely to report symptoms of drug abuse and PTSD and were less likely to endorse symptoms of current depression and anxiety. Having a regular medical provider covaried with elevated symptoms of lifetime major depression, suicide thoughts, trait anxiety, and PTSD and decreased symptoms of substance abuse and/or dependence.

Youth whose mothers were aged twenty or younger at the time of their births were more likely to report histories of suicide attempts than other youth. Respondents who believed that a relative(s) had a problem with alcohol use were more likely to report elevated symptoms for lifetime major depression, conduct disorder, and drug abuse and/or dependence, and current depression and were less inclined to report histories of suicide attempts. Youth who believed that a relative(s) had a problem with drug use more frequently reported elevated symptoms of lifetime major depression, alcohol abuse and/or dependence, PTSD, and trait anxiety and less often disclosed histories of suicide attempts than respondents who did not believe that any relatives had problems with drug use. Receipt of mental health services in the year preceding the interview tended to covary with history of suicide thoughts, PTSD, and conduct disorder.

Psychological Distress by Custodial Placement and Shelter Use

The odds of respondents who had spent at least one night in an emergency shelter in the past month having higher numbers of trait anxiety symptoms were 2.5 times that of respondents who had not spent a night in a shelter (Table 5.39). Respondents who had never spent time in foster care were 2.3, 2.8, and 2.4 times more likely to report higher numbers of symptoms of lifetime depression, to meet diagnostic criteria for lifetime depression caseness, and to disclose thoughts of suicide, respectively, than those who had spent time in foster care (Tables 5.39 and 5.41). The odds of respondents who had not spent time in juvenile detention meeting diagnostic criteria for current depression caseness and having histories of suicide thoughts were 3.8 and 2.1 times higher, respectively, than for those who had spent time in juvenile detention (Table 5.41). Participants who had spent time in a group home were 2.7 times more likely to meet diagnostic criteria for alcohol dependency and/or abuse caseness than were participants who had not spent time in a group home. Relationships between other measures of psychological distress and custodial placement were not statistically significant.

There was a trend in the data indicating that those who had spent time in juvenile detention were more likely to meet the diagnostic criteria for alcohol abuse and/or dependency caseness. Respondents who had been in group homes or foster care appeared to be less likely meet diagnostic criteria for current depression; and those who had been in foster care were less likely to meet diagnostic criteria for lifetime depression. Respondents who had never been in foster care or who had lived in group homes seemed more likely to report histories of suicide attempts. Youth who had not spent any of the 30 nights preceding the interview in an emergency shelter were more likely to report symptoms of conduct disorder and drug abuse and/or dependence and less likely to report symptoms of trait anxiety and current depression.

Psychological Distress by Homelessness Characteristics

In general, having problems finding clothes, food, and places to clean up was inversely related to substance abuse and/or dependency caseness. It is probable that these relationships are bidirectional, but this cannot be determined with cross-sectional survey data. The odds of respondents having problems finding clothes and places to clean up but not meeting diagnostic criteria for alcohol dependency and/or abuse caseness were four and two times greater, respectively, than for those who did not have these problems (Table 5.42). Participants who had difficulties finding food and places to clean up were 11 and 5 times less likely, respectively, to meet drug abuse and/or dependence diagnostic criteria than those who did not have these difficulties. Similar trends were noted for the relationships between problems finding clothes and drug abuse and/or dependence and between problems getting food and alcohol abuse and/or dependence.

Overall, respondents who had been temporarily homeless (one episode lasting less than one year), had left home on their own, and had been older at the time they first became homeless were less likely to meet substance abuse and/or dependence caseness criteria. Again, the cross-sectional nature of this data does not permit the determination of the direction of these relationships. In other words, it is unclear the extent to which substance abuse and/or dependence preceded and contributed to the respondent's homelessness and vice versa. The odds of respondents meeting alcohol abuse and/or dependence diagnostic criteria and being either episodically or chronically homeless and being told to leave home were 3, 4, and 2.3 times higher, respectively, than those who were temporarily homeless or who left home on their own (Table 5.42). Participants who first became homeless before age 14 were 2.7 times more likely to meet drug abuse and/or dependence diagnostic criteria. Similar trends were seen between age of first homelessness and alcohol dependence and/or abuse and between drug abuse and/or dependence, pattern of homelessness, and whether the respondent was asked to leave home. Youth who disclosed histories of symptoms of conduct disorder were more likely to have been asked to leave home than other youth. Cumulative lifetime exposure to homelessness positively covaried with symptoms of PTSD, substance abuse and/or dependence, and conduct disorder.

Psychological Distress by Disclosed Child Maltreatment

When examining the relationships between the various indicators of psychological distress and the three-category disclosed child maltreatment variable (Table 5.43), symptom counts and caseness seemed to be highest for those who disclosed histories of sexual assault (with or without physical assault). For current and lifetime depression and trait anxiety, there appeared to be no difference in the proportion of elevated symptom counts or caseness between those who reported no physical or sexual maltreatment and those who reported histories of physical assault. For other indicators of psychological distress, respondents who disclosed histories of physical assault had higher rates of caseness and elevated symptom counts than those who reported no maltreatment but lower rates than those who disclosed histories of sexual assault.

Examination of the odds ratios of the associations between the three-category child maltreatment variable and indicators of psychological distress demonstrated the heightened risk of psychopathology associated with the subtypes of maltreatment. Compared with youth who reported negative histories of sexual and physical assault, the odds of respondents disclosing histories of physical assault and having higher numbers of symptoms of lifetime depression, PTSD and drug abuse and/or dependence; histories of suicide thoughts; and meeting diagnostic criteria for conduct disorder caseness were 1.4, 2.0, 1.9, 5.0, and 2.1 times higher, respectively. Respondents who had disclosed histories of sexual assault (with or without physical assault) were 3.7, 20.9, 4.2, 6.8, and 5.6 times more likely to report higher numbers of symptoms of lifetime depression, PTSD and drug abuse and/or dependence; histories of suicide thoughts; and symptoms which meet diagnostic caseness criteria for conduct disorder than participants who reported negative histories of physical and sexual assault. Compared with youth who reported histories of physical assault, the odds of respondents disclosing histories of sexual assault and having higher numbers of symptoms of lifetime depression, PTSD and drug abuse and/or dependence; histories of suicide thoughts; and meeting diagnostic criteria for conduct disorder caseness were 2.7, 10.2, 2.2, 1.4, and 2.7 higher, respectively. Although not statistically significant, the cross-tabulations between alcohol abuse and/or dependence and child maltreatment showed the same trends discussed above.

There were no significant relationships between diagnoses for abuse and/or dependency of specific drugs and disclosure of child maltreatment. Due to the small number of respondents reporting no sexual or physical assault, the two-category child maltreatment variable was created which contrasts those who disclosed sexual assault from those who did not. The two-category child maltreatment variable is used in three-way analyses discussed later.

Analyses of the relationship of child maltreatment with specific symptoms of depression revealed trends for those who disclosed histories of sexual assault to also have a history of symptoms of appetite and/or weight loss, motor disturbances, fatigue, and guilt. Those who reported histories of physical assault often had histories of slowness of thoughts and thoughts of death. Respondents who disclosed histories of sexual assault were 2.5 times more likely to have had below average school grades compared with those who negative histories of sexual assault. Youth who disclosed histories of sexual or physical assault were less likely to report histories of gang involvement than those who recalled negative histories of child maltreatment.

Comorbidity of Psychological Distress by Disclosed Child Maltreatment[2]

Respondents who disclosed histories of physical assault had higher numbers of lifetime diagnoses than those who reported no maltreatment but lower numbers than those who disclosed histories of sexual assault (Table 5.44). Lifetime diagnoses include major depression, PTSD, alcohol abuse and/or dependence, drug abuse and/or dependence, and conduct disorder. The proportion of participants who reported histories of physical assault and who met diagnostic criteria for a current diagnosis of psychological distress (depression and/or trait anxiety) was similar to that of those who reported negative histories of child maltreatment but less than the proportion of those who reported histories of sexual assault. Specifically, the odds of respondents disclosing histories of sexual assault and meeting diagnostic criteria for 1-2 current or 3-4 lifetime diagnoses of psychological distress were 2.5 and 2.9 times higher, respectively, than those for respondents who reported negative histories of sexual assault. Below average school performance was associated with elevated symptoms and/or caseness for all psychological distress indicators, except lifetime alcohol abuse and/or dependence caseness. Respondents with below average school grades were 2.4 and 4 times more likely, respectively, to meet diagnostic criteria for caseness for lifetime drug abuse and/or dependence and conduct disorder. Having plans to return to school was inversely related to meeting diagnostic criteria for conduct disorder and positively related to symptoms of lifetime major depression.

Perceived Own and Relative's Health by Disclosed Child Maltreatment

The odds of respondents disclosing histories of sexual assault and perceptions of having a mental health problem or of a relative having a mental health problem were 3.8 times higher than for those who reported negative histories of sexual assault (Table 5.45). Youth reporting histories of sexual assault were five times more likely to describe their health since leaving home as "better" than were youth who reported negative histories of sexual assault.

Self-Protective Actions by Disclosed Child Maltreatment

The odds of respondents disclosing histories of sexual assault and avoiding certain people and carrying a weapon for protection were 2.3 times higher than for those who reported negative histories of sexual assault (Table 5.46). Compared with those who reported negative histories of sexual and physical assault, respondents who disclosed histories of physical or sexual assault tended to be more likely to also report that they slept during the day and avoided certain places in order to protect themselves from harm.

Comorbidity of Indicators of Psychological Distress

Eighty-five percent of the sample met diagnostic criteria for at least one current or lifetime indicator of psychological distress. Fifty-five percent of the respondents met diagnostic criteria for substance abuse and/or dependence and at least one other indicator of psychological distress. Two in three youth met diagnostic criteria for either drug and/or alcohol abuse and/or dependence; one in four youth met diagnostic criteria for both drug and alcohol abuse and/or dependence. Among respondents who met diagnostic criteria for caseness, significant covariation was found between alcohol abuse and/or dependence and conduct disorder; lifetime major depression and current depression; and lifetime drug abuse and/or dependence, alcohol abuse and/or dependence and conduct disorder (Table 5.47). The odds of respondents meeting diagnostic criteria for caseness on drug abuse and/or dependence as well as on alcohol abuse and/or dependence and on conduct disorder were 3.5 and 6.2 times higher, respectively, than for those who did not meet diagnostic criteria for drug abuse and/or dependence. Youth who met caseness criteria for alcohol abuse and/or dependence were eleven times more likely to meet diagnostic criteria for conduct disorder compared with youth who did not meet criteria for alcohol abuse and/or dependence. The odds of participants meeting diagnostic criteria for caseness on lifetime major depression and on current depression are three times higher than for those who did not meet lifetime depression diagnostic criteria.

In general, significant covariation was found among elevated symptoms of lifetime drug abuse and/or dependence and alcohol abuse and/or dependence and conduct disorder; alcohol abuse and/or dependence and conduct disorder; history of suicide attempts and lifetime PTSD; lifetime major depression and current depression, PTSD and trait anxiety; current depression, conduct disorder and trait anxiety; conduct disorder and trait anxiety; and PTSD and trait anxiety (Table 5.48). The odds of respondents having higher numbers of symptoms of drug abuse and/or dependence as well as higher numbers of symptoms of alcohol abuse and/or dependence, current depression, and conduct disorder were 2.6, 0.4 and 4.1 times higher, respectively, than for those who reported few symptoms of drug abuse and/or dependence. Youth who reported higher numbers of symptoms of alcohol abuse and/or dependence were eight times more likely to report higher symptoms of conduct disorder compared with youth who reported few symptoms of alcohol abuse and/or dependence. Respondents who disclosed histories of suicide attempts were three times more likely to report higher numbers of symptoms of PTSD. The odds of participants endorsing higher numbers of symptoms of lifetime major depression and of current depression, PTSD, and trait anxiety were 6.6, 3.4, and 5.3 times higher than for those who reported fewer lifetime depression symptoms. Youth who reported higher numbers of symptoms of current depression were 10.6 times more likely to report higher numbers of symptoms of trait anxiety but 2.3 times less likely to report higher numbers of symptoms of conduct disorder compared with those who endorsed fewer symptoms of current depression. The odds of respondents recalling few symptoms of conduct disorder and many symptoms of trait anxiety were 2.3 times higher than for those recalling many symptoms of conduct disorder. Participants disclosing higher numbers of PTSD symptoms were 2.2 times more likely to report higher numbers of trait anxiety symptoms than those reporting few symptoms of PTSD.

Comorbidity of Disclosed Indicators of Child Maltreatment

The odds of respondents who disclosed histories of physical assault also disclosing histories of witnessing domestic violence were 5.8 times higher than for those who reported negative histories of physical assault (Table 5.49). Youth who disclosed histories of sexual assault were 3.1 and 4.2 times more likely, respectively, to also disclose histories of neglect compared with those who reported negative histories of sexual assault. The odds of participants who disclosed histories of witnessing domestic violence also disclosing being neglect were 6.4 times higher than for those who reported negative histories of domestic violence.

Recalled Sequence[3] of Symptoms of Distress, Child Maltreatment, Homelessness and Risk-Taking

With the exception of conduct disorder, symptoms of other indicators of psychological distress and involvement in sex work seem to have begun after exposure to physical and/or sexual assaults for the majority of respondents (Table 5.50). The onset of symptoms of conduct disorder appear to be more evenly distributed across the three time periods: before, during, and after the year that physical and/or sexual assaults began. First symptoms of major depression, suicide thoughts and attempts, and alcohol dependence and/or abuse tended to occur either before or after the year of the first homelessness episode (Table 5.51). For most respondents, first symptoms of conduct disorder occurred before the first homelessness episode, and first symptoms of drug abuse and/or dependence, PTSD, and involvement in sex work occurred after the first homelessness episode. Three out of four of those who disclosed histories of sexual or physical assault recalled that the first assaults preceded their first homeless episodes. Virtually all respondents who met caseness criteria for conduct disorder and substance abuse and/or dependence reported that symptoms of conduct disorder occurred before the first symptoms of drug abuse and/or dependence (Table 5.52) and alcohol abuse and/or dependence (Table 5.53).

At least 50% of the respondents who qualified for dual diagnoses of major depression and substance abuse and/or dependence described that symptoms of major depression predated the first symptoms of substance abuse and/or dependence. The first symptoms of PTSD and involvement in sex work tended to be recalled as occurring in the same year or after the first symptoms of substance abuse and/or dependence. Half of those respondents with histories of suicide attempts and who met caseness criteria for alcohol abuse and/or dependence recalled the first suicide attempt as preceding the onset of symptoms of alcohol abuse and/or dependence. In contrast, 75% of the respondents with histories of suicide attempts and who met caseness criteria for drug abuse and/or dependence recalled the first suicide attempt as occurring either during or after the same year as the onset of symptoms of drug abuse and/or dependence appeared. Almost half of the respondents who met diagnostic criteria for both drug and alcohol abuse and/or dependence recalled that the first symptoms of alcohol abuse and/or dependence preceded those of drug abuse and/or dependence; for approximately one-third of the respondents, the first symptoms of both alcohol and drug abuse and/or dependence occurred in the same year.

Sexual Assault, Revictimization, and Risk-Taking[2]

Sexual Risk-Taking and Disclosed History of Sexual Assault

No significant association was found between number of sexual partners in the past year and history of sexual assault. However, the odds of youth reporting negative histories of sexual and physical assault also having greater numbers of sexual partners were 3.6 times higher than for those who reported histories of either physical or sexual assault (Table 5.54). Since 'sexual partner' was not defined for respondents, it is unclear whether respondents included casual or paying sexual partners in their estimates.

No significant association or trend was found between involvement in pornography and history of sexual assault. The odds of respondents disclosing histories of sexual assault and involvement in prostitution were 4.1 times higher than for those who reported negative histories of sexual assault (Table 5.55).

Sexual Revictimization by Demographic Characteristics and Homelessness History

Among those reporting histories of sexual assault, 65.6% had been assaulted more than once, 41.4% had been assaulted by more than one perpetrator, and 37.9% had been assaulted by more than one perpetrator more than once (Table 5.56). The odds of a respondent using an emergency shelter in the month prior to the interview and having a history of multiple sexual assault perpetrators were 6.4 times higher than those for a respondent not using an emergency shelter (Chi-square=5.038, $p<.05$, df=1). No statistically significant associations were found between revictimization variables and other sociodemographic or homelessness characteristics of the respondents. However, several trends were noted: female respondents seemed to be less likely to be sexually revictimized than men were; female survivors of sexual assault tended to have one sexual assault perpetrator and to have experienced one sexual assault. Respondents of color were more likely to be sexually assaulted more than once compared with white, non-Latino respondents. Older youth were more likely to have been sexually assaulted more than once; yet respondent age did not appear to substantially increase a youth's risk for having more than one sexual assault perpetrator. Respondents who were sexually revictimized were more likely to have been homeless (lifetime) for over one year compared with those who had been sexually victimized once by one perpetrator.

Sexual Risk-Taking by Sexual Revictimization

All three indicators of sexual revictimization: multiple assaults, multiple perpetrators, and multiple assaults and perpetrators combined were associated with involvement in prostitution (Table 5.57). The odds of respondents having histories of multiple sexual assaults, multiple perpetrators, and both multiple episodes and perpetrators and being involved in prostitution were 8.0, 5.0, and 4.9, respectively, higher than for sexual assault survivors who did not have histories of revictimization. History of multiple perpetrators and assaults combined was associated with involvement in pornography (Chi-square=3.329, $p<.10$, df=1).

Trends were noted in which men who had experienced multiple sexual assaults and multiple perpetrators were less likely to report using condoms regularly in the year preceding the interview than other male sexual assault survivors; yet sexually revictimized women were more likely to recall using condoms regularly in the year preceding the interview and less likely to have histories of pregnancy compared with women who had been assaulted once or assaulted by one perpetrator. Respondents with histories of sexual revictimization were more likely to have higher numbers of sexual partners within the year prior to the interview compared with respondents who had been sexually assaulted once or assaulted by one perpetrator.

Sexual Risk-Taking by Lifetime Homelessness Controlling for Demographic Characteristics[4]

The associations between lifetime homelessness, sexual revictimization, and indicators of sexual risk-taking were stratified on three demographic characteristics: sex, age, and race/ethnicity. Longtime homelessness (i.e., one year or greater lifetime) appeared to be most strongly associated with involvement in pornography for young (ages 13-15 years), white, non-Latinos and with involvement in prostitution for young, white, non-Latino, women in the sample (Tables 5.58-5.60). History of sexually transmitted disease, pregnancy, higher numbers of sexual partners (in the past year), and lack of use of condoms regularly in the year preceding the interview were most strongly associated with longtime homelessness for older youth (ages 16-17 years); younger youth of color; male respondents of color; and younger adolescents (ages 13-15 years), respectively, in the sample. The association between sexual revictimization and longtime homelessness was strongest for white, non-Latino, male youth in the sample. Sexual revictimization was inversely associated with histories of sexually transmitted disease for sexual assault survivors with shorter lifetime homelessness histories (i.e., less than one year). Pregnancy was inversely related to sexual revictimization among sexual assault survivors with longer lifetime homelessness (Table 5.61). Associations between sexual revictimization and use of condoms and number of sexual partners were not elaborated by stratifying on lifetime homelessness. Involvement in prostitution and history of pregnancy tended to co-occur among women who reported shorter lifetime homelessness; the association between histories of prostitution and sexually transmitted disease was strongest for respondents who had shorter lifetime homelessness (Table 5.62).

Psychological Distress by Sexual Revictimization

Sexual assault survivors with histories of single assaults were three times more likely to report higher numbers of lifetime depression symptoms compared with survivors who had been assaulted more than once (Table 5.63). The odds of sexual assault survivors having histories of multiple perpetrators or both multiple perpetrators and multiple assaults and meeting diagnostic criteria for conduct disorder caseness were twice as high as those for survivors having negative histories of revictimization.

Psychological Distress by History of Sexual Assault Controlling for Sociodemographic Mediators and Moderators[2]

Respondent Had Used Mental Health Services

In two-way analyses, receipt of mental health services in the year preceding the interview tended to be associated with increased symptomatology/likelihood of caseness for most indicators of psychological distress, except for suicide attempts and alcohol abuse and/or dependence, where there were no apparent relationships. The associations between disclosed history of sexual assault and higher numbers of current and lifetime indicators of psychological distress; i.e., suicide attempts; caseness for lifetime drug abuse and/or dependence, PTSD, major depression, current depression, and elevated symptom count for trait anxiety were the same or stronger for respondents who did not have histories of mental health service utilization and were inversely related for those who had received mental health services (Table 5.64). Similar patterns were noted for the relationship between elevated symptomatology in these indicators of psychological distress and history of sexual assault. The tendency for respondents with histories of sexual assault to meet diagnostic criteria for conduct disorder caseness remained unchanged whether or not they received mental health services; yet conduct disorder symptom count dropped in association with sexual assault for those who had received mental health services. In contrast, the association between alcohol abuse and/or dependence and history of sexual assault was strongest for respondents who had received mental health services; this was true for both alcohol abuse and/or dependence caseness and higher symptom counts. With the exception of alcohol abuse and/or dependence, psychological distress appears to be highest among sexual assault survivors who have not have mental health care.

Respondent Had a Regular Medical Provider

The relationships between having a history of sexual assault and number of current diagnoses, current depression caseness, and lifetime conduct disorder caseness were strengthened for respondents who did not have regular medical providers (Table 5.65). The opposite was true for the associations between sexual assault and greater numbers of symptoms of conduct disorder and current depression: the relationship was maintained or strengthened only among those who had regular medical providers. Associations between history of sexual assault and number of lifetime diagnoses, caseness and elevated symptom counts for lifetime alcohol and drug abuse and/or dependency, elevated trait anxiety symptom counts, and elevated PTSD symptom counts were stronger for youth who reported having regular medical providers.

Relative Had a Mental Problem

For some psychological distress indicators (i.e., caseness on major depression, alcohol abuse and/or dependence, and suicide attempts and higher numbers of symptoms of conduct disorder, alcohol abuse and/or dependence, and trait anxiety), being a sexual assault survivor was inversely related to distress among those who perceived that a relative had a mental health problem. (Table 5.66). Other significant indicators of psychological distress maintained or strengthened their relationships with sexual assault disclosure among respondents who did not think that any relatives had mental problems.

Relative Had an Alcohol Problem

The associations between disclosure of sexual assault and number of current and lifetime diagnoses, caseness and higher symptom counts for lifetime drug abuse and/or dependence, caseness and elevated symptom counts for lifetime PTSD, and current depression caseness were strongest for respondents who thought that a relative had an alcohol problem (Table 5.67). However, relationships between disclosure of sexual assault and suicide thoughts and attempts, caseness and higher symptom counts for lifetime alcohol abuse and/or dependence, caseness and elevated symptom counts for lifetime major depression, higher current depression symptom counts, and caseness and elevated symptom counts for conduct disorder were maintained or strongest for respondents who denied that any relatives had problems with alcohol.

Relative Had a Drug Problem

Relationships between disclosure of sexual assault and suicide thoughts and attempts, caseness and higher symptom counts for lifetime drug abuse and/or dependence, caseness and elevated symptom counts for lifetime alcohol abuse and/or dependence, lifetime major depression caseness, higher numbers of PTSD and current depression symptoms, and lifetime conduct disorder caseness were strongest for or maintained only for respondents who denied that any relatives had problems with drugs (Table 5.68). On the other hand, the associations between history of sexual assault and greater numbers of current diagnoses and PTSD caseness were strongest among participants who thought that a relative had a drug problem. For alcohol abuse and/or depression, major depression, and conduct disorder, history of sexual assault was inversely associated with distress among respondents who perceived that a relative had a drug problem.

Father's Educational Level

For higher numbers of current diagnoses, lifetime suicide attempts, caseness and elevated symptom counts for lifetime PTSD, and current depression caseness, the association between history of sexual assault and distress was maintained or strengthened among youth who reported that their fathers had at least twelfth grade educations (Table 5.69). In contrast, the relationships between sexual assault history and caseness and elevated symptom counts for lifetime alcohol and drug abuse and/or dependence, higher lifetime depression symptom counts, and caseness and elevated symptom counts for lifetime conduct disorder were strongest among respondents with fathers who had less than twelfth grade educations. Higher numbers of symptoms of current depression were associated with negative histories of sexual assault among respondents who had fathers with educations which were less than twelfth grade. Father's educational level appeared to suppress the relationship between greater numbers of lifetime diagnoses and history of sexual assault.

Length of Lifetime Homelessness

The relationships between history of sexual assault and lifetime suicide attempts, elevated trait anxiety symptom counts, and drug abuse and/or dependence caseness were stronger among respondents who had been homeless for one year or more (cumulatively) (Table 5.70). In contrast, associations between history of sexual assault and higher numbers of lifetime diagnoses, caseness and elevated symptom counts for lifetime alcohol abuse and/or dependence, major depression caseness, and PTSD caseness were maintained or strengthened for youth whose lifetime homelessness had lasted less than one year. History of sexual assault appeared to be related to having non-caseness status and lower symptoms of lifetime alcohol abuse and/or dependence among youth whose lifetime homelessness had lasted at least one year.

Respondent's Income

The associations between history of sexual assault and any current diagnoses, lifetime suicide thoughts and attempts, lifetime alcohol abuse and/or dependence caseness, elevated symptom counts for lifetime PTSD, caseness and higher symptom counts for lifetime major depression, and current depression caseness were maintained or strengthened for respondents who had incomes of $100 or greater in the month prior to the interview (Table 5.71). Among youth who reported monthly incomes which were less than $100, the relationships between history of sexual assault and higher numbers of lifetime psychological distress diagnoses and lifetime drug abuse and/or dependence caseness, caseness and higher symptom counts for lifetime conduct disorder, and current depression caseness were maintained or strengthened.

Difficulty Finding Clothing

The associations between history of sexual assault and higher numbers of lifetime diagnoses, elevated trait anxiety symptom counts, caseness and higher symptom counts for lifetime drug abuse and/or dependence, caseness and higher symptom counts for lifetime alcohol abuse and/or dependence, elevated lifetime PTSD symptom counts, higher symptom counts for lifetime conduct disorder, and higher symptom counts for current depression were maintained or strengthened among respondents who reported having many difficulties finding clothing (Table 5.72). Among youth who reported few difficulties finding clothing, the relationship between history of sexual assault and psychological distress was maintained or strengthened only for lifetime depression caseness and higher symptomatology and lifetime conduct disorder caseness.

Difficulty Finding a Place to Clean Up

The associations between history of sexual assault and higher numbers of lifetime diagnoses, lifetime major depression caseness, lifetime conduct disorder caseness, and elevated lifetime alcohol abuse and/or dependence symptom counts, and higher current depression symptom counts were maintained or strengthened among respondents who reported having many difficulties finding places in which to clean up (Table 5.73). Among youth who reported few difficulties finding places in which to clean up, the relationship between history of sexual assault and psychological distress was maintained or strengthened for indicators of current diagnoses, elevated trait anxiety symptoms, lifetime PTSD caseness, and higher lifetime drug abuse and/or dependence symptom counts.

Affiliation With a Street Gang

The associations between history of sexual assault and lifetime suicide thoughts and attempts, elevated lifetime PTSD symptom counts, and higher current depression symptom counts were maintained or strengthened for respondents who disclosed affiliations with street gangs (Table 5.74). Among youth who reported no affiliations with street gangs, the relationships between history of sexual assault and higher numbers of current and lifetime distress diagnoses, caseness and higher symptom counts for lifetime drug abuse and/or dependence, caseness and elevated symptom counts for lifetime alcohol abuse and/or dependence, lifetime PTSD caseness, lifetime major depression caseness, current depression caseness, and caseness and higher symptom counts for lifetime conduct disorder were maintained or strengthened.

Carrying a Weapon for Protection

The associations between history of sexual assault and current diagnoses, elevated trait anxiety symptom counts, lifetime suicide thoughts, caseness and higher symptom counts for lifetime major depression, lifetime conduct disorder caseness, and lifetime drug abuse and/or dependence caseness, and caseness and higher symptom counts for current depression were maintained or strengthened among respondents who reported carrying weapons for protection (Table 5.75). Among youth who did not carry weapons, the relationship between history of sexual assault and psychological distress was maintained or strengthened for indicators of higher numbers of lifetime diagnoses, lifetime suicide attempts, caseness and higher symptom counts for lifetime PTSD, caseness and elevated symptom counts for lifetime alcohol abuse and/or dependence, and higher lifetime drug abuse and/or dependence symptom counts, and caseness and higher symptom counts for lifetime conduct disorder. History of sexual assault was associated with non-caseness for lifetime PTSD and lower symptom counts for alcohol abuse and/or dependence among respondents who disclosed carrying a weapon for protection. History of sexual assault appeared to be related to having lower symptom counts for current depression among youth who did not carry a weapon for protection.

Psychological Distress by Characteristics of Assault[2]

Number of Diagnoses by Physical Assault Characteristics

The odds of respondents having histories of physical assault by multiple perpetrators and meeting diagnostic criteria for one or two current diagnoses were five times higher than for physical assault survivors who were victimized by single perpetrators (Table 5.76). Physical assault survivors who were victimized by life-threatening levels of violence and by many different modes of physical violence were 2.5 times more likely to have higher numbers of lifetime diagnoses compared with survivors who were assaulted by less-injurious and fewer methods of violence.

Although not statistically significant, physical assault survivors tended to meet diagnostic criteria for current diagnoses of psychological distress when the perpetrator(s) was a parent figure, the respondent was younger when the abuse began (2-10 years old), the frequency of abuse was high, and the number of types of physical assault endured was higher. Survivors tended to meet diagnostic criteria for 3-4 lifetime diagnoses when the perpetrator(s) included peers, there were multiple perpetrators, the respondent was younger when the abuse began (2-10 years old), the frequency of abuse was high, and the number of types of physical assault endured was higher.

Number of Diagnoses by Sexual Assault Characteristics

The odds of respondents meeting diagnostic criteria for one or two current diagnoses was six times higher for sexual assault survivors assaulted by parent figures than for survivors assaulted by others. The odds of respondents meeting diagnostic criteria for one or two current diagnoses was nine times higher for sexual assault survivors assaulted by peers than for survivors who were not (Table 5.77). Sexual assault survivors whose victimization included sexual penetration were 4.5 times more likely to have higher numbers of lifetime diagnoses compared with survivors whose assault did not included sexual penetration. Sexual assault survivors tended to meet diagnostic criteria for current diagnoses when the respondent was adolescent (i.e., 11-17 years old) when the abuse began and there were fewer types of sexúal assault endured. Survivors tended to meet diagnostic criteria for 3-4 lifetime diagnoses when the perpetrator(s) were not parent figures and the respondent was adolescent (i.e., 11-17 years old) when the abuse began.

Psychological Distress by Physical Assault Characteristics[5]

The odds of meeting diagnostic criteria for current depression caseness were 10 times higher for physical assault survivors having more than one perpetrator than for survivors who had one perpetrator (Table 5.78). Physical assault survivors who had peer perpetrators were three times more likely to meet diagnostic criteria for caseness on lifetime major depression compared with those who had been assaulted exclusively by adult perpetrators. The odds of physical assault survivors being adolescent at the first exposure (i.e., aged 11-17 years) and meeting diagnostic criteria for lifetime major depression caseness were 4 times higher than for those who were younger (i.e., aged 2-10 years). Physical assault survivors who had experienced life-threatening levels of violence were 5 times more likely to meet diagnostic criteria for lifetime major depression caseness. The odds of survivors having parent figure perpetrators and having histories of suicide thoughts and attempts were 3.6 and 2.8 times, respectively, higher than for survivors who had perpetrators who were not parent figures. Survivors who experienced life-threatening levels of violence were 3.5 and 2.8 times, respectively, more likely to meet diagnostic criteria for lifetime PTSD caseness and alcohol abuse and/or dependence than those who did not experience life-threatening levels of violence.

Although not statistically significant, caseness in current depression appeared to be associated with higher frequency of assaults, and caseness in lifetime depression seemed to be related to greater numbers of types of assaults. History of suicide attempts seemed to be associated with multiple perpetrators, adolescent age at first assault, greater frequency of assaults, and higher levels of violence. Lifetime PTSD caseness tended to covary with histories of multiple perpetrators and adolescent age at first assault. Lifetime alcohol abuse and/or dependence seemed to be related to being assaulted by multiple, peer, and non-parent perpetrators. Lifetime conduct disorder caseness appeared to covary with histories of parent and multiple perpetrators and younger age at first assault.

Elevated symptom counts of lifetime major depression, lifetime PTSD, and lifetime alcohol abuse and/or dependence were significantly related to being victimized by life-threatening levels of physical violence (Table 5.79). A trend was observed between elevated trait anxiety symptom counts and histories of life-threatening violent assaults. History of physical assaults by parent-figures seemed to be associated with higher symptom counts for trait anxiety and lifetime drug abuse and/or dependence. In contrast, history of non-parental figure perpetrators appeared to be associated with elevated symptoms of lifetime alcohol abuse and/or dependence and conduct disorder. Victimization by peer perpetrators covaried with higher symptom counts for lifetime depression and PTSD. History of multiple perpetrators seemed to be related to elevated symptom counts for trait anxiety, current depression, lifetime PTSD, and lifetime alcohol abuse and/or dependence. Adolescent age at first exposure to physical assaults (i.e., ages 11-17 years) appeared to covary with higher symptom counts for current depression and lifetime depression; yet younger age at first episode seems to be associated with elevated symptom counts for lifetime conduct disorder. With the exceptions of current and lifetime depression, higher frequency of physical assault episodes seemed to be associated with elevated symptom counts for all other indicators of psychological distress. Below average school performance seemed to be associated with assault histories which included multiple perpetrators and single assaults.

Psychological Distress by Characteristics of Sexual Assault[6]

The odds of survivors of sexual assault meeting diagnostic criteria for current depression and having histories of father and peer perpetrators were 8 and 6 times higher, respectively, than for those assaulted by adult perpetrators who were not their fathers or peers (Table 5.80). Meeting caseness criteria for lifetime PTSD was strongly associated with having non-father perpetrators among sexual assault survivors. The odds of survivors meeting diagnostic criteria for lifetime conduct disorder and having histories of multiple perpetrators were two times higher than for survivors with histories of single perpetrators. Survivors whose victimization included sexual penetration were 4.5 times more likely to meet caseness criteria for lifetime drug abuse and/or dependence compared with survivors whose victimization did not include penetration.

Trends which did not reach statistical significance were noted between other characteristics of sexual assault and caseness indicators of psychological distress. Histories which included non-father and peer perpetrators appeared to be related to meeting diagnostic criteria for lifetime depression. Victimization by fathers seemed to be associated with meeting diagnostic criteria for current depression, lifetime suicide thoughts and attempts, lifetime alcohol abuse and/or dependence, and lifetime conduct disorder. Adult age of perpetrators tended to covary with lifetime suicide attempts and lifetime alcohol abuse and/or dependence. Respondents with histories of sexual assault which included victimization by peer perpetrators tended to be associated with meeting diagnostic criteria for lifetime PTSD. Youth who had been assaulted by single perpetrators seemed to be more likely to have had suicide thoughts and attempts compared with those who had been victimized by multiple perpetrators. In contrast, survivors with histories of multiple perpetrators seemed more likely to meet caseness criteria for current depression. With the exceptions of alcohol abuse and/or dependence and suicide thoughts and attempts, adolescent age (i.e., ages 11-16 years) at first sexual assault appeared to be related to all caseness indicators of psychological distress. Survivors whose first assault occurred at a younger age (i.e., ages 3-9 years) were more likely to report histories of suicide thoughts and attempts compared with survivors whose exposure to sexual victimization began when they were adolescent.

Youth with histories of multiple sexual assaults were more likely to meet diagnostic criteria for lifetime depression and conduct disorder and to report histories of suicide thoughts and attempts compared with youth who had been victimized once. Less intrusive sexual victimization (i.e., no sexual penetration) tended to co-occur with lifetime depression caseness and suicide thoughts; whereas, more intrusive victimization (i.e., sexual penetration) tended to covary with lifetime PTSD and alcohol abuse and/or dependence caseness.

Elevated symptom counts of psychological distress were also significantly related to specific characteristics of sexual assault (Table 5.81). The odds of sexual assault survivors having non-father perpetrators and having higher symptom counts of drug abuse and/or dependence were 7 times higher than for those who had father perpetrators. Survivors who had been victimized once were 4 times more likely to have elevated symptom counts of lifetime depression compared with those who had been assaulted multiple times. Respondents with histories of a single sexual assault seemed to be more likely to endorse symptoms of current depression compared with those with histories of multiple assaults. Having adult perpetrators (without peer-aged perpetrators) seemed to covary with elevated lifetime PTSD symptom counts. Victimizations which included sexual penetration tended to co-occur with higher lifetime conduct disorder symptom counts. Other trends between characteristics of sexual assaults and the remaining symptom indicators of psychological distress tended to replicate those seen with caseness indicators. Below average school performance among sexual assault survivors appeared to be associated with history of peer perpetrators, sexual revictimization (i.e., multiple perpetrators and/or multiple episodes), and sexual penetration.

Psychological Distress by Whether Respondent Fought Back During Physical Assault

Fighting back during physical assaults was not significantly associated with caseness or elevated symptom counts of psychological distress (Table 5.82). However, survivors of physical assault who fought back during the assault were more likely to report elevated lifetime PTSD symptom counts, drug abuse and/or dependence, and conduct disorder and to meet diagnostic criteria for lifetime conduct disorder.

Psychological Distress by Sexual Assault Controlling for Decision to Leave Home

The associations between history of sexual assault and the presence of 1-2 current diagnoses, 3-4 lifetime diagnoses, caseness for lifetime alcohol and drug abuse and/or dependence, elevated lifetime conduct disorder symptom counts, and current depression caseness were maintained or strengthened among respondents who were told to leave home (Table 5.83). In contrast, relationships between history of sexual assault and suicide thoughts, trait anxiety, elevated drug abuse and/or dependence symptom counts, and caseness and higher symptom counts for lifetime major depression were maintained or strengthened among youth who left home on their own.

Disclosed Child Maltreatment by Respondent Sex

When each maltreatment type was considered independently of the others, the odds of female respondents disclosing histories of neglect and sexual assault were 3.5 and 3.2 times higher, respectively, than those for male respondents (Table 5.84). Although not statistically significant, the data suggest that male participants were slightly more likely to disclose histories of physical assault than were female participants and that female respondents were slightly more likely to disclose histories of witnessing domestic violence.

Assault Reporting and Subsequent Removal from Home by Respondent Sex

Among respondents who were assaulted by cohabiting individuals, sexual assaults appeared to be more likely to be reported to the authorities and reported sexual assaults were more likely to result in the removal of the survivor from the home when the survivor was female (Table 5.85). Although the physical assaults of female and male survivors were equally likely to be reported to authorities, physical assaults of female survivors appeared to be more likely to result in the removal of the survivor from the home.

Disclosed Characteristics of Sexual Assault by Respondent Sex

No statistically significant relationships were observed between disclosed characteristics of sexual assault and respondent sex (Table 5.86). Male survivors of sexual assault were slightly less likely to endure higher levels of physical violence and were slightly more likely to be the victim of sexual penetration by a non-parent perpetrator compared with female survivors.

Psychological Distress by Sexual Assault Controlling for Respondent Sex

The relationships between history of sexual assault and the presence of 1-2 current diagnoses; history of suicide thoughts; and elevated symptom counts for trait anxiety, lifetime drug abuse and/or dependence, and lifetime PTSD were maintained or strengthened among male respondents (Tables 5.87, 5.88 and 5.89). The associations between history of sexual assault and history of 3-4 lifetime diagnoses; lifetime suicide attempts; caseness for lifetime drug abuse and/or dependence, alcohol abuse and/or dependence, major depression, and conduct disorder; and elevated lifetime conduct disorder symptom counts were maintained or strengthened for female respondents. Elevated current depression symptom counts and lifetime conduct disorder caseness were inversely related to history of sexual assault among male respondents.

For female respondents, history of sexual assault appeared to be specifically related to current feelings of loneliness, hopelessness, and poor body image and to lifetime feelings of worthlessness (Table 5.83). However, history of sexual assault was inversely related to current feelings of self-hatred and self-blame, and worries about the future among female respondents. For male respondents, history of sexual assault seemed to be associated with current sleep and appetite problems, lifetime sleep problems, and history of prostitution.

In order to assess adaptation, the relationships between sexual assault and detainment by law enforcement and school performance were examined. For male youth, history of sexual assault tended to be associated with history of law enforcement detainment for suspicion of having committed minor offenses (e.g., status offense, loitering etc.), destroying property, prostitution, and substance-related offenses. For female youth, history of sexual assault covaried with being detained for suspicion of theft. History of sexual assault seemed to be inversely related to being detained for suspicion of committing a violent crime for both young men and young women in the sample. History of sexual assault seemed to covary with below average school performance; this appeared to be true exclusively for male respondents. History of sexual assault was weakly associated with above average school performance for female respondents.

Psychological Distress by Sexual Assault Controlling for Substance Abuse

In order to examine the effect of substance use as a coping mechanism rather than an indicator of psychological distress associated with sexual assault, analyses of distress by sexual assault were stratified by alcohol and drug abuse and/or dependence caseness. The relationships between history of sexual assault and lifetime suicide thoughts and attempts and elevated lifetime conduct disorder symptom counts were maintained or strengthened for respondents who met diagnostic criteria for alcohol abuse and/or dependence. In contrast, the associations between history of sexual assault and lifetime PTSD caseness, caseness and elevated symptom counts for lifetime depression, higher current depression symptom counts, and elevated trait anxiety symptom counts were maintained or strengthened for youth who did not meet diagnostic criteria for alcohol abuse and/or dependence.

The relationships between history of sexual assault, current depression caseness and elevated lifetime PTSD symptoms were maintained or strengthened for respondents who met diagnostic criteria for drug abuse and/or dependence. The associations between history of sexual assault and caseness and elevated symptom counts for lifetime major depression and lifetime conduct disorder were maintained or strengthened for participants who did not meet diagnostic criteria for drug abuse and/or dependence.

Notes

[1] Frequency distributions of some of the sociodemographic and psychological distress variables have been presented previously by the principal investigators of the Hollywood Homeless Youth Study (Robertson, 1989; Robertson, Greenblatt, Koegel, Mundy, 1990) and are reiterated here for the reader.

[2] Cross-tabulation cell differences which exceed 10% may be referred to as suggestive in the absence of a statistically significant Chi-square or Fisher's exact test. Chi-square values not reported in the text may be found in the tables.

[3] As assessed by respondent recall of age at first onset.

[4] Due to the lack of power to detect statistically significant associations in three-way analyses, three-way analyses are described by comparing the percentage differences between cells from zero-order tables (i.e., 2-way crosstabulations) with those from partial tables (i.e., 3-way tables). Trends noted here are used to generate hypotheses for future studies.

[5] Analyses were repeated for respondents reporting histories of physical assaults without sexual assaults. The findings and interpretations were similar to those presented here.

[6] Analyses were repeated for respondents reporting histories of sexual assaults with physical assaults. The findings and interpretations were similar to those presented here.

Results Summary

Sample Characteristics

In terms of modal demographic characteristics, the Hollywood Homeless Youth Sample may be described as predominantly male, 16-17 years old, Caucasian (non-Latino), and having out of state birthplaces. Most of the respondents reported having completed nine years or less of formal education with average performances, biological parents who were divorced but known to the respondent, biological parents who had completed 12 or more years of formal education, and a biological mother who was 20 years old or younger at the time of the respondent's birth. The majority of the sample had histories of institutional placements, usually multiple times and often including juvenile detention. Detention by law enforcement tended to be for non-violent offenses.

Homelessness
Almost half of the sample had been episodically homeless, i.e., homeless more than once but cumulatively less than one year. Nearly all respondents considered themselves "homeless". The proportion of youth who had been asked to leave home almost tripled between the first and most recent homelessness episodes. First homelessness episodes typically lasted less than 31 days and began when the respondent was younger than 14 years old. For approximately half of the sample, current homelessness episodes had lasted between 31 and 364 days at the time of the interview. Abandoned buildings were the sleeping locations of choice when respondents could not afford to pay for a place; the street and emergency shelters were ranked as second and third choices, respectively. Less than half of the youth reported spending the night in an emergency shelter in the past month or in the past year. Over half of the respondents had lived in more than one city and had been living in Los Angeles for one year or

less. Two-thirds of the respondents had spent at least one night in the home of a biological parent in the year preceding the interview. Although nearly all of the sample reported usually sleeping in Hollywood, few spent their entire days in Hollywood.

Subsistence and Basic Needs

Shelters and soup kitchens ranked first as main sources of food followed by paid meals. Over half of the respondents had experienced at least one day in the month prior to the interview with nothing to eat. A majority of the sample reported being employed in the past 30 days with legal employment and panhandling accounting for the most common sources of the sample's median $100 per month income. Although half of the youth had specific places and/or persons which provided their medical care, only one-third had financial coverage from either private medical insurance or Medi-Cal. Clothes and food were ranked above places to wash up and medical care as basic needs which were usually or sometimes difficult to obtain when homeless.

Indicators of Risk-Taking

Nearly one-third of the sample disclosed trading sex for money, food, shelter, or drugs. Half of the respondents reported having more than four sexual partners in the past year. Almost half of the women had been pregnant at least once. Among those who had been tested for HIV antibodies, 3.6% disclosed that they had tested positive. The vast majority of the sample seldom or never used any type of birth control in the past year. Nearly one in three youth disclosed histories of injecting drugs which were not prescribed for them, and one in five youth reported driving an automobile after or while consuming alcohol.

Perceived Health and Safety

Most of the respondents regarded their health as fair to poor, in general, and as the same or worse since becoming homeless. A majority of respondents reported using alcohol or drugs before becoming homeless. Most youth claimed that their substance use had not increased since becoming homeless. A minority of respondents thought that they had problems with mental health, drinking, or drug use. Half of the sample believed that a relative (usually a parent) had an alcohol problem, and approximately one-third believed that a relative had a mental health problem or a drug problem. Nearly all respondents reported taking specific actions to prevent being harmed; half of the sample disclosed that they carried weapons for protection.

Child Maltreatment

Nearly the entire sample disclosed histories of child maltreatment (i.e., neglect, physical or sexual assault, and/or witnessing domestic violence). Relatives were involved in the perpetration of the maltreatment for most respondents. Most of the maltreatment histories included physical assault and/or sexual assault. The vast majority of youth who disclosed histories of sexual assault (34%) also disclosed histories of physical assault. Of those who recalled histories of physical assault (79% of the sample), three in four had been exposed to assaults which were injurious or life-threatening, and a significant minority had been psychologically tortured by being tied up or locked in a small place. Nearly all respondents who disclosed histories of physical assault had been physically assaulted on multiple occasions, most had been assaulted by multiple perpetrators, and most had their first assaults before the age of eleven. Half of those who disclosed histories of sexual assault had been sexually penetrated during an assault, and over half had been assaulted by one perpetrator and on multiple occasions beginning after the age of ten. Most domestic violence episodes occurred between two specific adult relatives and were perpetrated by a father figure or the mother's boyfriend onto women (usually the respondents' mothers) and children of both sexes. Domestic assaults typically consisted of hitting, hurling objects, threatening with weapons, beating, and kicking; a few assaults progressed to stabbings, shootings, and/or sexual assaults. According to the respondents, most maltreatment went unreported to the child protection authorities and, consequently, few respondents were removed from the home for protection and even fewer perpetrators were arrested.

Psychological Distress

One out of five respondents met caseness criteria for current depression or lifetime PTSD, and one in four met caseness criteria for lifetime major depression. Among those who reported having symptoms of PTSD, seeing someone being murdered, being physically and/or sexually assaulted, and the deaths of loved ones were the most commonly cited traumatic experiences which were associated with the symptoms. Two-thirds of the sample disclosed having had thoughts of suicide, and almost half had attempted suicide. Nearly one-half of the youth met caseness criteria for alcohol abuse and/or dependence, and over one-third met caseness criteria for drug abuse and/or dependence. Among those respondents who met diagnostic criteria for drug abuse and/or dependence, criteria were most commonly met for cannabis, amphetamines, cocaine, and opiates. Almost half of the youth who met diagnostic criteria for drug abuse and/or dependence met criteria for more than one drug, and over three-quarters of the sample reported polydrug use in the six months preceding the interview. Over three in four drug using respondents reported using cannabis, psychedelics, cocaine, or amphetamines in the past year. Two out of three respondents met caseness criteria for conduct disorder (with symptoms occurring when housed and excluding running away). Less than one in ten youth met caseness criteria for trait anxiety disorder. Over three-quarters of the sample met caseness criteria for at least one indicator of lifetime psychological distress.

Sampling Strata

The street subsample was characterized as consisting of male youth aged 16-17 who had been born in the United States but not in California, been episodically homeless, reported higher numbers of symptoms of drug abuse and/or dependence, and met caseness criteria for lifetime conduct disorder. When comparing the drop-in center and shelter sample strata with the street sample stratum, one finds that drop-in centers tended to attract Caucasians born in the United States and shelters were more likely to contain young (aged 13-15 years) women of color who were not born in the United States. Drop-in centers had higher proportions of youth who had been told to leave home, were chronically homeless (i.e., more than one homelessness episode with lifetime homelessness equalling one year or more), and reported lower numbers of symptoms of current depression compared with the street sample stratum. Shelters, on the other hand, had higher proportions of youth who were homeless alone (vs. with friends), were temporarily homeless (i.e., one lifetime homelessness episode lasting less than one year), and reported greater numbers of symptoms of current depression, trait anxiety, and lifetime major depression.

Homelessness by Demographic Characteristics

The temporarily homeless tended to be 16-17 year old male youth and were equally likely to be of color as Caucasian. Compared with respondents who were temporarily homeless, episodically homeless youth were more likely to be young (aged 13-15 years) Caucasian men, and chronically homeless youth were more likely to be young (aged 13-15 years) Caucasian women.

Child Maltreatment by Demographic Characteristics

Compared with respondents who reported no histories of sexual or physical assault, survivors of physical assault were proportionately more likely to be men and survivors of sexual assault were more likely to be women whose fathers had completed less than 12 years of formal education.

Psychological Distress by Demographic, Placement, and Homelessness Characteristics

Youth who reported greater numbers of symptoms of trait anxiety tended to be young (aged 13-15 years) women who, in the month prior to the interview, had less than $100 in income and had spent the night in an emergency shelter. Elevated symptoms of lifetime major depression more likely disclosed by young (aged 13-15 years) women with less than $100 in income in the month prior to the interview who had never been in foster care. Histories of suicide thoughts were most often reported by women who had never been in foster care and who, in the month prior to the interview, had less than $100 in income and had spent at least one day with nothing to eat. The characteristics of respondents who disclosed histories of suicide attempts were the same as those with histories of suicide thoughts except they were more likely to be aged 16-17 years.

Youth who met criteria for current depression caseness were less likely to have histories of placements in institutional care. Similarly, youth who met criteria for lifetime major depression caseness tended to report no placements in foster care. In contrast, respondents who met criteria for caseness in alcohol abuse and/or dependence tended to disclose histories of placement in juvenile detention and group homes.

In general, having problems finding clothes, food, and places to clean up was inversely related to lifetime substance abuse and/or dependency caseness. Longer exposure to cumulative lifetime homelessness positively covaried with symptoms of lifetime substance abuse and/or dependence, conduct disorder, and PTSD. Age at onset of the first homelessness episode was inversely related to meeting diagnostic criteria for lifetime substance abuse and/or dependence. Youth who were asked to leave home were more likely to meet diagnostic criteria for lifetime conduct disorder and substance abuse and/or dependence.

Comorbidity of Indicators of Psychological Distress

Statistically significant comorbidity of diagnostic caseness was found between lifetime alcohol and drug abuse and/or dependence, current depression and lifetime major depression, and lifetime conduct disorder and lifetime drug and alcohol abuse and/or dependence. Significant comorbidity of elevated symptom counts was found between lifetime alcohol and drug abuse and/or dependence; current depression and lifetime major depression; lifetime conduct disorder and lifetime drug abuse and/or abuse, lifetime conduct disorder and alcohol abuse and/or dependence; lifetime PTSD and history of suicide attempt, lifetime PTSD and lifetime major depression; trait anxiety and lifetime major depression, trait anxiety and current depression, and trait anxiety and lifetime PTSD. Symptom counts for the following pairs of disorders were found to be inversely related to one another: current depression and lifetime drug abuse and/or dependence, lifetime conduct disorder and current depression, and trait anxiety and lifetime conduct disorder.

Comorbidity of Indicators of Child Maltreatment

Although all types of child maltreatment appeared to co-occur with one another, significant comorbidity was found between witnessing domestic violence and physical assault, witnessing domestic violence and sexual assault, neglect and sexual assault, and neglect and witnessing domestic violence.

Child Maltreatment and Psychological Distress

Compared with respondents who did not disclose histories of sexual assault, those who disclosed histories of sexual assault more frequently reported histories of suicide thoughts and attempts and high numbers of symptoms of trait anxiety, lifetime major depression, lifetime drug abuse and/or dependence, and PTSD; and these survivors were likely to meet caseness criteria for current depression and conduct disorder. Disclosure of a sexual assault history was also correlated with believing that the respondent and the respondent's relatives had mental health problems and that the respondent's health was better since leaving home. Survivors of sexual assault were more likely to report avoiding certain people and carrying weapons for protection.

Recalled Onset of Distress Relative to Maltreatment, Homelessness, and Substance Abuse

Relative to the onset of any maltreatment, symptoms of major depression, drug abuse and/or dependence, alcohol abuse and/or dependence, suicide thoughts and attempts, and PTSD were recalled as occurring later by a majority of maltreatment survivors. In addition, virtually all respondents who reported histories of involvement in sex work (i.e., pornography or prostitution) disclosed that the exposure to child maltreatment preceded their involvement in sex work.

Relative to the onset of the first homelessness episode, involvement in sex work and symptoms of lifetime major depression, lifetime drug and alcohol abuse and/or dependence, lifetime PTSD, and suicide thoughts and attempts were most often recalled as having begun in the same year or after. In contrast, physical or sexual assaults and symptoms of lifetime conduct disorder tended to precede the first homelessness episode.

The first symptoms of drug abuse and/or dependence were often recalled as occurring after the appearance of symptoms of major depression, suicide thoughts, conduct disorder, and alcohol abuse and/or dependence yet preceding suicide attempts, symptoms of PTSD, and involvement in sex work. Similarly, the first symptoms of alcohol abuse and/or dependence were often reported as occurring after the appearance of symptoms of major depression, suicide attempts, and conduct disorder yet preceding involvement in sex work and symptoms of PTSD.

Child Maltreatment, Sexual Revictimization, and Sexual Risk-Taking

With regard to sexual risk-taking, survivors of physical and/or sexual assault tended to report having fewer sexual partners in the year preceding the interview than were youth who reported negative histories of assault. Survivors of sexual assault were significantly more likely to report involvement in sex work than were survivors of physical assault. As mentioned earlier, although most sexual assault survivors had been exposed to multiple assaults, most had been assaulted by one perpetrator. Over one-third of sexual assault survivors had been assaulted more than once and by more than one perpetrator. Youth who had been sexually revictimized by either or both multiple assaults or multiple perpetrators were significantly more likely to engage in sex work.

Sexual Assault, Sexual Risk-Taking, and Lifetime Homelessness

Respondents who had histories of lifetime homelessness equalling one year or more were more likely to have posed for pornographic photographs or films, been involved in sex work, and been sexually revictimized. The relationships between longer lifetime homelessness, history of sexually transmitted diseases, and involvement in sex work were strengthened among women. In contrast, the relationships between longer lifetime homelessness, four or more sexual partners in the past year, and history of sexual revictimization were strengthened among men.

Relationships between longer lifetime homelessness, involvement in sex work, and pregnancy held only for younger respondents.

Among youth with shorter histories of lifetime homelessness, sexual revictimization appeared to be inversely related to history of sexually transmitted diseases and involvement in sex work seemed to be associated with history of pregnancy. Sexual revictimization appeared to be inversely related to pregnancies among youth with longer histories of lifetime homelessness.

Sexual Revictimization and Psychological Distress

Sexual revictimization and history of multiple perpetrators without multiple assaults were each associated with caseness in lifetime conduct disorder among sexual assault survivors. In contrast, history of a single sexual assault covaried with elevated numbers of symptoms of lifetime major depression.

Sexual Assault by Psychological Distress Controlling for:

Receipt of mental health services. The association of history of sexual assault with indicators of psychological distress tended to be mediated by whether the respondent had received mental health services in the year preceding the interview. Sexual assault survivors appeared to be more likely to report histories of suicide thoughts and attempts and to meet caseness criteria for drug abuse and/or dependence, lifetime PTSD, lifetime major depression, and current depression when no mental health services had been received. Similar patterns were maintained for high symptom counts of these indicators of psychological distress as well as for trait anxiety. In contrast, sexual assault survivors were more apt to report elevated symptoms and to meet caseness criteria of lifetime alcohol abuse and/or neglect when they had received mental health services.

Having a regular medical provider. Having a regular medical provider tended to have a somewhat different effect on the relationship between sexual assault and psychological distress. Individuals with histories of sexual assault were more likely to meet caseness criteria for lifetime drug and alcohol abuse and/or dependence when they had regular medical providers. Sexual assault survivors tended to report more symptoms of trait anxiety, lifetime drug and alcohol abuse and/or dependence, lifetime PTSD, lifetime conduct disorder, and current depression when they had regular medical providers. In contradiction, sexual assault survivors were more likely to meet caseness criteria for current depression and lifetime conduct disorder when they did not have a regular medical provider.

Relatives having mental health problems. Sexual assault survivors more often met caseness criteria and more often reported elevated symptoms for psychological distress when they believed that their relatives did not have mental health problems. Caseness criteria were more often met for lifetime drug abuse and/or dependence and conduct disorder and elevated symptoms were more frequently reported for lifetime drug abuse and/or dependence, PTSD, major depression, and conduct disorder for these survivors. In addition, survivors who did not believe that their relatives had mental health problems were more likely to report lifetime suicide thoughts and attempts than individuals who had not been exposed to sexual assault.

Relatives having alcohol problems. Sexual assault survivors who did not report that a relative had an alcohol problem were more likely to disclose elevated symptoms of lifetime alcohol abuse and/or dependence and conduct disorder, lifetime suicide thoughts and attempts, and symptoms meeting diagnostic criteria for lifetime alcohol abuse and/or dependence and major depression. Elevated symptoms of lifetime drug abuse and/or dependence were more often reported and caseness criteria for lifetime drug abuse and/or dependence and PTSD were more frequently met among sexual abuse survivors who did not believe that any relatives had alcohol problems.

Relatives having drug problems. Sexual assault survivors who did not believe that any relatives had drug problems more often reported elevated symptoms of lifetime drug and alcohol abuse and/or dependence, PTSD, and conduct disorder. Histories of suicide thoughts and attempts were more often disclosed and caseness criteria were more frequently met for lifetime alcohol abuse and/or dependence, major depression, and conduct disorder among sexual assault survivors who did not report that any relatives had drug problems.

Father's educational level. Sexual assault survivors more often reported elevated symptoms of lifetime drug and alcohol abuse and/or dependence, major depression, and conduct disorder and more frequently met caseness criteria for lifetime alcohol abuse and/or dependence when their father's educational level was less than 12th grade. In contrast, caseness criteria for lifetime PTSD, suicide attempts, and current depression were more often met among survivors whose fathers had completed 12 or more years of formal education.

Lifetime homelessness. Sexual assault survivors were more likely to report elevated symptoms of lifetime alcohol abuse and/or dependence and to meet caseness criteria for lifetime alcohol abuse and/or dependence and major depression if they had histories of lifetime homelessness equalling less than one year. Caseness criteria for lifetime drug abuse and/or dependence were more often met and suicide attempts were more frequently reported by survivors who had lifetime homelessness histories equalling one or more years.

Income in the past 30 days. Caseness criteria were more frequently met for lifetime drug abuse and/or dependence and conduct disorder and elevated symptoms of lifetime conduct disorder and current depression were more often reported among sexual assault survivors with incomes of less than $100. Survivors with incomes of $100 or more were more likely to report elevated symptoms of lifetime PTSD and depression and to disclose histories of suicide thoughts and attempts.

Problems finding clothing. Caseness criteria were more often met for lifetime drug and alcohol abuse and/or dependence and elevated symptoms of lifetime drug abuse and/or dependence, PTSD, and conduct disorder were more often reported among sexual assault survivors who regularly had difficulty finding clothing.

Membership in a street gang. Sexual assault survivors more frequently met caseness criteria for lifetime alcohol abuse and/or dependence, major depression, and conduct disorder and more often reported elevated symptoms of lifetime drug and alcohol abuse and/or dependence when they reported no street gang membership. Lifetime suicide attempts and elevated symptoms of lifetime PTSD were most often disclosed among survivors who acknowledged membership in a street gang.

Carrying a weapon for protection. Sexual assault survivors more often reported lifetime suicide attempts, elevated symptoms of lifetime alcohol abuse and/or dependence and conduct disorder and more frequently met caseness criteria for lifetime alcohol abuse and/or dependence and PTSD if they did not disclose weapon possession. Caseness criteria for current depression was most frequently met and elevated symptoms of trait anxiety, lifetime major depression, and current depression were most often reported by survivors who did carry weapons.

History of running away from home. Sexual assault survivors more frequently reported elevated symptoms of trait anxiety and more often met caseness criteria for lifetime major depression when they had run away from home. Elevated symptoms of lifetime alcohol abuse and/or dependence, PTSD, and conduct disorder, and current depression were more often reported among sexual assault survivors who had been told to leave home.

Substance abuse and/or dependence. Sexual assault survivors were less likely to meet caseness criteria for and report elevated symptoms of lifetime major depression and conduct disorder when they did not meet caseness criteria for drug abuse and/or dependence. Caseness criteria for current depression was most often met among sexual abuse survivors who also met diagnostic criteria for drug abuse and/or dependence. Survivors more frequently met caseness criteria for lifetime PTSD and major depression and more often reported elevated symptoms of lifetime major depression when they did not meet diagnostic criteria for alcohol abuse and/or dependence. History of suicide thoughts and attempts and elevated symptoms of lifetime conduct disorder were most commonly reported by survivors who met diagnostic criteria for alcohol abuse and/or dependence.

Psychological Distress by Characteristics of Physical Assaults

Survivors of physical assault were more likely to meet diagnostic criteria for 3-4 lifetime diagnoses of distress when their assaults involved life-threatening levels of violence, over 95 exposures, or multiple adult and peer perpetrators. Exposure to physical assaults by parents with an onset after age 10 tended to increase the probability that symptoms of several specific indicators of psychological distress would eventually be manifested. One notable exception is that symptoms of conduct disorder were reported more often among physical assault survivors who had first been assaulted when they were younger than 11 years old. Mediating characteristics varied somewhat depending on the indicator of distress, but the direction of the effects tended to remain stable. Multiple exposures (i.e., more than 95) tended to covary with indicators of all disorders except lifetime major depression, and life-threatening levels of violence tended to covary with all indicators of disorder except current depression, lifetime conduct disorder and drug abuse and/or dependence. Having been assaulted by a parent figure tended to be related to history of suicide thoughts and attempts. Physical assault survivors who reported that they fought back during physical assaults were less likely to report symptoms of trait anxiety but more apt to disclose symptoms of lifetime drug and alcohol abuse and/or dependence and conduct disorder.

Psychological Distress by Characteristics of Sexual Assaults

Survivors of sexual assault were more likely to meet diagnostic criteria for 3-4 lifetime diagnoses of distress when their assaults involved sexual penetration, exposure beginning after the age of 10 years, and non-parent perpetrators. Mediating characteristics varied somewhat depending on the indicator of distress, and the direction of the effects tended to vary considerably. For instance, history of sexual assaults perpetrated by the respondent's father tended to increase the probability that symptoms of current depression, lifetime alcohol abuse and/or dependence, conduct disorder, and suicide thoughts and attempts would be reported; yet symptoms of trait anxiety, lifetime major depression, drug abuse and/or dependence, and PTSD were more often reported among survivors who had been assaulted by persons other than their fathers. Suicide thoughts and attempts were most often reported by survivors who had been sexually assaulted on multiple occasions by their fathers beginning before the age of 10.

Child Maltreatment and Gender

Disclosure, Reporting to Authorities, Removal from Home, and Assault Characteristics

When examining each type of child maltreatment in isolation from the others, one finds that female respondents were significantly more likely to disclose histories of neglect and sexual assault and male respondents were slightly more likely to disclose histories of physical assault. Sexual assaults which victimized female youths were more often reported to the child protection authorities, especially if the alleged perpetrator lived in the youth's home. Female survivors of physical or sexual assault perpetrated by household residents were more likely to be removed from the home as a result of assault reports. Compared with female survivors of physical assault, male survivors tended to have earlier onsets of exposure to physical assault (i.e., at ages 3-10 years) and tended to be assaulted by multiple perpetrators. On the other hand, compared with male survivors of both sexual and physical assaults, female survivors tended to have been sexually assaulted once by a father figure and to have been physically assaulted multiple times by a single perpetrator with life-threatening force beginning in adolescence.

Assault and Psychological Distress

With regard to symptoms of psychological distress, female respondents who had been exposed to child maltreatment other than sexual assault were more likely to disclose current feelings of self-hatred and self-blame and to report being worried about the future compared with their male counterparts. Male survivors of sexual assault were more likely to report suicide thoughts and elevated symptoms of trait anxiety, lifetime drug abuse and/or dependence, and lifetime PTSD than female survivors. On the other hand, female sexual assault survivors more often reported suicide attempts and elevated symptoms of lifetime conduct disorder and current depression and more often met caseness criteria for lifetime drug abuse and/or dependence, major depression, and conduct disorder. More specifically, male sexual assault survivors more frequently reported symptoms of current sleep and appetite problems and lifetime symptoms of sleep problems and involvement in sex work. Female sexual assault survivors more often endorsed symptoms of current loneliness, hopelessness, and poor body image and lifetime symptoms of worthlessness and hopelessness.

Table 5.1 Demographic Characteristics of the Hollywood Homeless Youth Sample

Characteristics	%
Gender	
Male	61.5
Female	38.5
Age group (mean age = 16.1 years)	
13-15 years old	28.1
16-17 years old	71.9
Race/ethnicity	
White (non-Latino)	59.4
African-American (non-Latino)	14.6
Hispanic/Latino	12.5
Native American/Alaska Native	7.3
Asian/Pacific Islander	5.2
Other	1.0
Birthplace	
Los Angeles County	26.0
Other California county	13.5
Other state	46.9
Outside U.S.	13.5
Total *n*	96

Table 5.2 Educational Background of the Hollywood Homeless Youth Sample

Characteristics	%
Highest grade completed (mean grade = 9.2)	
1st-9th grade	54.2
10th-12th grade	45.8
Total *n*	83
Ever held back in school	
No	71.9
Yes	28.1
Total *n*	96
Ever in special education classes	
No	72.6
Yes	27.4
Total *n*	95
Overall grades in school	
A / B	26.1
C	42.0
D / F	31.8
Total *n*	88
Plans to return to school	
In school now	12.0
Plans to return	70.6
No plans to return	17.4
Total *n*	92

Table 5.3 Family History of the Hollywood Homeless Youth Sample

Characteristics	%
Biological parents'[a] marital history	
Divorced	58.1
Married, not divorced	26.7
Never married	14.0
Total *n*	86
Relationship with biological parents	
Knew both parents	82.9
Never knew father	7.9
Never knew mother	2.6
Never knew either parent	3.9
Adopted	2.6
Total *n*	76
Mortality of biological parents	
Mother still alive	86.0
Total *n*	88
Father still alive	89.0
Total *n*	81
Education of biological parents	
Father (mean = 11.7 years, median = 12.0 years)	
Up through 11th grade	32.9
12th grade or above	67.1
Total *n*	70
Mother (mean = 12.7 years, median = 12.0 years)	
Up through 11th grade	23.4
12th grade or above	76.6
Total *n*	77
Age of mother when R was born (mean = 21.4 years, median = 20.0 years, range = 13-39 years)	
≤ 20 years old	53.2
>20 years old	46.8
Total *n*	77
Number of living siblings	
0	31.9
1-2	40.7
3-12	27.5
Total *n*	91

[a] Among parents known to respondents.

Table 5.4 History of Institutional Placements of the Hollywood Homeless Youth Sample

Type of Placement	%
None	22.1
Foster care only	9.5
Group home only	6.3
Foster care and group home	6.3
Juvenile detention only	22.1
Juvenile detention and foster care	9.5
Juvenile detention and group home	8.4
Juvenile detention, foster care, and group home	15.8
Total *n*	95

Number of times in any placement among those who were in placement	
range	1-102
mean	9.5
median	4
Total *n*	73

Table 5.5 Detention[a] by Law Enforcement of the Hollywood Homeless Youth Sample

Number of times detained overnight	%
0	44.2
1	23.2
2	6.3
3	7.4
4	9.5
≥ 5	9.5
Total *n*	95

[a] Detained overnight in jail or juvenile hall.

Table 5.6 Reasons for Last Five Law Enforcement Detentions[a] in the Hollywood Homeless Youth Sample: Reason for Detention as the Unit of Analysis

	%	Total %
"Minor" offenses		34.8
Running away	17.6	
Trespassing	4.1	
To protect R	2.0	
Driving without a license	2.0	
Truancy	1.4	
Curfew violation	1.4	
Loitering	1.4	
Probation violation	1.4	
Incorrigibility	0.7	
False I.D.	0.7	
Lying to police officers	0.7	
Jaywalking	0.7	
AWOL from camp/placement	0.7	
Substance-related offenses		15.0
Drug dealing/use	11.5	
Driving while under the influence	1.4	
Drunk & disorderly	1.4	
Under the influence	1.4	
Destroying property		3.4
Arson	2.0	
Vandalism	1.4	
Theft		29.1
Stealing	9.5	
Grand theft auto	6.8	
Shoplifting	5.4	
Breaking & entering	4.7	
Robbery	2.0	
Burglary	0.7	
Sexual exploitation		1.4
Pimping	0.7	
Prostitution	0.7	
Violence-related offenses		17.1
Assault	12.2	
Carrying a concealed weapon	1.4	
Attempted murder	1.4	
Gang violence	1.4	
Rape	0.7	
Total number of reasons		148

[a] Detained overnight in jail or juvenile hall.

Table 5.7 Hierarchy of Reasons[a] for Last Five Detentions[b] in the Hollywood Homeless Youth Sample

	%
1. Minor offenses only	17.3
2. Substance-related ± 1	15.4
3. Destroyed property ± 1	
No substance-related offenses	1.9
Substance-related offenses	1.9
4. Theft ± 1, 3	
No substance-related offenses	25.0
Substance-related offenses	5.8
5. Violence ± 1, 3, 4	
No substance-related offenses	19.2
Substance-related offenses	13.5
Total *n*	52

[a] See Table 5.6 for descriptions of reason categories.

[b] Detained overnight in jail or juvenile hall.

Table 5.8 History of Homelessness[a] for the Hollywood Homeless Youth Sample

Characteristics	%
Amount of life homeless	
(mean = 440 days, median = 195 days)	
< 1 year	61.7
≥ 1 year	38.3
Total *n*	94
Number of times homeless	
(mode = 1 time, median = 4 times, mean = 7.3 times)	
1-4 times	51.1
≥ 5 times	48.4
Total *n*	94
Pattern of homelessness	
Temporary: 1 episode lasting < 365 days	16.8
Episodic: > 1 episode, lifetime homelessness < 365 days	45.3
Chronic: > 1 episode, lifetime homelessness ≥ 365 days	37.9
Total *n*	95
Considered self "homeless"[b]	92.0
Total *n*	88

[a] Homelessness = when R had no rented room, apartment, or house in which to sleep; [b] Eight percent of the respondents preferred to describe themselves as being something other than homeless, e.g.: "bummer," "about to be housed or sheltered," "free," "half & half," "street kid," and "on an adventure in Hollywood."

Table 5.9 Characteristics of First Episode[a] of Homelessness[b] for the Hollywood Homeless Youth Sample

Characteristics	%
Age (mean = 13.1 years)	
5-13 years old	51.6
14-17 years old	48.4
Total *n*	95
Told to leave home	14.0
Left home on own	86.0
Total *n*	93
Precipitating event	
Family conflict	50.0
Physical or sexual abuse	22.2
Wanted to be free, have no rules, be on own	6.7
Own alcohol or drug use	5.6
Wanted to go on journey, have an adventure, see world/L.A.; was bored	4.4
Wanted to be with friends	2.2
Didn't get along with roommates/friends	2.2
Abandoned/rejected by parents	2.2
Mom's alcohol problem	1.1
Felt family chore expectations were unfair	1.1
Family was evicted and became homeless	1.1
Tired of placement living situation	1.1
Total *n*	90
Number of days homeless (mean = 112.7, median = 14)	
≤ 30 days	68.8
31-364 days	21.5
1-6 years	9.7
Total *n*	93

[a] For 19 respondents, current homelessness episode was also their first.

[b] Homelessness = when R had no rented room, apartment, or house in which to sleep.

Table 5.10 Characteristics of Current Episode of Homelessness[a] for the Hollywood Homeless Youth Sample

Characteristics	%
Told to leave last home	35.1
Left home on own	64.9
Total *n*	94
Precipitating event	
Family conflict	36.3
Physical or sexual abuse	13.2
Didn't get along with roommates/friends, argument with girlfriend/boyfriend	11.0
Own alcohol or drug use	8.8
Wanted to be with friends/boyfriend/ girlfriend	5.5
Wanted freedom, to be on own, no rules	3.3
Felt unwanted by foster mom, friends, family	3.3
Wanted to see L.A.	2.2
AWOL from army in El Salvador	1.1
Arrested for fighting in group home	1.1
Evicted by law enforcement	1.1
Arrested too many times	1.1
Couldn't afford rent	1.1
To avoid going into foster home	1.1
Left group home after getting GED	1.1
Kicked out because wasn't selling enough drugs	1.1
Not enough money at home to support R	1.1
Kicked out by foster mom for planning to have abortion	1.1
To avoid going to youth authority	1.1
Wanted to see Grateful Dead concert	1.1
School said R had to repeat 2.5 grades	1.1
"Nothing left in Utah for me"	1.1
Dad's alcohol problem	1.1
Total *n*	91
Number of days homeless[b] (mean = 307 days, median = 90.0 days)	
≤ 30 days	30.4
31-364 days	46.8
1-7 years	22.8
Total *n*	92

(table continues)

Table 5.10 continued

	%
Homeless with someone	
With friends	53.2
Alone	46.8
Total *n*	94
Shelter	
Where usually sleep if cannot pay for a place	
Squat (abandoned building)	31.9
Street	18.1
Shelter	16.0
Car	10.6
Other	10.6
Family/friends	9.6
Beach	2.1
Hotel/motel	1.1
Total *n*	94
Number of nights spent in an emergency shelter in past month (mean = 6.1 nights)	
0	59.6
≥ 1	40.4
Total *n*	94

[a] Homelessness = when R had no rented room, apartment, or house in which to sleep.

[b] Homelessness = since R lived in a rented room, apartment, or house for 30 consecutive nights.

Table 5.11 Migration and Mobility of the Hollywood Homeless Youth Sample

	%	Total *n*
Respondent last moved to L.A. County:		
< 1 month ago	19.8	
1 month-1 year ago	32.5	
13 months-17 years ago	27.9	
Lived whole life in L.A.	19.8	
		86
Cumulative # years lived in L.A. County		
< 1 year	25.0	
1 year	15.9	
2-17 years	59.1	
		88
Total # intercity moves in 12 months (median = 2.5 times)		
0-2 times	42.7	
3-30 times	57.3	
		89
Spent ≥ 1 night in past year:		
On street/outdoors/public places	59.1	88
In squats	46.0	87
In shelter	40.4	89
In hotel/motel	22.7	88
In foster care	11.2	89
In group home	6.9	87
In institution	12.5	88
In family home	72.7	88
In other house/apartment	56.2	89
Other	17.2	87
% of sample that spent ≥ 1 night in the past year in a shelter, foster care, or group home		
No	54.2	
Yes	45.8	
		96

(table continues)

Table 5.11 continued

	%	Total *n*
# hours/day usually spent in Hollywood area		
24 hours	19.5	
< 24 hours	80.5	
		87
# days in past month spent in Hollywood area		
30 days	50.0	
< 30 days	50.0	
		88
Spent time in past month in:		
Downtown L.A. area	21.2	85
San Fernando Valley	18.8	85
Venice Beach/Westside	35.3	85
Other areas	22.4	85
Area usually sleep in		
Hollywood area	92.1	
Downtown L.A. area	1.1	
San Fernando Valley	4.5	
Venice Beach/Westside	1.1	
Other area	1.1	
Total *n*		89

Table 5.12 Main Source of Food for the Hollywood Homeless Youth Sample

	%	Total *n*
Main source of food:		95
Shelter/meal program	52.6	
Paid meal	31.6	
Relatives/friends	7.4	
Other[a]	5.3	
Dumpsters/street	2.1	
Market/store	1.1	
Experienced at least one day in the past 30 days with nothing to eat	56.8	95

[a] "Other" sources include food vouchers from a drop-in center, pimping, shoplifting, stealing, and exchanging sex for food.

Table 5.13 Subsistence Characteristics of the Hollywood Homeless Youth Sample

For past 30 days:		Total *n*
% employed	59.3%	91
Mean income	$ 196.38	85
Median income	$ 100.00	85
Main source of income[a]:		87
Legal job	27.6%	
Panhandling	19.5%	
Friends	13.8%	
Prostitution, pimping, pornography	11.5%	
Dealing drugs	11.5%	
Family	8.0%	
Other[b]	6.9%	
Receives no money	1.1%	

[a] No respondents claimed to receive income from general assistance/ welfare.

[b] "Other" sources include a youth shelter, "hit man work," "washing cars," "protecting a hooker friend from getting beaten up," "stealing then selling the product," and "babysitting before left home."

Table 5.14 Health Care Resources Awareness and Use in the Hollywood Homeless Youth Sample

	%	Total *n*
Have medical insurance (including MediCal)	34.1	88
Have a specific place and/or person providing medical care	51.3	78
In past year, received:		
Medical care	57.1	91
Help for a mental health problem	24.2	91
Help for alcohol use	15.5	84
Help for drug use	8.6	81
Ever spent the night at a:		
Mental hospital	24.7	93
Hospital or treatment facility for problems with alcohol	8.0	87
Hospital or treatment facility for problems with drugs	9.4	85
Living arrangements made for R when discharged from a(n):		
Alcohol treatment facility	50.0	6
Drug treatment facility	37.5	8

Table 5.15 Prevalence of Indicators of Sexual and Substance Use Risk-Taking in the Hollywood Homeless Youth Sample

Indicators of risk-taking	%	Total *n*
Number of sexual partners in past year (range = 0-≥95, median and mean = 4)		85
Traded sex for		
Money	29.3	92
Food or shelter	21.7	92
Drugs	10.6	85
Posed for sexual photographs or movies	7.8	90
Number of times pregnant		36
None	55.6	
1 time	25.0	
2-5 times	19.4	
Ever had sexually transmitted disease	18.6	86
Tested for HIV antibodies	29.2	96
Testing positive for HIV antibodies	3.6	28
Never got results	3.6	28
Frequency of birth control use in past year		91
Never	38.4	
Seldom	44.0	
Half of the time	8.8	
Most of the time	8.8	
Used birth control at last sexual encounter	50.5	91
Used condom at last sexual encounter	34.1	91
Ever drink and drive	19.5	87
Ever use needle to inject self with drugs	29.8	84

Table 5.16 Perceived Health of Self in the Hollywood Homeless Youth Sample

	%	Total *n*
Health of self		91
Good to excellent	27.5	
Fair to poor	72.5	
Health since became homeless		90
Worse	22.2	
Same	73.3	
Better	4.4	
Ever had mental health problem	33.0	94
Ever needed help with mental health problem	16.7	90
Ever thought was excessive drinker	27.9	86
Ever thought had drug problem	25.8	93
Used alcohol before first became homeless	70.1	87
Used drugs before first became homeless	74.7	83
Used more alcohol since became homeless	24.1	87
Used more drugs since became homeless	36.3	80

Table 5.17 Perceived Health of Relatives in the Hollywood Homeless Youth Sample

	%	Total *n*
Relative had mental health problem	32.2	90
Relative had alcohol problem	50.0	90
Mother	52.2	46
Father	73.9	46
Alcohol problem caused:		
Arguments	53.2	47
Violence towards R	42.6	47
Relative had drug problem	29.4	85
Mother	40.7	27
Father	55.6	27
Drug problem caused:		
Arguments	44.4	27
Violence towards R	33.3	27
Violence towards others	40.7	27
R to use drugs	25.9	27

Table 5.18 Daily Stressors of the Hollywood Homeless Youth Sample

	%	Total *n*
Actions taken to prevent being harmed		
Always with someone who is trusted	77.3	88
Avoided certain places	67.0	88
Avoided certain people	50.0	88
Carried a weapon	50.0	88
Slept during the day, stayed awake at night	23.9	88
Number of actions taken to stay safe		88
None	4.5	
1-2	42.0	
3-5	53.5	
Basic needs that were usually or sometimes difficult to obtain since becoming homeless		
Clothes	52.6	95
Food	49.5	95
Place to wash up	36.8	95
Medical care	31.9	94
Number of basic needs that were usually or sometimes difficult to obtain since becoming homeless		95
None	10.5	
1-2	43.2	
3-4	46.3	

Table 5.19 Hierarchical Distribution of Disclosed Child Maltreatment (i.e., Neglect, Assault, and Witnessing Domestic Violence[a]) in the Hollywood Homeless Youth Sample

	%
No maltreatment disclosed[b]	8.3
Non-specific neglect[c]	2.4
Physical neglect[d]	4.8
Physical assault[e] by:	
Non-relatives	13.1
Relatives	20.2
Both	16.7
Sexual assault[f] by:	
Non-relatives	16.7
Relatives	10.7
Both	7.1
Total *n*	84[g]

[a] Witnessing domestic violence was assessed with the question, "Have you ever seen anyone hit or physically hurt your mother, father, or your sisters or brothers or anyone else you lived with?"

[b] Respondents answered "no" to each of the four maltreatment screening questions; see notes a, c-f.

[c] Respondents answered "yes" to the question, "Did you ever feel neglected by your parent(s)?" but "no" to specific questions regarding physical neglect.

[d] Physical neglect refers to a respondent's perception of having inadequate food, clothing, shelter, or supervision, or being punished with physical neglect by their parent(s). Two respondents in this category also disclosed witnessing domestic violence.

[e] Respondents answered "yes" to the question, "Did anyone [i.e., relatives, family friends, caretakers or their relatives or friends, or strangers] . . . ever hit you or hurt you physically?" Category includes respondents who had also reported being neglected and/or witnessing domestic violence.

[f] Respondents answered "yes" to the question, "Did anyone [i.e., relatives, family friends, caretakers or their relatives or friends, or strangers] . . . ever mess with you sexually?" With one exception, all respondents in this category disclosed being survivors of more than one type of maltreatment. All except four reported being physically assaulted.

[g] Twelve respondents refused to answer any of the items on physical assault, sexual assault, or domestic violence; of these twelve respondents, seven refused to answer any items on neglect.

Table 5.20 Collapsed Hierarchical Distribution of Disclosed Child Maltreatment in the Hollywood Homeless Youth Sample

	%
No physical or sexual assault	15.5
Physical assault	50.0
Sexual assault ± physical assault	34.5
Total *n*	84

Table 5.21 Disclosed Child Neglect in the Hollywood Homeless Youth Sample

	%
None	31.5
Yes--unspecified	24.7
Yes--physical[a]	43.8
Total *n*	89[b]

[a] Physical neglect refers to respondent's perception of having inadequate food, clothing, shelter, or supervision, or being punished with physical neglect by parent(s).
[b] Seven respondents refused to answer the neglect section.

Table 5.22 Characteristics of Disclosed Child Physical Assault in the Hollywood Homeless Youth Sample

Characteristics	%
Disclosed history of physical assault[a]	79.3
Total *n*	84
Degree of violence	
Potentially injurious[b]	20.9
Injurious[c]	28.4
Life-threatening[d]	50.7
Total *n*	67
Psychological torture	
Tied up	16.4
Locked up	22.4
Total *n*	67
Number of different violent acts experienced	
1-4	52.2
5-10	47.8
Total *n*	67
Frequency of lifetime physical assault	
1x	6.5
≥ 2x	93.5
Total *n*	62
Age of respondent at first physical assault episode (median = 9 years old)	
2-10 years	66.1
11-17 years	33.9
Total *n*	62
Number of perpetrators	
1	32.3
≥ 2	67.7
Total *n*	65
Relation of perpetrator to respondent	
Adults only	50.0
Adults and peers	50.0
Father ± others (not mother)	25.8
Mother ± others (not father)	24.2
Father and mother ± others	27.3
Others only	22.7
Total *n*	66

[a] Not exclusive of other types of maltreatment.

[b] Potentially injurious = respondent was hit with hand, with an object, or was the target of a thrown object.

[c] Injurious = respondent was beaten, kicked, or burned.

[d] Life-threatening = respondent was threatened with a weapon, stabbed, or shot.

Table 5.23 Characteristics of Disclosed Child Sexual Assault in the Hollywood Homeless Youth Sample

Characteristics	%
Disclosed history of sexual assault[a]	34.5
Total *n*	84
Degree of intrusiveness hierarchy	
Perpetrator touched respondent	21.4
Respondent touched perpetrator	3.6
Oral contact	3.6
Genital contact	21.4
Penetration	50.0
Total *n*	28
Number of different intrusive acts ever experienced	
1-3	50.0
4-5	50.0
Total *n*	28
Frequency of lifetime sexual assault	
1x	32.1
2 - > 95x	67.9
Total *n*	28
Revictimization	
1 perpetrator or 1 assault episode	60.7
> 1 perpetrator and > 1 episode	39.3
Total *n*	28
Age of respondent at first sexual assault episode (median = 11 years old)	
3-9 years	42.9
11-16 years	57.1
Total *n*	28
Number of perpetrators	
1	58.6
2-6	41.4
Total *n*	29

(table continues)

Table 5.23 continued

	%
Relationship of perpetrator to respondent	
Adults only	65.5
Adults and peers	20.7
Peers only	13.8
Father ± others	31.0
Others only	69.0
Parent figure ± others	34.5
Others only	65.5
Relatives only: Adults and peers	27.6
Non-relatives only: Adults and peers	48.3
Both relatives and non-relatives	24.1
Total *n*	29

[a] Of the 29 respondents who disclosed being sexually assaulted, 25 also disclosed being physically assaulted. Classification is not exclusive of disclosed child neglect or witnessing violence in the home.

Table 5.24 Characteristics of Witnessing Violence in the Home in the Hollywood Homeless Youth Sample

Characteristics	%
Disclosed history of witnessing violence in the home	47.6
Total *n*	84
Relationship of participants	
Adult with adult only	50.0
Adult with child only	17.5
Child with child only	7.5
Adult with adult + adult with child or child with child	25.0
Relative with relative only	65.0
Non-relative with relative only	22.5
Both relative with relative and non-relative with relative	12.5
Total *n*	40
Number of dyads	
1[a]	75.0
> 1	25.0
Total *n*	40
Perpetrators[b]	
Father figure and/or mother's boyfriend ± others	77.5
Others only	22.5
Total *n*	40
Targets	%
Females only	
Mother figures only	37.5
Sisters only	2.5
Both mother and sister	2.5
Males only	
Father figures only	0.0
Brothers	10.0
Both females and males	
Adults only	12.5
Siblings only	12.5
Both-sex adults and siblings	2.5
Mother and siblings	20.0
Total *n*	40

(table continues)

Table 5.24 continued

Violent acts witnessed	%	Total *n*
Someone in the home was:		
Hit with a hand	95.0	40
Hit with an object	35.9	39
The target of a thrown object	40.0	40
Threatened with a weapon	28.2	39
Beaten	47.5	40
Kicked	39.5	38
Tied up	5.3	38
Locked in a small place	7.9	38
Burned	13.5	37
Stabbed or shot	13.2	38
Raped	13.2	38

[a] Four of these dyads had reciprocal directions of violence.

[b] Perpetrators include biological parents, stepparents, adoptive parents, mother's boyfriend, sister's boyfriend, siblings, a stranger, and a gang member.

Table 5.25 Responses to Maltreatment in the Hollywood Homeless Youth Sample

Responses	%	Total *n*
Fought perpetrator of physical assault	73.1	67
Left home because of maltreatment	41.6	77
Removed from home because of maltreatment	22.1	77
Left or removed from home because of maltreatment	50.6	77
Told to leave because of maltreatment	46.8	77

Number of times left or removed from home because of maltreatment	
Range	0-190
Mean	8
Mode	0
Median	1
Total *n*	77

Table 5.26 Reporting of Child Maltreatment to Authorities in the Hollywood Homeless Youth Sample

	%	Total *n*
Any maltreatment was reported	45.4	77[a]
Neglect was reported	17.1	35[b]
Physical assault was reported	35.5	62[b]
Sexual assault was reported	28.6	28[b]
Violence among others in the home was reported	39.5	38[b]

[a]Total n = the number of respondents who disclosed any maltreatment: i.e. neglect, assault, witnessing domestic violence, or combinations thereof. [b]Total n = the number of respondents who disclosed being victims of this particular type of maltreatment. Categories of maltreatment are not exclusive of one another.

Table 5.27 Removal of Respondent from Home as a Result of Reported Maltreatment in the Hollywood Homeless Youth Sample

	%	Total *n*
Removal for any maltreatment	48.6	35[a]
Removal for neglect	50.0	6[b]
Removal for physical assault by parent[c]	50.0	22[b]
Removal for sexual assault by parent[c]	25.0	8[b]
Removal for witnessing violence in the home	40.0	15[b]

[a]Total *n* = the number of respondents whose maltreatment was reported
[b]Total *n* = the number of respondents who disclosed that their maltreatment was reported. Categories of maltreatment are not exclusive of one another.
[c]It is unknown whether the parent perpetrator was also the respondent's custodian. Hence, removal of the respondent from the home may not have been necessary to avoid further maltreatment. However, only five of all reported maltreatment situations resulted in the perpetrator (regardless of the relationship with the respondent) being arrested.

Table 5.28 Prevalence of Indicators of Psychological Distress in the Hollywood Homeless Youth Sample

	%	Total *n*
Current		
Trait anxiety[a]	6.6	91
Depression[b] in past two weeks	22.7	88
Lifetime		
Post-traumatic stress disorder[c, d]	18.5	92
Depression[e]	26.3	95
Suicide thoughts	64.5	93
Suicide attempt	47.3	93
Alcohol dependence and/or abuse[e]	48.4	93
Drug dependence and/or abuse[e]	38.7	93
Conduct disorder[f]		
At any time		
Including running away as symptom	84.2	95
Excluding running away as symptom	71.6	95
When not homeless		
Including running away as symptom	81.1	95
Excluding running away as symptom	68.4	95

[a] Revised Children's Manifest Anxiety Scale equal to or greater than two standard deviations above the mean for age and sex-matched normative samples.

[b] Childhood Depression Inventory (CDI) score greater than or equal to 19.

[c] DSM-IIIR criteria for caseness were met as assessed by the Diagnostic Interview Schedule (DIS).

[d] Although DSM-IIIR criteria for caseness requires the presence of at least three symptoms of avoidance or numbing of stimuli associated with the trauma, the DIS only assesses two symptoms. Thus, two symptoms of avoidance or numbing of stimuli were required for caseness in this study.

[e] DSM-III criteria for caseness were met as assessed by the Diagnostic Interview Schedule (DIS). Diagnostic criteria for depression caseness did not differ significantly between the DSM-III and the DSM-IIIR. Most cases defined by the DSM-III as alcohol or drug abuse are classified as alcohol or drug dependence in the DSM-IIIR. The substance "abuse" diagnostic category has been retained in the DSM-IIIR to capture cases which do not qualify as dependence yet meet criteria for maladaptive patterns of use. Depression caseness includes severe cases (i.e., dysphoria and ≥ 4 symptom clusters) and excludes one case of severe grief and two cases of non-severe depression. Drug dependence and/or abuse caseness includes both severe and non-severe cases. The prevalence of severe drug dependence and/or abuse cases = 22.6% ($n = 93$).

[f] DSM-IIIR criteria for caseness were met as assessed by the Diagnostic Interview for Children & Adolescents (DICA).

Table 5.29 Prevalence of Multiple Diagnoses of Psychological Distress in the Hollywood Homeless Youth Sample

	%	Total *n*
Current diagnoses[a]		88
None	75.0	
1	20.5	
2	4.5	
Lifetime diagnoses[b]		93
None	17.2	
1	20.4	
2	20.4	
3	30.1	
4	11.8	

[a] DSM-III diagnostic criteria were met for current depression and/or trait anxiety. Diagnoses were assessed using the Revised Children's Manifest Anxiety Schedule for trait anxiety, and the Children's Depression Inventory for depression.

[b] DSM-IIIR diagnostic criteria were met for lifetime major depression, alcohol dependence and/or abuse, drug dependence and/or abuse, post-traumatic stress disorder, and/or conduct disorder while not homeless excluding running away as a symptom. Major depression, PTSD, and substance dependence/abuse were assessed using the Diagnostic Interview Schedule; conduct disorder was evaluated using the Diagnostic Interview for Children and Adolescents.

Table 5.30 Characteristics of Symptoms of Lifetime Depression[a] in the Hollywood Homeless Youth Sample

	%	Total *n*
Symptoms of dysphoria[b]	66.0	95
Symptoms of dysthymia[c]	30.0	95
Total number of symptom clusters		95
0	64.2	
1	0	
2	4.2	
3	2.1	
4	9.5	
5	5.3	
6	8.4	
7	5.3	
8	1.1	
Among those with history of major depressive episode, during worst depressive episode, had one or more symptoms of:		25
Guilt	92.0	
Sleep disturbance	80.0	
Thoughts of death	80.0	
Slow thoughts	68.0	
Disinterest in things usually enjoyed	68.0	
Loss of appetite/weight loss	64.0	
Motor disturbance	60.0	
Fatigue	44.0	

[a] As assessed by the Diagnostic Interview Schedule.

[b] Symptoms of depression for two weeks or more.

[c] Dysphoria for two years or more.

Table 5.31 Traumatic Experiences Which Produced Symptoms of Post-Traumatic Stress Disorder (PTSD) in the Hollywood Homeless Youth Sample

	%	Total *n*
Traumatic experience		62[a]
Saw person(s) killed	24.2	
Physical assault	16.1	
Death of friend(s) or family member(s)	14.5	
Sexual assault	11.3	
Saw person(s) being seriously injured	9.7	
Killed someone	4.8	
Almost assaulted, injured or abducted	4.8	
Satanic rituals with or without drug use	4.8	
Rejected by loved ones or asked to leave home	3.2	
Other[b]	3.2	
Injured someone	1.6	
Drug hallucination	1.6	
Number of traumatic experiences		40[c]
1	72.5	
> 1	27.5	

[a] Traumatic experience as the unit of analysis; 43 respondents had one or more symptoms of PTSD.

[b] Friend was abducted; R was bitten by a mouse.

[c] Respondent as the unit of analysis.

Table 5.32 Prevalence of Indicators of Lifetime Substance Abuse as Assessed by the DIS in the Hollywood Homeless Youth Sample

	%	Total *n*
Symptom count, any drug dependence and/or abuse		93
None	40.9	
1-7	59.1	
DSM-III diagnostic categories for drug abuse and dependence		93
No disorder	61.3	
Non-severe abuse, no dependence	4.3	
Non-severe dependence, no abuse	5.4	
Non-severe abuse and dependence	6.5	
Severe abuse, no dependence	4.3	
Severe dependence, no abuse	1.1	
Severe abuse and dependence	17.2	
Abuse and/or dependence of specific substances among respondents who met diagnostic criteria for any drug abuse and/or dependence	%	Total *n*
Cannabis	83.3	36
Amphetamines	33.3	36
Cocaine	22.2	36
Opiates	22.2	36
Hallucinogens	16.7	36
Barbiturates	13.9	36
Symptom count, any alcohol dependence and/or abuse	%	Total *n* 93
None	28.0	
1-10	72.0	

Table 5.33 Recent Drug Use in the Hollywood Homeless Youth Sample

	Among those who ever used		
	Used within past 6 months (%)	Used within past year (%)	Total *n*
Cannabis	85.6	94.0	83
Psychedelics	81.9	91.7	61
Cocaine	70.7	87.9	58
Amphetamines	70.7	82.8	58
Other narcotics	53.5	64.2	28
Barbiturates	44.0	56.0	25
Heroin	43.8	50.1	16
Inhalants	40.0	51.4	35
Tranquilizers	33.4	58.4	24

Table 5.34 Interview Location by Demographic Characteristics of the Hollywood Homeless Youth Sample

	Sex		Race/Ethnicity		Age in years		Birthplace		
Interview location	Male (%)	Female (%)	White (%)	Other (%)	13-15 (%)	16-17 (%)	CA (%)	Other U.S. (%)	Not U.S. (%)
1.Drop-in	52.5	45.9	63.2	30.8	55.6	47.8	44.7	58.7	33.3
2.Shelter	18.6	29.7	12.3	38.5	29.6	20.3	28.9	10.9	50.0
3.Street	28.8	24.3	24.6	30.8	14.8	31.9	26.3	30.4	16.7
Total n	59	37	57	39	27	69	38	46	12
Pearson Chi-Square	1.587		12.114**		3.058			9.610*	
(df)	(2)		(2)		(2)			(4)	
$OR_{1,2}$	--		6.423		--			Cramer's V = 0.224	
$OR_{2,3}$	--		0.400		--				
$OR_{1,3}$	--		2.569		--				

* $p < .10$
** $p < .01$

Table 5.35 Interview Location by Characteristics of Homelessness of the Hollywood Homeless Youth Sample

	How became homeless		Who with on the street		Lifetime homelessness		Pattern of homelessness[a]		
Interview location	Left (%)	Told to go (%)	Alone (%)	With another (%)	<1 yr (%)	≥1 yr (%)	Temporary (%)	Episodic (%)	Chronic (%)
1. Drop-in	44.3	63.6	40.9	58.0	41.4	66.7	56.3	34.9	66.7
2. Shelter	21.3	24.2	34.1	14.0	24.1	19.4	31.3	23.3	19.4
3. Street	34.4	12.1	25.0	28.0	34.5	13.9	12.5	41.9	13.9
Total n	61	33	44	50	58	36	16	43	36
Pearson Chi-Square	5.662*		5.483*		6.543**		11.931**		
(df)	(2)		(2)		(2)		(4)		
$OR_{1,2}$	0.791		0.290		0.500		Cramer's V = 0.251		
$OR_{2,3}$	0.310		2.728		0.501				
$OR_{1,3}$	0.245		0.790		0.250				

* $p < .10$
** $p < .05$

[a] Temporary = 1 episode lasting <365 days
Episodic = >1 episode, lifetime homelessness <365 days
Chronic = >1 episode, lifetime homelessness ≥365 days

Table 5.36 Interview Location by Indicators of Psychological Distress in the Hollywood Homeless Youth Sample

	Symptoms of major depression		Symptoms of anxiety		Caseness for current depression	
Interview location	Low (%)	High (%)	Low (%)	High (%)	No (%)	Yes (%)
1. Drop-in	50.9	48.8	56.5	40.0	54.4	35.0
2. Shelter	15.1	32.6	10.9	37.8	17.6	45.0
3. Street	34.0	18.6	32.6	22.2	27.9	20.0
Total *n*	53	43	46	45	68	20
Pearson Chi-Square	5.248*		8.990**		6.383**	
(df)	(2)		(2)		(2)	
$OR_{1,2}$	2.252		4.907		3.974	
$OR_{2,3}$	0.253		0.196		0.280	
$OR_{1,3}$	0.571		0.964		1.114	

* $p < .10$
** $p < .05$
Note: Low numbers of symptoms of lifetime major depression and trait anxiety reflect symptom scores which fall at or below a median of 12 on the Diagnostic Interview Schedule or 5 on the Revised Children's Manifest Anxiety Schedule. Caseness criterion for current depression is 19 symptoms or more as assessed by the Children's Depression Inventory.

Table 5.37 Homelessness by Demographic Characteristics in the Hollywood Homeless Youth Sample

	Sex		Age		Race/Ethnicity	
	Male (%)	Female (%)	13-15 yrs (%)	16-17 yrs (%)	White (%)	Non-white (%)
Pattern of homelessness[a]						
Temporary	16.9	16.7	11.1	19.1	14.3	20.5
Episodic	49.2	38.9	59.3	39.7	44.6	46.2
Chronic	33.9	44.4	29.6	41.2	41.1	33.3
Total *n*	59	36	27	68	56	39
Lifetime homelessness						
<1 year	65.5	55.6	70.4	58.2	58.9	65.8
≥1 year	34.5	44.4	29.6	41.8	41.1	34.2
Total *n*	58	36	27	67	56	38

[a]Temporary = 1 episode lasting <365 days
Episodic = >1 episode, lifetime homelessness <365 days
Chronic = >1 episode, lifetime homelessness ≥365 days

Table 5.38 Child Maltreatment by Selected Sociodemographic Characteristics in the Hollywood Homeless Youth Sample

	Sex		Father's education	
Child maltreatment	Male (%)	Female (%)	0-11th grade (%)	≥12th grade (%)
1. No physical or sexual assault	14.0	17.6	9.5	17.1
2. Physical assault	62.0	32.4	33.3	61.0
3. Sexual assault ± physical assault	24.0	50.0	57.1	22.0
Total *n*	50	34	21	41
Pearson Chi-square (df)	7.694** (2)		7.679** (2)	
$OR_{1,2}$	0.416		1.018	
$OR_{2,3}$	3.987		0.210	
$OR_{1,3}$	1.657		0.214	

* $p < .10$
** $p < .05$

Table 5.39 Symptoms[a] of Psychological Distress by Selected Demographic, Custodial Placement, and Homelessness Characteristics in the Hollywood Homeless Youth Sample

	Sex		Age		Income in past month		Foster care		Emergency shelter[b]		Had nothing to eat for ≥24 hrs[c]	
	Male	Female	13-15 yrs	16-17 yrs	<$100	≥$100	Never	Ever	No	Yes	No	Yes
Distress Symptoms	(%)	(%)	(%)	(%)	(%)	(%)	(%)	(%)	(%)	(%)	(%)	(%)
Trait anxiety[d]												
High count	41.8	61.1	57.7	46.2	62.2	38.6	49.1	50.0	39.6	62.2	55.3	45.3
Low count	58.2	38.9	42.3	53.8	37.8	61.4	50.9	50.0	60.4	37.8	44.7	54.7
Total *n*	55	36	26	65	37	44	53	38	53	37	38	53
Chi-square (df)	3.240* (1)		n.s.		4.450** (1)		n.s.		4.430** (1)		n.s.	
OR	2.187				2.617				0.398			
Major depression[e]												
High count	40.7	51.4	65.4	43.1	57.5	37.8	53.6	33.3	26.8	26.3	24.4	27.8
Low count	59.3	48.6	34.6	56.9	42.5	62.2	46.4	66.7	73.2	73.7	75.6	72.2
Total *n*	59	37	26	65	40	45	56	39	56	38	41	54
Chi-square (df)	n.s.		3.697* (1)		3.306* (1)		3.801* (1)		n.s.		n.s.	
OR			2.495		2.226		2.314					

(table continues)

Table 5.39 continued	Sex		Age		Income in past month		Foster care		Emergency shelter[b]		Had nothing to eat for ≥24 hrs[c]	
	Male	Female	13-15 yrs	16-17 yrs	<$100	≥$100	Never	Ever	No	Yes	No	Yes
Distress Symptoms	(%)	(%)	(%)	(%)	(%)	(%)	(%)	(%)	(%)	(%)	(%)	(%)
Major depression[e]												
High count	40.7	51.4	65.4	43.1	57.5	37.8	53.6	33.3	26.8	26.3	24.4	27.8
Low count	59.3	48.6	34.6	56.9	42.5	62.2	46.4	66.7	73.2	73.7	75.6	72.2
Total n	59	37	26	65	40	45	56	39	56	38	41	54
Chi-square (df)	n.s.		3.697* (1)		3.306* (1)		3.801* (1)		n.s.		n.s.	
OR			2.495		2.226		2.314					
Suicide thoughts[e]												
Ever	56.9	77.1	59.3	66.7	76.9	59.1	72.7	52.6	61.1	68.4	56.1	71.2
Never	43.1	22.9	40.7	33.3	23.1	40.9	27.3	47.4	38.9	31.6	43.9	28.8
Total n	58	35	27	66	39	44	55	38	54	38	41	52
Chi-square (df)	3.908** (1)		n.s.		2.995* (1)		3.964** (1)		n.s.		n.s.	
OR	0.392				2.304		2.400					

(table continues)

Table 5.39 continued	Sex		Age		Income in past month		Foster care		Emergency shelter[b]		Had nothing to eat for ≥24 hrs[c]	
	Male	Female	13-15 yrs	16-17 yrs	<\$100	≥\$100	Never	Ever	No	Yes	No	Yes
Distress Symptoms	(%)	(%)	(%)	(%)	(%)	(%)	(%)	(%)	(%)	(%)	(%)	(%)
Suicide attempts[e]												
Ever	37.9	62.9	33.3	53.0	59.0	40.0	51.8	40.5	46.3	47.4	29.3	61.5
Never	62.1	37.1	66.7	47.0	41.0	60.0	48.2	59.5	53.7	52.6	70.7	38.5
Total *n*	58	35	27	66	39	45	56	37	54	38	41	52
Chi-square	5.440**		2.982*		3.010*		n.s.		n.s.		9.577***	
(df)	(1)		(1)		(1)						(1)	
OR	0.360		0.443		2.159						0.259	

* $p < .10$, ** $p < .05$, *** $p < .01$

[a] Symptom counts were dichotomized at the median.

[b] Spent ≥1 night in shelter in past month.

[c] In past month.

[d] Measured by the Revised Children's Manifest Anxiety Scale.

[e] Measured by the Diagnostic Interview Schedule.

Table 5.40 Indicators of Psychological Distress by Perceived Problems with Alcohol, Drugs, and Mental Health Among Relatives

	Relative(s) perceived as having a problem with:					
	Alcohol		Drugs		Mental Health	
Lifetime distress	No (%)	Yes (%)	No (%)	Yes (%)	No (%)	Yes (%)
Depression[a]						
Low sx count	60.0	51.1	59.3	48.0	62.3	41.4
High sx count	40.0	48.9	40.7	52.0	37.7	58.6
Total n	45	45	59	25	61	29
Chi-square	n.s.		n.s.		3.485*	
(df)	(1)		(1)		(1)	
OR					2.341	
Suicide attempts[a]						
Never	47.7	56.8	48.3	62.5	61.7	32.1
Ever	52.3	43.2	51.7	37.5	38.3	67.9
Total n	44	44	58	24	60	28
Chi-square	n.s.		n.s.		6.670***	
(df)	(1)		(1)		(1)	
OR					3.396	
Drug abuse[a]						
Not case	75.6	48.9	69.5	36.0	73.3	41.4
Case	24.4	51.1	30.5	64.0	26.7	58.6
Total n	45	45	59	25	60	29
Chi-square	6.807***		8.175***		8.556***	
(df)	(1)		(1)		(1)	
OR	3.231		4.049		3.896	

(table continues)

Table 5.40
continued

Lifetime distress	Alcohol No (%)	Alcohol Yes (%)	Drugs No (%)	Drugs Yes (%)	Mental Health No (%)	Mental Health Yes (%)
	Relative(s) perceived as having a problem with:					
Anxiety[b]						
Low sx count	60.5	42.2	56.1	44.0	56.9	37.9
High sx count	39.5	57.8	43.9	56.0	43.1	62.1
Total n	43	45	57	25	58	29
Chi-square	2.929*		n.s.		2.782*	
(df)	(1)		(1)		(1)	
OR	2.093				2.160	
PTSD[a]						
Low sx count	52.3	51.1	56.9	48.0	62.7	31.0
High sx count	47.7	48.9	43.1	52.0	37.3	69.0
Total n	44	45	58	25	59	29
Chi-square	n.s.		n.s.		7.820***	
(df)	(1)		(1)		(1)	
OR					3.737	
Conduct disorder[c]						
Not case	33.3	33.3	35.6	16.0	42.6	13.8
Case	66.7	66.7	64.4	84.0	57.4	86.2
Total n	45	45	59	25	61	29
Chi-square	n.s.		3.225*		7.352***	
(df)	(1)		(1)		(1)	
OR			2.901		4.643	

*$p < .10$, **$p < .05$, ***$p < .01$, ****$p < .001$
[a]Symptoms and DSM-III caseness criteria assessed by the Diagnostic Interview Schedule; [b]Symptoms assessed by the Revised Children's Manifest Anxiety Scale; [c]DSM-IIIR caseness criteria assessed by the Diagnostic Interview for Children and Adolescents

Table 5.41 Indicators of Psychological Distress by History of Custodial Placement in the Hollywood Homeless Youth Sample

	History of Custodial Placements:					
	Juvenile detention		Group home		Foster home	
	No	Yes	No	Yes	No	Yes
Distress	(%)	(%)	(%)	(%)	(%)	(%)
Current depression[a]						
Case	35.0	12.5	27.5	15.2	28.0	15.8
Not case	65.0	87.5	72.5	84.8	72.0	84.2
Total *n*	40	48	51	33	50	38
Chi square	6.289*		n.s.		n.s.	
(df)	(1)					
OR	3.769					
Alcohol abuse[b]						
Case	41.5	53.8	40.0	64.7	45.5	52.6
Not case	58.5	46.2	60.0	35.3	54.5	47.4
Total *n*	41	52	55	34	55	38
Chi-square	n.s.		5.131*		n.s.	
(df)			(1)			
OR			0.364			
Major depression[b]						
Case	31.0	22.6	25.0	28.6	33.9	15.4
Not case	69.0	77.4	75.0	71.4	66.1	84.6
Total *n*	42	53	56	35	56	39
Chi-square	n.s.		n.s.		4.077**	
(df)					(1)	
OR					2.817	

* $p < .05$

[a] Measured by the Children's Depression Inventory.

[b] DSM-III caseness criteria as assessed by the Diagnostic Interview Schedule.

Table 5.42 Indicators of Substance Abuse[a] by Homelessness Characteristics in the Hollywood Homeless Youth Sample

	Problems getting clothes		Problems getting food		Place to clean up		Pattern of homelessness			Age first became homeless		How became homeless	
	No (%)	Yes (%)	No (%)	Yes (%)	No (%)	Yes (%)	Temporary (%)	Episodic (%)	Chronic (%)	5-13 yrs (%)	≥14 yrs (%)	Left (%)	Told to go (%)
Alcohol abuse &/or dependence													
Case	64.6	31.1	55.6	41.7	60.0	42.1	25.0	50.0	57.1	56.3	40.0	41.0	61.3
Not case	35.4	68.9	44.4	58.3	40.0	57.9	75.0	50.0	42.9	43.8	60.0	59.0	38.7
Total *n*	48	45	45	48	35	57	16	42	35	48	45	61	31
Chi-square	10.420***		n.s.		2.779*			4.622*		n.s.		3.397*	
(df)	(1)				(1)			(2)				(1)	
$OR_{1,2}$	4.043				2.063			0.333				0.439	
$OR_{2,3}$								0.751					
$OR_{1,3}$								0.250					

(table continues)

Table 5.42 continued

	Problems getting clothes		Problems getting food		Place to clean up		Pattern of homelessness			Age first became homeless		How became homeless	
	No (%)	Yes (%)	No (%)	Yes (%)	No (%)	Yes (%)	Temporary (%)	Episodic (%)	Chronic (%)	5-13 yrs (%)	≥14 yrs (%)	Left (%)	Told to go (%)
Drug abuse &/or dependence													
Case	45.8	31.1	64.4	14.6	60.0	24.6	18.8	40.5	46.7	50.0	26.7	32.8	48.4
Not case	54.2	68.9	35.6	85.4	40.0	75.4	81.3	59.5	54.3	50.0	73.3	67.2	51.6
Total n	48	45	45	48	35	57	16	42	35	48	45	61	31
Chi-square	n.s.		24.338*****		11.554****			n.s.		5.330**		n.s.	
(df)			(1)		(1)					(1)			
OR			10.581		4.598					2.745			

* $p < .10$, ** $p < .05$, *** $p < .01$, **** $p < .001$, ***** $p < .0001$

[a] DSM-III caseness criteria as assessed by the Diagnostic Interview Schedule.

Table 5.43 Indicators of Psychological Distress by Disclosed Child Maltreatment in the Hollywood Homeless Youth Sample

	3-category maltreatment			2-category maltreatment	
	1. No sexual or physical assault	2. Physical assault	3. Sexual ± physical assault	No sexual assault	Sexual ± physical assault
Distress	(%)	(%)	(%)	(%)	(%)
Trait anxiety[a]					
Low sx count	61.5	57.1	37.9	58.2	37.9
High sx count	38.5	42.9	62.1	41.8	62.1
Total *n*	13	42	29	55	29
Chi-square (df)		n.s.		3.117* (1)	
$OR_{1,2}$				2.277	
Current depression[b]					
Not case	83.3	85.0	65.5	84.6	65.5
Case	16.7	15.0	34.5	15.4	34.5
Total *n*	12	40	29	52	29
Chi-square (df)		n.s.		3.929** (1)	
$OR_{1,2}$				2.895	
Lifetime major depression[c]					
Low sx count	69.2	61.9	37.9	63.6	37.9
High sx count	30.8	38.1	62.1	36.4	62.1
Total *n*	13	42	29	55	29
Chi-square (df)		5.280* (2)		5.065** (1)	
$OR_{1,2}$		1.383		2.864	
$OR_{2,3}$		2.662			
$OR_{1,3}$		3.681			
Suicide thoughts[c]					
Never	61.5	43.9	7.1	48.1	7.1
Ever	38.5	56.1	92.9	51.9	92.9
Total *n*	13	41	28	54	28
Chi-square (df)		15.153**** (2)		13.788**** (1)	
$OR_{1,2}$		2.041		12.071	
$OR_{2,3}$		10.239			
$OR_{1,3}$		20.901			

(table continues)

Table 5.43 continued

	3-category maltreatment			2-category maltreatment	
	1. No sexual or physical assault (%)	2. Physical assault (%)	3. Sexual ± physical assault (%)	No sexual assault (%)	Sexual ± physical assault (%)
Suicide attempts[c]					
Never	69.2	53.7	35.7	57.4	35.7
Ever	30.8	46.3	64.3	42.6	64.3
Total *n*	13	41	28	54	28
Chi-square (df)		n.s.		3.471* (1)	
$OR_{1,2}$				2.426	
Lifetime drug abuse &/or dependence[c]					
None	61.5	45.2	27.6	49.1	27.6
≥1 symptom	38.5	54.8	72.4	50.9	72.4
Total *n*	13	42	29	55	29
Chi-square (df)		4.698* (2)		3.613* (1)	
$OR_{1,2}$		1.937		2.531	
$OR_{2,3}$		2.164			
$OR_{1,3}$		4.190			
Post-traumatic stress disorder[d]					
Low sx count	84.6	52.4	44.8	60.0	44.8
High sx count	15.4	47.6	55.2	40.0	55.2
Total *n*	13	42	29	55	29
Chi-square (df)		5.928* (2)		n.s.	
$OR_{1,2}$		4.990			
$OR_{2,3}$		1.356			
$OR_{1,3}$		6.769			
Conduct disorder[e]					
Not case	53.8	35.7	17.2	40.0	17.2
Case	46.2	64.3	82.8	60.0	82.8
Total *n*	13	42	29	55	29
Chi-square (df)		6.005** (2)		4.509** (1)	
$OR_{1,2}$		2.097		3.200	
$OR_{2,3}$		2.673			
$OR_{1,3}$		5.606			

* $p < .10$, ** $p < .05$, *** $p < .01$, **** $p < .001$

[a] Measured by the Revised Children's Manifest Anxiety Scale. [b] Caseness criterion for current depression is ≥19 symptoms as measured by the Children's Depression Inventory. [c] DSM-III criteria measured by the Diagnostic Interview Schedule. [d] DSM-IIIR criteria measured by the Diagnostic Interview Schedule. [e] DSM-IIIR criteria measured by the Diagnostic Interview for Children and Adolescents--symptomatic when not homeless, excluding runaway symptom.

Table 5.44 Comorbidity of Indicators of Psychological Distress by Disclosed Child Maltreatment in the Hollywood Homeless Youth Sample

Distress	3-category maltreatment			2-category maltreatment	
	1. No sexual or physical assault (%)	2. Physical assault (%)	3. Sexual ± physical assault (%)	No sexual assault (%)	Sexual ± physical assault (%)
Number of lifetime diagnoses[a]					
0-2	84.6	61.9	44.8	67.3	44.8
3-4	15.4	38.1	55.2	32.7	55.2
Total *n*	13	42	29	55	29
Chi-square (df)		6.096** (2)		3.970* (1)	
$OR_{1,2}$		3.381		2.530	
$OR_{2,3}$		2.002			
$OR_{1,3}$		6.769			
Number of current diagnoses[b]					
0	83.3	82.5	62.1	82.7	62.1
1-2	16.7	17.5	37.9	17.3	37.9
Total *n*	12	40	29	52	29
Chi-square (df)		n.s.		4.258* (1)	
$OR_{1,2}$				2.920	
$OR_{2,3}$					
$OR_{1,3}$					

* $p < .10$, ** $p < .05$, *** $p < .01$

[a]Includes major depression, PTSD, alcohol abuse and/or dependence, drug abuse and/or dependence, and/or conduct disorder

[b]Includes trait anxiety and/or current depression

Table 5.45 Perceived Own and Relative's Health by Disclosed Child Maltreatment in the Hollywood Homeless Youth Sample

	3-category maltreatment			2-category maltreatment	
Perceived health	1. No sexual or physical assault (%)	2. Physical assault (%)	3. Sexual ± physical assault (%)	No sexual assault (%)	Sexual ± physical assault (%)
Have mental health problem					
No	84.6	76.2	48.3	78.2	48.3
Yes	15.4	23.8	51.7	21.8	51.7
Total *n*	13	42	29	55	29
Chi-square (df)		8.109** (2)		7.786*** (1)	
$OR_{1,2}$		1.716		3.839	
$OR_{2,3}$		3.427			
$OR_{1,3}$		5.880			
Health since left home					
Worse	23.31	28.6	7.1	27.3	7.1
Better	76.9	71.4	92.9	72.7	92.9
Total *n*	13	42	28	55	28
Chi-square (df)		4.800* (2)		4.616** (1)	
$OR_{1,2}$		0.750		4.875	
$OR_{2,3}$		5.241			
$OR_{1,3}$		3.930			
Relatives have mental health problem					
No	100.0	70.0	46.4	76.9	46.4
Yes	--	30.0	53.6	23.1	53.6
Total *n*	12	40	28	52	28
Chi-square (df)		11.285*** (2)		7.569*** (1)	
$OR_{1,2}$		--		3.846	
$OR_{2,3}$		2.695			
$OR_{1,3}$		--			

* $p < .10$, ** $p < .05$, *** $p < .01$, **** $p < .001$

Table 5.46 Self-Protective Actions by Disclosed Child Maltreatment in the Hollywood Homeless Youth Sample

	3-category maltreatment			2-category maltreatment	
Self-protective actions	1. No sexual or physical assault (%)	2. Physical assault (%)	3. Sexual ± physical assault (%)	No sexual assault (%)	Sexual ± physical assault (%)
Sleep during the day					
No	92.3	77.5	69.0	81.1	69.0
Yes	7.7	22.5	31.0	18.9	31.0
Total *n*	13	40	29	53	29
Chi-square (df)		n.s.		n.s.	
Avoid certain places					
No	53.8	22.5	31.0	30.2	31.0
Yes	46.2	77.5	69.0	69.8	69.0
Total *n*	13	40	29	53	29
Chi-square (df)		n.s.		n.s.	
Avoid certain people					
No	84.6	45.0	34.5	54.7	34.5
Yes	15.4	55.0	65.5	45.3	65.5
Total *n*	13	40	29	53	29
Chi-square (df)		9.251***		3.077*	
$OR_{1,2}$		6.714		2.296	
$OR_{2,3}$		1.553			
$OR_{1,3}$		10.430			
Stay with trusted people					
No	15.4	30.0	117.2	26.4	17.2
Yes	84.6	70.0	82.8	73.6	82.8
Total *n*	13	40	29	53	29
Chi-square (df)		n.s.		n.s.	

(table continues)

Table 5.46 continued

Self-protective actions	3-category maltreatment: 1. No sexual or physical assault (%)	2. Physical assault (%)	3. Sexual ± physical assault (%)	2-category maltreatment: No sexual assault (%)	Sexual ± physical assault (%)
Carry a weapon					
No	61.5	52.5	34.5	54.7	34.5
Yes	38.5	47.5	65.5	45.3	65.5
Total n	13	40	29	53	29
Chi-square (df)		n.s.		3.077*	
$OR_{1,2}$				2.296	
$OR_{2,3}$					
$OR_{1,3}$					

* $p < .10$, ** $p < .05$, *** $p < .01$

Table 5.47 Comorbidity[a] of Caseness Among Measures of Psychological Distress[b] in the Hollywood Homeless Youth Sample

Caseness	Lifetime drug dependence &/or abuse[c]		Lifetime alcohol dependence &/or abuse[c]		Ever attempted suicide		Lifetime major depression[c]		Current depression[d]		Lifetime conduct disorder[e]	
	Not case (%)	Case (%)	Not case (%)	Case (%)	Not case (%)	Case (%)	Not case (%)	Case (%)	Not case (%)	Case (%)	Not case (%)	Case (%)
Lifetime alcohol dependence &/or abuse	37.3	67.6										
	$\chi^2 = 7.538$** OR = 3.521											
Ever attempted suicide	45.1	52.9	41.9	54.8								
Lifetime major depression	27.5	29.4	32.6	23.8	27.3	29.3						
Current depression	17.6	29.4	20.9	23.8	15.9	29.3	16.4	37.5				
							$\chi^2 = 4.421$* OR = 3.060					

(table continues)

Table 5.47 continued

Caseness	Lifetime drug dependence &/or abuse[c]		Lifetime alcohol dependence &/or abuse[c]		Ever attempted suicide		Lifetime major depression[c]		Current depression[d]		Lifetime conduct disorder[e]	
	Not case (%)	Case (%)	Not case (%)	Case (%)	Not case (%)	Case (%)	Not case (%)	Case (%)	Not case (%)	Case (%)	Not case (%)	Case (%)
Lifetime conduct disorder	54.9	88.2	46.5	90.5	63.6	73.2	70.5	62.5	68.2	68.4		
	χ^2 = 10.458** OR = 6.161		χ^2 = 18.947**** OR = 10.925									
Lifetime PTSD[f]	15.7	26.5	16.3	23.8	20.5	19.5	19.7	20.8	21.2	15.8	11.1	24.1

Total $n = 85$ for each analysis. * $p < .05$, ** $p < .01$, *** $p < .001$, **** $p < .0001$. [a] Association as measured by Pearson chi-square. [b] Caseness on anxiety is not included due to few cases ($n = 6$). [c] DSM-III criteria for caseness met as assessed by the Diagnostic Interview Schedule (DIS). Diagnostic criteria for depression caseness did not differ significantly between the DSM-III and the DSM-IIIR. Most cases defined by the DSM-III as alcohol or drug abuse are classified as alcohol or drug dependence in the DSM-IIIR. The substance "abuse" diagnostic category has been retained in the DSM-IIIR to capture cases which do not qualify as dependence yet meet criteria for maladaptive patterns of use. [d] Caseness as assessed by the Childhood Depression Inventory (CDI) = a score ≥ 19. [e] DSM-IIIR criteria for caseness met as assessed by the Diagnostic Interview for Children and Adolescents (DICA). Running away was not included as a symptom. Symptoms that were present when the respondent was not homeless were used to ascertain caseness. [f] Although DSM-IIIR criteria for caseness requires the presence of at least three symptoms of avoidance or numbing of stimuli associated with the trauma, the DIS only assesses two symptoms. Thus, two symptoms of avoidance or numbing of stimuli were required for caseness in this study.

Table 5.48 Comorbidity[a] of Symptom Counts Among Measures of Psychological Distress in the Hollywood Homeless Youth Sample

	Lifetime drug dependence &/or abuse[b]		Lifetime alcohol dependence &/or abuse[b]		Ever attempted suicide[b]		Lifetime major depression[b]		Current depression[c]		Lifetime conduct disorder[d]		Lifetime post-traumatic stress disorder[b]	
High sx count for	Low (%)	High (%)	Low (%)	High (%)	Low (%)	High (%)	Low (%)	High (%)	Low (%)	High (%)	Low (%)	High (%)	Low (%)	High (%)
Lifetime alcohol dependence &/or abuse	36.8	60.0												
	$\chi^2 = 4.821$** OR = 2.571													
Ever attempted suicide	45.7	50.0	40.9	55.3										
Lifetime major depression	48.6	44.0	50.0	38.3	45.5	46.3								

(table continues)

Table 5.48 continued

High sx count for	Lifetime drug dependence &/or abuse[b]		Lifetime alcohol dependence &/or abuse[b]		Ever attempted suicide[b]		Lifetime major depression[b]		Current depression[c]		Lifetime conduct disorder[d]		Lifetime post-traumatic stress disorder[b]	
	Low (%)	High (%)	Low (%)	High (%)	Low (%)	High (%)	Low (%)	High (%)	Low (%)	High (%)	Low (%)	High (%)	Low (%)	High (%)
Current depression	62.9	42.0	53.3	45.7	43.2	58.5	30.4	74.4						
	$\chi^2 = 3.583$* OR = 0.428						$\chi^2 =$ 16.290***** OR = 6.629							
Lifetime conduct disorder	34.3	68.0	28.3	76.6	50.0	58.5	56.5	51.3	64.3	44.2				
	$\chi^2 =$ 9.425*** OR = 4.073		$\chi^2 =$ 21.788***** OR = 8.308						$\chi^2 =$ 3.457* OR = 0.440					

(table continues)

Table 5.48 continued

High sx count for	Lifetime drug dependence &/or abuse[b]		Lifetime alcohol dependence &/or abuse[b]		Ever attempted suicide[b]		Lifetime major depression[b]		Current depression[c]		Lifetime conduct disorder[d]		Lifetime post-traumatic stress disorder[b]	
	Low (%)	High (%)	Low (%)	High (%)	Low (%)	High (%)	Low (%)	High (%)	Low (%)	High (%)	Low (%)	High (%)	Low (%)	High (%)
Lifetime post-traumatic stress disorder[b]	42.9	56.0	43.5	54.3	38.6	63.4	37.0	66.7	47.6	53.5	41.0	58.7		
					χ^2 = 5.213** OR = 2.753		χ^2 = 7.453*** OR = 3.412							
Trait anxiety[e]	57.1	46.0	55.6	43.5	45.5	56.1	32.6	71.8	23.8	76.7	61.5	41.3	40.5	60.5
							χ^2 = 12.966**** OR = 5.261		χ^2 = 23.818***** OR = 10.560		χ^2 = 3.457* OR = 0.440		χ^2 = 3.396* OR = 2.249	

(table continues)

Table 5.48 continued

Total $n = 85$ for each analysis.

* $p < .01$, ** $p < .05$, *** $p < .01$, **** $p < .001$, ***** $p < .0001$

[a] Association as measured by Pearson chi-square.

[b] As assessed by the Diagnostic Interview Schedule (DIS).

[c] As assessed by the Children's Diagnostic Inventory (CDI).

[d] As assessed by the Diagnostic Interview Schedule for Children and Adolescents.

[e] As assessed by the Revised Children's Manifest Anxiety Scale.

Table 5.49 Comorbidity of Disclosed Indicators of Child Maltreatment in the Hollywood Homeless Youth Sample

	Ever physically assaulted		Ever sexually assaulted		Ever witnessed domestic violence	
	No (%)	Yes (%)	No (%)	Yes (%)	No (%)	Yes (%)
Ever sexually assaulted	23.5	37.3				
Ever witnessed domestic violence	17.6	55.2	38.2	65.5		
	$\chi^2 = 7.676^{**}$ OR = 5.756		$\chi^2 = 5.688^{*}$ OR = 3.076			
Ever neglected	52.9	73.1	60.0	86.2	52.3	87.5
			$\chi^2 = 6.102^{*}$ OR = 4.167		$\chi^2 = 12.166^{***}$ OR = 6.391	

Total $n = 84$ for each analysis.

* $p < .05$, ** $p < .01$, *** $p < .001$

Table 5.50 Recalled Age of First Symptoms of Psychological Distress and Involvement in Sex Work by Age of First Physical or Sexual Assault in the Hollywood Homeless Youth Sample

	Relative to the first exposure to maltreatment, the first symptoms of psychological distress began:			
	Before (%)	In the same year (%)	After (%)	Total *n*
Major depression[a]	23.5	17.6	58.8	17
Drug abuse and/or dependence[a]	6.3	12.5	81.3	16
Drug abuse with or without dependence; ignore severity[a]	8.0	8.0	84.0	25
Suicide thoughts[b]	10.2	12.2	77.6	49
Suicide attempts[b]	8.6	14.3	77.1	35
Symptoms of conduct disorder[c]	40.4	25.5	34.0	47
Symptoms of post-traumatic stress disorder[b]	12.5	6.3	81.3	16
First used alcohol[a]	25.4	12.7	61.9	63
Alcohol abuse with or without dependence; ignore severity[a]	12.0	20.0	68.0	25
Involved in sex work[d]	3.8	3.8	92.3	26

[a] DSM-III criteria for caseness met as assessed by the Diagnostic Interview Schedule.

[b] Symptoms assessed by the Diagnostic Interview Schedule.

[c] Symptoms assessed by the Diagnostic Interview for Children and Adolescents.

[d] Includes exchanging sex for a place to stay, food, drugs, or money, or for posing for pornographic photographs or films.

Table 5.51 Recalled Age of First Symptoms of Psychological Distress, Child Maltreatment, and Involvement in Sex Work by Age of First Homeless Episode in the Hollywood Homeless Youth Sample

	Relative to the first homelessness episode, the first symptoms of psychological distress began:			
	Before (%)	In the same year (%)	After (%)	Total *n*
Major depression[a]	45.5	4. 5	50.0	22
Drug abuse and/or dependence[a]	28.6	23.8	47.6	21
Suicide thoughts[b]	44.3	14.8	41.0	61
Suicide attempts[b]	37.2	18.6	44.2	43
Symptoms of conduct disorder[c]	88.0	9.8	2.2	92
Symptoms of post-traumatic stress disorder[b]	27.9	14.0	58.1	43
Alcohol abuse with or without dependence; ignore severity[a]	36.1	19.4	44.4	36
Involved in sex work[d]	12.1	18.2	69.7	33
Physical or sexual assault	74.6	14.9	10.4	67
Physical assault	69.4	19.4	11.3	62
Sexual assault	71.4	10.7	17.9	28

[a] DSM-III criteria for caseness met as assessed by the Diagnostic Interview Schedule.

[b] Symptoms assessed by the Diagnostic Interview Schedule.

[c] Symptoms assessed by the Diagnostic Interview for Children and Adolescents.

[d] Includes exchanging sex for a place to stay, food, drugs, or money, or for posing for pornographic photographs or films.

Table 5.52 Recalled Age of First Symptoms of Psychological Distress and Involvement in Sex Work by Age of First Drug Abuse and/or Dependence Symptoms in the Hollywood Homeless Youth Sample

	Relative to the first symptoms of drug abuse and/or dependence, the first symptoms of psychological distress began:			
	Before (%)	In the same year (%)	After (%)	Total *n*
Major depression[a]	50.0	25.0	25.0	8
Suicide thoughts[b]	45.0	20.0	35.0	20
Suicide attempts[b]	25.0	31.3	43.8	16
Symptoms of conduct disorder[c]	97.1	2.9	0	34
Symptoms of post-traumatic stress disorder[b]	15.8	31.6	52.6	19
Alcohol abuse with or without dependence; ignore severity[a]	47.4	31.6	21.1	19
Involved in sex work[d]	22.2	27.8	50.0	18

[a] DSM-III criteria for caseness met as assessed by the Diagnostic Interview Schedule.
[b] Symptoms assessed by the Diagnostic Interview Schedule.
[c] Symptoms assessed by the Diagnostic Interview for Children and Adolescents.
[d] Includes exchanging sex for a place to stay, food, drugs, or money, or for posing for pornographic photographs or films.

Table 5.53 Recalled Age of First Symptoms of Psychological Distress and Involvement in Sex Work by Age of First Alcohol Abuse and/or Dependence Symptoms in the Hollywood Homeless Youth Sample

	Relative to the first symptoms of alcohol abuse and/or dependence, the first symptoms of psychological distress began:			
	Before (%)	In the same year (%)	After (%)	Total *n*
Major depression[a]	66.7	0	33.3	6
Suicide thoughts[b]	39.1	21.7	39.1	23
Suicide attempts[b]	50.0	15.0	35.0	20
Symptoms of conduct disorder[c]	91.7	5.6	2.8	36
Symptoms of post-traumatic stress disorder[b]	31.8	22.7	45.5	22
Involved in sex work[d]	18.8	18.8	62.5	16

[a]DSM-III criteria for caseness met as assessed by the Diagnostic Interview Schedule. [b]Symptoms assessed by the Diagnostic Interview Schedule. [c]Symptoms assessed by the Diagnostic Interview for Children and Adolescents. [d]Includes exchanging sex for a place to stay, food, drugs, or money, or for posing for pornographic photographs or films.

Table 5.54 Number of Sexual Partners[a] by Disclosed Child Maltreatment in the Hollywood Homeless Youth Sample

	No physical or sexual assault (%)	Physical and/or sexual assault (%)
Number of sexual partners[a]		
0-3	23.1	52.2
4->95	76.9	47.8
Total *n*	13	69
Chi-square (df)	3.713* (1)	
OR	0.275	

* $p < .10$
[a] In the past 12 months.

Table 5.55 Involvement in Sex Work by Sexual Assault in the Hollywood Homeless Youth Sample

	No sexual assault (%)	Sexual assault (%)
Traded sex[a]		
Never	78.2	46.4
Ever	21.8	53.6
Total *n*	55	28
Chi-square (df)	8.524* (1)	
OR	4.135	

* $p < .01$
[a] For food, shelter, drugs, or money.

Table 5.56 Distribution of Sexual Revictimization Characteristics in the Hollywood Homeless Youth Sample

	%	Total *n*
Number of times sexually assaulted		29
1	34.5	
2-95	65.5	
Number of perpetrators		29
1	58.6	
2-6	41.4	
Revictimization[a]		29
No	62.1	
Yes	37.9	

[a] >1 perpetrator and >1 assault.

Table 5.57 Involvement in Sex Work by Sexual Revictimization in the Hollywood Homeless Youth Sample

	Number of times sexually assaulted		Number of perpetrators		Revictimization[b]	
	1 (%)	2-95 (%)	1 (%)	2-6 (%)	No (%)	Yes (%)
Traded sex[a]						
Never	80.0	33.3	62.5	25.0	64.7	27.3
Ever	20.0	66.7	37.5	75.0	35.3	72.7
Total *n*	10	18	16	12	17	11
Chi-square (df)	5.600** (1)		3.877** (1)		3.743* (1)	
OR	8.000		5.000		4.889	

* $p < .10$, ** $p < .05$, *** $p < .01$

[a] For food, shelter, drugs, or money.

[b] >1 perpetrator and >1 assault.

Table 5.58 Sexual Risk-Taking and Sexual Revictimization by Lifetime Homelessness Controlling for Sex in the Hollywood Homeless Youth Sample

	Percentage change (≥1 year - <1 year lifetime homelessness)			
		Partial table: Sex		
	Zero-order table	Male	Female	Total *n*
Has posed for sexual photographs or films	11.1	11.1	12.5	89
Has traded sex for food, shelter, drugs or money	18.3	10.5	38.9	92
Has been sexually revictimized	25.0	46.4	15.3	28
Has had a sexually transmitted disease	8.8	6.4	13.2	85
Did not use condom at last sexual encounter	2.1	-9.3	7.5	89
≥4 sexual partners in lifetime	1.8	11.1	-3.5	88

Table 5.59 Sexual Risk-Taking and Sexual Revictimization by Lifetime Homelessness Controlling for Race in the Hollywood Homeless Youth Sample

	Percentage change (≥1 year - <1 year lifetime homelessness)			
		Partial table: Race		
	Zero-order table	White[a]	Non-white	Total *n*
Has posed for sexual photographs or films	11.1	19.7	-4.5	89
Has traded sex for food, shelter, drugs or money	18.3	25.9	5.3	92
Has been sexually revictimized	25.0	58.9	-17.5	28
Has been or is pregnant	10.0	-10.0	36.7	36
Has had a sexually transmitted disease	8.8	9.4	9.1	85
Did not use condom at last sexual encounter	2.1	-2.7	-3.1	89
≥4 sexual partners in lifetime	1.8	-5.9	14.2	88

[a] White, non-Latino.

Table 5.60 Sexual Risk-Taking and Sexual Revictimization by Lifetime Homelessness Controlling for Age in the Hollywood Homeless Youth Sample

	Percentage change (≥1 year - <1 year lifetime homelessness)			
		Partial table: Age		
	Zero-order table	13-15 yrs.	16-17 yrs.	Total *n*
Has posed for sexual photographs or films	11.1	25.0	6.1	89
Has traded sex for food, shelter, drugs or money	18.3	44.7	6.5	92
Has been sexually revictimized	25.0	33.3	20.0	28
Has been or is pregnant	10.0	50.0	-22.7	36
Has had a sexually transmitted disease	8.8	0	8.0	85
Did not use condom at last sexual encounter	2.1	9.7	2.0	89
≥4 sexual partners in lifetime	1.8	-16.8	4.7	88

Table 5.61 Sexual Risk-Taking by Sexual Revictimization Controlling for Lifetime Homelessness in the Hollywood Homeless Youth Sample

	Percentage change (sexual revictimization - no sexual revictimization)			
		Partial table: Lifetime homelessness		
	Zero-order table	<1 year	>1 year	Total *n*
Has had a sexually transmitted disease	-5.6	-25.0	0	27
Has been or is pregnant	-38.3	-7.1	-60.0	17
Did not use condom at last sexual encounter	13.3	8.3	16.6	28
≥4 sexual partners in lifetime	14.4	13.6	10.0	26

Table 5.62 Indicators of Sexual Risk-Taking by Involvement in Prostitution Controlling for Lifetime Homelessness in the Hollywood Homeless Youth Sample

	Percentage change (prostitution-no prostitution)			
		Partial table: Lifetime homelessness		
	Zero-order table	< 1 year	> 1 year	Total *n*
Has had a sexually transmitted disease	25.4	30.3	16.6	84
Has been or is pregnant	23.5	48.3	0	35
Did not use condom at last sexual encounter	16.0	20.0	13.7	88

Table 5.63 Indicators of Psychological Distress by Sexual Revictimization in the Hollywood Homeless Youth Sample

	Number of times sexually assaulted		Number of perpetrators		Revictimization[a]	
	1 (%)	2-95 (%)	1 (%)	2-6 (%)	No (%)	Yes (%)
# of symptoms of major depression[b]						
Low	20.0	52.6	35.3	41.7	38.9	45.5
High	80.0	47.4	64.7	58.3	61.1	54.5
Total *n*	10	19	17	12	18	11
Chi-square	2.876*		n.s.		n.s.	
(df)	(1)					
OR	0.225					
Conduct disorder[c]						
Not case	30.0	15.8	29.4	--	33.3	--
Case	70.0	84.2	70.6	100.0	66.7	100.0
Total *n*	10	19	17	12	18	11
Chi-square	n.s.		Fisher's exact*		Fisher's exact**	
(df)						
OR			2.00		1.917	

* $p < .10$, ** $p < .05$

[a] >1 perpetrator and >1 assault.

[b] Assessed by the Diagnostic Interview Schedule.

[c] DSM-IIIR criteria for caseness assessed by the Diagnostic Interview for Children and Adolescents. Running away was not included as a symptom. Symptoms that were present when the respondent was not homeless were used to ascertain caseness.

Table 5.64 Indicators of Psychological Distress by Sexual Assault Controlling for Receipt of Mental Health Services in the Hollywood Homeless Youth Sample

	Percentage change (sexual assault-no sexual assault)			
		Partial table: Received mental health services		
	Zero-order table	No	Yes	Total *n*
Diagnoses	χ^2, O.R.	χ^2, O.R.	χ^2, O.R.	
# of current diagnoses[a] 1-2	23.6 5.738**, 3.667	26.8 8.256***, 9.231	-21.4 n.s.	78
# of lifetime diagnoses[b] 3-4	22.5 3.897**, 2.534	19.0 4.796**, 3.385	-7.1 n.s.	81
Lifetime suicide thoughts[c]	41.9 14.091****, 12.500	49.2 13.465****, 21.600	3.2 n.s.	79
Lifetime suicide attempts[c]	22.0 3.516*, 2.455	38.1 7.799***, 5.075	-41.3 2.861*, 0.133	80
Lifetime drug abuse and/or dependence[c,d]	15.6 n.s.	26.8 4.026**, 3.045	-12.9 n.s.	81
Lifetime alcohol abuse and/or dependence[c, d]	16.7 n.s.	15.7 n.s.	35.7 n.s.	81
Lifetime PTSD[c, e, f]	7.2 n.s.	10.0 n.s.	-8.6 n.s.	81
Lifetime major depression[c, d]	10.6 4.890**, 2.842	13.8 n.s.	-17.1 n.s.	81

(table continues)

Table 5.64 continued

	Percentage change (sexual assault-no sexual assault)			
		Partial table: Received mental health services		
	Zero-order table	No	Yes	Total n
Diagnoses	χ^2, O.R.	χ^2, O.R.	χ^2, O.R.	
Current depression[g]	22.3 5.525**, 3.772	29.2 10.979****, 18.923	-31.4 n.s.	78
Lifetime conduct disorder[e, h]	23.2 4.575**, 3.252	21.1 n.s.	18.6 n.s.	81
High symptom counts	χ^2, O.R.	χ^2, O.R.	χ^2, O.R.	
Trait anxiety[i]	21.7 3.506*, 2.416	21.5 n.s.	-20.0 n.s.	81
Lifetime drug abuse and/or dependence[c]	22.4 3.840*, 2.625	24.8 3.338*, 2.927	12.9 n.s.	81
Lifetime alcohol abuse and/or dependence[c]	12.9 n.s.	13.5 n.s.	21.4 n.s.	81
Lifetime PTSD[c]	16.7 n.s.	29.9 4.872**, 3.429	-31.4 n.s.	81
Lifetime major depression[c]	25.6 n.s.	26.8 4.026**, 3.045	-1.4 n.s.	81
Lifetime conduct disorder[h]	19.3 2.803*, 2.217	24.0 3.075*, 2.708	2.9 n.s.	81
Current depression[g]	9.0 n.s.	9.6 n.s.	-30.0 n.s.	81

(table continues)

Table 5.64 continued

*p<.10, **p<.05, ***p<.01, ****p<.001

[a] Current depression and/or trait anxiety. [b] Any combination of the following diagnoses: major depression, substance abuse and/or dependence, post-traumatic stress disorder and/or conduct disorder. [c] Assessed by the Diagnostic Interview Schedule. [d] Met DSM-III criteria for caseness. [e] Met DSM-IIIR criteria for caseness. [f] Only 2 symptoms of avoidance or numbing were required for caseness. [g] Assessed by the Children's Depression Inventory. Caseness criterion is 19 or more symptoms. [h] Assessed by the Diagnostic Interview Schedule for Children & Adolescents. Caseness excludes symptoms of running away. All symptoms have occurred while the respondent was <u>not</u> homeless. [i] Assessed by the Revised Children's Manifest Anxiety Scale.

Table 5.65 Indicators of Psychological Distress by Sexual Assault Controlling for Having a Regular Medical Provider in the Hollywood Homeless Youth Sample

	Percentage change (sexual assault--no sexual assault)			
		Partial table: Have a regular medical provider		
	Zero-order table	No	Yes	Total *n*
Diagnoses	χ^2, O.R.	χ^2, O.R.	χ^2, O.R.	
# of current diagnoses[a] 1-2	20.7 3.887*, 3.025	32.9 4.525**, 6.133	9.8 n.s.	70
# of lifetime diagnoses[b] 3-4	16.3 n.s.	0 n.s.	33.4 4.208**, 4.375	72
Lifetime suicide thoughts[c]	40.0 11.873****, 10.957	37.5 3.552*, 7.000	38.8 7.259***, 13.600	70
Lifetime suicide attempts[c]	24.5 3.916*, 2.728	30.6 n.s.	25.8 n.s.	70
Lifetime drug abuse and/or dependence[c, d]	11.1 n.s.	3.7 n.s.	22.2 n.s.	72
Lifetime alcohol abuse and/or dependence[c, d]	15.6 n.s.	7.5 n.s.	27.8 2.857*, 3.250	72
Lifetime PTSD[c, e, f]	0.7 n.s.	-3.7 n.s.	0 n.s.	72
Lifetime major depression[c, d]	8.9 n.s.	7.4 n.s.	11.1 n.s.	72
Current depression[g]	19.3 3.700*, 3.083	32.9 4.525**, 6.133	10.2 n.s.	70

(table continues)

Table 5.65 continued

	Percentage change (sexual assault--no sexual assault)			
		Partial table: Have a regular medical provider		
	Zero-order table	No	Yes	Total *n*
Diagnoses	χ^2, O.R.	χ^2, O.R.	χ^2, O.R.	
Lifetime conduct disorder[e, h]	27.4 5.831**, 4.202	40.7 5.280**[j]	22.2 n.s.	72
High symptom counts	χ^2, O.R.	χ^2, O.R.	χ^2, O.R.	
Trait anxiety[i]	16.3 n.s.	0 n.s.	22.2 n.s.	72
Lifetime drug abuse and/or dependence[c]	17.1 n.s.	7.4 n.s.	27.8 2.857*, 3.250	72
Lifetime alcohol abuse and/or dependence[c]	13.4 n.s.	3.7 n.s.	27.8 2.857*; 3.250	72
Lifetime PTSD[c]	7.5 n.s.	-14.8 n.s.	22.2 n.s.	72
Lifetime major depression[c]	19.3 n.s.	14.9 n.s.	22.2 n.s.	72
Lifetime conduct disorder[h]	26.7 4.800**, 3.000	14.8 n.s.	44.5 7.200***, 7.000	72
Current depression[g]	8.9 n.s.	0 n.s.	22.3 n.s.	72

(table continues)

Table 5.65 continued

*p<.10, **p<.05, ***p<.01, ****p<.001

[a] Current depression and/or trait anxiety. [b] Any combination of the following diagnoses: major depression, substance abuse and/or dependence, post-traumatic stress disorder and/or conduct disorder. [c] Assessed by the Diagnostic Interview Schedule. [d] Met DSM-III criteria for caseness. [e] Met DSM-IIIR criteria for caseness. [f] Only 2 symptoms of avoidance or numbing were required for caseness. [g] Assessed by the Children's Depression Inventory. Caseness criterion is 19 or more symptoms. [h] Assessed by the Diagnostic Interview Schedule for Children & Adolescents. Caseness excludes symptoms of running away. All symptoms have occurred while the respondent was not homeless. [i] Assessed by the Revised Children's Manifest Anxiety Scale. [j] Unable to calculate odds ratio due to the presence of an empty cell.

Table 5.66 Indicators of Psychological Distress by Sexual Assault Controlling for a Relative Having a Mental Health Problem in the Hollywood Homeless Youth Sample

	Percentage change (sexual assault-no sexual assault)			
		Partial table: Relative had a mental disorder		
	Zero-order table	No	Yes	Total n
Diagnoses	χ^2, O.R.	χ^2, O.R.	χ^2, O.R.	
# of current diagnoses[a] 1-2	17.3 2.885*, 2.469	14.6 n.s.	15.0 n.s.	77
# of lifetime diagnoses[b] 3-4	24.8 4.747**, 2.846	26.2 3.453*, 3.429	1.7 n.s.	80
Lifetime suicide thoughts[c]	37.7 11.515****, 10.268	49.8 9.823***, 16.235	-7.1 n.s.	78
Lifetime suicide attempts[c]	19.9 2.776*, 2.241	38.4 5.991**, 5.062	-26.2 n.s.	78
Lifetime drug abuse and/or dependence[c, d]	15.0 n.s.	16.0 n.s.	-5.0 n.s.	80
Lifetime alcohol abuse and/or dependence[c, d]	15.1 n.s.	8.7 n.s.	18.3 n.s.	80
Lifetime PTSD[c, e, f]	7.9 n.s.	10.6 n.s.	3.3 n.s.	80
Lifetime major depression[c, d]	14.5 n.s.	13.5 3.284*, 3.542	-8.4 n.s.	80

(table continues)

Table 5.66 continued

	Percentage change (sexual assault-no sexual assault)			
		Partial table: Relative had a mental disorder		
	Zero-order table	No	Yes	Total *n*
Diagnoses	χ^2, O.R.	χ^2, O.R.	χ^2, O.R.	
Current depression[g]	15.8 n.s.	17.3 n.s.	8.3 n.s.	77
Lifetime conduct disorder[e, h]	24.4 4.866**, 3.373	26.9 2.895*, 3.333	3.4 n.s.	80
High symptom counts	χ^2, O.R.	χ^2, O.R.	χ^2, O.R.	
Trait anxiety[i]	18.4 n.s.	3.7 n.s.	31.6 2.769*, 3.850	80
Lifetime drug abuse and/or dependence[c]	21.0 3.420*, 2.500	19.0 n.s.	5.0 n.s.	80
Lifetime alcohol abuse and/or dependence[c]	13.2 n.s.	6.2 n.s.	18.3 n.s.	80
Lifetime PTSD[c]	15.1 n.s.	8.5 n.s.	0 n.s.	80
Lifetime major depression[c]	25.0 4.298**, 2.684	23.8 n.s.	8.4 n.s.	80
Lifetime conduct disorder[h]	23.9 4.161**, 2.657	31.5 4.154*, 3.733	-8.3 n.s.	80
Current depression[g]	7.4 n.s.	8.8 n.s.	3.3 n.s.	80

(table continues)

Table 5.66 continued

*$p<.10$, **$p<.05$, ***$p<.01$, ****$p<.001$

[a] Current depression and/or trait anxiety. [b] Any combination of the following diagnoses: major depression, substance abuse and/or dependence, post-traumatic stress disorder and/or conduct disorder. [c] Assessed by the Diagnostic Interview Schedule. [d] Met DSM-III criteria for caseness. [e] Met DSM-IIIR criteria for caseness. [f] Only 2 symptoms of avoidance or numbing were required for caseness. [g] Assessed by the Children's Depression Inventory. Caseness criterion is 19 or more symptoms. [h] Assessed by the Diagnostic Interview Schedule for Children & Adolescents. Caseness excludes symptoms of running away. All symptoms have occurred while the respondent was <u>not</u> homeless. [i] Assessed by the Revised Children's Manifest Anxiety Scale.

Table 5.67 Indicators of Psychological Distress by Sexual Assault Controlling for a Relative Having an Alcohol Problem in the Hollywood Homeless Youth Sample

	Percentage change (sexual assault-no sexual assault)			
		Partial table: Relative had an alcohol problem		
	Zero-order table	No	Yes	Total *n*
Diagnoses	χ^2, O.R.	χ^2, O.R.	χ^2, O.R.	
# of current diagnoses[a] 1-2	21.6 4.615**, 3.132	11.9 n.s.	27.0 3.570*, 3.800	78
# of lifetime diagnoses[b] 3-4	24.4 4.639**, 2.769	14.5 n.s.	30.7 3.858**, 3.592	81
Lifetime suicide thoughts[c]	39.9 14.091****, 12.500	50.0 8.580***[j]	36.0 5.794**, 6.875	79
Lifetime suicide attempts[c]	23.1 3.862**, 2.571	38.9 4.824**, 6.000	13.8 n.s.	79
Lifetime drug abuse and/or dependence[c, d]	17.5 n.s.	3.2 n.s.	22.0 n.s.	81
Lifetime alcohol abuse and/or dependence[c, d]	16.7 n.s.	38.2 4.713**, 5.067	0.9 n.s.	81
Lifetime PTSD[c, e, f]	7.2 n.s.	-4.7 n.s.	14.8 n.s.	81
Lifetime major depression[c, d]	12.7 n.s.	22.6 n.s.	2.9 n.s.	81

(table continues)

Table 5.67 continued

	Percentage change (sexual assault-no sexual assault)			
		Partial table: Relative had an alcohol problem		
	Zero-order table	No	Yes	Total n
Diagnoses	χ^2, O.R.	χ^2, O.R.	χ^2, O.R.	
Current depression[g]	20.2 4.360**, 3.158	15.8 n.s.	21.5 n.s.	78
Lifetime conduct disorder[e, h]	25.1 5.264**, 3.520	32.3 3.790*, 7.059	21.3 n.s.	81
High symptom counts	χ^2, O.R.	χ^2, O.R.	χ^2, O.R.	
Trait anxiety[i]	21.7 3.506*, 2.416	20.0 n.s.	18.9 n.s.	81
Lifetime drug abuse and/or dependence[c]	22.4 3.840*, 2.625	2.8 n.s.	35.5 5.487**, 5.455	81
Lifetime alcohol abuse and/or dependence[c]	12.9 n.s.	34.8 3.872**, 4.364	-3.4 n.s.	81
Lifetime PTSD[c]	16.7 n.s.	4.1 n.s.	26.3 2.815*, 2.946	81
Lifetime major depression[c]	25.6 4.890**, 2.842	32.6 3.532*, 3.889	17.6 n.s.	81
Lifetime conduct disorder[h]	21.3 3.379*, 2.396	31.3 3.135*, 3.778	13.3 n.s.	81
Current depression[g]	9.0 n.s.	18.8 n.s.	2.2 n.s.	81

(table continues)

(Table 5.67 continued)

$*p<.10$, $**p<.05$, $***p<.01$, $****p<.001$

[a] Current depression and/or trait anxiety. [b] Any combination of the following diagnoses: major depression, substance abuse and/or dependence, post-traumatic stress disorder and/or conduct disorder. [c] Assessed by the Diagnostic Interview Schedule. [d] Met DSM-III criteria for caseness. [e] Met DSM-IIIR criteria for caseness. [f] Only 2 symptoms of avoidance or numbing were required for caseness. [g] Assessed by the Children's Depression Inventory. Caseness criterion is 19 or more symptoms. [h] Assessed by the Diagnostic Interview Schedule for Children & Adolescents. Caseness excludes symptoms of running away. All symptoms have occurred while the respondent was not homeless. [i] Assessed by the Revised Children's Manifest Anxiety Scale. [j] Unable to calculate odds ratio due to the presence of an empty cell.

Table 5.68 Indicators of Psychological Distress by Sexual Assault Controlling for a Relative Having a Drug Problem in the Hollywood Homeless Youth Sample

	Percentage change (sexual assault-no sexual assault)			
		Partial table: Relative had a drug problem		
	Zero-order table	No	Yes	Total *n*
Diagnoses	χ^2, O.R.	χ^2, O.R.	χ^2, O.R.	
# of current diagnoses[a] 1-2	22.1 4.826**, 3.519	15.3 n.s.	33.3 2.794*, 5.000	72
# of lifetime diagnoses[b] 3-4	27.4 n.s.	27.0 3.684*, 3.125	-8.3 n.s.	75
Lifetime suicide thoughts[c]	44.8 14.869****, 13.636	51.4 14.018****[j]	32.3 n.s.	73
Lifetime suicide attempts[c]	21.7 3.193*, 2.416	36.6 6.344**, 5.000	-8.4 n.s.	73
Lifetime drug abuse and/or dependence[c, d]	10.2 n.s.	10.3 3.482*, 3.012	1.7 n.s.	75
Lifetime alcohol abuse and/or dependence[c, d]	13.2 n.s.	26.8 n.s.	-18.3 n.s.	75
Lifetime PTSD[c, e, f]	6.5 n.s.	2.4 n.s.	13.3 n.s.	75
Lifetime major depression[c, d]	14.4 n.s.	24.6 4.108**, 3.818	-11.7 n.s.	75

(table continues)

Table 5.68 continued

	Percentage change (sexual assault-no sexual assault)			
		Partial table: Relative had a drug problem		
	Zero-order table	No	Yes	Total *n*
Diagnoses	χ^2, O.R.	χ^2, O.R.	χ^2, O.R.	
Current depression[g]	20.7 4.717**, 3.695	18.4 2.903*, 3.718	23.3 n.s.	72
Lifetime conduct disorder[e, h]	18.3 2.839*, 2.607	34.6 6.346**, 6.737	-21.7 n.s.	75
High symptom counts	χ^2, O.R.	χ^2, O.R.	χ^2, O.R.	
Trait anxiety[i]	22.4 3.543*, 2.490	18.5 n.s.	28.3 n.s.	75
Lifetime drug abuse and/or dependence[c]	14.0 n.s.	15.3 n.s.	5.0 n.s.	75
Lifetime alcohol abuse and/or dependence[c]	8.9 n.s.	21.1 n.s.	-18.3 n.s.	75
Lifetime PTSD[c]	19.6 2.760*, 2.236	27.0 3.684*, 3.125	0 n.s.	75
Lifetime major depression[c]	24.5 4.265**, 2.727	24.2 2.892*, 2.727	20.0 n.s.	75
Lifetime conduct disorder[h]	13.2 n.s.	13.8 n.s.	-15.0 n.s.	75
Current depression[g]	6.8 n.s.	7.1 n.s.	1.7 n.s.	75

(table continues)

Table 5.68 continued

*$p<.10$, **$p<.05$, ***$p<.01$, ****$p<.001$

[a] Current depression and/or trait anxiety. [b] Any combination of the following diagnoses: major depression, substance abuse and/or dependence, post-traumatic stress disorder and/or conduct disorder. [c] Assessed by the Diagnostic Interview Schedule. [d] Met DSM-III criteria for caseness. [e] Met DSM-IIIR criteria for caseness. [f] Only 2 symptoms of avoidance or numbing were required for caseness. [g] Assessed by the Children's Depression Inventory. Caseness criterion is 19 or more symptoms. [h] Assessed by the Diagnostic Interview Schedule for Children & Adolescents. Caseness excludes symptoms of running away. All symptoms have occurred while the respondent was not homeless. [i] Assessed by the Revised Children's Manifest Anxiety Scale. [j] Unable to calculate odds ratio due to the presence of an empty cell.

Table 5.69 Indicators of Psychological Distress by Sexual Assault Controlling for Father's Educational Level in the Hollywood Homeless Youth Sample

	Percentage change (sexual assault-no sexual assault)			
		Partial table: Father's educational level		
	Zero-order table	0-11th grade	≥12th grade	Total *n*
Diagnoses	χ^2, O.R.	χ^2, O.R.	χ^2, O.R.	
# of current diagnoses[a] 1-2	17.0 n.s.	8.3 n.s.	24.4 n.s.	59
# of lifetime diagnoses[b] 3-4	25.3 3.595*, 2.817	38.9 3.500*, 8.000	34.0 3.255*, 4.500	62
Lifetime suicide thoughts[c]	29.0 5.444**, 5.760	24.2 n.s.	29.5 2.721*, 5.474	61
Lifetime suicide attempts[c]	16.2 n.s.	-1.1 n.s.	30.9 n.s.	61
Lifetime drug abuse and/or dependence[c, d]	22.1 n.s.	27.8 n.s.	22.9 n.s.	62
Lifetime alcohol abuse and/or dependence[c, d]	15.6 n.s.	38.9 3.500*, 8.000	21.5 n.s.	62
Lifetime PTSD[c, e, f]	14.0 n.s.	-5.5 n.s.	31.9 4.564**, 5.600	62
Lifetime major depression[c, d]	11.3 n.s.	11.1 n.s.	11.4 n.s.	62
Current depression[g]	12.2 n.s.	0 n.s.	24.4 n.s.	59

(table continues)

Table 5.69 continued

	Percentage change (sexual assault-no sexual assault)			
		Partial table: Father's educational level		
	Zero-order table	0-11th grade	≥12th grade	Total *n*
Diagnoses	χ^2, O.R.	χ^2, O.R.	χ^2, O.R.	
Lifetime conduct disorder[e, h]	24.7 3.999**, 3.840	50.0 5.452**, 10.000	20.1 n.s.	62
High symptom counts	χ^2, O.R.	χ^2, O.R.	χ^2, O.R.	
Trait anxiety[i]	8.5 n.s.	2.7 n.s.	3.8 n.s.	62
Lifetime drug abuse and/or dependence[c]	22.5 2.972*, 2.764	50.0 5.452**, 10.000	7.3 n.s.	62
Lifetime alcohol abuse and/or dependence[c]	10.7 n.s.	38.9 3.500*, 8.000	15.3 n.s.	62
Lifetime PTSD[c]	22.9 2.920*, 2.539	13.9 n.s.	29.2 n.s.	62
Lifetime major depression[c]	23.0 3.016*, 2.571	22.3 n.s.	13.1 n.s.	62
Lifetime conduct disorder[h]	22.6 2.898*,2.625	44.5 4.073**, 7.000	21.5 n.s.	62
Current depression[g]	-6.1 n.s.	-25.0 n.s.	5.6 n.s.	62

(table continues)

Table 5.69 continued

**p*<.10, ***p*<.05, ****p*<.01, *****p*<.001

[a] Current depression and/or trait anxiety. [b] Any combination of the following diagnoses: major depression, substance abuse and/or dependence, post-traumatic stress disorder and/or conduct disorder. [c] Assessed by the Diagnostic Interview Schedule. [d] Met DSM-III criteria for caseness. [e] Met DSM-IIIR criteria for caseness. [f] Only 2 symptoms of avoidance or numbing were required for caseness. [g] Assessed by the Children's Depression Inventory. Caseness criterion is 19 or more symptoms. [h] Assessed by the Diagnostic Interview Schedule for Children & Adolescents. Caseness excludes symptoms of running away. All symptoms have occurred while the respondent was <u>not</u> homeless. [i] Assessed by the Revised Children's Manifest Anxiety Scale. [j] Unable to calculate odds ratio due to the presence of an empty cell.

Table 5.70 Indicators of Psychological Distress by Sexual Assault Controlling for the Length of Lifetime Homelessness in the Hollywood Homeless Youth Sample

	Percentage change (sexual assault-no sexual assault)			
		Partial table: Lifetime homelessness		
	Zero-order table	< 1 year	≥ 1 year	Total *n*
Diagnoses	χ^2, O.R.	χ^2, O.R.	χ^2, O.R.	
# of current diagnoses[a] 1-2	22.0 4.689**, 3.092	19.9 n.s.	25.0 n.s.	80
# of lifetime diagnoses[b] 3-4	20.9 3.366*, 2.372	31.3 4.779**, 3.857	2.6 n.s.	83
Lifetime suicide thoughts[c]	40.7 13.209****, 11.607	41.7 9.369***[j]	42.9 5.088**, 7.071	81
Lifetime suicide attempts[c]	24.1 4.173**, 2.696	8.3 n.s.	46.5 6.261**, 12.500	81
Lifetime drug abuse and/or dependence[c, d]	13.7 n.s.	4.2 n.s.	26.7 n.s.	83
Lifetime alcohol abuse and/or dependence[c, d]	13.6 n.s.	25.7 3.090*, 2.922	-7.9 n.s.	83
Lifetime PTSD[c, e, f]	6.9 n.s.	10.5 n.s.	-1.3 n.s.	83
Lifetime major depression[c, d]	13.9 n.s.	24.4 3.326*, 3.222	-1.3 n.s.	83

(table continues)

Table 5.70 continued

	Percentage change (sexual assault-no sexual assault)			
		Partial table: Lifetime homelessness		
	Zero-order table	<1 year	≥1 year	Total *n*
Diagnoses	χ^2, O.R.	χ^2, O.R.	χ^2, O.R.	
Current depression[g]	20.3 4.314**, 3.056	16.6 n.s.	25.0 n.s.	80
Lifetime conduct disorder[e, h]	22.1 4.145**, 3.067	23.0 n.s.	20.1 n.s.	83
High symptom counts	χ^2, O.R.	χ^2, O.R.	χ^2, O.R.	
Trait anxiety[i]	22.5 3.747*, 2.504	18.1 n.s.	29.9 n.s.	83
Lifetime drug abuse and/or dependence[c]	20.5 3.203*, 2.411	21.6 n.s.	17.1 n.s.	83
Lifetime alcohol abuse and/or dependence[c]	10.0 n.s.	23.0 n.s.	-13.2 n.s.	83
Lifetime PTSD[c]	13.6 n.s.	16.7 n.s.	5.7 n.s.	83
Lifetime major depression[c]	24.3 4.453**, 2.705	29.9 3.957**, 3.457	18.4 n.s.	83
Lifetime conduct disorder[h]	20.7 3.165*, 2.325	20.8 n.s.	19.3 n.s.	83
Current depression[g]	9.8 n.s.	9.1 n.s.	10.9 n.s.	83

(table continues)

Table 5.70 continued

*$p<.10$, **$p<.05$, ***$p<.01$, ****$p<.001$

[a] Current depression and/or trait anxiety. [b] Any combination of the following diagnoses: major depression, substance abuse and/or dependence, post-traumatic stress disorder and/or conduct disorder. [c] Assessed by the Diagnostic Interview Schedule. [d] Met DSM-III criteria for caseness. [e] Met DSM-IIIR criteria for caseness. [f] Only 2 symptoms of avoidance or numbing were required for caseness. [g] Assessed by the Children's Depression Inventory. Caseness criterion is 19 or more symptoms. [h] Assessed by the Diagnostic Interview Schedule for Children & Adolescents. Caseness excludes symptoms of running away. All symptoms have occurred while the respondent was <u>not</u> homeless. [i] Assessed by the Revised Children's Manifest Anxiety Scale. [j] Unable to calculate odds ratio due to the presence of an empty cell.

Table 5.71 Indicators of Psychological Distress by Sexual Assault Controlling for Respondent Income in the Hollywood Homeless Youth Sample

	Percentage change (sexual assault-no sexual assault)			
		Partial table: Respondent income		
	Zero-order table	< $100	≥$100	Total *n*
Diagnoses	χ^2, O.R.	χ^2, O.R.	χ^2, O.R.	
# of current diagnoses[a] 1-2	19.4 3.517*, 2.857	-6.4 n.s.	42.0 8.918***, 11.500	71
# of lifetime diagnoses[b] 3-4	16.6 n.s.	30.8 3.208*, 3.733	5.6 n.s.	74
Lifetime suicide thoughts[c]	37.0 10.909****, 10.000	10.9 n.s.	57.7 12.923****[j]	72
Lifetime suicide attempts[c]	23.2 3.666*, 2.600	11.3 n.s.	31.0 3.586*, 3.600	73
Lifetime drug abuse and/or dependence[c, d]	11.6 n.s.	21.8 n.s.	5.6 n.s.	74
Lifetime alcohol abuse and/or dependence[c, d]	7.9 n.s.	2.6 n.s.	12.7 n.s.	74
Lifetime PTSD[c, e, f]	6.2 n.s.	10.9 n.s.	2.9 n.s.	74
Lifetime major depression[c, d]	11.8 n.s.	7.5 n.s.	17.0 n.s.	74

(table continues)

Table 5.71 continued

	Percentage change (sexual assault-no sexual assault)			
		Partial table: Respondent income		
	Zero-order table	<$100	≥$100	Total *n*
Diagnoses	χ^2, O.R.	χ^2, O.R.	χ^2, O.R.	
Current depression[g]	18.1 3.367*, 2.921	-0.8 n.s.	34.9 6.688***, 8.625	71
Lifetime conduct disorder[e, h]	16.9 n.s.	33.1 3.970**, 5.400	4.5 n.s.	74
High symptom counts	χ^2, O.R.	χ^2, O.R.	χ^2, O.R.	
Trait anxiety[i]	19.4 n.s.	18.8 n.s.	16.7 n.s.	74
Lifetime drug abuse and/or dependence[c]	21.4 3.283*, 2.500	27.5 n.s.	19.3 n.s.	74
Lifetime alcohol abuse and/or dependence[c]	3.6 n.s.	2.6 n.s.	5.2 n.s.	74
Lifetime PTSD[c]	14.5 n.s.	-2.6 n.s.	27.5 2.933*, 3.167	74
Lifetime major depression[c]	21.6 3.253*, 2.404	11.7 n.s.	27.5 2.933*, 3.167	74
Lifetime conduct disorder[h]	14.3 n.s.	32.7 3.478*, 3.900	1.3 n.s.	74
Current depression[g]	5.8 n.s.	16.9 n.s.	-5.2 n.s.	74

(table continues)

Table 5.71 continued

*$p<.10$, **$p<.05$, ***$p<.01$, ****$p<.001$

[a] Current depression and/or trait anxiety. [b] Any combination of the following diagnoses: major depression, substance abuse and/or dependence, post-traumatic stress disorder and/or conduct disorder. [c] Assessed by the Diagnostic Interview Schedule. [d] Met DSM-III criteria for caseness. [e] Met DSM-IIIR criteria for caseness. [f] Only 2 symptoms of avoidance or numbing were required for caseness. [g] Assessed by the Children's Depression Inventory. Caseness criterion is 19 or more symptoms. [h] Assessed by the Diagnostic Interview Schedule for Children & Adolescents. Caseness excludes symptoms of running away. All symptoms have occurred while the respondent was not homeless. [i] Assessed by the Revised Children's Manifest Anxiety Scale. [j] Unable to calculate odds ratio due to the presence of an empty cell.

Table 5.72 Indicators of Psychological Distress by Sexual Assault Controlling for Difficulty Finding Clothing in the Hollywood Homeless Youth Sample

	Percentage change (sexual assault-no sexual assault)			
		Partial table: Difficulty finding clothing		
	Zero-order table	High	Low	Total *n*
Diagnoses	χ^2, O.R.	χ^2, O.R.	χ^2, O.R.	
# of current diagnoses[a] 1-2	20.6 4.258**, 2.920	19.4 n.s.	22.8 n.s.	81
# of lifetime diagnoses[b] 3-4	22.5 3.970**, 2.530	26.7 3.051*, 3.033	4.2 n.s.	84
Lifetime suicide thoughts[c]	41.0 13.788****, 12.071	41.1 7.572***, 8.727	45.2 6.858**[j]	82
Lifetime suicide attempts[c]	21.7 3.471*, 2.426	23.2 n.s.	18.1 n.s.	82
Lifetime drug abuse and/or dependence[c, d]	15.6 n.s.	20.4 n.s.	1.0 n.s.	84
Lifetime alcohol abuse and/or dependence[c, d]	15.2 n.s.	10.1 n.s.	4.2 n.s.	84
Lifetime PTSD[c, e, f]	6.2 n.s.	8.6 n.s.	3.9 n.s.	84
Lifetime major depression[c, d]	12.7 n.s.	1.3 n.s.	30.6 3.617*, 4.167	84

(table continues)

Table 5.72 continued

	Percentage change (sexual assault-no sexual assault)			
		Partial table: Difficulty finding clothing		
	Zero-order table	High	Low	Total *n*
Diagnoses	χ^2, O.R.	χ^2, O.R.	χ^2, O.R.	
Current depression[g]	19.1 3.929**, 2.895	18.6 n.s.	22.8 n.s.	81
Lifetime conduct disorder[c, h]	22.8 4.509**, 3.200	14.5 n.s.	21.6 n.s.	84
High symptom counts	χ^2, O.R.	χ^2, O.R.	χ^2, O.R.	
Trait anxiety[i]	20.3 3.117*, 2.277	29.9 3.792*, 3.429	11.6 n.s.	84
Lifetime drug abuse and/or dependence[c]	21.5 3.613*, 2.531	25.9 3.367*, 3.810	4.8 n.s.	84
Lifetime alcohol abuse and/or dependence[c]	11.6 n.s.	10.1 n.s.	-2.3 n.s.	84
Lifetime PTSD[c]	15.2 n.s.	25.8 2.794*, 2.857	-1.9 n.s.	84
Lifetime major depression[c]	25.7 5.065**, 2.864	20.4 n.s.	34.5 3.658*, 4.242	84
Lifetime conduct disorder[h]	21.9 3.638*, 2.454	20.6 n.s.	7.7 n.s.	84
Current depression[g]	7.9 n.s.	15.1 n.s.	5.2 n.s.	84

(table continues)

Table 5.72 continued

**p*<.10, ***p*<.05, ****p*<.01, *****p*<.001

[a] Current depression and/or trait anxiety. [b] Any combination of the following diagnoses: major depression, substance abuse and/or dependence, post-traumatic stress disorder and/or conduct disorder. [c] Assessed by the Diagnostic Interview Schedule. [d] Met DSM-III criteria for caseness. [e] Met DSM-IIIR criteria for caseness. [f] Only 2 symptoms of avoidance or numbing were required for caseness. [g] Assessed by the Children's Depression Inventory. Caseness criterion is 19 or more symptoms. [h] Assessed by the Diagnostic Interview Schedule for Children & Adolescents. Caseness excludes symptoms of running away. All symptoms have occurred while the respondent was <u>not</u> homeless. [i] Assessed by the Revised Children's Manifest Anxiety Scale. [j] Unable to calculate odds ratio due to the presence of an empty cell.

Table 5.73 Indicators of Psychological Distress by Sexual Assault Controlling for Difficulty Finding a Place to Clean Up in the Hollywood Homeless Youth Sample

	Percentage change (sexual assault-no sexual assault)			
		Partial table: Availability of a place to clean up		
	Zero-order table	Low	High	Total *n*
Diagnoses	χ^2, O.R.	χ^2, O.R.	χ^2, O.R.	
# of current diagnoses[a] 1-2	20.3 4.057**, 2.852	28.6 2.851*, 4.000	13.7 n.s.	80
# of lifetime diagnoses[b] 3-4	23.7 4.421**, 2.679	11.5 n.s.	27.8 4.012*, 3.500	83
Lifetime suicide thoughts[c]	41.0 13.788****, 12.071	47.3 6.914***, 13.750	38.2 7.344***, 12.000	82
Lifetime suicide attempts[c]	20.9 3.198*, 2.348	25.5 n.s.	18.1 n.s.	81
Lifetime drug abuse and/or dependence[c, d]	16.8 n.s.	11.5 n.s.	15.3 n.s.	83
Lifetime alcohol abuse and/or dependence[c, d]	14.5 n.s.	11.5 n.s.	13.9 n.s.	83
Lifetime PTSD[c, e, f]	5.9 n.s.	12.0 n.s.	2.1 n.s.	83
Lifetime major depression[c, d]	14.1 n.s.	8.6 n.s.	18.1 n.s.	83

(table continues)

Table 5.73 continued

	Percentage change (sexual assault-no sexual assault)			
		Partial table: Availability of a place to clean up		
	Zero-order table	Low	High	Total *n*
Diagnoses	χ^2, O.R.	χ^2, O.R.	χ^2, O.R.	
Current depression[g]	18.8 3.746*, 2.829	20.9 n.s.	16.6 n.s.	80
Lifetime conduct disorder[e, h]	23.5 4.747**, 3.300	12.4 n.s.	28.5 3.794*, 3.877	83
High symptom counts	χ^2, O.R.	χ^2, O.R.	χ^2, O.R.	
Trait anxiety[i]	19.5 2.863*, 2.206	30.3 2.783*, 3.536	11.9 n.s.	83
Lifetime drug abuse and/or dependence[c]	22.4 3.887*, 2.625	25.6 2.839*, 6.000	14.6 n.s.	83
Lifetime alcohol abuse and/or dependence[c]	10.8 n.s.	5.9 n.s.	11.1 n.s.	83
Lifetime PTSD[c]	16.3 n.s.	11.5 n.s.	16.7 n.s.	83
Lifetime major depression[c]	26.9 5.519**, 3.014	22.6 n.s.	29.2 3.861**, 3.333	83
Lifetime conduct disorder[h]	22.9 3.967*, 2.561	19.2 n.s.	23.6 n.s.	83
Current depression[g]	7.1 n.s.	-3.8 n.s.	15.3 n.s.	83

(table continues)

Table 5.73 continued

*p<.10, **p<.05, ***p<.01, ****p<.001

[a] Current depression and/or trait anxiety. [b] Any combination of the following diagnoses: major depression, substance abuse and/or dependence, post-traumatic stress disorder and/or conduct disorder. [c] Assessed by the Diagnostic Interview Schedule. [d] Met DSM-III criteria for caseness. [e] Met DSM-IIIR criteria for caseness. [f] Only 2 symptoms of avoidance or numbing were required for caseness. [g] Assessed by the Children's Depression Inventory. Caseness criterion is 19 or more symptoms. [h] Assessed by the Diagnostic Interview Schedule for Children & Adolescents. Caseness excludes symptoms of running away. All symptoms have occurred while the respondent was not homeless. [i] Assessed by the Revised Children's Manifest Anxiety Scale.

Table 5.74 Indicators of Psychological Distress by Sexual Assault Controlling for Gang Affiliation in the Hollywood Homeless Youth Sample

	Percentage change (sexual assault-no sexual assault)			
		Partial table: Member of gang		
	Zero-order table	No	Yes	Total *n*
Diagnoses	χ^2, O.R.	χ^2, O.R.	χ^2, O.R.	
# of current diagnoses[a] 1-2	20.3 4.057**, 2.852	35.3 5.215**, 5.133	8.3 n.s.	80
# of lifetime diagnoses[b] 3-4	23.7 4.421**, 2.679	32.4 4.309**, 4.278	14.0 n.s.	83
Lifetime suicide thoughts[c]	40.1 13.209****, 11.607	32.4 4.096**, 7.562	47.6 9.773***, 17.500	81
Lifetime suicide attempts[c]	20.9 3.198*, 2.348	-11.1 n.s.	45.2 8.396***, 9.545	81
Lifetime drug abuse and/or dependence[c, d]	16.8 n.s.	21.2 n.s.	11.5 n.s.	83
Lifetime alcohol abuse and/or dependence[c, d]	16.3 n.s.	24.8 n.s.	4.8 n.s.	83
Lifetime PTSD[c, e, f]	7.7 n.s.	16.0 n.s.	0.4 n.s.	83
Lifetime major depression[c, d]	12.3 n.s.	21.2 n.s.	5.8 n.s.	83

(table continues)

Table 5.74 continued

	Percentage change (sexual assault-no sexual assault)			
		Partial table: Member of gang		
	Zero-order table	No	Yes	Total *n*
Diagnoses	χ^2, O.R.	χ^2, O.R.	χ^2, O.R.	
Current depression[g]	18.8 3.746*, 2.829	27.7 3.361*, 3.771	12.5 n.s.	80
Lifetime conduct disorder[e, h]	23.5 4.747**, 3.300	41.7 6.286**, 7.333	4.4 n.s.	83
High symptom counts	χ^2, O.R.	χ^2, O.R.	χ^2, O.R.	
Trait anxiety[i]	19.5 2.863*, 2.206	19.2 n.s.	21.7 n.s.	83
Lifetime drug abuse and/or dependence[c]	22.4 3.887**, 2.625	34.0 4.143**, 4.444	11.1 n.s.	83
Lifetime alcohol abuse and/or dependence[c]	12.6 n.s.	24.8 n.s.	-2.9 n.s.	83
Lifetime PTSD[c]	16.3 n.s.	-0.8 n.s.	30.3 3.635*, 3.520	83
Lifetime major depression[c]	25.1 4.763**, 2.782	22.8 n.s.	29.4 3.612*, 3.490	83
Lifetime conduct disorder[h]	22.9 3.967*, 2.561	28.8 3.285*, 3.500	13.5 n.s.	83
Current depression[g]	7.1 n.s.	0.2 n.s.	14.0 n.s.	83

(table continues)

Table 5.74 continued

$^{*}p<.10$, $^{**}p<.05$, $^{***}p<.01$, $^{****}p<.001$

[a] Current depression and/or trait anxiety. [b] Any combination of the following diagnoses: major depression, substance abuse and/or dependence, post-traumatic stress disorder and/or conduct disorder. [c] Assessed by the Diagnostic Interview Schedule. [d] Met DSM-III criteria for caseness. [e] Met DSM-IIIR criteria for caseness. [f] Only 2 symptoms of avoidance or numbing were required for caseness. [g] Assessed by the Children's Depression Inventory. Caseness criterion is 19 or more symptoms. [h] Assessed by the Diagnostic Interview Schedule for Children & Adolescents. Caseness excludes symptoms of running away. All symptoms have occurred while the respondent was not homeless. [i] Assessed by the Revised Children's Manifest Anxiety Scale.

Table 5.75 Indicators of Psychological Distress by Sexual Assault Controlling for Carrying a Weapon in the Hollywood Homeless Youth Sample

	Percentage change (sexual assault-no sexual assault)			
		Partial table: Carries weapon		
	Zero-order table	No	Yes	Total *n*
Diagnoses	χ^2, O.R.	χ^2, O.R.	χ^2, O.R.	
# of current diagnoses[a] 1-2	19.9 3.856**, 2.784	-0.7 n.s.	33.1 5.199**, 5.400	79
# of lifetime diagnoses[b] 3-4	23.1 4.158**, 2.606	49.3 8.136***, 8.944	1.6 n.s.	82
Lifetime suicide thoughts[c]	41.0 13.639****, 12.037	31.7 3.043*, 4.286	43.5 10.351***[j]	80
Lifetime suicide attempts[c]	22.0 3.516*, 2.455	40.7 4.886**, 6.182	9.8 n.s.	80
Lifetime drug abuse and/or dependence[c, d]	18.1 n.s.	12.4 n.s.	19.3 n.s.	82
Lifetime alcohol abuse and/or dependence[c, d]	15.6 n.s.	35.9 4.303**, 4.714	-5.7 n.s.	82
Lifetime PTSD[c, e, f]	5.6 n.s.	39.7 7.172***, 8.667	-15.5 n.s.	82
Lifetime major depression[c, d]	11.9 n.s.	12.4 n.s.	14.9 n.s.	82

(table continues)

Table 5.75 continued

	Percentage change (sexual assault-no sexual assault)			
		Partial table: Carries weapon		
	Zero-order table	No	Yes	Total *n*
Diagnoses	χ^2, O.R.	χ^2, O.R.	χ^2, O.R.	
Current depression[g]	18.5 3.564*, 2.763	2.8 n.s.	27.8 3.872**, 4.364	79
Lifetime conduct disorder[e, h]	22.4 4.336**, 3.150	31.4 3.295*, 6.353	16.4 n.s.	82
High symptom counts	χ^2, O.R.	χ^2, O.R.	χ^2, O.R.	
Trait anxiety[i]	20.7 n.s.	4.8 n.s.	34.0 4.968**, 4.163	82
Lifetime drug abuse and/or dependence[c]	23.3 4.180**, 2.726	28.6 n.s.	15.4 n.s.	82
Lifetime alcohol abuse and/or dependence[c]	11.8 n.s.	32.4 3.395*, 3.938	-9.9 n.s.	82
Lifetime PTSD[c]	15.6 n.s.	22.1 n.s.	10.9 n.s.	82
Lifetime major depression[c]	24.4 4.463**, 2.700	15.2 n.s.	34.0 4.968**, 4.163	82
Lifetime conduct disorder[h]	22.1 3.671*, 2.478	32.1 3.077*, 3.818	13.2 n.s.	82
Current depression[g]	6.1 n.s.	-15.2 n.s.	21.5 n.s.	82

(table continues)

Table 5.75 continued

**p*<.10, ***p*<.05, ****p*<.01, *****p*<.001

[a] Current depression and/or trait anxiety. [b] Any combination of the following diagnoses: major depression, substance abuse and/or dependence, post-traumatic stress disorder and/or conduct disorder. [c] Assessed by the Diagnostic Interview Schedule. [d] Met DSM-III criteria for caseness. [e] Met DSM-IIIR criteria for caseness. [f] Only 2 symptoms of avoidance or numbing were required for caseness. [g] Assessed by the Children's Depression Inventory. Caseness criterion is 19 or more symptoms. [h] Assessed by the Diagnostic Interview Schedule for Children & Adolescents. Caseness excludes symptoms of running away. All symptoms have occurred while the respondent was not homeless. [i] Assessed by the Revised Children's Manifest Anxiety Scale. [j] Unable to calculate odds ratio due to the presence of an empty cell.

Table 5.76 Number of Diagnoses of Psychological Distress by Characteristics of Physical Assault in the Hollywood Homeless Youth Sample

	Relationship with perpetrator		Age of perpetrator		Number of perpetrators		Age at first exposure		Frequency		Number of types of physical assault		Degree of violence	
	Parents ± others (%)	Others (%)	Adults only (%)	Adult & peers (%)	1 (%)	≥2 (%)	2-10 yrs (%)	11-17 yrs (%)	1-95 (%)	>95 (%)	1-4 (%)	5-10 (%)	Routine or injurious (%)	Life threat-ening (%)
# of current diagnoses														
0	70.0	80.0	75.8	68.8	90.5	65.1	67.5	81.0	78.1	65.5	77.1	64.5	71.9	70.6
1-2	30.0	20.0	24.2	31.3	9.5	34.9	32.5	19.0	21.9	34.5	22.9	35.5	28.1	29.4
Total *n*	50	15	33	32	21	43	40	21	32	29	35	31	32	34
Chi-square	n.s.		n.s.		4.652**		n.s.		n.s.		n.s.		n.s.	
OR					5.089									

(table continues)

Table 5.76 continued

	Relationship with perpetrator		Age of perpetrator		Number of perpetrators		Age at first exposure		Frequency		Number of types of physical assault		Degree of violence	
	Parents ± others (%)	Others (%)	Adults only (%)	Adult & peers (%)	1 (%)	≥2 (%)	2-10 yrs (%)	11-17 yrs (%)	1-95 (%)	>95 (%)	1-4 (%)	5-10 (%)	Routine or injurious (%)	Life threatening (%)
# of lifetime diagnoses														
0-2	54.9	53.3	63.6	45.5	66.7	50.0	58.5	52.4	59.4	50.0	65.7	43.8	66.7	44.1
3-4	45.1	46.7	36.4	54.5	33.3	50.0	41.5	47.6	40.6	50.0	34.3	56.3	33.3	55.9
Total *n*	51	15	33	33	21	44	41	21	32	30	35	32	33	34
Chi-square	n.s.		n.s.		n.s.		n.s.		n.s.		3.261*		3.443*	
OR											2.464		2.533	

Table 5.77 Number of Diagnoses of Psychological Distress by Characteristics of Sexual Assault in the Hollywood Homeless Youth Sample

	Relationship with perpetrator		Age of perpetrator		Number of perpetrators		Age at first exposure		Frequency		Penetration	
	Parents ± others (%)	Others (%)	Adults only (%)	Adult & peers (%)	1 (%)	≥2 (%)	2-10 yrs (%)	11-17 yrs (%)	1-95 (%)	>95 (%)	No (%)	Yes (%)
# of current diagnoses												
0	33.3	75.0	78.9	30.0	64.7	58.3	66.7	56.3	70.0	63.2	71.4	57.1
1-2	66.7	25.0	21.1	70.0	35.3	41.7	33.3	43.8	30.0	36.8	28.6	42.9
Total *n*	9	20	19	10	17	12	12	16	10	19	14	14
Chi-square	4.577**		6.667***		n.s.		n.s.		n.s.		n.s.	
OR	0.167		8.750									
# of lifetime diagnoses												
0-2	55.6	40.0	42.1	50.0	47.1	41.7	58.3	37.5	50.0	47.4	64.3	28.6
3-4	44.4	60.0	57.9	50.0	52.9	58.3	41.7	62.5	50.0	52.6	35.7	71.4
Total *n*	9	20	19	10	17	12	12	16	10	19	14	14
Chi-square	n.s.		n.s.		n.s.		n.s.		n.s.		3.590*	
OR											4.500	

Table 5.78 Psychological Distress (Caseness) by Characteristics of Physical Assault in the Hollywood Homeless Youth Sample

	Relationship with perpetrator		Age of perpetrator		Number of perpetrators		Age at first exposure		Frequency		Degree of violence	
Distress caseness	Parents ± others (%)	Others (%)	Adults only (%)	Adult & peers (%)	1 (%)	≥2 (%)	2-10 yrs (%)	11-17 yrs (%)	1-95 (%)	>95 (%)	Routine or injurious (%)	Life threat-ening (%)
Current depression												
Not case	72.0	86.7	75.8	75.0	95.2	67.4	72.5	81.0	81.3	69.0	75.0	73.5
Case	28.0	13.3	24.2	25.0	4.8	32.6	27.5	19.0	18.8	31.0	25.0	26.5
Total *n*	50	15	33	32	21	43	40	21	32	29	32	34
Chi-square	n.s.		n.s.		6.075**		n.s.		n.s.		n.s.	
OR					9.655							
Lifetime depression												
Not case	66.7	66.7	78.8	54.5	66.7	68.2	78.0	47.6	62.5	70.0	84.8	52.9
Case	33.3	33.3	21.2	45.5	33.3	31.8	22.0	52.4	37.5	30.0	15.2	47.1
Total *n*	51	15	33	33	21	44	41	21	32	30	33	34
Chi-square	n.s.		4.364**		n.s.		5.885**		n.s.		7.923***	
OR			3.095				3.911				4.978	

(table continues)

Table 5.78 continued

Distress caseness	Relationship with perpetrator		Age of perpetrator		Number of perpetrators		Age at first exposure		Frequency		Degree of violence	
	Parents ± others (%)	Others (%)	Adults only (%)	Adult & peers (%)	1 (%)	≥2 (%)	2-10 yrs (%)	11-17 yrs (%)	1-95 (%)	>95 (%)	Routine or injurious (%)	Life threatening (%)
Lifetime suicide thoughts												
Not case	24.0	53.3	24.2	37.5	38.1	27.9	27.5	28.6	31.3	24.1	34.4	27.3
Case	76.0	46.7	75.8	62.5	61.9	72.1	72.5	71.4	68.7	75.9	65.6	72.7
Total *n*	50	15	33	32	21	43	40	21	32	29	32	33
Chi-square	4.661**		n.s.		n.s.		n.s.		n.s.		n.s.	
OR	0.276											
Lifetime suicide attempts												
Not case	42.0	66.7	43.8	51.5	57.1	44.2	50.0	38.1	51.6	40.0	54.8	41.2
Case	58.0	33.3	56.3	48.5	42.9	55.8	50.0	61.9	48.4	60.0	45.2	58.8
Total *n*	50	15	32	33	21	43	40	21	31	30	31	34
Chi-square	2.814*		n.s.		n.s.		n.s.		n.s.		n.s.	
OR	0.362											

(table continues)

Table 5.78 continued

Distress caseness	Relationship with perpetrator		Age of perpetrator		Number of perpetrators		Age at first exposure		Frequency		Degree of violence	
	Parents ± others (%)	Others (%)	Adults only (%)	Adult & peers (%)	1 (%)	≥2 (%)	2-10 yrs (%)	11-17 yrs (%)	1-95 (%)	>95 (%)	Routine or injurious (%)	Life threatening (%)
Lifetime PTSD												
Not case	74.5	80.0	78.8	72.7	85.7	70.5	78.0	66.7	75.0	73.3	87.9	67.6
Case	25.5	20.0	21.2	27.3	14.3	29.5	22.0	33.3	25.0	26.7	12.1	32.4
Total *n*	51	15	33	33	21	44	41	21	32	30	33	34
Chi-square	n.s.		n.s.		n.s.		n.s.		n.s.		3.945**	
OR											3.467	
Lifetime alcohol abuse/ dependence												
Not case	54.9	40.0	57.6	45.5	61.9	45.5	53.7	57.1	56.3	50.0	63.6	38.2
Case	45.1	60.0	42.4	54.5	38.1	54.5	46.3	42.9	43.7	50.0	36.4	61.8
Total *n*	51	15	33	33	21	44	41	21	32	30	33	34
Chi-square	n.s.		n.s.		n.s.		n.s.		n.s.		4.323**	
OR											2.827	

* $p < .10$, ** $p < .05$, *** $p < .01$, **** $p < .001$

Table 5.79 Psychological Distress (Symptom Counts) by Characteristics of Physical Assault in the Hollywood Homeless Youth Sample

	Relationship with perpetrator		Age of perpetrator		Number of perpetrators		Age at first exposure		Frequency		Degree of violence	
Distress symptom counts	Parents ± others (%)	Others (%)	Adults only (%)	Adult & peers (%)	1 (%)	≥2 (%)	2-10 yrs (%)	11-17 yrs (%)	1-95 (%)	>95 (%)	Routine or injurious (%)	Life threatening (%)
Lifetime depression												
Low	49.0	53.3	57.6	42.4	52.4	50.0	58.5	38.1	46.9	53.3	66.7	38.2
High	51.0	46.7	42.4	57.6	47.6	50.0	41.5	61.9	53.1	46.7	33.3	61.8
Total *n*	51	15	33	33	21	44	41	21	32	30	33	34
Chi-square											5.426**	
OR											3.231	
Lifetime PTSD												
Low	45.1	46.7	54.5	36.4	57.1	40.9	46.3	38.1	46.9	36.7	66.7	26.5
High	54.9	53.3	45.5	63.6	42.9	59.1	53.7	61.9	53.1	63.3	33.3	73.5
Total *n*	51	15	33	33	21	44	41	21	32	30	33	34
Chi-square	n.s.		n.s.		n.s.		n.s.		n.s.		10.884****	
OR											5.556	

(table continues)

Table 5.79 continued

Distress symptom counts	Relationship with perpetrator		Age of perpetrator		Number of perpetrators		Age at first exposure		Frequency		Degree of violence	
	Parents ± others (%)	Others (%)	Adults only (%)	Adult & peers (%)	1 (%)	≥2 (%)	2-10 yrs (%)	11-17 yrs (%)	1-95 (%)	>95 (%)	Routine or injurious (%)	Life threatening (%)
Lifetime alcohol abuse /dependence												
Low	52.9	40.0	54.5	45.5	61.9	43.2	51.2	57.1	56.3	46.7	60.6	38.2
High	47.1	60.0	45.5	54.5	38.1	56.8	48.8	42.9	43.7	53.3	39.4	61.8
Total n	51	15	33	33	21	44	41	21	32	30	33	34
Chi-square	n.s.		n.s.		n.s.		n.s.		n.s.		3.353*	
OR											2.485	

* $p < .10$, ** $p < .05$, *** $p < .01$, **** $p < .001$

Table 5.80 Psychological Distress (Caseness) by Characteristics of Sexual Assault in the Hollywood Homeless Youth Sample

Distress caseness	Relationship with perpetrator: Father ± others (%)	Relationship with perpetrator: Others only (%)	Age of perpetrator: Adults only (%)	Age of perpetrator: Adult & peers (%)	Number of perpetrators: 1 (%)	Number of perpetrators: 2-6 (%)	Age at first exposure: 3-9 yrs (%)	Age at first exposure: 11-16 yrs (%)	Frequency: 1 (%)	Frequency: ≥ 2 (%)	Penetration: No (%)	Penetration: Yes (%)
Current depression												
Not case	33.3	80.0	78.9	40.0	70.6	58.3	75.0	56.3	70.0	68.4	71.4	64.3
Case	66.7	20.0	21.1	60.0	29.4	41.7	25.0	43.8	30.0	31.6	28.6	35.7
Total n	9	20	19	10	17	12	12	16	10	19	14	14
Chi-square	Fisher's Exact**		Fisher's Exact**		n.s.		n.s.		n.s.		n.s.	
OR	0.125		5.625									
Lifetime PTSD												
Not case	100.0	70.0	84.2	70.0	82.4	75.0	91.7	68.8	80.0	78.9	85.7	71.4
Case	0	30.0	15.8	30.0	17.6	25.0	8.3	31.3	20.0	21.1	14.3	28.6
Total n	9	20	19	10	17	12	12	16	10	19	14	14
Chi-square	Fisher's Exact*		n.s.		n.s.		n.s.		n.s.		n.s.	
OR	--											

(table continues)

Table 5.80 continued

Distress caseness	Relationship with perpetrator		Age of perpetrator		Number of perpetrators		Age at first exposure		Frequency		Penetration	
	Father ± others (%)	Others only (%)	Adults only (%)	Adult & peers (%)	1 (%)	2-6 (%)	3-9 yrs (%)	11-16 yrs (%)	1 (%)	≥ 2 (%)	No (%)	Yes (%)
Lifetime drug abuse/ dependence												
Not case	55.6	50.0	52.6	50.0	52.9	50.0	58.3	50.0	60.0	52.6	71.4	35.7
Case	44.4	50.0	47.4	50.0	47.1	50.0	41.7	50.0	40.0	47.4	28.6	64.3
Total n	9	20	19	10	17	12	12	16	10	19	14	14
Chi-square	n.s.		n.s.		n.s.		n.s.		n.s.		3.590*	
OR											4.500	
Lifetime conduct disorder												
Not case	0	25.0	15.8	20.0	29.4	0	25.0	12.5	30.0	15.8	14.3	21.4
Case	100.0	75.0	84.2	80.0	70.6	100.0	75.0	87.5	70.0	84.2	85.7	78.6
Total n	9	20	19	10	17	12	12	16	10	19	14	14
Chi-square	n.s.		n.s.		Fisher's Exact*		n.s.		n.s.		n.s.	
OR	--				2.000							

* $p < .10$, ** $p < .05$, *** $p < .01$, **** $p < .001$

Table 5.81 Psychological Distress (Symptom Counts) by Characteristics of Sexual Assault in the Hollywood Homeless Youth Sample

	Relationship with perpetrator		Age of perpetrator		Number of perpetrators		Age at first exposure		Frequency		Penetration	
Distress symptom counts	Father ± others (%)	Others only (%)	Adults only (%)	Adult & peers (%)	1 (%)	2-6 (%)	3-9 yrs (%)	11-16 yrs (%)	1 (%)	≥2 (%)	No (%)	Yes (%)
Trait anxiety												
Low	44.4	35.0	42.1	30.0	29.4	50.0	33.3	43.8	30.0	42.1	35.7	50.0
High	55.6	65.0	57.9	70.0	70.6	50.0	66.7	56.3	70.0	57.9	64.3	50.0
Total *n*	9	20	19	10	17	12	12	16	10	19	14	14
Chi-square	n.s.		n.s.		n.s.		n.s.		n.s.		n.s.	
OR												
Lifetime depression												
Low	55.6	30.0	42.1	30.0	35.3	41.7	41.7	37.5	20.0	52.6	28.6	57.1
High	44.4	70.0	57.9	70.0	64.7	58.3	58.3	62.5	80.0	47.4	71.4	42.9
Total *n*	9	20	19	10	17	12	12	16	10	19	14	14
Chi-square	n.s.		n.s.		n.s.		n.s.		2.876*		n.s.	
OR									0.225			

(table continues)

Table 5.81 continued

Distress symptom counts	Relationship with perpetrator		Age of perpetrator		Number of perpetrators		Age at first exposure		Frequency		Penetration	
	Father ± others (%)	Others only (%)	Adults only (%)	Adult & peers (%)	1 (%)	2-6 (%)	3-9 yrs (%)	11-16 yrs (%)	1 (%)	≥2 (%)	No (%)	Yes (%)
Lifetime drug abuse/ dependence												
Low	55.6	15.0	26.3	30.0	17.6	41.7	33.3	25.0	30.0	31.6	35.7	21.4
High	44.4	85.0	73.7	70.0	82.4	58.3	66.7	75.0	70.0	68.4	64.3	78.6
Total *n*	9	20	19	10	17	12	12	16	10	19	14	14
Chi-square	5.110**		n.s.		n.s.		n.s.		n.s.		n.s.	
OR	7.083											

$*p < .10$, $** p < .05$

Table 5.82 Psychological Distress by Whether Respondent Fought Back During Physical Abuse in the Hollywood Homeless Youth Sample

	Fought	
Symptom count	No (%)	Yes (%)
Anxiety		
Low	40.0	53.1
High	60.0	46.9
Total *n*	20	49
Chi-square	n.s.	
Current depression		
Low	45.0	51.0
High	55.0	49.0
Total *n*	20	49
Chi-square	n.s.	
Lifetime PTSD		
Low	55.0	44.9
High	45.0	55.1
Total *n*	20	49
Chi-square	n.s.	
Lifetime drug abuse/dependence		
Low	50.0	32.7
High	50.0	67.3
Total *n*	20	49
Chi-square	n.s.	
Lifetime conduct disorder		
Low	55.0	44.9
High	45.0	55.1
Total *n*	20	49
Chi-square	n.s.	
Lifetime alcohol abuse/dependence		
Not case	60.0	49.0
Case	40.0	51.0
Total *n*	20	49
Chi-square	n.s.	

Table 5.83 Indicators of Psychological Distress by Sexual Assault Controlling for Whether Respondent Ran Away From Home in the Hollywood Homeless Youth Sample

	Percentage change (sexual assault-no sexual assault)			
		Partial table: How left home		
	Zero-order table	Left	Told to go	Total n
Diagnoses	χ^2, O.R.	χ^2, O.R.	χ^2, O.R.	
# of current diagnoses[a] 1-2	22.0 4.689**, 3.092	19.8 2.801*, 3.015	28.9 n.s.	80
# of lifetime diagnoses[b] 3-4	20.9 3.366*, 2.372	16.7 n.s.	30.9 n.s.	83
Lifetime suicide thoughts[c]	40.7 13.209****, 11.607	44.7 11.008****, 18.000	31.9 n.s.	81
Lifetime suicide attempts[c]	24.1 4.173**, 2.696	24.3 2.939*, 2.694	25.0 n.s.	81
Lifetime drug abuse and/or dependence[c, d]	13.7 n.s.	9.4 n.s.	25.7 n.s.	83
Lifetime alcohol abuse and/or dependence[c, d]	13.6 n.s.	8.9 n.s.	27.6 n.s.	83
Lifetime PTSD[c, e, f]	6.9 n.s.	2.8 n.s.	12.5 n.s.	83
Lifetime major depression[c, d]	13.9 n.s.	23.3 3.733*, 3.333	-6.6 n.s.	83
Current depression[g]	20.3 4.314**, 3.056	17.9 n.s.	28.9 n.s.	80

(table continues)

Table 5.83 continued

	Percentage change (sexual assault-no sexual assault)			
		Partial table: How left home		
	Zero-order table	Left	Told to go	Total *n*
Diagnoses	χ^2, O.R.	χ^2, O.R.	χ^2, O.R.	
Lifetime conduct disorder[e, h]	22.1 4.145**, 3.067	21.7 n.s.	24.3 n.s.	83
High symptom counts	χ^2, O.R.	χ^2, O.R.	χ^2, O.R.	
Trait anxiety[i]	22.5 3.747*, 2.504	28.3 4.134**, 2.267	7.9 n.s.	83
Lifetime drug abuse and/or dependence[c]	20.5 3.203*, 2.411	25.6 3.376*, 2.917	11.8 n.s.	83
Lifetime alcohol abuse and/or dependence[c]	10.0 n.s.	3.3 n.s.	27.6 n.s.	83
Lifetime PTSD[c]	13.6 n.s.	7.8 n.s.	23.7 n.s.	83
Lifetime major depression[c]	24.3 4.453**, 2.705	26.1 3.511*, 2.918	18.4 n.s.	83
Lifetime conduct disorder[h]	20.7 3.165*, 2.325	12.8 n.s.	38.2 3.283*, 5.143	83
Current depression[g]	9.8 n.s.	5.0 n.s.	20.4 n.s.	83

(table continues)

Table 5.83 continued

**p*<.10, ***p*<.05, ****p*<.01, *****p*<.001

[a] Current depression and/or trait anxiety. [b] Any combination of the following diagnoses: major depression, substance abuse and/or dependence, post-traumatic stress disorder and/or conduct disorder. [c] Assessed by the Diagnostic Interview Schedule. [d] Met DSM-III criteria for caseness. [e] Met DSM-IIIR criteria for caseness. [f] Only 2 symptoms of avoidance or numbing were required for caseness. [g] Assessed by the Children's Depression Inventory. Caseness criterion is 19 or more symptoms. [h] Assessed by the Diagnostic Interview Schedule for Children & Adolescents. Caseness excludes symptoms of running away. All symptoms have occurred while the respondent was not homeless. [i] Assessed by the Revised Children's Manifest Anxiety Scale.

Table 5.84 Disclosed Child Maltreatment by Respondent Sex in the Hollywood Homeless Youth Sample

	Sex	
	Male (%)	Female (%)
Neglect		
No	41.5	16.7
Yes	58.5	83.3
Total *n*	53	36
Chi-square	6.136*	
OR	3.548	
Physical assault		
No	17.0	26.5
Yes	83.0	73.5
Total *n*	53	34
Chi-square	n.s.	
Sexual assault		
No	76.0	50.0
Yes	24.0	50.0
Total *n*	50	34
Chi-square	6.052*	
OR	3.167	
Witnessed domestic violence		
No	56.0	47.1
Yes	44.0	52.9
Total *n*	50	34
Chi-square	n.s.	

* $p < .05$

Table 5.85 Assault Reporting and Removal From Home by Respondent Sex in the Hollywood Homeless Youth Sample

	Sex	
	Male (%)	Female (%)
Physical assault reported		
No	64.9	64.0
Yes	35.1	36.0
Total *n*	37	25
Chi-square	n.s.	
Sexual assault reported		
No	83.3	62.5
Yes	16.7	37.5
Total *n*	12	16
Chi-square	n.s.	
Removed for physical assault[a]		
No	84.8	73.9
Yes	15.2	26.1
Total *n*	33	23
Chi-square	n.s.	
Removed for sexual assault[a]		
No	100.0	62.5
Yes	0	37.5
Total *n*	6	8
Chi-square	2.864*	
OR	--	

[a]Among respondents who had been assaulted by someone living in their homes

Table 5.86 Disclosed Characteristics of Sexual Assault by Respondent Sex in the Hollywood Homeless Youth Sample

	Sex	
	Male (%)	Female (%)
Degree of violence		
Low	45.5	35.7
High	54.5	64.3
Total *n*	11	14
Chi-square	n.s.	
Perpetrator		
Parents ± others	57.1	62.5
Others only	42.9	37.5
Total *n*	21	8
Chi-square	n.s.	
Penetration		
No	45.5	52.9
Yes	54.5	47.1
Total *n*	11	17
Chi-square	n.s.	
Age at first exposure		
3-9 years	41.7	43.8
11-16 years	58.3	56.3
Total *n*	12	16
Chi-square	n.s.	

Table 5.87 Indicators of Psychological Distress by Sexual Assault Controlling for Indicators of Alcohol Abuse and/or Dependence in the Hollywood Homeless Youth Sample

	Percentage change (sexual assault-no sexual assault)			
		Partial table: Alcohol abuse and/or dependence[a, b]		
	Zero-order table	Not case	Case	Total n
Diagnoses	χ^2, O.R.	χ^2, O.R.	χ^2, O.R.	
Lifetime suicide thoughts[a]	41.0 13.788****, 12.071	30.2 3.359*, 4.412	50.0 11.259****[h]	82
Lifetime suicide attempts[a]	21.7 3.471*, 2.426	9.4 n.s.	29.5 3.317*, 3.600	82
Lifetime PTSD[a, c, d]	6.2 n.s.	14.0 n.s.	-3.9 n.s.	84
Lifetime major depression[a, b]	12.7 n.s.	25.0 2.862*, 3.184	2.3 n.s.	84
Current depression[e]	19.1 3.929**, 2.895	14.7 n.s.	23.2 n.s.	81
Lifetime conduct disorder[c, f]	22.8 4.509**, .3200	16.0 n.s.	18.2 3.251*[h]	84

(table continues)

Table 5.87 continued

	Percentage change (sexual assault-no sexual assault)			
		Partial table: Alcohol abuse and/or dependence[a, b]		
	Zero-order table	Not case	Case	Total n
High symptom counts	χ^2, O.R.	χ^2, O.R.	χ^2, O.R.	
Trait anxiety[g]	20.3 3.117*, 2.277	31.4 3.722*, 4.000	13.6 n.s.	84
Lifetime PTSD[a]	15.2 n.s.	17.4 n.s.	10.8 n.s.	84
Lifetime major depression[a]	25.7 5.065**, 2.864	40.5 6.148**, 5.833	13.6 n.s.	84
Lifetime conduct disorder[f]	20.7 3.638*, 2.454	9.6 n.s.	21.5 2.720*, 4.000	84
Current depression[e]	7.9 n.s.	13.0 n.s.	4.5 n.s.	84

*p<.10, **p<.05, ***p<.01, ****p<.001

[a]Assessed by the Diagnostic Interview Schedule. [b]Met DSM-III criteria for caseness. [c]Met DSM-IIIR criteria for caseness. [d]Only 2 symptoms of avoidance or numbing were required for caseness. [e] Assessed by the Children's Depression Inventory. Caseness criterion is 19 or more symptoms. [f]Assessed by the Diagnostic Interview Schedule for Children & Adolescents. Caseness excludes symptoms of running away. All symptoms have occurred while the respondent was not homeless. [g]Assessed by the Revised Children's Manifest Anxiety Scale. [h]Unable to calculate odds ratio due to the presence of an empty cell.

Table 5.88 Indicators of Psychological Distress by Sexual Assault Controlling for Indicators of Drug Abuse and/or Dependence in the Hollywood Homeless Youth Sample

	Percentage change (sexual assault-no sexual assault)			
		Partial table: Drug abuse and/or dependence[a, b]		
	Zero-order table	Not case	Case	Total *n*
Diagnoses	χ^2, O.R.	χ^2, O.R.	χ^2, O.R.	
Lifetime suicide thoughts[a]	41.0 13.788****, 12.071	39.2 7.276**, 11.900	45.2 6.787**, 13.500	82
Lifetime suicide attempts[a]	21.7 3.471*, 2.426	18.3 n.s.	24.8 n.s.	82
Lifetime PTSD[a, c, d]	6.2 n.s.	2.5 n.s.	6.4 n.s.	84
Lifetime major depression[a, b]	12.7 n.s.	30.5 5.278**, 4.521	-11.9 n.s.	84
Current depression[e]	19.1 3.929*, 2.895	-3.8 n.s.	45.3 7.235***, 10.000	81
Lifetime conduct disorder[c, f]	22.8 4.509**, .3200	34.1 5.018**, 4.706	-3.2 n.s.	84

(table continues)

Table 5.88 continued

	Percentage change (sexual assault-no sexual assault)			
		Partial table: Drug abuse and/or dependence[a, b]		
	Zero-order table	Not case	Case	Total n
High symptom counts	χ^2, O.R.	χ^2, O.R.	χ^2, O.R.	
Trait anxiety[g]	20.3 3.117*, 2.277	19.5 n.s.	19.9 n.s.	84
Lifetime PTSD[a]	15.2 n.s.	8.9 n.s.	19.9 n.s.	84
Lifetime major depression[a]	25.7 5.065**, 2.864	38.2 6.266**, 5.077	11.1 n.s.	84
Lifetime conduct disorder[f]	20.7 3.324*, 2.332	21.1 n.s.	4.7 n.s.	84
Current depression[e]	7.9 n.s.	7.4 n.s.	7.1 n.s.	84

**p*<.10, ***p*<.05, ****p*<.01, *****p*<.001

[a]Assessed by the Diagnostic Interview Schedule. [b]Met DSM-III criteria for caseness. [c]Met DSM-IIIR criteria for caseness. [d]Only 2 symptoms of avoidance or numbing were required for caseness. [e] Assessed by the Children's Depression Inventory. Caseness criterion is 19 or more symptoms. [f]Assessed by the Diagnostic Interview Schedule for Children & Adolescents. Caseness excludes symptoms of running away. All symptoms have occurred while the respondent was <u>not</u> homeless. [g]Assessed by the Revised Children's Manifest Anxiety Scale.

Table 5.89 Indicators of Psychological Distress by Sexual Assault Controlling for Respondent Sex in the Hollywood Homeless Youth Sample

	Percentage change (sexual assault-no sexual assault)			
		Partial table: Respondent sex		
	Zero-order table	Male	Female	Total *n*
Diagnoses	χ^2, O.R.	χ^2, O.R.	χ^2, O.R.	
# of current diagnoses[a] 1-2	20.6 4.258**, 2.920	21.9 3.036*, 3.875	11.8 n.s.	81
# of lifetime diagnoses[b] 3-4	22.5 3.970**, 2.530	15.8 n.s.	41.1 6.585**, 8.438	84
Lifetime suicide thoughts[c]	48.5 13.788****, 12.071	41.0 8.588**, 14.438	23.2 2.972*, 6.250	82
Lifetime suicide attempts[c]	21.7 3.471*, 2.426	3.9 n.s.	28.4 2.972*, 3.852	82
Lifetime drug abuse and/or dependence[c, d]	15.6 n.s.	13.6 n.s.	35.3 5.885**, 11.200	84
Lifetime alcohol abuse and/or dependence[c, d]	15.2 n.s.	13.6 n.s.	23.5 n.s.	84
Lifetime PTSD[c, e, f]	6.2 n.s.	6.6 n.s.	11.7 n.s.	84
Lifetime major depression[c, d]	12.7 n.s.	-4.4 n.s.	23.6 n.s.	84

(table continues)

Table 5.89 continued

	Percentage change (sexual assault-no sexual assault)			
		Partial table: Respondent sex		
	Zero-order table	Male	Female	Total *n*
Diagnoses	χ^2, O.R.	χ^2, O.R.	χ^2, O.R.	
Current depression[g]	19.1 3.929*, 2.895	16.4 n.s.	11.8 n.s.	81
Lifetime conduct disorder[e, h]	22.8 4.509**, 3.200	-19.7 n.s.	23.6 5.846**, 5.958	84
High symptom counts	χ^2, O.R.	χ^2, O.R.	χ^2, O.R.	
Trait anxiety[i]	20.3 3.117*, 2.277	24.1 n.s.	5.9 n.s.	84
Lifetime drug abuse and/or dependence[c]	21.5 3.613*, 2.531	33.8 4.635**, 8.000	23.5 n.s.	84
Lifetime alcohol abuse and/or dependence[c]	11.6 n.s.	10.9 n.s.	17.6 n.s.	84
Lifetime PTSD[c]	15.2 n.s.	15.8 n.s.	5.9 n.s.	84
Lifetime major depression[c]	25.7 5.065**, 2.864	26.7 2.771*, 3.033	17.6 n.s.	84
Lifetime conduct disorder[h]	21.9 3.638*, 2.454	22.4 n.s.	35.3 4.371**, 4.643	84
Current depression[g]	7.9 n.s.	-19.7 n.s.	23.6 n.s.	84

(table continues)

Table 5.89 continued

*$p<.10$, **$p<.05$, ***$p<.01$, ****$p<.001$

[a] Current depression and/or trait anxiety. [b] Any combination of the following diagnoses: major depression, substance abuse and/or dependence, post-traumatic stress disorder and/or conduct disorder. [c] Assessed by the Diagnostic Interview Schedule. [d] Met DSM-III criteria for caseness. [e] Met DSM-IIIR criteria for caseness. [f] Only 2 symptoms of avoidance or numbing were required for caseness. [g] Assessed by the Children's Depression Inventory. Caseness criterion is 19 or more symptoms. [h] Assessed by the Diagnostic Interview Schedule for Children & Adolescents. Caseness excludes symptoms of running away. All symptoms have occurred while the respondent was <u>not</u> homeless. [i] Assessed by the Revised Children's Manifest Anxiety Scale.

VII
Discussion[1]

It must be recognized that the causes and consequences of homelessness in the general and youth populations are numerous, complex, and dynamic. Understanding homelessness requires the study of both macro and micro-level social, economic, political, and health systems as well as the individual who is homeless. The macro-level factors which profoundly contribute to homelessness include the growth of poverty, the erosion of welfare benefits, the reduction of decent low- and moderate-income housing, the decline of employment opportunities, and the political shifting of responsibility for poverty relief, equalization of economic opportunity, and protection of individual liberty. To focus exclusively on the characteristics of the family and/or the homeless individual could result in victim blaming and the reinforcement of negative stereotypes rather than recognizing that these homeless are affected by and react to changes in the macrostructures of mainstream society and the microstructure changes in the culture of street life. The structure and limitations of research funding have encouraged researchers to conduct cross-sectional and retrospective research on service-utilizing homeless individuals rather than longitudinal examinations of persons and families at-risk for homelessness and the systems which affect them. *This study's cross-sectional descriptive results must be kept in perspective with regard to the larger societal forces which affect homeless youth and their families in the United States.*

Descriptive Characteristics of the Sample and the Sampling Strata

Sample Demographic Characteristics

Compared with the general youth population aged 13-17 living in Los Angeles County, the Hollywood Homeless Youth Sample (HHYS) is disproportionately male, older, white and Native American. Among 13-17 year old persons living in Los Angeles County in 1990, 52% were male; 34% aged 16-17 years; 34% white, 12% black, 43% Hispanic, 0.3% American Indian, and 11% Asian (1990 U.S. Census STF3B files). Latino and Asian youth are underrepresented in the HHYS. The HHYS may underrepresent Latino and Asian youth by underrepresenting immigrant youth, in general. The proportion of HHYS respondents who reported that they were born outside the United States is 14%; whereas, the proportion of Los Angeles County residents of all ages who have birthplaces outside the United States is 33% (U.S. Census STF3B, 1990). The mean grade level completed in the HHYS was 9.2, 28% had been held back at some point in school, and 27% had been in a special education program (vs. 0.34% and 0.35% for Los Angeles Unified School District students, kindergarten through 12th grade, 1992/1993 retention and special education statistics, respectively, *Fall 1993 Annual School Program Survey*. L.A.U.S.D.)

When comparing the demographic characteristics of the HHYS sample with those collected at intake to youth shelters in Hollywood (Pennbridge et al., 1990), it is apparent that the HHYS shelter stratum contains a greater proportion of youth of color, particularly Asian and African American, who were born outside of California than would be expected. Compared with reported demographic characteristics of clients contacted through street outreach and drop-in services in Hollywood, the HHYS combined drop-in center and street site stratum contains a greater proportion of Caucasian youth and fewer Latinos/Hispanics and African Americans and more Native Americans. It is difficult to know what these discrepancies represent. It is plausible that the HHYS demographics reflect a seasonal variation in the demographic characteristics of the local homeless youth population, a much discussed but poorly documented phenomenon.

Many attributes of a sample of homeless youth interviewed in Chicago were comparable to those observed in the HHYS. For instance, nearly 50% of the homeless youth interviewed in Chicago believed that a cohabitant had had an alcohol problem compared with 50% of the HHYS (Chicago Coalition for the Homeless, 1993). About one in four respondents in Chicago had been expelled from school compared with 37% in the HHYS, and one in three Chicago homeless youth had been held back at least one year compared with 28% of the HHYS. Whether these characteristics are stable across time and across samples of homeless youth in different geographic regions remains to be seen.

Sampling

One of the prevailing difficulties in doing research among the homeless is obtaining a sample which truly represents the population. Since no 'master list' of homeless persons exists and because the homeless tend to be fairly mobile, it is difficult to estimate the probability of a homeless individual being sampled. Sampling homeless persons from street sites can be quite dangerous and costly, as well. Consequently, many studies have relied on sampling homeless individuals from service sites such as soup kitchens and shelters. This is adequate to describe those among the homeless who utilize such services, but sampling exclusively from service sites does not represent those who do not use social or medical services. Forty percent of the HHYS would not have been represented in the survey if the sample had been limited to shelter users.

The two primary types of social services designed for and used by homeless youth in Hollywood are shelters and drop-in centers. Anecdotal evidence suggested that shelters and drop-in centers did not attract the same homeless youth. Therefore, for some analyses, the HHYS sample was stratified across three sampling site types: shelters, drop-in centers, and street sites. Youth encountered at the three types of interview location did indeed tend to differ from one another. Perhaps due to the low tolerance for which youth shelters and other providers have for antisocial behavior and substance use, the HHYS street subsample contained the greatest proportion of youth with symptoms of substance abuse and conduct disorder. Consistent with data from the housed population in which symptoms of substance abuse and conduct disorder often covary with being male (Offord, 1985), the street subsample was predominantly male.

Compared with the street subsample, shelters appeared to more often attract youth who were temporarily homeless, were alone, were endorsing symptoms of lifetime and current depression and anxiety, were survivors of maltreatment (particularly sexual assault) and were characterized as young (aged 13-15 years) immigrant women of color who had incomes of less than $100 in the month preceding the interview. These youth may be the least able to cope with the challenges and dangers of street life due to their relative inexperience with American street culture, lack of social support, lack of tangible coping resources, relative youth, and psychological fragility. Studies which have described the prevalence of child maltreatment and symptoms of psychological distress among homeless youth in shelters may have underestimated the proportion of the larger homeless youth population which is chronically homeless and has symptoms of conduct disorder and substance abuse and overestimated the prevalence of child maltreatment, depression and anxiety.

Youth who disclosed engaging in same-sex sexual activities or who identified themselves as gay, lesbian, or bisexual were more likely to be interviewed on the street and in drop-in centers than in shelters. Homosexual and bisexual youth often report being homeless because of conflicts about their sexual orientation. After experiencing rejection in their homes and communities, homosexual and bisexual youth may avoid using services designed for heterosexual youth in order to evade additional conflict around their sexual orientation. Given the increased prevalence of symptoms of drug abuse and/or dependence and conduct disorder and histories of sexual assault compared with heterosexual youth, programs and facilities which are designed specifically for and are attractive to gay, lesbian, and bisexual youth may be critical to their abilities for departure from street life. Since these data were collected, a new youth shelter has opened in Hollywood which is administered by a local gay and lesbian organization.

The chronically homeless were most often interviewed at drop-in sites. For studies attempting to track youth over time beginning early in the youth's homelessness, sampling strategies which rely exclusively on drop-in centers would be less productive than those which perhaps oversample in shelters and street sites. This is not to suggest that a tremendous overlap of individuals between location types may not exist. Overall, the data support the notion that sampling sources will influence the degree to which any subpopulation is represented by a sample and will dictate the description of the population as a whole.

Child Maltreatment

As previously described in the homeless and runaway youth literature, the prevalence of lifetime exposure to child neglect, domestic violence, physical abuse and sexual abuse was high compared to national averages (Kennedy, 1991). At 68%, 79%, and 34%, the lifetime prevalences of neglect, physical abuse, and sexual abuse in the HHYS substantially exceed the 1992 national annual incidences of maltreatment among reported and substantiated cases involving minor children of 52%, 23%, and 14%, respectively (U.S.D.H.H.S., N.C.C.A.N., 1994). Of course, one would expect lifetime prevalences to surpass annual incidences of maltreatment. Finkelhor (1994) reports that the most reliable studies of the national lifetime prevalence of childhood sexual assault among adults estimate that approximately 20% of all women and between 5 and10% of all men have been sexually assaulted before the age of 18. At 50% for women and 24% for men, the prevalences of childhood sexual assault among the youth of the HHYS far exceed the national estimates in the general adult population. Prevention and intervention programs and policies aimed at youth at risk for maltreatment, running away or homelessness should be designed with these maltreatment rates among homeless youth in mind.

Almost all (92%) of those who participated in the child maltreatment sections disclosed histories of maltreatment; and nearly all (87%) who disclosed histories of child maltreatment described being physically assaulted. This suggests that child maltreatment in general and physical assault in particular may be two of several critical antecedents to youth homelessness, assuming that lifetime prevalences of childhood physical assault in the general population are not as high as those observed in the HHYS.

For nearly 80% of the survivors of physical assault, the level of violence experienced was at least injurious, if not life-threatening. Over half of those who disclosed histories of maltreatment described that the maltreatment was a factor in their leaving home, voluntarily or not. Anecdotal reports suggest that much, if not a majority, of child maltreatment does not get reported to child protection authorities. Given the stigma associated with child neglect and abuse and domestic violence and the myth that adolescents do not require protection from child maltreatment and exploitation, it is not surprising that fewer than half of the respondents who allege histories of child maltreatment knew of any reports to authorities. Neglect and sexual assault were less often reported to authorities than physical assaults; this may be partially due to the inherent difficulties in proving childhood sexual assault and the less obvious cases of neglect.

Lifetime prevalences of child maltreatment among other samples of homeless and runaway youth were quite comparable to those found in the HHYS when similar methodology was used. Seventy-five percent of the homeless youth interviewed in Chicago disclosed histories of physical abuse by their caretakers (vs. 79% of the HHYS reporting histories of physical assaults by anyone), and 17% (vs. 18% of the HHYS) reported histories of sexual abuse by their relatives (Chicago Coalition for the Homeless, 1993). Seventeen percent of the youth in Chicago disclosed having been locked in small spaces (vs. 18% in the HHYS).

Consistent with the results of some studies (Wyatt, Newcomb, and Riederle, 1993), history of child maltreatment was inversely related to the educational level of the father. Having a father who had not completed high school appeared to be a risk factor for sexual assault, in particular. Some researchers who have explored the role of family socioeconomic status in the maltreatment of children in more detail than was done in the Hollywood Homeless Youth Study indicate that it is extreme poverty which places a family at risk for exposure to child maltreatment (Finkelhor, 1994). It is impossible to determine from the HHYS data whether it is the father's education, per se, which puts youth at greater risk for sexual assault or if father's educational level is merely a proxy for socioeconomic status.

As in other studies (Finkelhor, 1990), women were more likely to disclose histories of sexual assault, and men more frequently described histories of physical assault in the HHYS. The variation in rates of disclosed sexual assault across gender is most likely due to both an actual difference in exposure as well as a dissimilarity in tendencies to disclose histories of sexual assault. Neglect, physical assault, sexual assault, and witnessing domestic violence covaried with one another. If the HHYS is representative of other homeless youth, service providers should be aware of the high likelihood of exposure to multiple types of child maltreatment among homeless youth. As with other studies which have found that family drug use is a risk factor for sexual assault (Beitchman et al., 1991 and 1992), a HHYS respondent who believed that a relative had a problem with mental health, alcohol use, or drug use was more likely to have disclosed a history of sexual assault.

Fewer respondents disclosed histories of sexual assault than physical assault, yet nearly all of those who described histories of sexual assault also reported histories of physical assault. Therefore, the only comparison available which had some degree of statistical power, vis a vis sample size, was between those who had been sexually assaulted and those who had not been sexually assaulted among a sample with a high lifetime prevalence of child maltreatment, particularly physical assaults, and an unknown lifetime prevalence of psychological abuse. Due to the limited sample size, exposure patterns to every different combination of maltreatment could not be partialled out and examined; moderate exposure heterogeneity with regard to neglect and witnessing domestic violence within dichotomous categories was unavoidable.

Child Maltreatment, Sexual Revictimization, and Risk-Taking

One out of three respondents had been tested for HIV-antibodies; 3.6% of those tested were positive for HIV-antibodies (vs. seroprevalence rates of 0.85% among military applicants under 20 years of age from Los Angeles, Burke et al., 1990; 0.29% among 16-21 year old Job Corps participants from California, St. Louis et al., 1989; and 1.09% among 13-24 year old patients of Los Angeles County STD and Family Planning clinics, The Los Angeles County Adolescent HIV/AIDS Strategic Plan, 1993). Four to six percent of the homeless and runaway youth population in the United States is estimated to be HIV infected (Stricof, Kennedy, Nattel, Weisfuse, and Novick, 1991). Given the high prevalence of sexual assault, prostitution, and unprotected sexual activities, homeless youth are at increased risk for exposure to HIV compared to the housed adolescent population.

Contrary to the literature that suggests that child sexual abuse or sexual revictimization may predispose survivors to engage in sexual acts with greater numbers of partners (Wyatt, 1992), there were no observed differences in the numbers of sexual partners described by survivors of physical assault compared with those of survivors of sexual assault. Respondents who did *not* disclose histories of physical or sexual assault reported the highest number of sexual partners in the year preceding the interview. This result may reflect an unintended interpretation of the question about numbers of 'sexual partners'; for the respondents, 'sexual partners' may connote only those partners with whom the respondent had an emotional relationship. Anecdotal evidence from other studies of homeless youth suggest that homeless youth often make fine distinctions between persons with whom they have sexual relations.

Consistent with other studies (Silbert and Pines, 1983), analyses between child maltreatment variables and involvement in sex work revealed that histories of sexual assault and sexual revictimization covaried positively with participation in pornography and prostitution. History of sexual assault appeared to be a stronger risk factor for involvement in prostitution among young men than among young women. History of sexual assault, per se, was not related to participation in pornography; however, sexual revictimization was related to participation in pornography. Although homelessness, in and of itself, exerts strong economic pressures which favor participation in sex work, it appears that history of sexual assault increases the odds that homeless youth will engage in sex work. It is unclear why history of sexual assault may be a stronger risk factor for engaging in prostitution for young men than young women or why young men were more often sexually revictimized than young women. Compared with young women, perhaps young men have a higher psychological need for control in interpersonal encounters which may drive them toward re-experiencing the assault experience under controlled conditions via prostitution to regain their sense of power. It may be that the increased participation in prostitution by male sexual assault survivors placed them in increased danger of being revictimized.

One may speculate that survivors of sexual assault in general and sexual revictimization in particular may be the least psychologically able to assert themselves in interpersonal negotiations, especially for the purposes of protection. Women with histories of sexual assault were more likely to report histories of pregnancies compared with women who had not been sexually assaulted, yet sexual revictimization was not related to pregnancy. History of sexual assault, but not sexual revictimization, appeared to covary with history of sexually transmitted diseases, particularly for women. Although use of birth control in the past year, in general, and specifically use of a condom were unrelated to history of sexual assault, they were less frequently reported by those sexual assault survivors who had been revictimized. The seemingly contradictory results observed in the HHYS may be due to (1) a lack of statistical power necessary to observe the expected relationships, (2) a lack of respondent knowledge regarding his or her history of asymptomatic and symptomatic STD infections, (3) stronger relationships between sexual revictimization and lack of use of birth control and condoms among men than women and (4) a weak relationship between history of sexual assault and lack of use of condoms among women. The observed gender differences in risk-taking may reflect differences in exposure to sexual assaults. For young women in the HHYS, a single sexual assault perpetrated by a parent may have been sufficient to impair the development of self-protective behaviors. For young men, multiple exposures by non-parents may have resulted in the impairment of the development of self-protective behaviors.

Involvement in prostitution was also a risk factor for pregnancy. It is known that, at least at the time of this study, prostitutes would often be offered more compensation for engaging in sexual acts *without* using a condom. However, youth who engaged in prostitution were *more* likely to report regular use of birth control in general and use of condoms specifically during the year preceding the interview than youth who did not prostitute; this was particularly true for youth who had histories of sexual abuse. Regular use of birth control and condoms in the last year were positively related to a history of pregnancy and were unrelated to a history of sexually transmitted diseases. Perhaps it is the experience of pregnancy which encouraged the use of birth control. The sample size was insufficient to assess the relationship between prostitution, birth control use, and pregnancy among female sexual assault survivors.

As expected, given the economic and perhaps social pressure to engage in sex work and sexual risk-taking, length of homelessness was positively related to sexual revictimization and sexual risk-taking, but this covariation was moderated by respondent gender. Lifetime cumulative homelessness of one year or greater appeared to be a risk factor for involvement in sex work and sexually transmitted diseases, especially among women. Whereas, longer lifetime homelessness seemed to put men at increased risk for greater numbers of sexual partners and sexual revictimization. Lifetime cumulative homelessness did not appear to be related to use of birth control, in general, or of condoms, in particular. The data suggest that the course of entry into sex work for homeless young men differs somewhat from that of homeless young women. Perhaps young men enter into sex work earlier in the course of homelessness than young women and thereby have a longer period of exposure to various sexual partners who may initiate a sexual assault. In other words, for men, homelessness, rather than the length of homelessness, may determine involvement in sex work, and length of involvement in sex work vis-a-vis length of homelessness may affect exposure to numerous sexual partners and to sexual revictimization. For women, on the other hand, length of homelessness may determine entry into sex work and exposure to STDs (perhaps via sex work).

Sexual assault survivors whose fathers had higher than average educations (i.e., high school graduate or greater) were more likely to be sexually revictimized than those whose fathers had lower educations. Wyatt and colleagues (1993) suggest that, for women, this association may be strongest when the initial sexual assault is extrafamilial and that revictimization may be facilitated by the higher work demands often associated with those with higher educations which results in the father's physical and/or emotional absence necessary to support and protect the child after the first sexual assault. The lack of paternal support after the first sexual assault may have contributed to the lowering of the child's self-esteem, thereby putting the child at risk for sexual revictimization.

Consistent with Wyatt's findings (1993), incest survivors were at increased risk for sexual revictimization when their father's educational level was lower than average. Wyatt and her colleagues postulate that female incest survivors whose fathers had lower educations were vulnerable to sexual revictimization because they may not have learned the skills necessary to protect themselves from further revictimization despite adequate levels of self-esteem.

Antecedents to Homelessness

Without information on the economic and social stressors of the families of the respondents, it is impossible to estimate the influence of societal macrolevel structural changes or microlevel interpersonal changes on the homelessness of the youth in the sample. Few youth attributed their departures from home specifically to family homelessness or poverty, and despite the widespread belief that family members had problems with substance use and/or mental health, few attributed their homelessness directly to these factors. Although most respondents reported that the *event(s)* which precipitated their leaving home was family conflict or child maltreatment, nearly two-thirds attributed the *cause* of their current homelessness or inability to establish their own residences to a lack of tangible resources such as a job, money, identification, and housing.

Most minor youth do not qualify for general assistance on their own, and only 10 percent of the sample had completed the process of becoming legally emancipated. It is not surprising, then, to find that only one percent of the sample reported receiving general assistance in the 30 days prior to the interview. With welfare reform as a high political priority these days, it is unlikely that policymakers will widen the entrance to welfare to include minor youth who are not living with their parents or guardians.

Contrary to the belief that, for all, homelessness is an agreeable and freely chosen lifestyle, few (6%) reported that their homelessness was desirable. For the nearly one-third of the sample who reported that their current homeless was due to family crisis or the inability to 'get along with others', supported family reunification may be the best intervention for all parties if support includes any necessary structural as well as psychosocial support for the family. For others with untenable or nonexistent family support, assistance towards independent living might be suitable and desirable. As with homeless adults, the histories and characteristics of homeless youth are quite heterogenous.

Unfortunately, public policy has tended to be unidimensional with regard to publicly supported interventions for homeless and runaway youth by favoring either institutionalization or family reunification, depending on the political climate. Placement of a youth with underfunded and undersupported foster families and group homes may result in the youth's reexposure to child maltreatment. Institutionalization of homeless youth may mean incarceration in facilities for juvenile offenders. It is undoubtedly a reflection of the political perspective of homeless youth as potential law breakers in California that mandates that state funding for homeless and runaway youth be housed in the Office of Criminal Justice Planning. Involvement in the 'system', i.e., foster, group or juvenile justice care, does not guarantee that a youth will be taught non-violent conflict resolution techniques or job skills or will be given the opportunities in which to raise self-esteem. Involvement in the 'system' certainly does not prevent homelessness among a substantial number of youth. Although only six-percent of the respondents reported leaving foster or group care before their most recent episode of homelessness, roughly one-third of those who had been in foster care, group care, or juvenile detention overnight spent the night following their most recent departure from care on the street or in an emergency shelter. Clearly, our systems of institutionalized care for youth need assistance in preventing premature departures by youth and subsequent homelessness. Since most (two-thirds) of the respondents had experienced multiple episodes of homelessness, it would appear that efforts toward preventing recurrent homelessness were ineffective for the youth in the HHYS.

When the HHYS is stratified across patterns of homelessness, i.e., temporary, episodic, or chronic, the demographic patterns observed for the whole sample shift according to stratum. Of particular interest are the demographic characteristics of the chronically homeless in the HHYS: young (aged 13-15), white-non-Latino, and female. One might be concerned that the chronically homeless youth might be at particular risk for adult homelessness. If the HHYS is representative of the homeless youth population in Los Angeles, do its young, white, chronically homeless women represent those homeless youth who are at greatest risk for becoming homeless adult women (who are often with children), a rapidly growing subpopulation among homeless adults?

To the author's knowledge, no one has tracked a sample of homeless youth long enough to establish what proportion of homeless youth remain or become homeless again during adulthood. Given that homeless adults and adolescents often share childhood histories of frequent institutional placements and exposure to family violence and child maltreatment, it seems probable that homelessness during adolescence is a risk factor for adult homelessness. Researchers of homeless adults have reported that some of their respondents had histories of homelessness as minor adolescents (McChesney, 1987; Susser, Streuning, and Conover, 1987; Vander Kooi, 1983). Interviews with a nationally representative sample of adult household members revealed that parental neglect and either physical or sexual abuse significantly increased the odds of prior homelessness among respondents (Struening and Link, 1997). In addition, a recent study of homeless women with severe mental illness revealed that survivors of child sexual abuse were more likely to become homeless during childhood (Davies-Netzley, Hurlburt, and Hough, 1996). The strength of adolescent homelessness as a risk factor for adult homelessness is currently unknown, however.

Psychological Distress

Studies of lifetime prevalences of indicators[2] of psychological distress among community and school samples of adolescents have found rates of major depression to vary from 4-9%, alcohol abuse 32%, drug abuse 10%, generalized anxiety 4%, and PTSD 6% (Reinherz et al., 1993; Whitaker et al., 1990). The lifetime prevalence of conduct disorder among the general child/adolescent (i.e., under 18 years of age) population has been estimated at 2-9% for female children and 6-16% for male children (American Psychiatric Association, *DSM-IV*, 1994). Assuming that measurement of psychological distress among the HHYS was relatively valid and reliable (internal consistency reliabilities, as measured by Cronbach's alpha, ranged from .70 to .90 among the respondents of the HHYS), lifetime prevalences of indicators of psychological distress exceeded the rates found in the general adolescent population. The proportion of the HHYS which met diagnostic criteria was: 26% for major depression, 48% for alcohol abuse and/or dependence, 39% for drug abuse and/or dependence, 7% for trait anxiety, 18% for PTSD, and 68-84% for conduct disorder (depending on the criteria used). At 64% and 47%, the lifetime prevalences for suicide thoughts and attempts dramatically surpassed those found among adults in Wave II of the Los Angeles Epidemiologic Catchment Area (ECA) project (12% and 4%, respectively) (Sorenson and Rutter, 1991). The elevated rates of reported symptoms of psychological distress may be due to the methodology employed as well as the extremely high prevalence of acute and chronic exposure to traumatic (e.g., child maltreatment and street violence) and daily stressors (e.g., deprivation of food, clothing, shelter, and safety) among the HHYS.

Nearly all of the traumatic experiences cited as causes for reported symptoms of PTSD involved violence. Much speculation has linked the exposure to violence at home and on the street with subsequent symptoms of psychological distress and participation in violence among homeless youth. However, the processes by which these events are linked are still undefined. It is probable that, as suggested by other studies, early exposure to aggressive interpersonal interaction contributes to the likelihood that a predisposed individual will use aggression in their own interpersonal interactions by mechanisms including, but not limited to: modeling, stress-induction, and sensitization (Cummings and El-Sheikh, 1991). Data presented by Cummings and El-Sheikh suggest that emotional and behavioral responses to angry home environments vary across children, that these responses remain relatively stable over time, and that unresolved (i.e., concluding without apology or compromise) and hostile (i.e., involving violence against objects or persons) conflicts result in the highest levels of anger and distress as reported by the children studied.

Comorbidity of diagnostic caseness was remarkably high: 26% of the sample met diagnostic criteria for *both* drug and alcohol abuse, 61% of the sample met criteria for *one or both* drug and alcohol abuse, 55% of the respondents met diagnostic criteria for substance abuse and/or dependence plus one other indicator of psychological distress, and 85% met diagnostic criteria for at least one current or lifetime psychological disorder (vs. 26% in a community sample of adolescents, Fergusson et al., 1993). Clearly, polydrug abuse can make detoxification and addiction recovery more complicated, a fact well known to substance abuse treatment providers. Accurate diagnosis of addictions at intake for substance abuse treatment is, therefore, crucial to proper acute and follow-up care. Multiple diagnoses of psychological disorders can further complicate effective treatment.

Comorbidity among indicators of psychological distress was evident for both diagnostic caseness and symptom counts. As observed in other studies (Fergusson, Horwood, and Lynskey, 1993) and discussed in the most recent version of the *Diagnostic and Statistical Manual of Mental Disorder* (American Psychiatric Association, *DSM-IV*, 1994), alcohol and drug abuse and/or dependence covaried with each other and with conduct disorder, and anxiety disorders (i.e., PTSD and trait anxiety) covaried with each other and with mood disorders (i.e., lifetime major depression, current depression, and suicide attempts) within the HHYS. In addition, symptoms of mood disorders covaried with symptoms of substance abuse and/or dependence, probably a reflection of the mood regulating and disregulating functions of drugs and alcohol.

Symptoms of trait anxiety and major depression were inversely related to alcohol abuse and/or dependence. This finding is consistent with reports that alcohol use may be inversely related to symptoms of depression over short periods of time (Aneshensel and Huba, 1984). Alcohol abuse and/or dependence may afford the sedation necessary to reduce symptoms of trait anxiety but would be expected to exacerbate symptoms of depression. However, depressed individuals may be attracted to the numbing properties of alcohol when painful affect is experienced. Symptoms of trait anxiety were inversely related to symptoms of drug abuse and/or dependence and conduct disorder. Substance use may attenuate the symptoms of anxiety thereby facilitating antisocial actions, and persons with trait anxiety may tend to avoid substance abuse and antisocial behaviors. Symptoms of PTSD, on the other hand, were positively related to symptoms of substance abuse and/or dependence, particularly drug abuse, and conduct disorder. Participation in a drug-abusing and antisocial subculture of the streets may increase the likelihood of exposure to traumatic events which may induce symptoms of PTSD. Symptoms of PTSD may be attenuated by drug use; and efforts to gain control over one's exposure to the traumatic stress of victimization may lead a youth into antisocial activities.

Demographic Factors and Psychological Distress

Several sociodemographic factors were examined for their potential relationships with psychological distress. Consistent with other studies of the relationship between gender and endorsement of symptoms of psychological distress (e.g., as cited in the American Psychiatric Association, *DSM-IV*, 1994), young women from the HHYS were more likely to endorse symptoms associated with mood (i.e., current and lifetime major depression and suicide thoughts and attempts) and anxiety disorders (i.e., trait anxiety and PTSD). Male respondents, on the other hand, more often reported externalizing symptoms of distress, i.e., substance abuse and/or dependence and conduct disorder. It is unknown whether this represents actual gender differences in exposure to stress, symptoms of distress, or in the willingness to report various symptoms of distress or a combination of these factors.

Older youth were more likely to disclose previous suicide attempts and symptoms of substance abuse and/or dependence and PTSD and were less likely to report symptoms of current depression. Compared with younger respondents, older youth are probably more likely to have been exposed to the types of acute stressors which can trigger symptoms of PTSD and more likely to have been exposed to longer durations of homelessness and substance use.

Lower than average income in the month preceding the interview (i.e., less than $100) tended to covary with symptoms of mood and anxiety disorders, yet higher than average income tended to covary with symptoms of substance abuse and/or dependence. Although few respondents earned enough money to independently acquire housing and support themselves, those who earned less than average may have been despondent over their lack of financial resources. Youth who reported symptoms of substance use may have been more likely to be involved in the selling of illicit drugs which may account for the association between higher incomes and substance use. Employment, in and of itself, was not a strong or consistent predictor of any indicator of psychological distress.

Higher than average education (i.e., 10th grade or higher) was associated with an increased likelihood that respondents would report symptoms of lifetime major depression and PTSD but a decreased likelihood that they would endorse symptoms of current depression. Some developmental psychologists (Green and Larson, 1991) suggest that increased cognitive maturity among children and adolescents may facilitate enhanced insight regarding internal experience and emotion which may be manifested as symptoms of internalized distress; yet these cognitively mature children and adolescents are also more apt to have highly developed skills in affect regulation, thus limiting the duration of the distress. It seems likely that cognitive maturity covaries with educational level.

The proportion of the HHYS which had been held back in school or had attended special education classes was exponentially higher than that of the Los Angeles Unified School District student population (L.A.U.S.D., 1992/1993). History of repeated grades and attendance in special education classes were weak or inconsistent predictors of symptoms of psychological distress. In general, youth who had poor or failing grades more often reported symptoms of all evaluated indicators of psychological distress than youth who had good to excellent grades. Without additional information, it is difficult to know how school performance and placement reflected and affected a respondent's overall emotional and cognitive adaptation. Nearly one-third of the HHYS had received poor to failing grades overall, yet 83% of the sample reported that they were either attending school at the time of the interview (12%) or were planning to return to school (71%). This suggests that some of the youth who had had difficult times in school were resilient enough to return or to plan on returning to school. A college degree was the goal of many who wanted to continue their education, a goal not often associated with those who wish to remain on the fringes of mainstream society. Having plans to return to school covaried with elevated symptoms of lifetime depression and PTSD and decreased symptoms of alcohol abuse, conduct disorder, and suicide attempts.

Family Characteristics and Psychological Distress

At 69%, the divorce rate among the married parents of the respondents greatly exceeds the 13% divorce rate among the ever-married in the general population of Los Angeles County aged 15 years or older (U.S. Census STF3B, 1990) and the 50% lifetime divorce rate among marriages which is described in the popular press. The extent to which the HHYS parental divorce rate compares with that of other parents of 13-17 year-olds was not established. Parental divorce has been recognized as a potentially severe acute stressor for children which may be accompanied by chronic stress arising from resultant poverty, new or overcrowded living quarters, change of schools, and continued family arguments or parental discord (American Psychiatric Association, 1987). Although history of parental divorce did not appear to be positively related to any indicator of psychological distress, it should be regarded as a plausible contributor to the multiple sources of stress for the respondents of the HHYS. Roughly one in ten respondents had also experienced the potentially extreme stress of either the loss of a mother or a father or both. Death of one's biological father appeared to put youth at increased risk for symptoms of substance abuse and conduct disorder.

Over half of the respondents had been born to mothers who were 20 years old or younger at the time of their birth. Given that childbirth during adolescence may place young women at increased risk for curtailed or delayed education and poverty and may place their children at increased risk for neglect and abuse, age of mother at the respondent's birth was examined as a potential covariate of indicators of psychological distress. Age of mother at birth (i.e., 20 years or younger) tended to vary inversely with a respondent's history of suicide attempts. Younger age of mother at birth was correlated with a respondent's father's lack of a high school education, another potential risk factor for family poverty, distress, and violence, and covaried with a respondent's history of child neglect, placement in foster care, and increased cumulative lifetime homelessness for the respondent. Age of mother at the respondent's birth may have contributed both directly and indirectly to the veritable constellation of potential stressors present in the lives of many respondents and may have been a risk factor for youth homelessness.

The proportion of parents who completed high school closely mirrored that of the general population over 25 years of age residing in Los Angeles County (U.S. Census STF3B, 1990). Contrary to studies which suggest an inverse relationship between socioeconomic status and risk of psychological distress (Gore, Aseltine, and Colton, 1992; Rutter, 1975), youth with fathers who had completed 12 or more grades/years of education were more likely to report symptoms of lifetime major depression, trait anxiety, and current depression. Some researchers speculate that education may facilitate problem recognition and the reporting of distress symptoms (Yokopenic, Clark, and Aneshensel, 1983). No trends were observed between mother's education and symptoms of psychological distress.

Perceived Psychological Distress of Relatives and Youth Psychological Distress

Why some youth respond to stress and distress with substance use or antisocial behaviors is not well understood. Relationships between perceived substance abuse among relatives and symptoms of psychological distress were analyzed in an attempt to uncover the role of behavior modeling of substance use by relatives in the development of symptoms of substance abuse among youth. Respondents who held the belief that a relative had problems with alcohol use appeared to be at decreased risk for suicide attempts but increased risk for symptoms of trait anxiety, lifetime major depression, current depression, conduct disorder, and drug abuse and/or dependence. Youth who perceived that a relative had a drug or a mental health problem were more likely to endorse symptoms of all indicators of psychological distress except current depression. Familial drug use seemed to put youth at decreased risk for suicide attempts, yet familial mental illness put youth at increased risk for suicide thoughts and attempts. Contrary to expectations arising from social learning theory (Bandura, 1977), youth who had been exposed to familial alcohol abuse were no more likely to express symptoms of alcohol abuse than youth who had not been exposed to familial alcohol abuse. However, exposure to familial drug use covaried with a youth's symptoms of drug abuse and/or dependence. The conflict and violence which were described as being precipitated by a relative's substance abuse undoubtedly contributed to the overall stress experienced by the youth.

Institutionalized Care and Psychological Distress

Two-thirds of the HHYS had histories of institutionalized care (including group care and juvenile detention and excluding foster care and psychiatric hospitalization). Whereas the lifetime prevalences of the institutionalization of 13-17 year olds in the general population of Los Angeles County are unknown, the point prevalence institutionalization of minor children in Los Angeles County was 0.6% in 1990. The rate of institutionalization among the HHYS most certainly exceeds that in the general adolescent population.

As another potential source of stress, institutionalization was examined in two ways: the types of institutions (including juvenile detention, foster and group care) and the number of separate episodes in any type of placement. One-third of the sample had experienced multiple types of placements. History of juvenile detention or foster or group care as well as the number of individual placements were associated with the presence or absence of symptoms lifetime psychological distress. The results suggest that juvenile detention and foster care may be associated with protection against depression and suicide but that juvenile detention and group care may introduce increased risk for conduct disorder. Placement in juvenile detention and group care may result from preexisting symptoms of conduct disorder and may expose youth to an environment where socially unacceptable behaviors may be learned.

In addition, juvenile detention and group care appear to be associated with increased risk for substance abuse and/or dependence. It is unknown whether or not it is the increased reliance on substance use which decreases depressive symptomatology in juvenile detention and if the substance use is for the purpose of mood control. Also unknown is whether the onset of substance abuse precedes placement or occurs during placement or after placement has been terminated. Foster and group care were associated with better than average school grades, and, of the three types of placement examined, foster care appeared to be, potentially, the most protective placement against symptoms of psychological distress.

Youth who have been placed two or more times in any institutionalized care seem to be at increased risk for symptoms of anxiety, substance abuse and/or dependence, and conduct disorder. History of group care and multiple placements in any institutionalized care were related to an increased likelihood that respondents would experience episodes of homelessness earlier and more frequently in their lives as well as longer cumulative lifetime homelessness. It has been suggested that children living through multiple placements have had their attachment to their primary caregiver severed so many times that attachment to anyone may be difficult and may result in problems establishing and maintaining social relationships later in life. Difficulty with attachment in social relationships may predispose these children to homelessness by making cohabitation, employment, and help-seeking more trying for all involved.

From a macrolevel perspective, children who have few strong social ties when they are released from institutionalized care are also likely to have fewer tangible resources with which to establish an independent home. Unfortunately, programmed psychosocial and tangible assistance during the transition from institutionalized care during childhood to family or independent living has been noticeably absent or, at best, inadequate. Planned transitional assistance would be particularly important if, in fact, placement in juvenile detention and group care substantially increases the risk for preexisting, concurrent, or antecedent substance abuse and/or dependence. Given that nearly half of the sample had spent at least one night in an emergency shelter or foster or group care in the year preceding the interview, contact with 'the youth care system' did not prevent these youth from becoming homeless.

Subsistence Needs and Psychological Distress

Difficulty obtaining food, clothing, or a place to clean up was inversely related to symptoms of substance abuse and conduct disorder, even after controlling for income levels. Substance use somehow either facilitated access to these daily essentials or made their absence less noticeable. Of the things which respondents did to protect themselves while living on the street, carrying a weapon was most strongly and consistently associated with various indicators of psychological distress. Namely, respondents who reported that they carried a weapon for protection were more likely to endorse symptoms of lifetime suicide thoughts, substance abuse and/or dependence and conduct disorder and current depression. Possessing a weapon may be particularly necessary for individuals who are involved in antisocial activities such as robbery, who are involved in the purchase or sale of controlled substances, or whose safety is regularly compromised because of being under the influence of drugs and/or alcohol. Given an observed positive association between weapon possession and income, weapon possession appears to be tangibly rewarding. Ironically, weapon possession was inversely related to having problems obtaining food and a place to clean up. This apparent relationship may be a reflection of the tendency for aggressive youth to either avoid or be turned away from youth services, such as shelters, which provide food and places to shower.

Service Utilization and Psychological Distress

Youth with symptoms of lifetime major depression, suicide thoughts, conduct disorder, PTSD, trait anxiety, and current depression were more likely to report use of mental health services in the year preceding the interview, although belief that they had a mental health problem did not covary with symptoms of conduct disorder or substance use. Perhaps youth perceive substance use and the symptoms associated with conduct disorder as necessary for survival on the street rather than as evidence of a mental health disorder.

Consistent with some of the literature on medical service utilization (Gortmaker and Gore, 1982), receipt of medical services in the year preceding the interview covaried with symptoms of all indicators of psychological distress, except substance abuse. However, having a regular medical provider seemed to be protective against elevated symptoms of substance abuse. It is unclear from the data whether having a regular medical provider indicates a greater frequency of medical visits and/or an established relationship with a particular provider or is a proxy for some other measure of stability. Exposure to medical providers on a regular basis may facilitate the recognition of signs of substance abuse by the provider and the initiation of intervention. Physicians may be less inclined, at least initially, to suspect the existence of mental health disorders when the presenting somatic symptoms are less pronounced and/or are easily explained by organic illness. Perhaps substance abusing and/or dependent youth are less likely to seek medical care for fear of having their abuse or addiction discovered. On the other hand, previous contacts with the medical system may have been perceived negatively because of discussions about substance abuse and discouraged regular contact with medical providers.

Street Gang Affiliation and Psychological Distress

Gang affiliation appeared to be a risk factor for substance abuse and/or dependence; particularly alcohol, cannabis, and amphetamines; conduct disorder; and PTSD as well as a protective factor against current depression. Substance use may have warded off any symptoms of depression or anxiety. Youth with symptoms of trait anxiety seemed to be more protected against gang affiliation than those without symptoms of trait anxiety.

Mobility and Migration

Respondents were quite mobile: over half had experienced between 3 and 30 intercity moves in the year preceding the interview and only half had spent the past month in Hollywood. When in Los Angeles, few (20%) respondents spent their entire days in the Hollywood area. Despite the apparent mobility of the respondents, almost all usually slept in Hollywood. Perhaps this is due to the reputation of Hollywood as a hub for street youth and, because of this, is the home of many youth-serving agencies. Researchers attempting to quantify and describe the homeless population in a given geographic area will, therefore, be challenged to carefully define the criteria for enumeration and description. In addition, the data suggest that homeless youth cannot be considered merely a local issue.

Suggested Relationships Between Psychological Distress, Child Maltreatment,and Youth Homelessness

Sequencing of Symptom Onset

Although one may legitimately dispute the validity of recalled ages at onset of events and symptoms, they are often all that are available in cross-sectional studies, and they may be useful in suggesting patterns for further study. In the HHYS, symptoms of conduct disorder were equally likely to be recalled as occurring before or after the year of the first exposure to maltreatment. The antisocial behaviors associated with conduct disorder may have precipitated some forms of child maltreatment when parental attempts to discipline the child accelerated. Virtually all respondents recalled that other symptoms of psychological distress appeared after their first exposure to maltreatment; this recalled sequence of events suggests that the maltreatment was perceived as distressing and that it may have been perceived as playing a role in the etiology of some symptoms of psychological distress which appeared subsequently. Approximately equal proportions of respondents recalled that symptoms of major depression, suicide thoughts and attempts, and alcohol abuse and/or dependence had their onset before their first homelessness episode as after their first homelessness episode. If the recollections are accurate, the data refute the notion that all homeless persons are mentally ill before the onset of homelessness and support the perspective that some dimensions of psychological distress may be both a cause and a consequence of homelessness.

Other dimensions of psychological distress, such as drug abuse and/or dependence and PTSD, were described as occurring either during the same year as the first homelessness episode or after by a majority of respondents. If this sequence is accurate, homelessness may be a risk factor for symptoms of drug abuse and/or dependence and PTSD among maltreated youth. The tendency for symptoms of alcohol abuse and/or dependence to be recalled as preceding symptoms of drug abuse and/or dependence, coupled with the sample's high rates of comorbidity of alcohol and drug abuse, implicates alcohol as a potential 'gateway' to drug use among the respondents. Symptoms of major depression were most often recalled as preceding symptoms of either alcohol or drug abuse and/or dependence; this is a symptom sequence which contributes evidence for the hypothesis that substance use may be a coping mechanism for those experiencing symptoms of depression. Symptoms of drug abuse and/or dependence were often recalled as appearing before the first attempt at suicide, the first involvement in pornography or prostitution, and first symptom of PTSD. It has been suggested by many homeless youth service providers as well as the youth themselves that drug use facilitates the dissociated mental state necessary for involvement in sex work; however, drug use which is adaptive for surviving the experience of non-violent sex work may be a risk factor for re-exposure to sexual and physical assaults. Drug use, which may have initially been somewhat adaptive in the control of depressive or anxious moods, may evolve into an undesirable addiction or maladaptive coping which puts the youth at risk for exposure to drug-related violence and more frequent and worse symptoms of psychological distress, including attempts at suicide.

Child Maltreatment and Psychological Distress

With the exception of current depression, symptoms of psychological distress generally increased across categories of maltreatment with the lowest frequency of symptoms occurring among those who reported no physical or sexual assaults, a moderate frequency of symptoms occurring among those who reported histories of physical assault, and the highest frequency of symptoms occurring among those who reported histories of sexual assault. For current depression, the highest frequency of symptoms occurred among youth disclosing histories of sexual assault. In the child maltreatment literature, physical and sexual assaults have been associated with symptoms of a wide variety of indicators of psychological distress. It is unclear whether these data represent a direct association between exposure to child maltreatment and psychological distress or associations of child maltreatment and psychological distress with a third undefined construct.

The progressive increase in rates of psychological distress observed across HHYS respondents categorized by child maltreatment exposure (i.e., no sexual or physical assaults, physical assaults, and sexual assaults-usually with physical assaults) suggest that, for this sample, maltreatment exposure which includes physical assault is more distressing than maltreatment which does not or an absence of maltreatment but is less distressing than maltreatment exposure which includes sexual assault as well as physical assault. From the perspective of constructivist self-development theory (i.e., CSD theory) (McCann and Pearlman, 1990), it may be that the sample's child maltreatment exposure categories represent a hierarchy of challenges to the self and its resources, needs, and schemas.

The proportions of assault survivors whose onset of exposure to physical assaults occurred before the age of eleven was equivalent across the physical assault and sexual assault categories. Therefore, differences in developmental stage at exposure to physical assaults are less likely to account for the variation in distress between physical assault and sexual assault survivors.

Due to the small size of the HHYS and the high lifetime prevalence of child maltreatment, most comparisons were made between youth who had been sexually assaulted (most of whom also had been physically assaulted) and youth who had not been sexually assaulted (most of whom had been physically assaulted, however). A much larger sample size would be required to partial out the specific psychological effects of each subtype of child maltreatment and compare them with each other. It is doubtful that, among the homeless youth population, there are any youth who have entirely escaped exposure to neglect, emotional, physical, or sexual abuse, or family violence, so studies of child maltreatment among homeless youth may never be able to find a suitable maltreatment-free comparison group within the homeless youth population. Since homelessness itself covaries with psychological distress, it must be considered in the context of understanding the effects of past child maltreatment on the lifetime prevalence of symptoms of psychological distress.

Homelessness and Psychological Distress

The HHYS was comprised of relatively few (17%) newcomers to homelessness. Although almost two-thirds of the sample reported cumulative lifetime homelessness of less than one year, most respondents had experienced multiple episodes of homelessness. Half of the sample had been exposed to homelessness by the age of thirteen. It appears that departures from home which resulted in homelessness usually began as the youth's idea but were increasingly endorsed or requested by the parents/caretakers with progressive episodes. This shift from unilateral to bilateral endorsement of the youth's leaving home may represent the exhaustion of coping resources needed to stabilize the family home. Youth who were told to leave home the last time they departed were more likely to report symptoms of substance abuse and/or dependence and conduct disorder, whereas youth who left home on their own were more likely to endorse symptoms of depression and PTSD. It seems probable that, if youth exhibited the disruptive symptoms of conduct disorder or substance abuse while living at home, they would be at greater risk for being asked to leave home. Youth who were asked to leave home by their parents/caretakers were more likely to have been hospitalized overnight for mental illness, possibly by parents who have depleted their own coping resources and are attempting to regain control over their children. The development of symptoms of depression and PTSD among youth who left home on their own may reflect reactions to conflict, maltreatment or other stressors in the home and/or to stressors encountered on the street.

Five parameters of homelessness were analyzed for their potential relationships with psychological distress: age at first homelessness, number of episodes of homelessness, cumulative lifetime homelessness, pattern of homelessness (i.e., temporary, episodic, or chronic), and whether the youth was accompanied by friends. Elevated symptoms of and caseness for substance abuse and/or dependence covaried with longer episodes of current homelessness (over 30 days), greater numbers of episodes of homelessness (over four), longer lifetime homelessness, younger age at first homelessness (younger than 14 years), and episodic or chronic homelessess. Elevated symptoms of conduct disorder appeared to covary with the parameters of homelessness in a similar pattern to substance abuse, however age at first homelessness tended to be older. Being homeless with friends appears to covary with lower than average numbers of symptoms of and non-caseness for conduct disorder. It is likely that this is a reciprocal relationship in which those with conduct disorder have difficulty maintaining friendships and social pressure from friends may reduce the likelihood that a youth will behave in socially unacceptable ways.

The data suggest that trait anxiety and current depression symptoms subside with time during a current episode of homelessness but that current depression becomes more likely if homelessness becomes chronic rather than temporary. Indicators of major depression and suicide thoughts were reported more often among youth who had experienced fewer than five episodes of homelessness at older ages (over 13 years old) and whose lifetime homelessness was less than one year. The risk of suicide attempts appeared to increase if the current episode of homelessness exceeded one month in duration and decrease if the youth was episodically homeless (vs. temporarily or chronically). This would suggest that brief episodic homelessness is less distressing than the first episode or the impact of long-term homelessness.

In sum, homeless youth may be most vulnerable to symptoms of depression and suicide attempts both early *and* late in their courses of homelessness. Depression early in homelessness may be due to the harsh survival skills learning curve that a youth must quickly navigate and master. Depression later in homelessness may result from declining hope for a stable and independent future and an exhaustion of coping resources necessary for survival on the streets. The data strongly suggest that risk for substance abuse and/or dependence increases as the duration of homelessness lengthens. Substance use may satisfy many needs for homeless youth: affect control, appetite suppression, boredom reduction, and assistance with dissociation from unpleasant and unsafe survival behaviors, living conditions, and environments.

Sexual Revictimization by Psychological Distress

Youth who had been sexually revictimized were more likely to report symptoms of conduct disorder than youth who had been sexually assaulted once or by one perpetrator. Sexual revictimization may covary with symptoms of conduct disorder because exposure to physical assaults, although less often life-threatening, tended to occur earlier in life for revictimized youth than for other survivors of sexual assault. Respondents who had been sexually assaulted by one perpetrator or on one occasion more frequently endorsed symptoms of lifetime major depression than those who had been revictimized, perhaps because the sexual assaults more often occurred before adolescence among survivors who were not revictimized.

Sexual Assault by Psychological Distress Controlling for

Receipt of Mental Health Services

Among the general sample, receipt of mental health services in the year preceding the interview was associated with an increase in symptoms of all indicators of psychological distress, except alcohol abuse. However, for survivors of sexual assault, receipt of mental health services was associated with a reduction in most of the measured symptoms of psychological distress. Of course, the direction of these relationships cannot be known from cross-sectional data. One interpretation of these data is that mental health intervention assisted the sexual assault survivors in coping with and adapting to their environment. However, it cannot be determined from these data whether it was the mental health intervention, per se, or something else about the self-selected individuals themselves which lowered their symptoms associated with lifetime psychological distress. For instance, psychological distress in the general sample may have prompted youth to seek mental health care, but psychological distress among sexual assault survivors may have encouraged respondents to both seek out mental health care and remain in treatment longer. It may be due to the tendency for sexual assault survivors to experience multiple symptoms of distress which influences them to stay in therapy longer than other maltreatment survivors or other homeless youth, in general.

Notably unaltered by receipt of mental health services were symptoms of alcohol abuse and/or dependence, yet, as with other measures of psychological distress, symptoms of drug abuse were lower in those survivors who had received mental health services in the year preceding the interview. Three or more explanations are plausible: (1) coping skills acquired during therapy were ineffective against alcohol abuse, (2) alcohol use and abuse are more openly tolerated in American society than drug use, and/or (3) help-seeking was more frequent among those with the most severe problems.

Having a Regular Medical Provider

Having a regular medical provider mediated the relationship between history of sexual assault and psychological distress. History of sexual assault appeared to be a risk factor for increased symptoms of psychological distress, i.e., anxiety, substance abuse, PTSD, conduct disorder, and current depression, among respondents who claimed to have regular medical providers. It is possible that, for sexual assault survivors, high levels of psychological distress are accompanied by somatic symptoms which prompt the individual to seek medical care. A somewhat ambiguous finding was that sexual assault survivors were more likely to meet diagnostic criteria for current depression and lifetime conduct disorder than youth who had not been sexually assaulted when they did *not* have a regular medical provider. Although it is plausible that conduct disordered youth with a sexual assault history may feel alienated from seeking any services which are equated with a mainstream lifestyle and which require trust of adults, it is unclear why depressed survivors of sexual assault are less likely to have regular medical providers. Symptoms of depression are usually associated with increased medical service utilization in the general population. For youthful survivors of sexual assault, however, the somatic symptoms of depression may be ameliorated by concurrent substance use or the psychological symptoms may be severe enough to be immobilizing.

Relatives Having Alcohol, Drug, or Mental Health Problems

The belief that relatives (usually parents) had problems with substance use or mental health mediated the relationship between history of sexual assault and psychological distress. In general, the relationship between history of sexual assault and psychological distress was weakest among youth who believed that relatives had problems with substance use or mental health. It may be that the belief that a relative has a problem with mental health or substance use reflects an attribution of blame for the youth's sexual assault to those problems or those relatives with those problems. Sexually assaulted youth who do not believe that any relatives have problems with substance use or mental health may be more likely to blame themselves for their assaults and suffer more symptoms of psychological distress. Alternatively, the stress of having relatives who have difficulties with substance use and/or mental illness may compete with exposure to child maltreatment in explaining variation in psychological distress.

Father's Educational Level

Among youth whose fathers had not completed 12th grade, history of sexual assault was a risk factor for symptoms of substance abuse, conduct disorder, and major depression. In contrast, youth whose father's educational levels were greater than or equal to 12th grade educations, history of sexual assault was a risk factor for symptoms of PTSD, current depression, and suicide attempts. As suggested by Wyatt and her colleagues (1993), perhaps sexually assaulted youth with more educated fathers are more likely to be aware of the stigma of sexual assault, especially incest, and to blame themselves for their assaults which would result in decreases in self-esteem and increases in internalizing symptoms of distress. Wyatt speculates that, on the other hand, sexual assault survivors with less educated fathers may be less likely to blame themselves for the assaults and more likely to emulate modeled externalizing symptoms of distress.

Lifetime Homelessness

History of sexual assault covaried with symptoms of alcohol abuse and/or dependence and major depression among youth whose lifetime duration of homelessness was less than one year and with symptoms of drug abuse and/or dependence and suicide attempts among respondents whose lifetime duration of homelessness was one year or longer. It seems that, over time, the appearance of symptoms of psychological distress among homeless persons may follow a sequence from more internalizing symptoms to more externalizing symptoms, and this sequence may be particularly true for sexual assault survivors. The shift in types of symptoms of psychological distress which are experienced may reflect the influence of acculturation to street life, i.e., a way of life which may include more antisocial activities and values, some of which are perceived as necessary for survival. As in the general population, it appears that, for homeless youth, symptoms of alcohol abuse and/or dependence tend to precede symptoms of drug abuse and/or dependence and that symptoms of major depression tend to precede suicide attempts.

Income in the Past 30 Days and Problems Finding Clothing
Income in the past 30 days and clothing availability, both indicators of tangible resources available to the respondent, tended to mediate the relationship between sexual assault history and psychological distress. History of sexual assault was more often associated with externalizing symptoms of distress when respondents had less than $100 in income in the month preceding the interview and had problems finding adequate clothing. Conversely, history of sexual assault was more often associated with internalizing symptoms of distress when respondents had more tangible resources. These observations may reflect the enhanced likelihood among sexual assault survivors for externalizing symptoms of distress to appear later in the course of homelessness, when tangible and other resources may be diminished.

The endorsement of particular symptoms of psychological distress may be influenced by the particular street subculture with which a respondent is involved. In addition, externalizing symptoms of distress, such as the robbing, stealing and lying associated with conduct disorder, may facilitate the acquisition of tangible resources, or, in the case of substance abuse, use of psychoactive substances may make the absence of tangible resources less noticeable and more tolerable. From this perspective, externalizing symptoms of distress during times of hardship may be adaptive. Internalizing symptoms of distress may be a 'luxury' that can be better afforded among those with greater basic resources.

The association between externalizing symptoms of psychological distress and the absence of tangible resources might be anticipated for all homeless youth in the sample, but only the relationship between inadequate clothing and externalizing symptoms of distress was found among the general sample. Youth who reported symptoms of drug abuse and/or dependence and conduct disorder were more likely to have incomes exceeding $99 the month prior to the interview. Homeless youth often acquire their clothes from local youth-serving agencies, many of whom are reluctant to serve individuals who have antisocial behavior problems or are abusing substances and whose highly structured services often are difficult for youth with externalizing symptoms of distress to accommodate or are found to be alienating. In the general HHYS, higher incomes were associated with externalizing symptoms of distress (i.e., drug abuse and/or dependence and conduct disorder) only among women, and internalizing symptoms (i.e., current and lifetime depression, anxiety, PTSD, and suicide attempts) were related to lower incomes for both sexes. It is unclear why this is the case since young women were as likely to participate in prostitution, a source of money and drugs, as young men.

Carrying a Weapon for Protection and Membership in a Street Gang
Not surprisingly, for the sample as a whole, externalizing symptoms of distress were more often associated with respondents who claimed to carry weapons for protection and who alleged to be members of street gangs than respondents who did not. Gang membership, by virtue of its association with aggressive group behaviors and substance use, may both appeal to individuals who are externalizing their distress and may foster the externalization of distress among its members. Among survivors of sexual assault, however, externalizing symptoms of distress were more frequently reported among those who did *not* carry weapons and who were *not* members of a street gang. It is possible that gang membership is a proxy for access to certain tangible resources and for personal safety actions which may afford survivors the 'luxury' of internalizing distress. For sexual assault survivors who are resource and safety 'poor', externalizing symptoms of distress may be adaptive in both expressing distress and in acquiring resources and perceived safety.

Running Away from Home
Externalizing symptoms of psychological distress were most often associated with history of sexual assault when the individual had been told to leave home, and internalizing symptoms were most often observed among survivors who had left home on their own. It is likely that any externalizing symptoms of distress which were expressed at home contributed to the breakdown in the relationship between the caretaker and the youth and thus contributed to the youth's being asked to leave the home. In addition, being asked to leave home may trigger especially potent feelings of betrayal and abandonment in someone who has been sexually violated and may be perceived as blame and punishment by the caretaker for involvement in the sexual assault. These feelings and perceptions may trigger self-destructive behaviors such as substance

abuse and/or rage against others manifested as the antisocial acts associated with conduct disorder.

Substance Abuse and/or Dependence

Symptoms of conduct disorder and suicide thoughts and attempts were most often associated with history of sexual assault among youth who also endorsed symptoms of alcohol abuse and/or dependence, whereas symptoms of major depression and PTSD were most frequently related to history of sexual assault among youth who did not have symptoms of alcohol abuse and/or dependence. It may be that, for sexual assault survivors, alcohol abuse contributed to affect control and the disinhibition necessary for the externalization of some distress in the form of antisocial behavior. The comorbidity of indicators of psychological distress which is observed in the general sample may simply be more specified and exaggerated among sexual assault survivors due to their higher levels of distress overall.

Symptoms of major depression and conduct disorder were most often associated with history of sexual assault among youth who did not endorse symptoms of drug abuse and/or dependence, yet symptoms of current depression appeared to be related to history of sexual assault for youth who did report symptoms of drug abuse and/or dependence. Perhaps, for sexual assault survivors, drug use is more often for the purpose of self-medication or affect control, hence its association with symptoms of current depression. It is unclear, though, why symptoms of major depression and conduct disorder would be most strongly related to sexual assault history specifically among those who did not disclose symptoms of lifetime drug abuse and/or dependence. Perhaps the relationships between major depression, conduct disorder, and sexual assault are obscured in the presence of drug abuse because of the strong correlations between major depression and drug abuse and between conduct disorder and drug abuse.

Gender

History of sexual assault covaried with anxiety disorders (i.e., lifetime PTSD and trait anxiety), sexual risk-taking (i.e., involvement in pornography and prostitution), suicide thoughts, symptoms of drug abuse and/or dependence (as well as diagnostic caseness specifically for cannabis, perhaps for the purpose of anxiety reduction) and somatic complaints (i.e., disturbances of sleep and appetite) more frequently among young men than young women. Young women who had histories of sexual assault, on the other hand, more often reported symptoms of mood disorders (i.e., current depression, lifetime major depression, and suicide attempts), conduct disorder (general disorder as described by the DSM-IIIR and aggressive subtype as described by the DSM-III), and met diagnostic criteria for drug abuse and/or dependence than young male survivors.

The tendency to more frequently detect covariation between internalizing symptoms of distress and female gender and externalizing symptoms of distress and male gender in community samples and in the HHYS may reflect, among other things, gender differences in reporting tendencies, socialized norms regarding expressions of distress, role strains, and hormonal influences. Some of the observed gender-related distress symptom patterns may not be easily explained by differences in sex role socialization, role strain, or hormones, alone. For instance, symptoms of PTSD and anxiety disorders were more often endorsed by women in the general HHYS, yet they were more prevalent among male survivors of sexual assault. Perhaps anxiety is a more socially acceptable or hormonally compatible type of internalized psychological distress for men to experience and/or report than depression when distress is high, as in sexual assault survivors of the HHYS. In addition, young men were more often sexually assaulted by multiple non-parent perpetrators, characteristics associated with symptoms of PTSD. Female survivors of sexual assault may be predisposed to symptoms of aggressive conduct disorder because of their more frequent concurrent exposure to life-threatening levels of violence, although at an older age, compared with male sexual assault survivors. Exposure to life-threatening levels, in general, tended to prompt respondents to fight back; fighting back during physical assaults was positively associated with symptoms of conduct disorder and substance abuse and inversely associated with symptoms of anxiety. It cannot be known from these data whether symptoms of conduct disorder precede and enable fighting back during physical assaults or whether the symptoms developed as a result of the assault exposure.

Perhaps exposure to sexual assaults elicit somewhat distinct responses from survivors who are attempting to regain their sense of control, depending on the characteristics of the assault and their psychological impact.

Compared with young women, for instance, young men tended to be sexually assaulted by multiple non-parent perpetrators on multiple occasions and may perceive the assault exposures as having been under their control (e.g., because they are adolescent males and/or because they may have experienced sexual arousal during the assault). Like female sexual assault survivors, male sexual assault survivors were most often assaulted by men; male survivors may view this as evidence that they are perceived to be homosexual. Male sexual assault survivors may, therefore, engage in sexual risk-taking, such as prostitution, in order to reenact the assault under controlled conditions in order to experience endorphin release and/or to regain a sense of power and control over sexual encounters. Young women, on the other hand, tended to be sexually assaulted by a father figure and to be exposed to more violent physical assaults which may disrupt many basic psychological developmental processes such as the need for safety and trust as well as encourage the progression of an aggressive and protective style of interpersonal interaction, perhaps as a means of maintaining control over future exposures to victimization. For both men and women, reexposure to victimizing encounters may invoke powerful emotions, such as anxiety and depression, which may be managed or avoided with drug use. Drugs may have been used for different purposes among men and women who are survivors of sexual assault in the HHYS. For instance, female survivors may have used drugs in self-destructive patterns consistent with their higher rates of suicide attempts; whereas male survivors may have used drugs for purposes of anxiety control consistent with their elevated rates of cannabis abuse and/or dependence.

Characteristics of Physical and Sexual Assaults, Psychological Distress, and Constructivist Self-Development Theory

Exposure to the extreme stress of a physical or sexual assault before adolescence may interfere with the development of a coping repertoire which includes self-soothing strategies essential for a person to tolerate strong affect and maintain positive self-esteem. It may be that the earlier the exposure to assaults, the more affected one's basic cognitive schemas regarding one's expectations of others and the world and, for those threatened with physical annihilation, the more diminished one's ability to empathize with the hardships of others. For youth with early exposure to sexual assaults without life-threatening physical assaults, a reduction in negative affect tolerance may result in symptoms of self-destruction and/or self-medication such as suicide attempts or substance abuse. Early exposure to physical assaults, on the other hand, may result in more anti-social behaviors associated with the social learning of such behaviors during interpersonal conflict facilitated by a reduction in empathy.

Assaults perpetrated by primary caretakers would be expected to be the most damaging to an individual's sense of self-esteem and the needs for trust, safety, and intimacy with others, since the first reflections of oneself as a worthwhile being is in the eyes of the primary caretaker and the first intimate relationship or attachment is with the caretaker. These processes appear to be the most compatible with symptoms of depression. Assaults by multiple perpetrators (simultaneous or not) may induce strong fear and severely challenge the need for safety and power over relationships with the environment, processes compatible with symptoms of PTSD and anxiety. It also seems plausible that the more a survivor perceives that the core self is being violated or damaged, as in sexual penetration, and the more a survivor feels that the psychological and/or physical self is being threatened with annihilation, as in life-threatening physical violence and sexual penetration, the more that individual may fight back for survival and experience symptoms of PTSD, anxiety, and depression.

Disclosure, Reporting to Authorities, Removal from Home, and Assault Characteristics by Gender

Consistent with the literature on child abuse, young women were more likely to disclose histories of sexual assault than were young men (Finkelhor et al., 1990). Young women also more frequently reported histories of neglect than did young men. The tendency for women to disclose histories of sexual assault and neglect more frequently than men may reflect actual differences in exposure and/or differences in willingness to recognize and disclose such treatment. In western cultures, boys and girls are often taught from an early age that femininity is equated with vulnerability and the easy expression of emotions and that masculinity is expressed as self-reliance, invulnerability, and the control of emotions. Perhaps male respondents are uneasy viewing themselves as 'victims' of anything, especially anything sexual since this may induce suspicion of homosexual tendencies.

In keeping with our cultural view of women and girls as vulnerable creatures in need of protection, female sexual assault survivors were more likely to have their assaults reported and more likely to be removed from the home for either sexual or physical assaults than were male assault survivors. Given that young men seem to find their childhood assaults no less distressing than women do, this practice appears to neglect the welfare of our male children.

Contributions to the Research Literature

Although this study was not designed to investigate all causes and consequences of homelessness among youth or all causes and consequences of child maltreatment among homeless youth, it has contributed to the body of descriptive knowledge about homeless youth. In addition, the study included youth who were not utilizing services at the time of the interview, an often overlooked sector in previous studies of homeless youth.

In particular, the study has queried in a systematic and standardized way about homelessness history, child maltreatment, indicators of psychological distress, and risk-taking. Several types of child maltreatment were assessed which facilitated a more careful description of the exposure categories and perhaps a better understanding of observed differences between exposure categories than has been done in many studies of child maltreatment. In contrast to studies which have reported physicians' subjective assessments of psychological distress and studies which have assessed only depression, the Hollywood Homeless Youth Study measured multiple indicators of psychological distress using standardized instruments designed to measure mental health in the general community and interviewers trained in survey methodology, adolescent psychology, and psychiatric epidemiology. The conceptualization of the data and their analyses have been undertaken from an epidemiological perspective, such as the concepts that dose of exposure may be related to response and that the strengths of relationships may be understood as odds ratios.

Examination of both symptom counts and diagnostic caseness for indicators of psychological distress more often than not resulted in similar conclusions. Diagnostic categories have the advantage that they are more highly correlated with clinician diagnoses than symptom categories and, as such, may represent psychopathology which is more severe and in need of clinical intervention. Use of symptom counts allows for prediction of both subclinical and clinical levels of distress. Subclinical cases of distress may represent individuals who may not be functioning in the most adaptive ways and who may benefit from some level of intervention. Subclinical cases may progress to clinical caseness or may spontaneously resolve without intervention.

Problem Behavior Theory

Research on problem behavior theory suggests that the onset and intensity of problem behaviors may be predicted by an adolescent's personal values and expectations and by the adolescent's perception of peer and role model approval of a given problem behavior (Jessor and Jessor, 1977). An adolescent's personal values and expectations with regard to achievement, independence, deviance, religion, and society are believed to interact with perceived peer/role model approval for problem behaviors to influence the adolescent's tendency to move away from conventional or mainstream attitudes, values, expectations, and behaviors. The HHYS data suggest that, for adolescents, increased exposure to institutionalized care in juvenile detention facilities or group homes, to homelessness in general, and to street gang membership in particular, may encourage substance abuse and antisocial behavior via the perceived approval for such activities among peers and the internalization of non-conventional values, attitudes, and expectations which are consistent with such problem behaviors. The observed relationship between perceived modeling of drug abuse by a relative and respondent drug abuse may be mediated by a shift in values which favor such behavior.

Socialization

Several of the observed associations in the data may represent social learning processes. For instance, the earlier the onset of exposure to physical assaults, the more likely the respondent was to report symptoms of conduct disorder; this association may represent the learning of aggressive responses to interpersonal conflict. Exposure to sexual assault in general, and to sexual revictimization in particular, increased the odds that a respondent would be engaged in sex work (i.e., pornography and prostitution). It is difficult to ascertain from this data the degree to which early exposure to sexual assault may socialize a child to relate to others in sexualized manners which enable later involvement in prostitution and pornography vs. the degree to which exposure to sex work may increase the probability of being sexually assaulted.

The perception that a relative had a drug problem was related to increased symptoms of drug abuse among respondents; an association which suggests that, aside from the potential for genetic predispositions to drug abuse, drug use may be a learned coping strategy. Symptoms of substance abuse and conduct disorder appeared to escalate as cumulative lifetime homelessness lengthened, with symptoms of alcohol abuse often preceding those of drug abuse. Perhaps both substance use and antisocial behavior are encouraged by the socialization and acculturation processes which are adaptive for survival on the street. For instance, the perception that most friends used drugs significantly increased the risk that a respondent would report symptoms consistent with a diagnosis of drug abuse and/or dependence. Positive associations observed between exposure to institutionalized care in juvenile detention facilities and group homes, street gang affiliation, and symptoms of substance abuse and conduct disorder also may reflect patterns of socialization.

Female sexual assault survivors tended to endorse different symptoms of psychological distress than male sexual assault survivors. The tendency for young men and women to endorse different symptoms of distress may be due to gender-based variations in (1) exposure to and appraisal of maltreatment and other stressors and strains, (2) socially acceptable coping strategies and expressions of distress, and (3) the biochemical origins and expressions of emotion. In addition, the data suggest that sexual assaults perpetrated on the female respondents were more likely to be reported to child protection authorities than were sexual assaults perpetrated on the male respondents; among youth who were over ten years of age at the time of maltreatment onset, reports to child protection authorities more often resulted in the removal of the respondent from the home when the respondent was female. The more frequent reporting and removal of female child maltreatment survivors may reflect a culturally learned tendency to protect females more than males.

Stress and Coping

The limited measures of key constructs of transactional, structural, and resiliency stress models coupled with the cross-sectional design and small sample size of the study do not allow analyses which may test the fit of the data to these models. However, a few relevant speculations may be made from the data. The data suggest that homeless youth used coping strategies which (1) altered their physical relationship to stressors (e.g., leaving home to escape conflict and/or maltreatment), (2) altered their perceived relationship to a stressor (e.g., fighting back during physical assaults), and (3) managed emotional distress (e.g., substance use to alter moods and reduce tension). Arguably, some of the coping strategies used may be perceived to be symptoms of psychological distress in response to stressors or stressors in themselves.

All homeless youth may be presumed to have experienced some loss of valued relationships, belongings, or roles in the process of becoming homeless. The mechanism by which homeless youth transition into and out of social roles embedded in the street culture is unknown. Consequently, the impacts that these role transitions and losses have on the development of psychological distress among homeless youth have not been explored.

Aneshensel and Gore (1991) postulated that the normal developmental tasks associated with adolescence influence physical and mental health via their effects on the adolescent's roles and relationships. Unfortunately, little is known from the HHYS data about how exposure to maltreatment and homelessness may have affected the developmental progression of the youth in the sample.

Structural models of stress predict that stressors increase a person's vulnerability to psychological distress via their exacerbation of role strains and subsequent diminishment of self-esteem and sense of control. Consistent with this model, youth who had survived exposure to sexual assaults or who reported elevated symptoms of trait anxiety, lifetime major depression, or lifetime drug abuse and/or dependence were more likely to report diminished self-esteem as measured by items from the Children's Depression Inventory (Cronbach's alpha=.56 for self-esteem subscale). Self-esteem appeared to mediate the relationship between exposure to sexual assault and psychological distress but not necessarily in the expected directions. The relationships between exposure to sexual assault and elevated symptoms of trait anxiety and PTSD were most pronounced among youth who reported lower levels of self-esteem. Inexplicably, the relationships between exposure to sexual assault and elevated symptoms of lifetime major depression, alcohol abuse and/or dependence, conduct disorder, and history of suicide attempts were most pronounced among respondents who reported higher levels of self-esteem.

The young women did not appear to be any more or less distressed than the young men in the sample, regardless of exposure status to sexual assaults; the young women merely endorsed different symptoms of psychological distress. Therefore, the idea that women are somehow more vulnerable to stress than men was not supported by these data. Of all of the tested factors which may affect the relationship between exposure to sexual assault and psychological distress, receipt of mental health services in the year prior to the interview appeared to have the most beneficial effect in ameliorating the distress symptoms associated with exposure to sexual assault.

Four Traumagenic Dynamics

Finkelhor and Browne's (1988) model of the traumagenic dynamics involved in sexual abuse appears to overlap considerably with constructivist self-development theory, yet its simplicity reminds us of some of the key sexual assault characteristics which were associated with specific symptoms of distress. The four traumagenic dynamics model predicts that sexual assaults which involve traumatic sexualization, betrayal, stigmatization, and powerlessness will be the most psychologically damaging for the survivor. Consistent with this model, the HHYS data suggest that exposure to life-threatening levels of force is associated with higher numbers of lifetime psychiatric diagnoses and exposure to sexual penetration is associated with higher numbers of current and lifetime psychiatric diagnoses. The model predicts that exposure to life-threatening levels of force and sexual penetration may provoke particularly high levels of distress which may be elaborated as problems with sexual satisfaction, intimacy and trust in relationships. Life-threatening levels of force may also induce a sense of powerlessness in sexual assault survivors which could explain its relationship with elevated symptoms of PTSD. Powerlessness may result in a reduced sense of self-efficacy in the ability to protect oneself and subsequent involvement in aggressive antisocial behavior or exposure to revictimization, depending on the survivor's needs for control and sense of helplessness. Sexual assaults perpetrated by a parent were found to be associated with the presence of current symptoms of psychological distress and a history of suicide thoughts and attempts; these associations may be mediated by the survivor's sense of intentional betrayal by someone who was trusted.

Internalization of the cultural stigma associated with being a sexual assault survivor may be more pronounced for young men because of the cultural expectation for men to be able to protect themselves from harm. Stigmatization may be particularly intense if the sexual assault involved implicit rather than explicit force and if any physiological pleasure was derived from the experience. The internalized stigma may motivate a sexual assault survivor to associate with other stigmatized persons such as the homeless, sex workers, drug abusers, alcoholics, gang members, and criminals.

Constructivist Self Development Theory

Constructivist self development theory (i.e., CSD theory, McCann and Pearlman, 1990) appears to be adequate to explain the associations between child maltreatment exposure and psychological distress in homeless youth. Whether CSD theory is the best model for this purpose remains to be seen. If the findings described here are representative of other homeless youth, it seems unlikely that there is a need for an entirely new model of stress and coping which is specific to homeless youth. In the absence of knowledge of stressor appraisals by respondents and other variables of the stress process, it is difficult to know whether departing home because of severe family conflict and/or maltreatment represents avoidant coping or adaptation or both.

Consistent with other studies of the effects of child maltreatment, exposure to physical assaults appeared to increase the risk for the appearance of anti-social behaviors, and exposure to sexual assaults appeared to increase the risk for the appearance of all measured indicators of distress and some indicators of sexual risk-taking. Also consistent with other studies of child maltreatment was the finding that demographic characteristics such as gender, family characteristics such as substance abuse, and assault characteristics such as relationship to perpetrator often moderated or mediated the type and amount of distress expressed. The HHYS data suggest that psychological distress may be both a cause and a consequence of homelessness and maltreatment history. New to the literature is the contribution of the contextual effect of street life on the relationship between history of assault exposure and history of psychological distress. Since the child abuse literature and anecdotal evidence from homeless youth both suggested that substance use may be employed as a coping mechanism during times of distress, substance abuse was examined separately as an indicator of psychological distress and as an indicator of coping. Arguably, displaying specific symptoms of psychological distress may have significant benefits for homeless persons (e.g., avoidance of victimization, admission into a shelter etc.) and may, therefore, be used as coping mechanisms. The extent to which substance abuse contributed directly or indirectly to further psychological distress could not be determined.

Study Limitations

Since the sample was drawn from a snowball list of geographic sites where homeless youth congregate in Hollywood, generalizations cannot necessarily be made about other homeless youth or about other maltreated youth who are not exposed to homelessness. Due to the snowball list of sites, the independence of data collected from different respondents, although likely, cannot be guaranteed. The study employed a cross-sectional design which does not allow for causal analyses. Questions about historical events and their timing were subject to recall bias.

Recollection of symptoms of past psychological distress may have been affected by the presence of internal symptom cues (e.g., current depression or illness) or external stress cues (e.g., stressors associated with homelessness) (Aneshensel, Estrada, Hansell, and Clark, 1987). Limited statistical power demanded that both trends and statistically significant relationships be considered for interpretation and hypothesis generation. Sensitive or stigmatized feelings or behaviors or experiences (such as child maltreatment) may have been underreported. Some respondents may have been psychologically unable to recall exposure to particularly traumatic events or the details of these events. Due to a modest sample size, this study could not factor out the individual or interactive effects of different combinations of child maltreatment exposure and contextual factors of street life on psychological distress or the independent developmental effects on the expression of specific symptoms of distress. In addition, exposure to child maltreatment, service utilization, and psychological distress were not validated by other measurement sources such as records from child protection agencies, records from youth service providers, or clinical assessments.

Unmeasured constructs which may explain some of the associations suggested by the data cannot be ruled out. Some of these unmeasured constructs may include: (1) parental/caretaker attachment, (2) social isolation, (3) social support, (4) coping skills and resources, (5) organic causes of mental illness, (6) substance-induced mental illness, (7) seasonal and temporal variability among characteristics of homeless youth and street life, (8) recency of exposure to assaults, (9) patterns of assault histories such as whether exposure to multiple perpetrators occurred simultaneously or separately, whether the assaults perpetrated by non-cohabitants occurred during a homelessness episode or institutionalized care, frequency of assaults by specific perpetrators and contexts, reactions to assault disclosure if assaults were disclosed etc., (10) triggers to and context of substance use, (11) exposure to psychological abuse, (12) constructs specific to CSD theory: self-esteem, IQ, empathy, psychological needs, and basic cognitive schemas (13) appraisal and symbolic meaning of potentially stressful events and coping resources, (14) psychological and physical development before, during, and after exposure to child maltreatment, (15) resiliency and adaptation other than the absence of distress and school performance, (16) social roles and role strain, and (17) attributions about exposure to child maltreatment. Finally, a larger sample size would enable a more finely tuned analyses of the impact of different types of maltreatment exposure at various developmental stages of childhood and adolescence.

Hypotheses Generated by the Study

The HHYS data suggest that the dimensions of homelessness context and history, psychological distress and risk-taking, child maltreatment, and sociodemographic and family characteristics are often reciprocally interrelated and that homelessness, sociodemographic and family characteristics may moderate or mediate the relationship between child maltreatment and psychological distress (Figure 1).

Selected hypotheses:

1. Length of homelessness is positively and reciprocally related to psychological distress

2. Lack of tangible resources is positively and reciprocally related to psychological distress among homeless youth

3. Service utilization is positively related to internalizing symptoms of psychological distress among homeless youth

4. Among homeless youth, the relationship between exposure to physical assaults and sexual assaults during childhood and specific symptoms of psychological distress is mediated by the characteristics of the assault exposure.

5. Among homeless youth, the relationship between exposure to physical assaults and sexual assaults during childhood and specific symptoms of psychological distress is moderated by survivor gender.

6. Among homeless youth, the relationship between exposure to physical assaults and sexual assaults during childhood and specific

symptoms of psychological distress is moderated by the educational level of the survivor's father.

7. Among homeless youth, the relationship between exposure to physical assaults and sexual assaults during childhood and specific symptoms of psychological distress is moderated by the perception that a relative has a problem with substance use and/or mental illness.

8. Among homeless youth, the relationship between exposure to physical assaults and sexual assaults during childhood and specific symptoms of psychological distress is mediated by substance use.

9. Among homeless youth, the relationship between exposure to physical assaults and sexual assaults during childhood and specific symptoms of psychological distress is mediated by receipt of mental health services.

10. Among homeless youth, the relationship between exposure to physical assaults and sexual assaults during childhood and specific symptoms of psychological distress is mediated by length of homelessness.

11. Among homeless youth, the relationship between exposure to sexual assault during childhood and sexual risk-taking is mediated by the duration of exposure to homelessness.

12. Among homeless youth, the relationship between exposure to sexual assault during childhood and sexual risk-taking is moderated by gender.

Future Studies

In addition to examining the unmeasured constructs and the hypotheses mentioned above, future studies of homeless youth should broaden their definitions of homelessness to include those youth who are at risk for homelessness (e.g., youth in placement) and those youth who associate with street youth. Attempts should be made to obtain a modified area probability sample of shelters, drop-in centers, natural hang-outs, and sweeps of selected census blocks (a refinement of the sample described in this study). Ideally, a separate study should determine the effects of sampling done at various hours of the day, days of the week, seasons, years, and geographic regions. Duplicate interviews should be scrupulously avoided. Data collection methods which require minimal literacy should be used.

General Policy Implications

Primary health care is concerned with attaining a level of health for individuals and their communities which will enable them to lead socially and economically productive lives (World Health Organization, 1978). Health is defined here as a 'state of complete physical, mental, and social well-being, and not merely the absence of disease or infirmity' and is viewed as a fundamental human right which should be supported by governments. Given the rates of exposure to child maltreatment and psychological distress among homeless youth and their elevated risks for exposure to physical and sexual revictimization, disease, and pregnancy while living on the streets, we have woefully failed to assist these young persons in attaining a level of health compatible with productive self-determination in mainstream American society. Three strategies which may improve the health of homeless youth and youth at-risk for homelessness include: (1) closing the entries to youth homelessness and widening the exits from youth homelessness, (2) refusing to support policies which are inherently biased against fair treatment for youth, the poor, or homeless persons, and (3) creating a single government agency or bureau which is responsible for the well-being of all children and adolescents and a coordinated and supported intrastate and interstate child protection policy.

Closing the doors to homelessness among youth would include family economic and social support programs as well as mental health and substance abuse treatment for family members in need and increased support and monitoring of children in institutionalized care. For instance, current strengths-based wrap-around projects which coordinate comprehensive community support services for youth at risk and their families using flexible funds may effectively close many of the doors to homelessness and other problems among youth.

Some local child protection authorities have chosen to prioritize the use of ever-dwindling funds towards preventing deaths and serious injuries among the youngest children. From a secondary prevention perspective, this is an understandable position. Little funding is available for tracking maltreated youth from local communities who have run away from home or from placement, and virtually no funds are available for assisting maltreated youth who originate from other counties, states, or countries. As a society, is it acceptable to underfund a child protective organization to the extent that it can do little in the way of primary prevention of child maltreatment for any children and minimal prevention for older children and adolescents? Considering the potential sequelae for maltreatment exposure include increased risk-taking and poorer mental and physical health among our young people, today's starving of the child protective services may result in the compromised development of many of our children.

Although public awareness of child maltreatment appears to have increased dramatically over the past decade, much work remains to be done. For instance, child protective authorities are not strong in every community, and they do not have easy access to data and assistance from authorities from other communities throughout the nation. Effective primary, secondary, and tertiary child maltreatment prevention programs are not available to children of all developmental stages. All expectant parents and families are not educated and supported in their childrearing. Family education and support should be affordable and accessible to everyone but perhaps particularly to adolescent parents, and it must, at minimum, include: (1) instruction in reasonable expectations for child behavior and positive caretaking and discipline practices which are consistent with a child's developmental stage, (2) skills training in conflict resolution between adults, (3) job-training and employment programs, (4) safe housing, (5) reliable and safe public transportation, (6) child care and respite care, and (7) strategies to strengthen existing social support. Family support programs may benefit all families by preparing them for the inevitable stressful periods and may prevent maladaptive coping, child maltreatment, domestic violence, and the premature departure of youth from the home.

Widening the exits from youth homelessness encompasses the provision of more work and training opportunities for youth of all ages; the payment of a livable wage and the assurance of safe work environments in proximity to high-quality affordable child care; the provision of comprehensive national health care coverage which is accessible without parental permission (two-thirds of the HHYS were without private or public health care coverage); the support for more community-based not-for-profit ownership and management of affordable, decent, and safe housing; the existence of transitional living programs which use flexible funds, are coordinated with integrated mental health and substance abuse services, have sufficient funding for hiring, training, and maintaining qualified staff, are able to provide follow-up support by tracking and monitoring youth, and are sensitive to the complex experiences and needs of homeless youth (see Cauce et al., 1994 and Schram and Giovengo, 1991 for programs which incorporate some of these qualities);

Several public policies have been implemented or suggested in the recent past which appear to be biased against youth or homeless people. For instance, many communities have passed anti-panhandling ordinances which will force homeless persons to engage in riskier and less legal behaviors for survival. Some communities have also passed ordinances forbidding sleeping in public places, thus forcing homeless persons into unsafe and unhygienic abandoned buildings and other places. In addition, many states continue to lower the age at which a juvenile may be tried and incarcerated as an adult for alleged criminal activity; thus, placing the juvenile in adult settings with potentially increased risk of victimization and decreased odds of rehabilitation.

A single government agency responsible for the well-being of all children and youth could integrate the activities of child welfare agencies, educational districts, health districts, and juvenile justice programs to prevent the loss of children to the streets. Housing programs for homeless and runaway youth in criminal justice agencies, as is done in California, limits the community's perspective of homeless youth and limits the spectrum of responses to those which entail juvenile justice strategies. As

Werner (1992) concluded from her extensive longitudinal research on resiliency among high-risk children in Kauai, formal policies and interventions should focus on building and reinforcing the protective factors (such as informal ties to friends, relatives, and community and the availability of educational and career opportunities for growth) as well as on ameliorating the risk factors in a child's life. A new government agency charged with overseeing the healthy maturation of all children and youth could be responsible for the development of regional policies and funding for services and research which are specific to youth at risk (see The California Child, Youth and Family Coalition, 1990, for examples) and should endeavor to instill individuals and their communities with a sense of responsibility for the well-being of all young people in the community.

Closing Comment

For those readers who remain unconvinced of the importance of understanding the experiences of homeless youth:

"Those of us who work with (homeless youth) regularly are invariably struck by their tenacity, resourcefulness, and intelligence - qualities typically absent from the stereotypic image of the drifting sociopathic delinquent. One could argue that they have exhibited exceptional initiative and creativity in arriving at difficult solutions to intolerable burdens of abuse and disorder at home. The persistence of these attributes in spite of the disorder and depression in their lives is evidence of the human potential that remains. . .Apart from the importance of serving a seriously underserved population, knowledge of them will help us understand their place in the spectrum of alienating processes that affect our young people." (Deisher and Rogers, 1991)

Notes

[1] The modest sample size did not allow for complex multivariate analyses of the relationships between child maltreatment, psychological distress, and mediators or moderators. Consequently, univariate and bivariate results are discussed with the goal of *hypothesis generation* for

future studies. Given that the sample size lacked statistical power to demonstrate significant differences of more moderate to subtle magnitudes, results which were found to be statistically significant at $p < .10$ and results which suggested potential relationship trends (i.e., differences in proportion of 10% or greater) will both be discussed in this section.

[2] With the exception of trait anxiety and current depression, all other indicators of psychological distress were based on lifetime prevalences. In order to examine sub-clinical distress, substance abuse and/or dependence, conduct disorder, PTSD, current depression, and major depression were assessed by dichotomized symptom counts split at the median as well as by diagnostic caseness (according to either the DSM-III or the DSM-IIIR).

Figure 1 Suggested Relationships Between Sociodemographic and Family Characteristics, Homelessness, Child Maltreatment, and Psychological Distress in the Hollywood Homeless Youth Sample

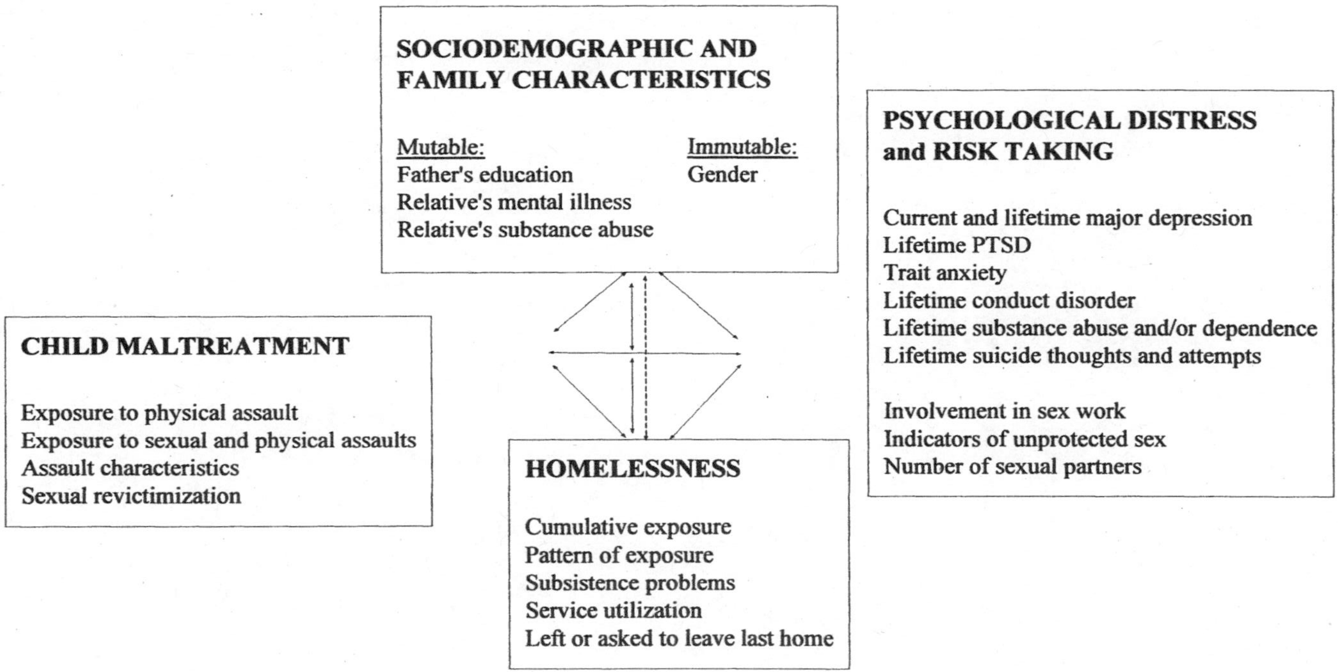

VIII
References

Abramson, L., Seligman, M., & Teasdale, J. (1978). Learned helplessness in humans: Critique and reformulation. *Journal of Abnormal Psychology*, *87*, 49-74.

Achenback, T., & Edelbrock, C. (1981). Behavioral problems and competencies reported by parents of normal and disturbed children aged four through sixteen. *Monographs of the Society for Research in Child Development*, *46*(188).

Adams-Tucker, C. (1981). A socioclinical overview of 28 sex-abused children. *Child Abuse and Neglect*, *5*, 361-367.

Adams-Tucker, C. (1982). Proximate effects of sexual abuse in childhood: A report on 28 children. *American Journal of Psychiatry*, *139*, 1252-1256.

Adams, G. R., & Munro, G. (1979). Portrait of the North American runaway: A critical review. *Journal of Youth and Adolescence*, *8*(3), 359-373.

Ageton, S. S. (1983). *Sexual assault among adolescents*. Lexington, MA: Lexington Books.

Allen, D. M., & Tarnowski, K. J. (1989). Depressive characteristics of physically abused children. *Journal of Abnormal Child Psychology*, *17*(1), 1-11.

American Association for Protecting Children. (1988). *Highlights of official child neglect and abuse reporting 1986*. Denver, CO: American Humane Association.

American Psychiatric Association. (1968). *Diagnostic and statistical manual of mental disorders, Second Edition*. Washington, D.C.: American Psychiatric Association.

American Psychiatric Association. (1980). *Diagnostic and statistical manual of mental disorders, Third Edition*. Washington, D.C.: American Psychiatric Association.

American Psychiatric Association. (1987). *Diagnostic and statistical manual of mental disorders, Third Edition- Revised*. Washington, D.C.: American Psychiatric Association.

American Psychiatric Association. (1994). *Diagnostic and statistical manual of mental disorders, Fourth Edition*. Washington, D.C.: American Psychiatric Association.

Aneshensel, C. S. (1985). The natural history of depressive symptoms: Implications for psychiatric epidemiology. In J. Greenley (Ed.), *Research in community and mental health* (Vol. 5). Greenwich, CT: JAI Press.

Aneshensel, C. S., & Gore, S. (1991). Development, stress and role-restructuring: Social transitions of adolescence. In J. Eckenrode (Ed.), *The social context of coping*. New York: Plenum.

Aneshensel, C. S., & Stone, J. D. (1982). Stress and depression: A test of the buffering model of social support. *Archives of General Psychiatry*, *39*, 1392-1396.

Angold, A. (1988). Childhood and adolescent depression: I. Epidemiological and aetiological aspects. *British Journal of Psychiatry*, *152*, 601-617.

Anthony, E. J. (1974). The syndrome of the psychologically invulnerable child. In E. J. Anthony & C. Koupernik (Eds.), *The child in his family: children at psychiatric risk* (pp. 529-544). New York: Wiley.

Augoustinos, M. (1987). Developmental effects of child abuse: Recent findings. *Child Abuse and Neglect*, *11*, 15-27.

Bagley, C., & Ramsay, R. (1985, February). *Disrupted childhood and vulnerability to sexual assault: Long-term sequels with implications for counselling.* Paper presented at the Conference on Counseling the Sexual Abuse Survivor, Winnipeg, Canada.

Bagley, C., & Ramsay, R. (1986). Sexual abuse in childhood: Psychosocial outcomes and implications for social work practice. *Journal of Social Work and Human Sexuality, 4*, 33-47.

Bandura, A. (1977). Self-efficacy: Toward a unifying theory of behavioral change. *Psychological Review, 84*, 191-215.

Barahal, R. M., Waterman, J., & Martin, H. (1981). The social cognitive development of abused children. *Journal of Consulting and Clinical Psychology, 49*, 508-516.

Barrera, M. (1981). Social support's role in the adjustment of pregnant adolescents: Assessment issues and findings. In B. Gottleib (Ed.), *Social networks and social support in community mental health* (pp. 69-96). Newbury Park, CA: Sage.

Baum, A., Singer, J. E., & Baum, C. S. (1981). Stress and the environment. *Journal of Social Issues, 37*(1), 4-35.

Beitchman, J. H., Zucker, K. J., Hood, J. E., daCosta, G. A., & Akman, D. (1991). A review of the short-term effects of child sexual abuse. *Child Abuse and Neglect, 15*, 537-556.

Beitchman, J. H., Zucker, K. J., Hood, J. E., daCosta, G., Akman, D., & Cassavia, E. (1992). A review of the long-term effects of child sexual abuse. *Child Abuse and Neglect, 16*, 101-118.

Berliner, L., & Conte, J. (1990). The process of victimization: The victims' perspective. *Child Abuse and Neglect, 14*, 29-40.

Billings, A. C., & Moos, R. H. (1982). Stressful life events and symptoms: A longitudinal model. *Health Psychology, 1*(2), 99-117.

Billings, A. C., & Moos, R. H. (1985). Psychosocial processes of remission in unipolar depression: Comparing depressed patients with matched community controls. *Journal of Consulting and Clinical Psychology, 3*, 314-325.

Boney-McCoy, S. & Finkelhor, D. (1995). Prior victimization: A risk factor for child sexual abuse and for PTSD-related symptomatology among sexually abused youth. *Child Abuse and Neglect, 19*, 1401-1421.

Bourque, L. B., & Back, K. W. (1977). Life graphs and life events. *Journal of Gerontology, 32*, 669-674.

Brems, C., & Johnson, M. E. (1989). Problem-solving appraisal and coping style: The influence of sex-role orientation and gender. *Journal of Psychology, 123*(2), 187-194.

Brennan, T., Huizinga, D., & Elliot, D. (1978). *The social psychology of runaways*. Lexington, MA: Lexington.

Brent, D. A. (1995). Risk factors for adolescent suicide and suicidal behavior: Mental and substance abuse disorders, family environmental factors, and life stress. *Suicide and Life Threatening Behavior, 25(Suppl)*, 52-63.

Breslau, N., Davis, G. C., Andreski, P., & Peterson, E. (1991, March). Traumatic events and posttraumatic stress disorder in an urban population of young adults. *Archives of General Psychiatry, 48*, 216-222.

Briere, J. (1984). *The effects of childhood sexual abuse on later psychological functioning: Defining a post-sexual abuse syndrome.* Paper presented at the Third National Conference on Sexual Victimization of Children, Washington, D.C.

Briere, J. (1992). *Child abuse trauma: Theory and treatment of the lasting effects*. Newbury Park: Sage.

Briere, J., & Elliott, D. M. (1994). Immediate and long-term impacts of child sexual abuse. *The Future of Children, 4*(2), 54-69.

Briere, J., Evans, D., Runtz, M., & Wall, T. (1988). Symptomatology in men who were molested as children: A comparison study. *American Journal of Orthopsychiatry, 58*(3), 457-461.

Briere, J., & Runtz, M. (1988). Symptomatology associated with childhood sexual victimization in a nonclinical adult sample. *Child Abuse and Neglect, 12*, 51-59.

Briere, J., & Runtz, M. (1990). Differential adult symptomatology associated with three types of child abuse histories. *Child Abuse and Neglect, 14*, 357-364.

Brown, A., Pelcovitz, D., & Kaplan, S. (1983). *Child witnesses of family violence: A study of psychological correlates.* Paper presented at the meeting of the American Psychological Association, Anaheim, CA.

Brown, G. W. (1974). Meaning, measurement, and stress of life events. In B. S. Dohrenwend & B. P. Dohrenwend (Eds.), *Stressful life events: Their nature and effects* (pp. 217-244). New York: Wiley.

Brown, G. W., Andrews, B., Harris, T. A., Alder, Z., & Bridge, L. (1986). Social support, self-esteem and depression. *Psychological Medicine, 16*, 813-831.

Brown, G. W., & Harris, T. (1978). *Social origins of depression.* London: Tavistock.

Brown, J. D., & Siegel, J. M. (1988). Attributions for negative life events and depression: The role of perceived control. *Journal of Personality and Social Psychology, 54*(2), 316-322.

Browne, A., & Finkelhor, D. (1986). Impact of child sexual abuse: A review of the research. *Psychological Bulletin, 99*(1), 66-77.

Bruns, C., & Geist, C. S. (1984). Stressful life events and drug use among adolescents. *Journal of Human Stress, 9*, 135-139.

Burgess, A. W., Hartman, C. R., McCausland, M. P., & Powers, P. (1984). Response patterns in children and adolescents exploited through sex rings and pornography. *American Journal of Psychiatry, 141*, 656-662.

Burgess, A. W., Hartman, C. R., & McCormack, A. (1986). Adolescents at risk. In A. Burgess (Ed.), *Youth at risk: Understanding runaway and exploited youth* (pp. 1-8). Washington, D.C.: National Center for Missing and Exploited Children.

Burgess, A. W., Hartman, C. R., & McCormack, A. (1987). Abused to abuser: Antecedents of socially deviant behaviors. *American Journal of Psychiatry, 144*, 1431-1436.

Burgess, A. W., & Holmstrom, L. L. (1975). Sexual trauma of children and adolescents: Pressure, sex, secrecy. *Nursing Clinics of North America, 10*(3), 551-563.

Burgess, A. W., & Holmstrom, L. L. (1979). Adaptive strategies and recovery from rape. *American Journal of Psychiatry, 136*, 1278-1282.

Burke, D., Brudage, J., Goldenbaum, M., Gardner, L., Peterson, M., Visintine, R., & Redfied, R. (1990, April 18). Human Immunodeficiency Virus infections in teenagers. Seroprevalence among applicants to U.S. Military Service. The Walter Reed Retrovirus Research Group. *Journal of the American Medical Association, 263(15)*, 2074-2077.

Burnam, M. A., Stein, J. A., Golding, J. M., Siegel, J. M., Sorenson, S. B., Forsythe, A. B., & Telles, C. A. (1988). Sexual assault and mental disorders in a community population. *Journal of Consulting and Clinical Psychology, 56*(6), 843-850.

California Child, Youth and Family Coalition. (1990). *A comprehensive policy for runaway/homeless youth in the state of California: A position paper.* Sacramento, CA: The California Child, Youth and Family Coalition.

Carlson, E. B., Furby, L., Armstrong, J., & Shlaes, J. (1997). A conceptual framework for the long-term psychological effects of traumatic childhood abuse. *Child Maltreatment, 2*(3), 272-295.

Caton, C. L. (1986). The homeless experience in adolescent years. In E. Bassuk (Ed.), *The mental health needs of homeless persons* (pp. 63-70). San Francisco: Jossey-Bass.

Cauce, A. M., Morgan, C. J., Wagner, V., Moore, E., Sy, J., Wurzbacher, K., Weeden, K., Tomlin, S., & Blanchard, T. (1994). Effectiveness of intensive case management for homeless adolescents: Results of a 3-month follow-up. *Journal of Emotional and Behavioral Disorders, 2*(4), 219-227.

Cavaiola, A. A., & Schiff, M. (1988). Behavioral sequelae of physical and/or sexual abuse in adolescents. *Child Abuse and Neglect, 12*, 181-188.

Chicago Coalition for the Homeless. (1993). *Alone after dark: A survey of homeless youth in Chicago.* Chicago: Author.

Cicchetti, D., Rogosch, F. A., Lynch, M., & Holt, K. D. (1993). Resilience in maltreated children: Processes leading to adaptive outcome. *Development and Psychopathology, 5*, 629-647.

Claussen, A. H., & Crittenden, P. M. (1991). Physical and psychological maltreatment: Relations among types of maltreatment. *Child Abuse and Neglect, 15*, 5-18.

Cohen-Sandler, R., Berman, A. L., & King, R. A. (1982). Life stress and symptomatology: Determinants of suicidal behavior in children. *Journal of the American Academy of Child Psychiatry, 21*, 178-186.

Cohen, F. S., & Densen-Gerber, J. (1982). A study of the relationship between child abuse and neglect and drug addiction in 178 patients: Preliminary results. *Child Abuse and Neglect, 6*, 383-387.

Cohen, J. A., & Mannarino, A. P. (1988). Psychological symptoms in sexually abused girls. *Child Abuse and Neglect, 12*, 571-577.

Cohen, L. H., Burt, C., & Bjorck, J. (1987). Life stress and adjustment: Effects of life events experienced by young adolescents and their parents. *Developmental Psychology, 23*, 583-592.

Collings, S. J. (1995). The long-term effects of contact and noncontact forms of child sexual abuse in a sample of university men. *Child Abuse & Neglect, 19,* 1-6.

Compas, B. E., Davis, G. E., & Forsythe, C. J. (1985). Characteristics of life events during adolescence. *American Journal of Community Psychology, 13*(6), 677-691.

Compas, B. E., Wagner, B. M., Slavin, L. A., & Vannatta, K. (1986). A prospective study of life events, social support, and psychological symptomatology during the transition from high school to college. *American Journal of Community Psychology, 14*, 241-257.

Conte, J. R., & Schuerman, J. R. (1987). Factors associated with an increased impact of child sexual abuse. *Child Abuse and Neglect, 11*, 201-211.

Coons, P. M. (1986a). Child abuse and multiple personality disorder: Review of the literature and suggestions for treatment. *Child Abuse and Neglect, 10*, 455-462.

Coons, P. M. (1986b). Psychiatric problems associated with child abuse: A review. In J. J. Jacobson (Ed.), *Psychiatric sequelae of child abuse: Reconnaissance of child abuse and neglect evaluation, prospects, recommendations* (pp. 169-200). Springfield, Illinois: Charles C. Thomas.

Crowe, R. R. (1974). An adoption study of antisocial personality. *Archives of General Psychiatry, 31*, 785-791.

Cummings, E. M., & El-Sheikh, M. (1991). Children's way of coping with angry environments: A process-oriented approach. In E. M. Cummings, A. L. Greene & K. H. Karraker (Eds.), *Life-span developmental psychology: Perspectives on stress and coping* (pp. 131-150). Hillsdale, New Jersey: Lawrence Erlbaum.

Curran, D. K. (1987). *Adolescent suicidal behavior.* Washington, D.C.: Hemisphere.

Davies-Netzley, S., Hurlburt, M. S., & Hough, R. L. (1996). Childhood abuse as a precursor to homelessness for homeless women with severe mental illness. *Violence and Victims, 11*(2), 129-142.

Deisher, R., & Rogers, W. (1991). The medical care of street youth. *Journal of Adolescent Health, 12*(7), 500-503.

DeLongis, A., Coyne, J. C., Dakof, G., Folkman S., & Lazarus, R. S. (1982). Relationship of daily hassles, uplifts, and major life events to health status. *Health Psychology, 1*, 119-136.

Dembo, R., Dertke, M., La Voie, L., Borders, S., Washburn, M., & Schmeidler, J. (1987). Physical abuse, sexual victimization and illicit drug use: A structural analysis among high risk adolescents. *Journal of Adolescence, 10*, 13-33.

Dennis, D. L. (1987). *Research methodologies concerning homeless persons with serious mental illness and/or substance abuse disorders.* Albany, NY: New York State Office of Mental Health, Bureau of Survey and Evaluation Research.

Dodge, K. A., & Frame, C. L. (1982). Social cognitive biases and deficits in aggressive boys. *Child Development, 53*, 620-635.

Dodge, K. A., Murphy, R. R., & Buchsbaum, K. (1984). The assessment of intention-cue detection skills in children: Implications for developmental psychopathology. *Child Development, 55*, 163-173.

Doerfler, L. A., Felner, R. D., Rowlison, R. T., Raley, P. A., & Evans, E. (1988). Depression in children and adolescents: A comparative analysis of the utility and construct validity of two assessment measures. *Journal of Consulting and Clinical Psychology, 56(5)*, 769-772.

Dressler, W. (1985). The social and cultural context of coping: Action, gender and symptoms in a southern black community. *Social Science and Medicine, 21*(5), 499-506.

Dunn, J. (1980). Individual differences in temperament. In M. Rutter (Ed.), *Scientific foundations of developmental psychiatry* (pp. 101-109). London: Heinemann Medical.

Edwards, P. W., & Donaldson, M. A. (1989). Assessment of symptoms in adult survivors of incest: A factor analytic study of the responses to childhood incest questionnaire. *Child Abuse and Neglect, 13*, 101-110.

Egeland, B., Carlson, E., & Sroufe, L. A. (1993). Resilience as process. *Development and Psychopathology, 5,* 517-528.

Egeland, B., & Sroufe, L. A. (1981). Attachment and early maltreatment. *Child Development, 52,* 44-52.

Ellis, R. H., & Milner, J. S. (1981). Child abuse and locus of control. *Psychological Reports, 48,* 507-510.

Emery, R. E. (1989). Family violence. *American Psychologist, 44*(2), 321-328.

Famularo, R., Fenton, T., Kinscherff, R., & Augustyn, M. (1996). Psychiatric comorbidity in childhood posttraumatic stress disorder. *Child Abuse & Neglect, 20,* 953-961.

Farber, E. D., & Joseph, J. A. (1985). The maltreated adolescent: Patterns of physical abuse. *Child Abuse and Neglect, 9,* 201-206.

Farber, E. D., Kinast, C., McCoard, W. D., & Falkner, D. (1984). Violence in families of adolescent runaways. *Child Abuse and Neglect, 8,* 295-299.

Farber, E. D., Showers, J., Johnson, C. F., Joseph, J.A., & Oshins, L. (1984). The sexual abuse of children: A comparison of male and female victims. *Journal of Clinical Child Psychology, 13,* 294-297.

Farr, R. K., Koegel, P., & Burnam, M. A. (1986). *A study of homelessness and mental illness in the skid row area of Los Angeles.* Los Angeles, CA: Los Angeles County Department of Mental Health.

Feitel, B., Margetson, N., Chamas, J., & Lipman, C. (1992, February). Psychosocial background and behavioral and emotional disorders of homeless and runaway youth. *Hospital and Community Psychiatry, 43*(2),155-159.

Femina, D. D., Yeager, C. A., & Lewis, D. O. (1990). Child abuse: Adolescent records vs. adult recall. *Child Abuse and Neglect, 14,* 227-231.

Fergusson, D. M., Horwood, L. J., & Lynskey, M. T. (1993, November). Prevalence and comorbidity of DSM-III-R diagnoses in a birth cohort of 15 year olds. *Journal of the American Academy of Child and Adolescent Psychiatry, 32(6),* 1127-1134.

Fergusson, D.M., Horwood, L.J., & Lynskey, M.T. (1996). Childhood sexual abuse and psychiatric disorder in young adulthood: II. Psychiatric outcomes of childhood sexual abuse. *Journal of the*

American Academy of Child and Adolescent Psychiatry, 35(10), 1365-1374.

Finkelhor, D. (1979). *Sexually victimized children.* New York: The Free Press.

Finkelhor, D. (1984). *Child sexual abuse.* New York: The Free Press.

Finkelhor, D. (1986). Designing new studies. In D. Finkelhor, S. Araji, L. Baron, A. Browne, S. D. Peters & G. E. Wyatt (Eds.), *A sourcebook on child sexual abuse* (pp. 60-88). Beverly Hills, CA: Sage.

Finkelhor, D. (1994). The international epidemiology of child sexual abuse. *Child Abuse and Neglect, 18*(5), 409-417.

Finkelhor, D., & Baron, L. (1986). High risk children. In D. Finkelhor, S. Araji, L. Baron, A. Browne, S. D. Peters & G. E. Wyatt (Eds.), *A sourcebook on child sexual abuse* (pp. 60-88). Beverly Hills, CA: Sage.

Finkelhor, D., & Browne, A. (1988). Initial and long-term effects: A conceptual framework. In K. Faller (Ed.), *Child sexual abuse* (pp. 180-198). New York: Columbia University.

Finkelhor, D., Hotaling, G., Lewis, I., & Smith, C. (1990). Sexual abuse in a national survey of adult men and women: Prevalence, characteristics, and risk factors. *Child Abuse and Neglect, 14*, 19-28.

Foa, E. B., Steketee, G. S., & Rothbaum, B. O. (1989). Behavioral/cognitive conceptualization of post-traumatic stress disorder. *Behavior Therapy, 20,* 155-176.

Folkman, S., & Lazarus, R. S. (1980, September). An analysis of coping in a middle-aged community sample. *Journal of Health and Social Behavior*, 21, 219-239.

Fonagy, P., Steele, M., Steele, H., Higgitt, A., & Target, M. (1994). The Emanuel Miller Memorial Lecture 1992: The theory and practice of resilience. *Journal of Child Psychology and Psychiatry and Allied Disciplines, 35,* 231-257.

Fondacaro, M. R., & Moos, R. H. (1987). Social support and coping: A longitudinal analysis. *American Journal of Community Psychology, 15*(5), 653-673.

Fontana, A., & Dovidio, J. F. (1984). The relationship between stressful life events and school related performances of Type A and Type B adolescents. *Journal of Human Stress, 10*, 50-54.

Frank, E., & Anderson, B. P. (1987). Psychiatric disorders in rape victims: Past history and current symptomatology. *Comprehensive Psychiatry*, *28*(1), 77-82.

Freeman-Longo, R. E. (1986). The impact of sexual victimization on males. *Child Abuse and Neglect*, *10*, 411-414.

Freud, S. (1893). Studies on hysteria. In J. Strachey (Ed.), *Complete psychological works* (1959, Vol. 2). London: Hogarth Press.

Friedrich, W. N., Beilke, R. L., & Urquiza, A. J. (1988). Behavior problems in young sexually abused boys: A comparison study. *Journal of Interpersonal Violence*, *3*, 21-28.

Friedrich, W., Reams, R., & Jacobs, J. (1982). Depression and suicidal ideation in early adolescence. *Journal of Youth and Adolescence*, *11*, 403-407.

Fromoth, M. E. (1983, August). The Long Term Psychological Impact of Childhood Sexual Abuse. Unpublished doctoral dissertation. Auburn University, Auburn, AL.

Fromuth, M. E. (1986). The relationship of childhood sexual abuse with later psychological and sexual adjustment in a sample of college women. *Child Abuse and Neglect*, *10*, 5-15.

Fromuth, M. E., & Burkhart, B. R. (1989). Long-term psychological correlates of childhood sexual abuse in two samples of college men. *Child Abuse and Neglect*, *13*, 533-542.

Gad, M. T., & Johnson, J. H. (1980). Correlates of adolescent life stress as related to race, SES, and levels of perceived social support. *Journal of Clinical Child Psychology*, *9*, 13-16.

Galambos, N. L., & Dixon, R. A. (1984). Adolescent abuse and the development of personal sense of control. *Child Abuse and Neglect*, *8*, 285-293.

Garbarino, J. (1980). Defining emotional maltreatment: The message is the meaning. *Journal of Psychiatric Treatment and Evaluation*, *2*, 105-110.

Garbarino, J. (1988). *The psychologically battered child.* San Francisco: Jossey-Bass.

Garbarino, J., & Vondra, J. (1989). Psychological maltreatment: Issues and perspectives. In M. R. Brassard, R. Germain & S. N. Hart (Eds.),

Psychological maltreatment of children and youth (pp. 25-44). New York: Pergamon.

Garmezy, N. (1974). The study of competence in children at risk for severe psychopathology. In E. J. Anthony & C. Koupernik (Eds.), *The child in his family: Children at psychiatric risk* (pp. 77-98). New York: Wiley.

Garmezy, N. (1987). Stress, competence, and development: Continuities in the study of schizophrenic adults, children vulnerable to psychopathology, and the search for stress-resilient children. *American Journal of Orthopsychiatry*, *57*(2), 159-174.

Garmezy, N. (1988). Stressors of childhood. In N. Garmezy & M. Rutter (Eds.), *Stress, coping, and development in children* (pp. 43-84). Baltimore, MD: Johns Hopkins University Press.

Garmezy, N., Masten, A., & Tellegen, A. (1984). The study of stress and competence in children: A building block for developmental psychopathology. *Child Development*, *55*, 97-111.

Gelles, R. J. (1983). An exchange/social control theory. In D. Finkelhor (Ed.), *The dark side of families: Current family violence research* (pp. 151-165). Beverly Hills: Sage.

George, C., & Main, M. (1979). Social interactions of young abused children: Approach, avoidance, and aggression. *Child Development*, *50*, 306-318.

German, D. E., Habenicht, D. J., & Futcher, W. G. (1990). Psychological profile of the female adolescent incest victim. *Child Abuse and Neglect*, *14*, 429-438.

Gersten, J. C., Langner, T. S., Eisenberg, T. G., & Orzeck, L. (1974). Child behavior and life events: Desirable change or change per se. In B. S. Dohrenwend & B. P. Dohrenwend (Eds.), *Stressful life events: Their nature and effects* (pp. 159-170). New York: John Wiley.

Giovannoni, J., & Billingsley, A. (1970). Child neglect among the poor: A study of parental adequacies in families of three ethnic groups. *Child Welfare*, *49*, 196-204.

Gold, E. R. (1986). Long-term effects of sexual victimization in childhood: An attributional approach. *Journal of Consulting and Clinical Psychology*, *54*(4), 471-475.

Goldwert, M. (1986). Childhood seduction and the spiritualization of psychology: The case of Jung and Rank. *Child Abuse and Neglect, 10*, 555-557.

Gomes-Schwartz, B., Horowitz, J. M., & Sauzier, M. (1985). Severity of emotional distress among sexually abused preschool, school-age, and adolescent children. *Hospital and Community Psychiatry, 36*, 503-508.

Goodman, L.A., Dutton, M.A., & Harris, M. (1997). The relationship between violence dimensions and symptom severity among homeless, mentally ill women. *Journal of Traumatic Stress, 10*(1), 51-70.

Goodwin, J. (1981). Suicide attempts in sexual abuse victims and their mothers. *Child Abuse and Neglect, 5*, 217-221.

Gorcey, M., Santiago, J., & McCall-Perez, F. (1986). Psychological consequences for women sexually abused in childhood. *Social Psychiatry, 21*, 129-133.

Gore, S., Aseltine, R. H., & Colton, M. E. (1992, June). Social structure, life stress and depressive symptoms in a high school-aged population. *Journal of Health and Social Behavior, 33*(2), 97-113.

Gorman, D. M. (1993). A review of studies comparing checklist and interview methods of collection in life event research. *Behavioral Medicine, 19*(2), 66-73.

Gortmaker, S., & Gore, S. (1982). Stress and the utilization of health services: A time series and cross-sectional analysis. *Journal of Health and Social Behavior, 23*, 25-38.

Green, A. H. (1983). Dimension of psychological trauma in abused children. *Journal of the American Academy of Child Psychiatry, 22*(3), 231-237.

Green, A. H. (1988). Child maltreatment and its victims: A comparison of physical and sexual abuse. *Psychiatric Clinics of North America, 11*(4), 591-610.

Green, A. H. (1993). Child sexual abuse: Immediate and long-term effects and intervention. *Journal of the American Academy of Child and Adolescent Psychiatry, 32*(5), 890-902.

Green, A. H. (1995). Comparing child victims and adult survivors: Clues to the pathogenesis of child sexual abuse. *Journal of The American Academy of Psychoanalysis, 23,* 655-670.

Greenberg, M. T., Siegel, J. M., & Leitch, C. J. (1983). The nature and importance of attachment relationships to parents and peers during adolescence. *Journal of Youth and Adolescence, 12*, 373-386.

Greene, A., & Larson, R. W. (1991). Variation in stress reactivity during adolescence. In E. M. Cummings, A. L. Greene & K. H. Karraker (Eds.), *Life-span developmental psychology: Perspectives on stress and coping* (pp. 195-212). Hillsdale, New Jersey: Lawrence Erlbaum.

Greene, J.M., & Ringwalt, C.L. (1996). Youth and familial substance use's association with suicide attempts among runaway and homeless youth. *Substance Use and Misuse, 31*(8), 1041-1058.

Groth, N. A. (1978). Guidelines for assessment and management of the offender. In A. Burgess, N. Groth, S. Holmstrom & S. Sgroi (Eds.), *Sexual assault of children and adolescents* (pp. 25-42). Lexington, MA: Lexington Books.

Gruber, K. J., & Jones, R. J. (1983). Identifying determinants of risk of sexual victimization of youth: A multivariate approach. *Child Abuse and Neglect, 7*, 17-24.

Gruber, K. J., Jones, R. J., & Freeman, M. H. (1982, Fall). Youth reactions to sexual assault. *Adolescence, 17*(67), 541-551.

Hall, E. R., & Flannery, P. J. (1984). Prevalence and correlates of sexual assault experiences in adolescents. *Victimology: an International Journal, 9*(3-4), 398-406.

Hamilton, S., & Fagot, B. I. (1988). Chronic stress and coping styles: A comparison of male and female undergraduates. *Journal of Personality and Social Psychology, 55*(5), 819-823.

Hammen, C., Mayol, A., deMayo, R., & Marks, T. (1986). Initial symptom levels and the life-event-depression relationship. *Journal of Abnormal Psychology, 95*(2), 114-122.

Hartman, C. R., Burgess, A. W., & McCormack, A. (1987). Pathways and cycles of runaways: A model for understanding repetitive runaway behavior. *Hospital and Community Psychiatry, 38*(3), 292-299.

Hartman, M., Leon, G. R., & Finn, S. E. (1987). Sexual abuse experiences in a clinical population: Comparisons of familial and nonfamilial abuse. *Psychotherapy, 24*(2), 154-159.

Haugaard, J. J., & Emery, R. E. (1989). Methodological issues in child sexual abuse research. *Child Abuse and Neglect, 13*, 89-100.

Helzer, J. E., & Robins, L. N. (1988). The diagnostic interview schedule: Its development, evolution, and use. *Social Psychiatry and Psychiatric Epidemiology, 23*, 6-16.

Heppner, P. P., Reeder, B. L., & Larson, L. M. (1983). Cognitive variables associated with personal problem solving appraisal: Implications for counseling. *Journal of Counseling Psychology, 30*(4), 537-545.

Herjanic, B., & Reich, W. (1982). Development of a structured psychiatric interview for children: Agreement between child and parent on individual symptoms. *Journal of Abnormal Child Psychology, 10(3)*, 307-324.

Herman, D. B., Susser, E. S., Struening, E. L., & Link, B. L. (1997). Adverse childhood experiences: Are they risk factors for adult homelessness? *American Journal of Public Health, 87*, 249-255.

Herman, J., Russell, D., & Trocki, K. (1986). Long-term effects of incestuous abuse in childhood. *American Journal of Psychiatry, 143*(10), 1293-1296.

Herrenkohl, E. C., Herrenkohl, R. C., & Egolf, B. (1994). Resilient early school-age children from maltreating homes: Outcomes in late adolescence. *American Journal of Orthopsychiatry, 64*, 301-309.

Hibbard, R. A., Brack, C. J., Rauch, S., & Orr, D. P. (1988). Abuse, feelings, and health behaviors in a student population. *American Journal of Diseases in Children, 142*, 326-330.

Hibbard, R. A., & Hartman, G. L. (1992). Behavioral problems in alleged sexual abuse victims. *Child Abuse and Neglect, 16*, 755-762.

Higgins, D.J., & McCabe, M.P. (1994). The relationship of child sexual abuse and family violence to adult adjustment: Toward an integrated risk-sequelae model. *Journal of Sex Research, 31*(4), 255-266.

Hoffman-Plotkin, D., & Twentyman, C. T. (1984). A multimodal assessment of behavioral and cognitive deficits in abused and neglected preschoolers. *Child Development, 55*, 794-802.

Holman, E. A., & Stokols, D. (1994). The environmental psychology of child sexual abuse. *Journal of Environmental Psychology, 14*, 237-252.

Holmes, S. J., & Robins, L. N. (1988, February). The role of parental disciplinary practices in the development of depression and alcoholism. *Psychiatry, 51*, 24-36.

Horowitz, M. J. (1986). *Stress response syndromes*. Northvale, N.J.: Jason Aronson.

Horowitz, M., Schaffer, C., Hiroto, D., Wilner, N., & Levin B. (1977). Life event questionnaires for measuring presumptive stress. *Psychosomatic Medicine, 39*, 413-431.

Hudgens, R. W., Robins, E., & Delong, W. B. (1970). The reporting of recent stress in the lives of psychiatric patients. *British Journal of Psychiatry, 117*, 635-643.

Hughes, H. M. (1988). Psychological and behavioral correlates of family violence in child witnesses and victims. *American Journal of Orthopsychiatry, 58*(1), 77-88.

Hutchings, B., & Mednick, S. A. (1974). Registered criminality in the adoptive and biological parents of registered male adoptees. In S. A. Mednick & B. Hutchings (Eds.), *Genetics, environment and psychopathology* (pp. 215-227). Amsterdam: North-Holland.

Institute of Medicine. (1988). *Homelessness, health, and human needs*. Washington, D.C.: National Academy.

Isherwood, J., Adam, K. S., & Hornblow, A. R. (1982). Life event stress, psychosocial factors, suicide attempt and auto-accident proclivity. *Journal of Psychosomatic Research, 26*(3), 371-383.

Jaffe, P. G., Hurley, D. J., & Wolfe, D. (1990). Children's observations of violence: I. Critical issues in child development and intervention planning. *Canadian Journal of Psychiatry, 35*, 466-470.

Janet, P. (1889). *L'automatisme psychologique*. Paris: Balliere.

Janus, M., Burgess, A. W., & McCormack, A. (1987). Histories of sexual abuse in adolescent male runaways. *Adolescence, 22*(86), 405-417.

Janus, M., McCormack, A., Burgess, A.W., & Hartman, C. (1987). *Adolescent runaways: Causes and consequences.* Lexington, MA: Lexington Books.

Johnson, J. H. (1986). *Life events as stressors in childhood and adolescence*. Newbury Park: Sage.

Johnson, J. H., & Bradlyn, A. S. (1988). Life events and adjustment in childhood and adolescence: Methodological and conceptual issues. In L. H. Cohen (Ed.), *Life events and psychological functioning: Theoretical and methodological issues* (pp. 64-95). Beverly Hills, CA: Sage.

Jones, E. D., & McCurdy, K. (1992). The links between types of maltreatment and demographic characteristics of children. *Child Abuse and Neglect, 16*, 201-215.

Jones, L. P. (1988). A typology of adolescent runaways. *Child and Adolescent Social Work, 5*(1), 16-29.

Joshi, N. P., & Scott, M. (1988). Drug use, depression, and adolescents. *Pediatric Clinics of North America, 35*(6), 1349-1365.

Jumper, S.A. (1995). A meta-analysis of the relationship of child sexual abuse to adult psychological adjustment. *Child Abuse and Neglect, 19*(6), 715-728.

Justice, B., & Justice, R. (1979). *The broken taboo*. New York: Human Sciences Press.

Kagan, J. (1988). Stress and coping in early development. In N. Garmezy & M. Rutter (Eds.), *Stress, coping, and development in children* (pp. 191-216). Baltimore, MD: Johns Hopkins University Press.

Kalmuss, D. (1984, February). The intergenerational transmission of marital aggression. *Journal of Marriage and the Family, 46*(1), 11-19.

Kandel, D. B. (1982). Epidemiological and psychosocial perspectives on adolescent drug use. *Journal of the Academy of Child Psychiatry, 21*(4), 328-347.

Kandel, D. B., & Davies, M. (1982). Epidemiology of depressive mood in adolescents: An empirical study. *Archives of General Psychiatry, 39*, 1205-1212.

Kanner, A. D., Coyne, J. C., Schaefer, C., & Lazarus, R. S. (1981). Comparison of two modes of stress measurement: Daily hassles and uplifts versus major life events. *Journal of Behavioral Medicine, 14*, 1-39.

Kazdin, A. E. (1988). Childhood depression. In E. J. Mash & L. G. Terdal (Eds.), *Behavioral assessment of childhood disorders.* (pp. 157-195). New York: Guilford Press.

Kazdin, A. E., Moser, J., Colbus, D., & Bell, R. (1985). Depressive symptoms among physically abused and psychiatrically disturbed children. *Journal of Abnormal Psychology, 94,* 298-307.

Kelley, S. J. (1986). Learned helplessness in the sexually abused child. *Issues in Comprehensive Pediatric Nursing, 9,* 193-207.

Kendall-Tackett, K.A., Williams, L.M., & Finkelhor, D. (1993). Impact of sexual abuse on children: A review and synthesis of recent empirical studies. *Psychological Bulletin, 13,* 164-180.

Kennedy, M. R. (1991). Homeless and runaway youth mental health issues: No access to the system. *Journal of Adolescent Health, 12,* 576-579.

Kessler, R. C. (1997). The effects of stressful life events on depression. *Annual Review of Psychology, 48,* 191-214.

Kessler, R. C., & McLeod, J. D. (1984). Sex differences in vulnerability to undesirable life events. *American Sociological Review, 49,* 620-631.

Kessler, R. C., & McRae, J. A. (1981, August). Trends in the relationship between sex and psychological distress: 1957-1976. *American Sociological Review, 46,* 443-452.

Kessler, R. C., Price, R. H., & Wortman, C. B. (1985). Social factors in psychopathology: Stress, social support, and coping processes. *Annual Review of Psychology, 36,* 531-572.

Kinard, E. M. (1982). Experiencing child abuse: Effects on emotional adjustment. *American Journal of Orthopsychiatry, 52*(1), 82-91.

Kipke, M. D., Montgomery, S., & MacKenzie, R. G. (1993). Substance use among youth seen at a community-based health clinic. *Journal of Adolescent Health, 14,* 289-294.

Kobasa, S. C., Maddi, S. R., & Kahn, S. (1982). Hardiness and health: A prospective study. *Journal of Personality and Social Psychology, 42,* 168-177.

Kolko, D. J., Moser, J. T., & Weldy, S. R. (1988). Behavioral/emotional indicators of sexual abuse in child psychiatric inpatients: A controlled comparison with physical abuse. *Child Abuse and Neglect, 12*, 529-541.

Krug, R. S. (1989). Adult male report of childhood sexual abuse by mothers: Case descriptions, motivations and long-term consequences. *Child Abuse and Neglect, 13*, 111-119.

Kurtz, P. D., Kurtz, G. L., & Jarvis, S. V. (1991, Fall). Problems of maltreated runaway youth. *Adolescence, 26(103)*, 543-555.

Lamb, S. & Edgar-Smith, S. (1994). Aspects of disclosure: Mediators of outcome of childhood sexual abuse. *Journal of Interpersonal Violence, 9*, 307-326.

Lamphear, V. S. (1986). The psychological adjustment of maltreated children: Methodological limitations and guidelines for future research. *Child Abuse and Neglect, 10*, 63-69.

Lang, D. J. (1977). Imagery in therapy: An information processing analysis of fear. *Behavioral Therapy, 8*, 862-886.

Lazarus, R. S. (1975). The self-regulation of emotion. In L. Levi (Ed.), *Emotions: Their parameters and measurement*. New York: Raven.

Lazarus, R. S., & Cohen, J. B. (1977). Environmental stress. In I. Altman & J. F. Wohlwill (Eds.), *Human behavior and environment* (Vol. 1). New York: Plenum.

Lazarus, R. S., & Folkman, S. (1984). *Stress, appraisal, and coping*. New York: Springer.

Leadbeater, B. J., Blatt, S. J., & Quinlan, D. M. (1995). Gender-linked vulnerabilities to depressive symptoms, stress, and problem behaviors in adolescents. *Journal of Research on Adolescence, 5*(1), 1-29.

Leiter, J., Myers, K.A., & Zingraff, M.T. (1994). Substantiated and unsubstantiated cases of child maltreatment: Do their consequences differ? *Social Work Research, 18*(2), 67-82.

Lewis, D. O., Pincus, J. H., & Glaser, G. H. (1979). Violent juvenile delinquents: Psychiatric, neurological, psychological, and abuse factors. *Journal of the American Academy of Child Psychiatry, 18*, 307-319.

Lindberg, F. H., & Distad, L. J. (1985). Survival responses to incest: Adolescents in crisis. *Child Abuse and Neglect, 9*, 521-526.

Lipsett, L. (1983). Stress in infancy: Toward understanding the origins of coping behavior. In N. Garmezy & M. Rutter (Eds.), *Stress, coping, and development in children* (pp. 161-190). New York: McGraw-Hill.

Loeber, R., Weisman, W., & Reid, J. (1983). Family interactions of assaultive adolescents, stealers, and nondelinquents. *Journal of Abnormal Child Psychology, 11*, 1-14.

Los Angeles County Adolescent HIV Consortium. (1993). *The Los Angeles County adolescent HIV/AIDS strategic plan.* Los Angeles: Author.

Los Angeles Unified School District. (1993). *Fall 1993 annual school program survey.* Los Angeles: Author.

Luthar, S. (1993). Annotation: Methodological and conceptual issues in research on childhood resilience. *Journal of Child Psychology and Psychiatry and Allied Disciplines, 34*, 441-453.

Luthar, S., & Zigler, E. (1991). Vulnerability and competence: A review of research on resilience in childhood. *American Journal of Orthopsychiatry, 61*(1), 6-22.

Lyons, J. A. (1987). Posttraumatic stress disorder in children and adolescents: A review of the literature. *Developmental and Behavioral Pediatrics, 8*(6), 451-467.

Lyons, J. A. (1991). Strategies for assessing the potential for positive adjustment following trauma. *Journal of Traumatic Stress, 4*(1), 93-111.

Maccoby, E. E., & Martin, J. A. (1983). Socialization in the context of the family: Parent-child interaction. In E. M. Hetherington (Ed.), *Handbook of child psychology* (Vol. IV, pp. 1-101). New York: John Wiley.

MacFarlane, K. (1978). The victimization of women. In J. R. Chapman & M. Gates (Eds.), *Sexual abuse of children* (pp. 81-109). Beverly Hills, CA: Sage.

Main, M., & George, V. (1985). Responses of abused and disadvantaged toddlers to distress in agemates: A study in the day care setting. *Developmental Psychology, 21*, 407-412.

Masten, A. S., Garmezy, N., Tellegren, A., Pellegrini, D. S., Larkin, K., & Larsen, A. (1988). Competence and stress in school children: The moderating effects of individual and family qualities. *Journal Child Psychology Psychiatry, 29*(6), 745-764.

Maxwell, B. E. (1992). Hostility, depression, and self-esteem among troubled and homeless adolescents in crisis. *Journal of Youth and Adolescence, 21*(2), 139-150.

Mensch, B. S., & Kandel, D. B. (1988). Underreporting of substance use in a national longitudinal youth cohort. Individual and interviewer effects. *Public Opinion Quarterly, 52*, 100-124.

McCann, I. L., & Pearlman, L. A. (1990). *Psychological trauma and the adult survivor: Theory, therapy, and transformation.* New York: Brunner/Mazel.

McCann, I. L., Sakheim, D. K., & Abrahamson, D. J. (1988, October). Trauma and victimization: A model of psychological adaptation. *The Counseling Psychologist, 16(4)*, 531-594.

McChesney, K. (1987). *Characteristics of the residents of two inner-city emergency shelters for the homeless.* Los Angeles: City of Los Angeles, Office of the City Attorney.

McCormack, A., Janus, M., & Burgess, A. W. (1986). Runaway youths and sexual victimization: Gender differences in an adolescent runaway population. *Child Abuse and Neglect, 10*, 387-395.

McKirnan, D. J., & Johnson, T. (1986). Brief report: Alcohol and drug use among 'street' adolescents. *Addictive Behaviors, 11*, 201-205.

Metalsky, G. I., Halberstadt, L. J., & Abramson, L. Y. (1987). Vulnerability to depressive mood reactions: Toward a more powerful test of the diathesis-stress and causal mediation components of the reformulated theory of depression. *Journal of Personality and Social Psychology, 52*(2), 386-393.

Meyer, C. B., & Taylor, S. E. (1986). Adjustment to rape. *Journal of Personality and Social Psychology, 50*(6), 1226-1234.

Mian, M., Wehrspann, W., Klajner-Diamond, H., LeBaron, D., & Winder, C. (1986). Review of 125 children 6 years of age and under who were sexually abused. *Child Abuse and Neglect, 10*, 223-229.

Mrazek, P. J., & Mrazek, D. A. (1987). Resilience in child maltreatment victims: A conceptual exploration. *Child Abuse and Neglect, 11*, 357-366.

Mullen, P. E., Martin, J. L., Anderson, J. C., Romans, S. E., & Herbison, G. P. (1994). The effect of child sexual abuse on social, interpersonal, and sexual function in adult life. *British Journal of Psychiatry, 165,* 35-47.

Mullins, L. L., Siegel, L. J., & Hodges, K. (1985). Cognitive problem solving and life event correlates of depressive symptoms in children. *Journal of Abnormal Child Psychology, 13,* 305-314.

Murphy, L. B., & Moriarty, A. E. (1976). *Vulnerability, coping, and growth: From infancy to adolescence.* New Haven: Yale University.

National Network of Runaway and Youth Services, Inc. (1985). *To whom do they belong?* Washington, D.C.: Author.

Navarre, E. L. (1987). Psychological maltreatment: The core component of child abuse. In M. R. Brassard, R. Germain & S. N. Hart (Eds.), *Psychological maltreatment of children and youth* (pp. 45-56). New York: Pergamon.

Neiman, L. (1988). A critical review of resiliency literature and its relevance to homeless children. *Children's Environmental Quarterly, 5*(1), 17-25.

Newberger, C. M., & De Vos, E. (1988). Abuse and victimization: A life-span developmental perspective. *American Journal of Orthopsychiatry, 58*(4), 505-511.

Newberger, E. H., Newberger, C. M., & Hampton, R. L. (1983). Child abuse: The current theory base and future research needs. *Journal of the American Academy of Child Psychiatry, 22*(3), 262-268.

Offord, D. R. (1985, December). Child psychiatric disorders: Prevalence and perspectives. *Symposium on Child Psychiatry, 8(4).*

Ollendick, T. H., & Yule, W. (1990). Depression in British and American children and its relation to anxiety and fear. *Journal of Consulting and Clinical Psychology, 58(1),* 126-129.

Olson-Raymer, G. (1986). *California's runaway and homeless youth population.* Sacramento, CA: the California Child, Youth, and Family Coalition.

Opinion Research Corporation. (1976). *National statistical survey on runaway youth.* [A report for the U.S. Dept. of Health, Education, and Welfare.] Princeton, NJ: Author.

Ormel, J., & Sanderman, R. (1989). Life events, personal control and depression. In A. Steptoe & A. Appels (Eds.), *Stress, personal control and health.* Brussels-Luxembourg: John Wiley.

Park, C. L., & Folkman, S. (1997). Meaning in the context of stress and coping. *Review of General Psychology, 1,* 115-144.

Parke, R. D., & Slaby, R. G. (1983). The development of aggression. In E. M. Hetherington (Ed.), *Handbook of child psychology* (Vol. IV, pp. 547-641). New York: John Wiley.

Patterson, J. M., & McCubbin, H. I. (1987). Adolescent coping style and behaviors: Conceptualization and measurement. *Journal of Adolescence, 10,* 163-186.

Paykel, E. S. (1974). Life stress and psychiatric disorder: Applications of the clinical approach. In B. S. Dohrenwend & B. P. Dohrenwend (Eds.), *Stressful life events: Their nature and effects* (pp. 135-149). New York: Wiley.

Paykel, E. S. (1978). Contribution of life events to causation of psychiatric illness. *Psychological Medicine, 8,* 245-253.

Pearlin, L. I. (1985). Social process and social supports. In S. Cohen & L. Syme (Eds.), *Social support and health* (pp. 43-60). New York: Academic Press.

Pearlin, L. I., & Lieberman, M. A. (1979). Social sources of emotional distress. In R. Simmons (Ed.), *Research in community and mental health* (Vol. 1, pp. 217-248). Greenwich, Conn.: JAI Press.

Pearlin, L. I., Lieberman, M. A., Menaghan, E. G., & Mullan, J. T. (1981, December). The stress process. *Journal of Health and Social Behavior, 22,* 337-356.

Pearlin, L. I., & Schooler, C. (1978, March). The structure of coping. *Journal of Health and Social Behavior, 19,* 2-21.

Pennbridge, J. N., Yates, G. L., David, T. G., & MacKenzie, R. G. (1990). Runaway and homeless youth in Los Angeles County. *Journal of Adolescent Health Care, 11,* 159-165.

Peters, J. J. (1976). Children who are victims of sexual assault and the psychology of offenders. *American Journal of Psychotherapy, 30,* 398-421.

Peters, R. D., McMahon, R. J., & Quinsey, V. L. (Editors). (1992). *Aggression and violence throughout the life-span* (pp. 1-346). Newbury Park: Sage.

Peters, S. D. (1988). Child sexual abuse and later psychological problems. In G. E. Wyatt & G. J. Powell (Eds.), *Lasting effects of child sexual abuse* (pp. 101-117). Newbury Park, CA: Sage.

Peters, S. D., Wyatt, G. E., & Finkelhor, D. (1986). Prevalence. In D. Finkelhor, S. Araji, L. Baron, A. Browne, S. D. Peters & G. E. Wyatt (Eds.), *Soucebook on child sexual abuse* (pp. 15-59). Beverly Hills, CA: Sage.

Pierce, R., & Pierce, L. H. (1985). The sexually abused child: A comparison of male and female victims. *Child Abuse and Neglect*, *9*, 191-199.

Powers, J. L., & Eckenrode, J. (1988). The maltreatment of adolescents. *Child Abuse and Neglect*, *12*, 189-199.

Powers, J. L., Eckenrode, J., & Jaklitsch, B. (1990). Maltreatment among runaway and homeless youth. *Child Abuse and Neglect*, *14*, 87-98.

Powers, J. L., & Jaklitsch, B. W. (1989). Psychological and behavioral effects of maltreatment. In *Understanding survivors of abuse: Stories of homeless and runaway adolescents* (pp. 21-28). Lexington, Massachusetts: Lexington Books.

Pursley, M. (1981). *Runaway youth situation in Los Angeles County: A general overview*. Los Angeles: United Way Planning Council.

Pynoos, R. S., Frederick, C., Nader, K., Arroyo, W., & Steinberg, A. (1987). Life threat and posttraumatic stress in school-age children. *Archives of General Psychiatry*, *44*, 1057-1063.

Radloff, L. S., & Rae, D. S. (1979). Susceptibility and precipitating factors in depression: Sex differences and similarities. *Journal of Abnormal Psychology*, *88*(2), 174-181.

Reinherz, H. Z., Giaconia, R. M., Lefkowitz, E. S., Pakiz, B., & Frost, A. K. (1993, March). Prevalence of psychiatric disorders in a community population of older adolescents. *Journal of the American Academy of Child and Adolescent Psychiatry, 32(2)*, 369-377.

Reynolds, C. R. (1980). Concurrent validity of what I think and feel: The revised children's manifest anxiety scale. *Journal of Consulting and Clinical Psychology. 48(6)*, 774-775.

Reynolds, C. R., & Richmond, B. O. (1978). What I think and feel: A revised measure of Children's Manifest Anxiety. *Journal of Abnormal Child Psychology, 6(2)*, 271-280.

Rieker, P. P., & Carmen, E. H. (1986). The victim-to-patient process: The disconfirmation and transformation of abuse. *American Journal of Orthopsychiatry, 56*(3), 360-370.

Rimsza, M. E., Berg, R. A., & Locke, C. (1988). Sexual abuse: Somatic and emotional reactions. *Child Abuse and Neglect, 12*, 201-208.

Robertson, M. J. (1989). *Homeless youth in Hollywood: Patterns of alcohol use* [Report for the National Institute on Alcohol Abuse and Alcoholism]. Berkeley: University of California.

Robertson, M. J. (1991). Homeless youth: An overview of recent literature. In J.H. Kryder-Coe, L.M. Salamon, & J.M. Molnar (Eds.) *Homeless children and youth: A new American dilemma.* (pp. 151-165) New Brunswick: Transaction Press.

Robertson, M. J., Greenblatt, M., Koegel, P., & Mundy, P. (1990, 11/August). *Characteristics and circumstances of homeless adolescents in Hollywood.* Paper presented at the Annual Meeting of the American Psychological Association. Boston, MA.

Robertson, M. J., Ropers, M. H., & Boyer, R. (1984). *Emergency shelter for the homeless in Los Angeles County.* Los Angeles: University of California at Los Angeles School of Public Health.

Robertson, M. J., Ropers, R. H., & Boyer, R. (1985). *The homeless in Los Angeles County: An empirical assessment.* Los Angeles: University of California at Los Angeles School of Public Health.

Robins, L. N., Helzer, J. E., Weissman, M. M., Orvaschel, H., Gruenberg, E., Burke, J. D., & Regier, D. A. (1984, October). Lifetime prevalence of specific psychiatric disorders in three sites. *Archives of General Psychiatry, 41*, 949-958.

Roesler, T. A., & McKenzie, N. (1994). Effects of childhood trauma on psychological functioning in adults sexually abused as children. *The Journal of Nervous and Mental Disease, 182*(3), 145-150.

Rosario, M., Shinn, M., Morch, H., & Huckabee, C. B. (1988). Gender differences in coping and social supports: Testing socialization and role constraint theories. *Journal of Community Psychology, 16*, 55-69.

Rossi, P. H. (1989). Counting the homeless and the extremely poor. In *Down and out in America: The origins of homelessness* (pp. 45-82). Chicago: The University of Chicago Press.

Rothman, J., & David, T. (1985). *Status offenders in Los Angeles County: Focus on runaway and homeless youth.* [Report for the Bush Program in Child and Family Policy]. Los Angeles: University of California.

Rotter, J. B. (1975). Some problems and misconceptions related to the construct of internal versus external control of reinforcement. *Journal of Consulting and Clinical Psychology, 43*, 56-67.

Ruch, L. O., & Chandler, S. M. (1982). The crisis impact of sexual assault on three victim groups: Adult rape victims, child rape victims, and incest victims. *Journal of Social Service Research, 5*(1/2), 83-100.

Ruddick, S. (1988). Debunking the dream machine: The case of street kids in Hollywood California. *Children's Environments Quarterly, 5*(1), 8-16.

Rudin, M. M., Zalewski, C., & Bodmer-Turner, J. (1995). Characteristics of child sexual abuse victims according to perpetrator gender. *Child Abuse & Neglect, 19,* 963-973.

Russell, D. E. (1986). *The secret trauma: Incest in the lives of girls and women.* New York: Basic Books.

Russell, D. E., Schurman, R. A., & Trocki, K. (1988). The long-term effects of incestuous abuse: A comparison of Afro-Americans and White American victims. In G. E. Wyatt & G. J. Powell (Eds.), *Lasting effects of child sexual abuse* (pp. 119-134). Newbury Park, CA: Sage.

Rutter, M. (1977). Individual differences. In M. Rutter & L. Hersov (Eds.), *Child psychiatry: Modern approaches* (pp. 3-21). Oxford: Blackwell Scientific.

Rutter, M. (1979). Protective factors in children's responses to stress and disadvantage. In M. W. Kent & J. E. Rolf (Eds.), *Primary prevention of psychopathology: Social competence in children* (Vol. 3). Hanover, New Hampshire: University Press of New England.

Rutter, M. (1981). Stress, coping and development: Some issues and some questions. *Journal of Child Psychology and Psychiatry, 22*(4), 323-356.

Rutter, M. (1987). Psychosocial resilience and protective mechanisms. *American Journal of Orthopsychiatry, 57*(3), 316-331.

Rutter, M., Cox, A., & Tupling, C. (1975). Attainment and adjustment in two geographical areas: 1.: The prevalence of psychiatric disorder. *British Journal of Psychiatry, 126*, 493-509.

Rutter, M., Yule, B., Quinton, D., Rowlands, O., Yule, W., & Berger, M. (1975). Attainment and adjustment in two geographical areas: III. Some factors accounting for area differences. *British Journal of Psychiatry, 126*, 520-533.

SAS User's Guide: Basics, Version 5 Edition. (1985). Cary, NC: SAS Institute Inc.

Schaefer, M. R., Sobieraj, K., & Hollyfield, R. L. (1988). Prevalence of childhood physical abuse in adult male veteran alcoholics. *Child Abuse and Neglect, 12*, 141-149.

Schellenbach, C. J., & Guerney, L. F. (1987). Identification of adolescent abuse and future intervention prospects. *Journal of Adolescence, 10*, 1-12.

Schram, D. D., & Giovengo, M. A. (1991). Evaluation of Threshold: An independent living program for homeless adolescents. *Journal of Adolescent Health, 12*, 567-572.

Schweitzer, R. D., & Hier, S. J. (1993). Psychological maladjustment among homeless adolescents. *Australian and New Zealand Journal of Psychiatry, 27*, 275-280.

Seidner, A., & Calhoun, K. S. (1984, August). *Childhood sexual abuse factors related to differential adult adjustment.* Paper presented at the Second National Conference for Family Violence. Durham, NC.

Seifer, R., & Sameroff, A. J. (1987). Multiple determinants of risk and invulnerability. In E. J. Anthony & B. J. Cohler (Eds.), *The invulnerable child* (pp. 51-69). New York: Guilford Press.

Seligman, M. E. (1975). *Helplessness: On depression, development and death.* San Francisco: Freeman.

Selye, H. (1973, November-December). The evolution of the stress concept. *American Scientist, 61*, 692-699.

Shaffer, D., & Caton, C. L. (1984). *Runaway and homeless youth in New York City: A report to the Ittleson Foundation.* New York: Division of Child Psychiatry, New York State Psychiatric Institute and Columbia University College of Physicians and Surgeons.

Shane, P. (1989). Changing patterns among homeless and runaway youth. *American Journal of Orthopsychiatry*, *59*(2), 208-214.

Shapiro, S. (1987). Self-mutilation and self-blame in incest victims. *American Journal of Psychotherapy*, *61*(1), 46-54.

Sibthorpe, B., Drinkwater, J., Gardner, K., & Bammer, G. (1995). Drug use, binge drinking and attempted suicide among homeless and potentially homeless youth. *Australian and New Zealand Journal of Psychiatry, 29*(2), 248-256.

Siegel, J. M., Burnam, M. A., Stein, J., Golding, J., & Sorenson, S. B. (1986). *Sexual assault and psychiatric disorder: Phase II analyses*. Washington, D.C.: National Institute of Mental Health, Antisocial and Violent Behavior Branch.

Siegel, J. M., Sorenson, S. B., Golding, J. M., Burnam, M. A., & Stein, J. A. (1987). The prevalence of childhood sexual assault: The Los Angeles Epidemiological Catchment Area Project. *American Journal of Epidemiology*, *126*(6), 1141-1153.

Silbert, M. H., & Pines, A. M. (1983, July-August). Early sexual exploitation as an influence in prostitution. *Social Work*, pp. 185-289.

Silver, R. L., & Wortman, C. B. (1980). Coping with undesirable life events. In J. Garber & M. E. Seligman (Eds.), *Human helplessness: Theory and applications*. New York: Academic Press.

Simons, R. L., & Whitbeck, L. B. (1991, September). Sexual abuse as a precursor to prostitution and victimization among adolescent and adult homeless women. *Journal of Family Issues, 12(3)*, 361-379.

Sirles, E. A., Smith, J. A., & Kusama, H. (1989). Psychiatric status of intrafamilial child sexual abuse victims. *Journal of the American Academy of Child and Adolescent Psychiatry*, *28*(2), 225-229.

Smart, R. G., & Walsh, G. W. (1993, Spring). Predictors of depression in street youth. *Adolescence, 28(109)*, 41-53.

Smart, R., Adlaf, E. M., Porterfield, K. M., & Canale, M. D. (1990). *Drugs, youth, and the street.* [Report to the Addiction Research Foundation of Ontario].

Smucker, M. R., Craighead, W. E., Craighead, L. W., & Green, B. J. (1986). Normative and reliability data for the children's depression inventory. *Journal of Abnormal Child Psychology, 14(1)*, 25-39.

Sorenson, S. B., & Rutter, C. M. (1991). Transgenerational patterns of suicide attempt. *Journal of Consulting and Clinical Psychology, 59*(6), 861-866.

Sorenson, S. B., & Siegel, J. M. (1992). Gender, ethnicity, and sexual assault: Findings from a Los Angeles study. *Journal of Social Issues, 48*(1), 93-104.

Sorenson, S. B., Siegel, J. M., Golding, J. M., & Stein, J. A. (1991). Repeated sexual victimization. *Violence and Victims, 6*(4), 299-308.

Sowder, B. J. (1985). *Disasters and mental health: Selected contemporary perspectives*. Rockville, MD: National Institutes of Mental Health.

Spaccarelli, S. (1994). Stress, appraisal, and coping in child sexual abuse: A theoretical and empirical review. *Psychological Bulletin, 116*(2), 340-362.

Spaccarelli, S. (1995). Measuring abuse stress and negative cognitive appraisals in child sexual abuse: Validity data on two new scales. *Journal of Abnormal Child Psychology, 23*(6), 703-727.

Spaccarelli, S., & Kim, S. (1995). Resilience criteria and factors associated with resilience in sexually abused girls. *Child Abuse and Neglect, 19*(9), 1171-1182.

Spielberger, C. D. (1973). *State-trait anxiety inventory for children.* Palo Alto, California: Consulting Psychologists Press.

Spirito, A., Overholser, J., & Stark, L. J. (1989). Common problems and coping strategies II: Findings with adolescent suicide attempters. *Journal of Abnormal Child Psychology, 17*(2), 213-221.

St. Louis, M., Hayman, C., & Miller, C. et al. (1989). *HIV infection in disadvantaged adolescents in the United States: Findings from the Job Corps screening programs.* Paper presented at the Fifth International Conference on AIDS. Montreal.

Stanford Center for the Study of Families, (1991, November). Homeless teenagers. In *The Stanford Studies of homeless families, children and youth* (pp. 29-31). Stanford, CA: Stanford Center for the Study of Families, Children and Youth.

Stark, E., & Flitcraft, A. H. (1988). Women and children at risk: A feminist perspective on child abuse. *International Journal of Health Services, 18*(1), 97-118.

Stark, L. J., Spirito, A., Williams, C. A., & Guevremont, D. C. (1989). Common problems and coping strategies I: Findings with normal adolescents. *Journal of Abnormal Child Psychology, 17*(2), 203-212.

Starr, R. (1982). A research-based approach to the prediction of child abuse. In R. H. Starr (Ed.), *Child abuse prediction: Policy implications* (pp. 105-134). Cambridge, MA: Ballinger.

Steele, B. F. (1986). Notes on the lasting effects of early child abuse throughout the life cycle. *Child Abuse and Neglect, 10*, 283-291.

Stefanidis, N., Pennbridge, J., MacKenzie, R., & Pottharst, K. (1992, July). Runaway and homeless youth: The effects of attachment history on stabilization. *American Journal of Orthopsychiatry*, pp. 442-446.

Stein, J. A., Golding, J. M., Siegel, J. M., Burnam, M. A., & Sorenson, S. B. (1988). Long-term psychological sequelae of child sexual abuse: The Los Angeles Epidemiologic Catchment Area Study. In G. E. Wyatt & G. J. Powell (Eds.), *Lasting effects of child sexual abuse* (pp. 135-154). Beverly Hills: Sage.

Stiffman, A. R. (1989). Physical and sexual abuse in runaway youths. *Child Abuse and Neglect, 13*, 417-426.

Stiffman, A. R., Earls, F., Powell, J., & Robins, L. N. (1987, Summer). Correlates of alcohol and illicit drug use in adolescent medical patients. *Contemporary Drug Problems*, 295-314.

Stillion, J. M., McDowell, E. E., & May, J. H. (1989). Suicide in adolescence and young adulthood. In *Suicide across the life span: Premature exits* (pp. 85-123). New York: Hemisphere.

Stone, A. A., Helder, L., & Schneider, M. S. (1988). Coping with stressful events: Coping dimensions and issues. In Lawrence H. Cohen (Ed.), *Life events and psychological functioning: Theoretical and methodological issues* (pp. 182-210). Beverly Hills, CA: Sage.

Straker, G., & Jacobson, R. S. (1981). Aggression, emotional maladjustment and empathy in the abused child. *Developmental Psychology, 17*(6), 762-765.

Stricof, R., Kennedy, J., Nattell, T., Weisfuse, I., & Novick, L. (1991). HIV seroprevalence in a facility for runaway and homeless adolescents. *American Journal of Public Health, 81*, 50-53.

Summit, R. C. (1983). The child sexual abuse accomodation syndrome. *Child Abuse and Neglect*, *7*, 177-193.

Summit, R. C. (1988). Hidden victims, hidden pain: Societal avoidance of child sexual abuse. In G. E. Wyatt & G. J. Powell (Eds.), *Lasting effects of child sexual abuse* (pp. 39-60). Beverly Hills: Sage.

Susser, E., Streuning, E., & Conover, S. (1987). Childhood experiences of homeless men. *American Journal of Psychiatry*, *144*, 1599-1601.

Swearington, E. M., & Cohen, L. H. (1985). Life events and psychological distress: A prospective study of young adolescents. *Developmental Psychology*, *21*(6), 1045-1054.

Tarter, R. E., Hegedus, A. E., Winsten, N. E., & Alterman, A. I. (1984). Neuropsychological, personality, and familial characteristics of physically abused delinquents. *Journal of the American Academy of Child Psychiatry*, *23*, 668-674.

Tennant, C., & Bebbington, P. (1978). The social causation of depression: A critique of the work of Brown and his colleagues. *Psychological Medicine*, *8*, 565-575.

Tennant, C., Bebbington, P., & Hurry, J. (1981). The role of life events in depressive illness: Is there a substantial causal relation? *Psychological Medicine*, *11*, 379-389.

Thoits, P. A. (1983). Dimensions of life events that influence psychological distress: An evaluation and synthesis of the literature. In H. B. Kaplan (Ed.), *Psychological stress: Trends in theory and research*. New York: Academic Press.

Thoits, P. A. (1986, April). Multiple identities: Examining gender and marital status differences in distress. *American Sociological Review*, *51*, 259-272.

Thoits, P. A. (1995). Identity-relevant events and psychological symptoms: A cautionary tale. *Journal of Health and Social Behavior*, *36*, 72-82.

Thoits, P. A. (1995). Stress, coping, and social support processes: Where are we? What next? *Journal of Health and Social Behavior*. (Extra issue), 53-79.

Timmer, D. A., Eitzen, D. S., & Talley, K. D. (1994). *Paths to homelessness: Extreme poverty and the urban housing crisis*. Boulder, CO: Westview.

Tong, L., Oates, K., & McDowell, M. (1987). Personality development following sexual abuse. *Child Abuse and Neglect*, *11*, 371-383.

Toro, P. A. (1982). Developmental effects of child abuse: A review. *Child Abuse and Neglect*, *6*, 423-431.

Toth, S. L., Manly, J. T., & Cicchetti, D. (1992). Child maltreatment and vulnerability to depression. *Development and Psychopathology*, *4*, 97-112.

Tufts' New England Medical Center: Division of Child Psychiatry. (1984). *Sexually exploited children: Service and research project*. Washington, D.C.: U.S. Department of Justice, Office of Juvenile Justice and Delinquency Prevention.

Ulbrich, P. M., Warheit, G. J., & Zimmerman, R. S. (1989, March). Race, socioeconomic status, and psychological distress: An examination of differential vulnerability. *Journal of Health and Social Behavior, 30*, 131-146.

United States Department of Health and Human Services. (1981). *Study findings: National study of the incidence and severity of child abuse and neglect* (DHHS Pub. no. 81-80325). Washington, D.C.: National Center on Child Abuse and Neglect.

United States Department of Health and Human Services. (1983). *Runaway and homeless youth: National program inspection.* (Region X Office of the Inspector General). Washington, D.C.

United States Department of Health and Human Services. (1988). *Study findings: Study of national incidence and prevalence of child abuse and neglect*. Washington, D.C.: National Center on Child Abuse and Neglect.

United States Department of Health and Human Services. (1994). *1992 National annual incidence and prevalence of child abuse and neglect*. Washington, D.C.: National Center on Child Abuse and Neglect.

Urquiza, A.J., & Goodlin-Jones, B.J. (1994). Child sexual abuse and adult revictimization with women of color. *Violence and Victims, 9*(3), 223-32.

van der Kolk, B. A., Brown, P., & van der Hart, O. (1989). Pierre Janet on post-traumatic stress. *Journal of Traumatic Stress*, *2*(4), 365-378.

van Houten, T., & Golembiewski, G. (1978). *Life stress as a predictor of alcohol abuse and/or runaway behavior*. Washington, D.C.: American Youth Work Center.

Vander Kooi, R. (1983). *Youths without homes: A survey of Chicago street youths and their agencies*. Chicago: Chicago Community Trust.

Vander Mey, B. J. (1988). The sexual victimization of male children: A review of previous research. *Child Abuse and Neglect, 12*, 61-72.

Vilhjalmsson, R. (1993). Life stress, social support and clinical depression: A reanalysis of the literature. *Social Science and Medicine, 37*(3), 331-342.

Wagner, B. M., Compas, B. E., & Howell, D. C. (1988). Daily and major life events: A test of an integrative model of psychosocial stress. *American Journal of Community Psychology, 16*(2), 189-205.

Walker, L. E., & Browne, A. (1985). Gender and victimization by intimates. *Journal of Personality, 53*(2), 179-195.

Wallerstein, J. S., & Kelly, J. B. (1980). *Surviving the break up: How children and parents cope with divorce*. New York: Basic Books.

Weiner, B. (1979). A theory of motivation for some classroom experiences. *Journal of Educational Psychology, 71*, 3-25.

Welner, Z., Reich, W., Herjanic, B., Jung, K. G., & Amado, H. (1987). Reliability, validity, and parent-child agreement studies of the diagnostic interview for children and adolescents (DICA). *Journal of the American Academy of Child and Adolescent Psychiatry, 26(5)*, 649-653.

Werner, E. E. (1984, November). Resilient children. *Young Children*, 68-72.

Werner, E. E. (1986). The concept of risk from a developmental perspective. *Advances in Special Education, 5*, 1-23.

Werner, E. E. (1992). The children of Kauai: Resiliency and recovery in adolescence and adulthood. *Journal of Adolescent Health, 13*, 262-268.

Werner, E., & Smith, R. S. (1982). *Vulnerable, but invincible: A longitudinal study of resilient children and youth*. New York: McGraw Hill.

Wertlieb, D., Weigel, C., & Feldstein, M. (1987a). Stress, social support, and behavior symptoms in middle childhood. *Journal of Clinical Child Psychology, 16*(3), 204-211.

Wertlieb, D., Weigel, C., Springer, T., & Feldstein, M. (1987b). Temperament as a moderator of children's stressful experiences. *American Journal of Orthopsychiatry, 57*(2), 234-245.

Whitaker, A., Johnson, J., Shaffer, D., Rapoport, J. L., Kalikow, K., Walsh, B. T., Davies, M., Braiman, S., & Dolinsky, A. (1990). Uncommon troubles in young people: Prevalence estimates of selected psychiatric disorders in a nonreferred adolescent population. *Archives of General Psychiatry, 47*, 487-496.

Widom, C.S., & Kuhns, J.B. (1996). Childhood victimization and subsequent risk for promiscuity, prostitution, and teenage pregnancy: A prospective study. *American Journal of Public Health, 86*(11), 1607-1612.

Williams, L.M. (1995). Recall of childhood trauma: A prospective study of women's memories of child sexual abuse: Correction. *Journal of Consulting and Clinical Psychology, 63*(3), 343.

Wills, T.A., McNamara, G., & Vaccaro, D. (1995). Parental education related to adolescent stress-coping and substance use: Development of a mediational model. *Health Psychology, 14*(5), 464-478.

Wilson, K.G., Stelzer, J., Bergman, J.N., Kral, M.J., Inayatullah, M., & Elliott, C.A. (1995). Problem solving, stress, and coping in adolescent suicide attempts. *Suicide and Life-Threatening Behaviors, 25*(2), 241-252.

Wolfe, D. A. (1987). *Child abuse: Implications for child development and psychopathology* (pp. 97-121). Beverly Hills, CA: Sage.

Wolfe, D. A., & Mosk, M. D. (1983). Behavioral comparisons of children from abusive and distressed families. *Journal of Consulting and Clinical Psychology, 51*(5), 702-708.

Wolfe, V.V. & Birt, J. (1995). The psychological sequelae of child sexual abuse. In T.H. Ollendick & R. J. Prinz (Eds.), *Advances in Clinical Child Psychology* (Vol. 17). New York: Plenum.

Wolock, I., & Horowitz, B. (1979). Child maltreatment and material deprivation. *Social Service Review, 53*, 175-194.

Wood, B., Orsak, C., Murphy, M., & Cross, H. J. (1996). Semistructured child sexual abuse interviews: Interview and child characteristics related to credibility of disclosure. *Child Abuse & Neglect, 20,* 81-92.

World Health Organization (1978). *Primary Health Care* [Report to the International Conference on Primary Health Care: Alma Ata, USSR]. Geneva: Author (1-79).

Wortman, C. B. (1983). Coping with victimization: Conclusions and implications for future research. *Journal of Social Issues, 39*, 197-223.

Wozencraft, T., Wagner, W., & Pellegrin, A. (1991). Depression and suicidal ideation in sexually abused children. *Child Abuse and Neglect, 15*, 505-511.

Wyatt, G. E. (1985). The sexual abuse of Afro-Americans and white American women in childhood. *Child Abuse and Neglect, 9*, 507-519.

Wyatt, G. E. (1986). *The aftermath of child sexual abuse.* Unpublished manuscript.

Wyatt, G. E., Guthrie, D., & Notgrass, C. M. (1992). Differential effects of women's child sexual abuse and subsequent sexual revictimization. *Journal of Consulting and Clinical Psychology, 60*(2), 167-173.

Wyatt, G. E., Newcomb, M. D., & Riederle, M. H. (1993). *Sexual abuse and consensual sex: Women's developmental patterns and outcomes.* Newbury Park: Sage.

Wyatt, G. E., & Peters, S. D. (1986). Issues in the definition of child sexual abuse in prevalence research. *Child Abuse and Neglect, 10*, 231-240.

Wynkoop, T. F., Capps, S. C., & Priest, B. J. (1995). Incidence and prevalence of child sexual abuse: A critical review of data collection procedures. *Journal of Child Sexual Abuse, 4*(2), 49-66.

Yates, G. L., MacKenzie, R. G., Pennbridge, J. N., & Cohen, E. (1988). A risk profile comparison of runaway and non-runaway youth. *American Journal of Public Health, 78*, 820-821.

Yokopenic, P. A., Clark, V. A., & Aneshensel, C. S. (1983, January). Depression, problem recognition, and professional consultation. *Journal of Nervous and Mental Disease, 171(1)*, 15-23.

Zimrin, H. (1986). A profile of survival. *Child Abuse and Neglect*, *10*, 339-349.

Index